The Oregon Trail Revisited

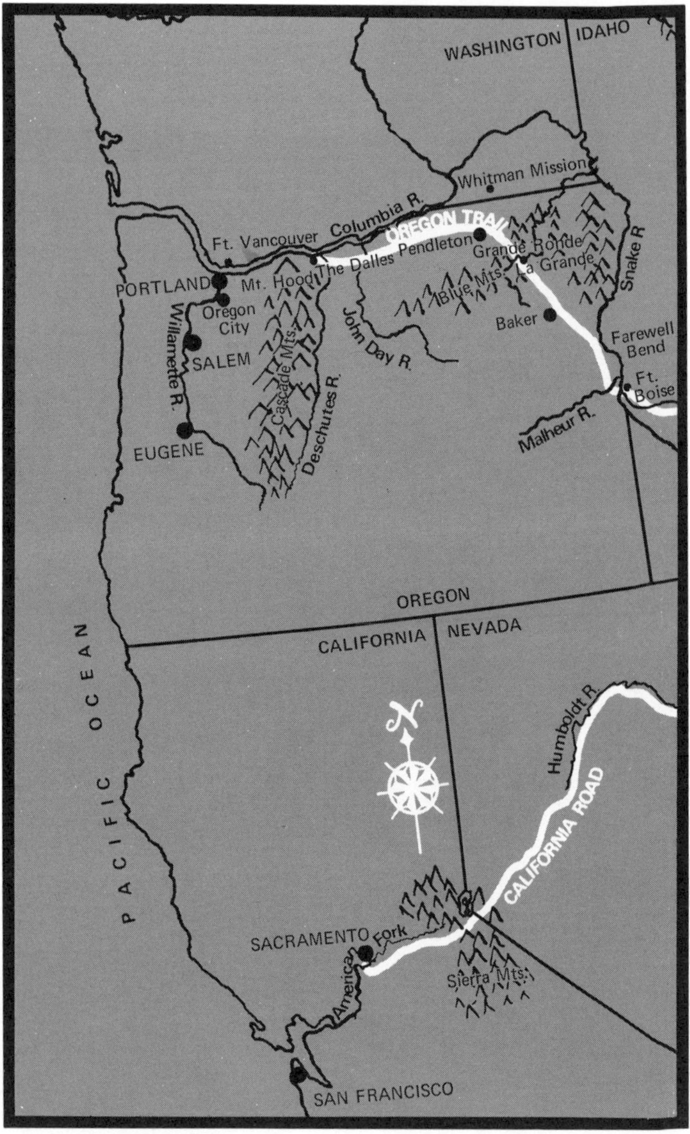
WASHINGTON
IDAHO
Whitman Mission
Columbia R.
OREGON TRAIL
Ft. Vancouver
The Dalles
Pendleton
Grande Ronde
La Grande
Snake R.
PORTLAND
Mt. Hood
Blue Mts.
Oregon City
Baker
Willamette R.
SALEM
Cascade Mts.
John Day R.
Farewell Bend
Ft. Boise
Deschutes R.
Malheur R.
EUGENE
OREGON
CALIFORNIA
NEVADA
PACIFIC OCEAN
N
Humboldt R.
CALIFORNIA ROAD
SACRAMENTO
Fork
American
Sierra Mts.
SAN FRANCISCO

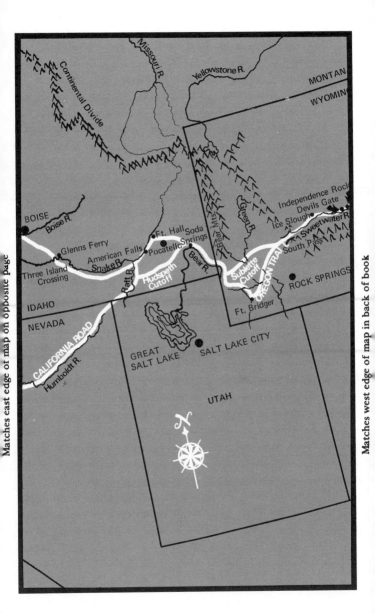

Other books by the author:

The Old Cathedral
1965 (2nd edition, 1980)

The Story of Old Ste. Genevieve
1967 (2nd edition, 1973; 3rd edition, 1976;
4th edition, 1987)

History of the Hazelwood School District
1977

Legacy: The Sverdrup Story
1978

Leif Sverdrup: Engineer Soldier At His Best
1980

Maps Of The Oregon Trail
1982 (2nd edition, 1983)

The Oregon Trail Revisited

Gregory M. Franzwa

Foreword by
George B. Hartzog Jr.
Director, National Park Service
United States Department of the Interior

The Patrice Press

Library of Congress Cataloging-in-Publication Data

Franzwa, Gregory M.
   The Oregon Trail revisited / Gregory M. Franzwa:
   foreword by George B. Hartzog, Jr.
   p.   cm.

   Bibliography: p.
   Includes index.
   ISBN 0-935284-57-5. ISBN 0-935284-58-3 (pbk.)

   1. Oregon Trail—History. 2. West (U.S.)—
Description and travel—1981- —Guidebooks. 3.
Automobiles—Road guides—West (U.S.) 4. Historic
sites—West (U.S.)—Guidebooks. I. Title.
F597.F73 1988
917.8′0433—dc19   88-1027
                                          CIP

Published by
The Patrice Press
1810 N. Grant Rd./Suite 108/Tucson, AZ 85745

To Laura,
who made it all possible

Contents

Preface &
Acknowledgments

This book is written in two parts; the first a broad history of the Oregon Trail and its impact upon the course of American events of the 19th century; followed by a brief and general outline of its route. The second and larger part of the book is a detailed guide designed to direct the reader to the exact points where the old trail crosses the public roadways of today. This section is interlaced with historical data pertinent to the specific areas being visited.

The book is the product of several field trips into the American West from 1968 through the early part of 1972, amplified by countless days of study in St. Louis.

The effort obviously was work, but it didn't seem like it at the time. The typical day in the field began shortly after dawn and all too often didn't end until 18 hours later. After working on the trail until dusk, the tapes would be transcribed and combined with the notes taken over the preceding months and years, with eight to 10 pages of manuscript being produced per day in this manner.

The project was shot through with little mysterie. Why, for instance, were certain historical markers located miles away from where they ought to be? Why are ruts visible in one spot and completely invisible 100 yards away, with all climate and land use conditions seemingly identical?

These and countless hundreds of other problems have been ironed out. Only a few remain, and we are now satisfied that the book is in reasonably good shape. There still may be errors, or at least substantial differences in opinion. Other editions will be published in succeeding years and those who question portions of the text are requested to communicate with the publishers so that the differences may be resolved.

We owe many favors to the people who helped us during the course of this adventure, and the rest of these remarks are devoted to an acknowledgment of their efforts on our behalf.

The people from the historical societies were of considerable assistance to us. Robert W. Richmond of the Kansas State Historical Society steered us to the elusive Blue Mound and over the long obscure trail through downtown Topeka. Donald D. Snoddy of the Nebraska society provided us with reams of material for study in their handsome building in Lincoln. Mrs. Katherine Halverson of the Wyoming society should have closed up for the afternoon, as all patriotic organizations of Cheyenne do on the first day of Frontier Days, but she didn't. She stayed at her desk as we labored through stacks of Paul Henderson's priceless maps and closed up the building only after we had finished our work.

Merle W. Wells, director of the Idaho society, read our manuscript and devoted a lot of time in helping us understand where our suppositions about the British, which were garnered from several 19th century sources, were wrong wrong wrong, and he is right. Barbara Friedman of the Oregon society devoted much of one day during an early trip to Portland to help us find our way around some particularly knotty problems.

Much of the time spent in literary research was put in at the Missouri Historical Society in St. Louis. We are especially grateful to Mrs. Arthur W. Felt and Mrs. Fred C. Harrington Jr. of the society's library for their efforts on our behalf.

There are two people in Jackson Co., Mo., who deserve special recognition. (Jackson Co. is by far the most difficult section of the trail to track down.) William A. Goff, the capable author and editor of the Westport Historical Society *Quarterly,* is one of them. Bill helped from the very beginning, making the society's archives available, touring through old Westport, and finally pulling a ton of mistakes from the manuscript.

Mrs. Frank E. Fowler gets most of the credit for the material around Independence, Mo. As director of archives for the Jackson County Historical Society, Mrs. Fowler was quite content to catalog and sift her literary materials until we came along. She became interested in helping find the critical locations, to such a degree that we felt like the sorcerer's apprentice — we don't know how to turn her off. Our files are stuffed full of material she prepared especially for this project, all assembled with great scholarship.

There are other smaller societies all the way along the trail whose members have been helpful. Like the Jefferson County, Nebraska group, which has made their whole county a living museum through the device of a one-mil tax for that purpose. Miss Estaline Carpenter of Fairbury is one of the spark plugs of that organization, and she offered her help to us most willingly. We were tempted to accept her offer of an aircraft tour, declining only because the touring public might not want to do this. Flights are available for $10 at the Fairbury airport. Jefferson County is loaded with Oregon Trail ruts visible from the air.

The National Park Service people were most generous in their help. Director Hartzog's foreword is gratefully acknowledged, as is the help of his superintendents at such sites as Scotts Bluff and Ft. Laramie. John R. Miele, the acting director of the Whitman Mission National Historic Site; and Elt Davis, director of Fort Vancouver National Historic Site, spent a lot of their own time on our behalf and we thank them for it.

Two libraries in St. Louis have a surprising volume of general data pertinent to the Oregon Trail; the fine Central Public Library in downtown St. Louis and the delightful Mercantile Library, one of the country's finest private libraries. Peggy Smith, of the Missouri Valley Room of Kansas City's Public Library, provided expert documentation in pulling out the last of the bugs in Jackson County, then proceeded to give the revised draft one hell of a critical reading, and it is the better for it.

The Oregon Trail passes through much of five states, and the governors of those states deserve a special vote of thanks for their help in many areas: Hon. Cecil D. Andrus of Idaho, Hon. Robert E. Docking of Kansas, Hon. J. James Exon of Nebraska, Hon. Tom McCall of Oregon, and Hon. Stanley K. Hathaway of Wyoming.

Much credit should go to the anonymous engineers of the State Highway Commissions of Idaho and Oregon, who walked for years to pin down the route of the trail in their two states, and then published fine little booklets of strip maps to record their efforts.

Our photographic problems were solved in great part by E. O. (Buck) Miller of W. Schiller & Co., who provided valuable advice on several occasions. Our twin Konica cameras, acquired on his recommendation, survived total emersion in the slimy mud of the Independence Crossing of the Big Blue River in Kansas and still perform like new. Apex Photo Service processed our color work with expertise. We printed up the black and white negatives ourselves, using the darkroom of Mark Thomson's Banner Printing Co. of St. Charles, Mo.

William H. Hasse of Holiday Rambler Corporation saw to it that we were able to buy, on short notice, the sort of trailer that would see us through the last summer of field work with a minimum of living expense and a maximum of comfort. His dealer, Bill Thomas of Bill Thomas Camper Sales, made certain that we were equipped with all safety devices, then trained us in trailering to such a degree that he probably saved our lives.

James R. Graff of the Kampgrounds of America (KOA) organization provided us with a VIP card, enabling us to sponge off a number of campgrounds from Kansas on west. These included the Topeka KOA; Casper, Cheyenne, Chugwater and Lyman KOAs in Wyoming; Boise, Burley, Jerome and Lava Hot Springs in Idaho; and Cascade Locks in Oregon. The savings and comfort afforded by these installations was as much appreciated by hard working writers as by relaxing vacationers.

We thank our dear aunt, Miss Katherine Franzwa, and her friends, Preston B. and Marguerite Reed of Baker,

Oregon, who sent material from local sources and then accompanied us up on the Ruckles Flat, where we found the trail just as the emigrants left it.

We thank also Vernon Sternberg, founder and director of the Southern Illinois University Press, who shared his vast knowledge of publishing beautiful books with us. We hope a little of that rubbed off. Lord knows he tried.

And we thank Harold Warp, who allowed us to reproduce some of his fine collection of paintings by William H. Jackson.

Mrs. Mary Hayes caught countless grammatical and typographical errors in the manuscript — we thank her profusely although we must say she certainly is picky.

Our attorney and friend, Carroll J. Donohue, has our gratitude for reading the manuscript in its entirety and giving it the green light.

Many other people helped us but there simply isn't room to list them here and they wouldn't want us to either. Some took a couple of hours off to help. Some answered lengthy letters with detailed explanations. Some opened doors (figuratively) and gates (literally) for us. They all made their contributions, and this is a better book because they did.

We can recall reading a book published back in 1943 which mentioned a nationally-known authority on the trail, Paul C. Henderson, from Bridgeport, Nebraska. Subsequent references to him turned up in later books. Examination of the Annals of the Wyoming Historical Society revealed that Paul or his wife Helen were represented, either as authors or authorities, in virtually every issue for more than a decade.

It wasn't until the last year of our research that we realized that Mr. Henderson was not only quite alive, he was more active than ever — a tough, virile westerner, a one-man historical society on the trails of the American West.

The Hendersons liked what we are doing. They befriended us and agreed to read the manuscript. Since then they have provided a flood of cassette tapes, slides of their exquisite maps, photographs and other data from their vast storehouse of archival materials in Bridgeport.

—*Gregory M. Franzwa*
July 17, 1972

PREFACE TO SUBSEQUENT EDITIONS

They have gone in pickups and sedans and Jeeps, on bicycles and motorcycles, on horses and on foot. Families go, students go, clubs go. Literally thousands of people have gone to see the Oregon Trail with this book in hand. Hundreds of them have corresponded with me and many have accepted the invitation to advise where highways change and, in some cases, where mistakes were made in the text. Consequently, much of this book differs from the earlier editions, and it now is as perfect as I know how to make it. Yet, in two weeks a bridge might wash away, a gravel road might be paved, or a highway number could change.

Some of those who took much of their time to help bring the book up to date are, in alphabetical order: Robert L. Berry, Barbara Burgess, John Burns, Daniel Connell, Lynn A. Corson, Sr. Eleanor Craig, Bill and Gay Davison, Ruth Donaldson, Ronald O. Downs, Reg Duffin, Nancy Ehrlich, Norma J. Eid, Joe Fairfield, Polly Fowler, Porter French, Bill Goff, Arch and Naomi Gordon, R. P. Howard, M.D., Stanley B. Kimball, Ph.D., Stanley Kowalkowski, Rev. Edward J. Kowrach, Dorman Lehman, John A. Mann, Richard Marius, Charles W. Martin, Ronald H. Martin, Robert Murray, Samuel G. Neis, Jr., Mark Nelson, Frank Peters, E. Chilton Phoenix, Bob Picker, Peter L. Samson, Lizzie Sells, Cornelia Shields, Peter M. Stephan, Emory Strong, Morty Sumberg, Harry C. Underwood, Clyde Wallace, Merle Wells, Ferris D. White, and Art Yenson. I am especially indebted to Ray Schoch, who always provides carefully documented papers after his trips along the trail.

I am most appreciative of the dozens of book reviews, particularly those by Frank Peters of the *St. Louis Post-Dispatch* and Don Russell of the *Brand Book* of the Chicago Westerners. We also acknowledge the good taste of the American Association for State and Local History, whose judges awarded this effort their "Certificate of Commendation" for 1973.

—Gregory M. Franzwa
January 1988

Foreword

by GEORGE B. HARTZOG JR.
Director, National Park Service
United States Department of the Interior

In recent years we Americans have enjoyed the excitement of watching men conquer the thresholds of outer space. Through the magic of modern communication, we have witnessed the first human excursions to the moon.

Perhaps because of these wonders, it is difficult to comprehend that just over a century ago Oregon and California seemed as remote as the moon does today. Americans once ventured to the western edge of the continent as they now do into space. But they did not merely pause and return. They stayed and populated the land, and they helped to build America.

Today, when most of us are content to let a few daring individuals conquer the universe, it is easy to forget that the West was not conquered by a handful of trained adventurers. Ordinary Americans traveled the Oregon Trail by the hundreds of thousands, seeking a better life in the form of farmland they could call their own. Half a million of them crossed the Continental spine at the great South Pass.

It took courage to venture into a strange and forbidding land, drawn only by a promise of a better life. Pioneers on the Oregon Trail faced many obstacles — climate and terrain, distance, Indians, hardship and sickness, scarcity of food and water, to name only a few. Amateurs in the wilderness, they profited by their experience, buried their dead — more than 30,000 still lie along the trail — and pushed on to build the comfortable America their descendants have inherited.

We of the National Park Service are charged with preserving some of the landmarks of the Oregon Trail. Chimney Rock, Scotts Bluff, Fort Laramie, and Whitman Mission stand today as reminders of the trail's past. Other sites have been designated National Historic Landmarks as a result of National Park Service studies. As this book shows so well, however, the story of the Oregon Trail is greater than these few outstanding places. It was mile on mile of toil, pain, adventure — and hope. Mr. Franzwa recounts this story, and he gives us a splendid guide book so that all may visit the many scenes of this great epic.

Read this book and reflect on qualities that shaped America, especially the perseverance and courage of ordinary citizens who created a nation out of a strange wilderness. Under the guidance of Mr. Franzwa, we may stand at South Pass, witnessing in our imagination the migrations of the past, and sensing the quiet determination that characterized our forebears.

Washington, D.C.
March, 1972

The Oregon Trail Revisited

Part 1

CHAPTER 1   HISTORY OF THE OREGON TRAIL

Oregon in 1820 was a lot of things to a lot of people, but one thing it wasn't — the Oregon with the boundaries we know today. It started somewhere in the Rocky Mountains (it is a fact that no one knew exactly where) and proceeded west to the Pacific Ocean. On the south, at the 42nd parallel, was Mexico, or more specifically that part of Mexico known as California. On the north, 54°40', and Russian territory. That was about as close as anyone could get but that was close enough.

The American people knew the things that were important. Such as, the land was full of beaver, and beaver pelts were nothing less than hairy money. You could get there from St. Louis, but as Meriwether Lewis and William Clark had reported in 1806, it was one helluva job. The Missouri River will take you near there if you are in no big hurry — it goes almost everywhere else first. The Columbia, the Great River of the West, abounded in salmon, and somebody ought to be able to make a living off of that some way.

And most important, there was a valley out there; a long, wide one where the ground was more fertile than anywhere else on earth. There was plenty of rainfall, it was warm in the winter, comfortable in the summer, and the Indians couldn't care less if any white man came around — there was plenty of land along the Willamette for everybody.

The land in between? That was something else. Clark's journal is not flattering; time and again he noted a lack of forestation. Zebulon Pike journeyed to Colorado in 1806 and published four years later, and an awaiting nation learned that the great plains were utterly worthless. Stephen Long gave them a name — the "Great American Desert", and it stuck. In 1821 the United States stopped at the western boundary of the new State of Missouri. The desert started there and didn't end until the great front range of the Rocky Mountains broke the monotony, 600 miles to the west.

At the time it was deemed a major misfortune that the land of the Louisiana Purchase was the barren land; and only the land of Oregon was valuable. It would appear that President Thomas Jefferson was indeed not much of a real estate man, as the New Englanders had charged. England, still detested by Yankee Doodle, was the boss in Oregon.

The Governor and Company of Adventurers of England Trading Into Hudson's Bay, or the Hudsons Bay Co. for short, had fought the equally British Northwest Company to a standoff, and the crown forced a merger, with the former surviving. Thus was formed the single monopolistic force in the fur trade in North America, John Bull still in command.

The American John Jacob Astor had no thought of colonization when he decided to buck the British in the fur trade. He wanted only money and its attendant power. He launched a two-pronged attack — the barque *Tonquin* rounded the Horn and headed for the bar of the Columbia, while simultaneously Wilson Price Hunt and a party of men called "Astorians" journeyed overland through the interior West to the mouth of the Columbia, and Astoria was formed. The *Tonquin* was destroyed. Rendezvous was never effected, but Astoria was an American reality and stayed American until the War of 1812.

In 1812 Robert Stuart found the Oregon Trail, only in reverse. Stuart, an Astorian, took a company of men back across the continent to report the loss of the *Tonquin* to Astor in New York. With the exception of a wild goose chase just west of the continental divide, he took what became known as the Oregon Trail. He didn't actually traverse the South Pass. Undoubtedly he was following Indian trails all the way, and probably those trails were a little too fresh for comfort on that last haul over the wide, rolling knoll that separates Atlantic and Pacific waters. Stuart took one look at the Indian signs and elected to go a few miles to the south, and picked the trail up again on the Sweetwater.

Stuart left Astoria on June 29, 1812, and arrived in St. Louis 10 months later, on April 30, 1813. He spent the winter near the Wyoming-Nebraska border. On May 15, 1813, the *Missouri Gazette* (St. Louis) had this to say about the expedition:

"By information received from these gentlemen, it appears that a journey across the continent of North America might be performed with a waggon, there being no obstruction on the whole route that any person would dare call a mountain in addition to its being much the most direct and short one to go from this place to the mouth of the Columbia River. Any future party who may undertake this journey, and are tolerably acquainted with the different places, where it would be necessary to lay up a small stock of provisions, would not be impeded, as in all probability they would not meet with an Indian to interrupt their progress; although on the other route more north, there are almost insurmountable barriers."

A nation started to wonder . . .

William Henry Ashley was a Virginian who settled in Ste. Genevieve immediately after the Louisiana Purchase. He had enjoyed varied careers; surveyor, land speculator, merchant and a manufacturer of gunpowder. He moved to the bustling town of St. Louis, 60 miles up the Mississippi, and gained prominence there. On Feb. 13, 1822 he ran a celebrated help wanted ad in the *Missouri Gazette:*

"To Enterprising Young Men: The Subscriber wishes to engage ONE HUNDRED MEN to ascend the river Missouri to its source, there to be

employed for one, two or three years. For
particulars, enquire of Major Andrew Henry, near
the Lead Mines, in the county of Washington (who
will ascend with and command the party) or to the
subscriber at St. Louis."

This was the same Andrew Henry who had led a
brigade of the Missouri Fur Co. to the Three Forks of
the Missouri (above Yellowstone Park) in 1810.

Somebody read that ad to a gangling, raw-boned kid
who lived west of town, and Jim Bridger signed up for
his first trip to the mountains.

That was the real beginning of the American fur
trade, and the fur trade was the beginning of the West.
In 1823, Ashley beefed up his outfit, bringing in Tom
(Broken Hand) Fitzpatrick, Jed Smith, Bill Sublette, and
Jim Clyman. It was Clyman who, later that winter, made
his way over the South Pass, the low meadow in a low
mountain range destined to figure prominently in the
expansion of the United States.

The next summer (1824) Ashley started the
technique of the rendezvous, where thousands of red
and white trappers would bring their peltry to a single
spot, trade it to the factors in exchange for money,

National Park Service

*Smith, Sublette and Jackson caravan leaving St. Louis
for continental divide in 1830.*

whiskey, beads, food — anything they wanted as long as they were gypped. The rendezvous system prospered for a dozen years, until the world craze for beaver hats evaporated.

It was in the 1830s that the course of Oregon emigration was changed. In 1830 Jed Smith, Bill Sublette and Dave Jackson took a caravan of 81 men from St. Louis to the rendezvous in the Wind River Mountains, at the mouth of the Popo Agie River, near present Riverton, Wyo. All were mounted on mules. The difference between this and earlier caravans was this one rolled on wheels; 10 wagons drawn by four mules each, and two one-mule dearborns. A dozen beef cattle and one milk cow completed the caravan.

They didn't roll over the mountains but at least they got to them. A nation hungry for news from this thrilling land noted this, and waited until somebody could get a wagon all the way.

Wagon transport was absolutely essential to mass emigration. The wagons were needed to haul a family's personal possessions, to transport the provisions not only for the five-month haul but to sustain the family until the crops planted the following spring were harvested. The wealthy could emigrate by sailing ship around the Horn and up the west coast, or by ship to Panama, across the neck of land by pack mule, and by ship to the Pacific Northwest. The cost either way was $300 a head. By wagon a whole family, their personal belongings and their livestock, could move to the West for $200. The nation waited and watched.

They didn't have to wait long. In 1832 Capt. Benjamin E. Bonneville, on leave from the U.S. Army, assembled a train at Ft. Osage on the eastern edge of Jackson Co., Mo., and moved west by land — past the new Blue Mills landing northeast of Independence, over the bottoms of the Missouri River, across the rock ledges in what is now downtown Kansas City, and onto the old Chouteau fur trail to the mountains. His wagons crossed the divide at the familiar South Pass, headed to the northwest. He built his fort in western Wyoming, on the Green.

That was enough to excite the nation. Now the dreamers could dream reality. In 1836 they would see Dr. Marcus Whitman take wheels (only two, but still wheels) almost to the Columbia and that proved something; but the farmers of Iowa, Virginia and Georgia already knew all they wanted to know. The West was open. Wagons could move there if they were built right. And in a few years they themselves would quit this vale of tears and get out there in the promised land where they belonged.

Why, asked many an Easterner, would a man want to abandon all he had worked for to emigrate to Oregon? Men had come to Missouri, removed the scrub oak, built cabins and forced a blade through the tough and unyielding prairie turf. Each year a few more acres, each year a few more dollars. Their families were under way, their prosperity seemed assured.

England, hated England, still was predominant in the Pacific Northwest. A joint occupational treaty had been signed in 1818, and it is true that, by 1840 at least, the Americans outnumbered the British, who had nothing but furs in mind. But England still held sway. Oregon wasn't in the United States; it wasn't even United States territory. England clearly had the right of prior occupancy, going all the way back to Sir Francis Drake.

The same forces were at work on the man from Missouri which had eaten on his forebears in New England a generation back. Men dissatisfied with Massachusetts gave it up and broke ground in New Hampshire. Men from Ohio and Virginia went to Kentucky. Men from Kentucky went to Missouri.

There were other, more tangible reasons for going West. There was a stunning national panic in 1837, and the price of improved farm land sunk to anywhere from $25 on down to $5 an acre. Those who recovered from 1837 were hit even harder by the 1842 depression. Those who lived in or near the cities found the industrial revolution taking hold; work in the factories was unrewarding and there was always the danger of layoffs. The air was filthy; the water was polluted. Taxes were up, hours were long, wages were down.

By 1842 wheat had fallen to 15 cents a bushel and

you couldn't give the corn away. Jesse Applegate sold a whole steamboat load of bacon for $100; other farmers burned it for fuel. Bankrupt merchants would pay in scrip, and farmers found their income was about 50 cents a day worth of paper, which might or might not be worth anything at all.

Lindsay Applegate, a gentle man, came west partly because he feared the social unrest, the pro-slavery mobs in particular. Another man, interviewed late in his life, said he came west "because the thing wasn't fenced in and nobody dared to keep me off."

Missouri's senators had more influence on the western movement than anyone else in government. Thomas Hart Benton, one of Missouri's first senators, was seated in December 1821, and from that day forward the chamber rang with his expansionist rhetoric. He was the foremost proponent of acquisition of the Oregon Territory until his colleague, Alexander Buckner, died in 1833.

The brilliant young doctor from Ste. Genevieve, Lewis F. Linn, stepped into service as Missouri's other senator until his death a decade later, and Linn and Benton collaborated constantly on the Oregon question.

It was Linn, in fact, who introduced the territorial bill in Congress, on Feb. 7, 1838. He kept the bill alive for the rest of his life, but unfortunately his life wasn't long enough. Cholera had laid half his constituency low in the old town of Ste. Gene-

Daguerreotype by Matthew Brady of Sen. Thomas Hart Benton, taken about the time of "The Oregon Question."

vieve; the good doctor responded to his first obligation, came home, and took the cholera himself. The gauntlet reverted to the old warrior, Benton, in 1843.

Benton had some ideas about keeping the Oregon

question in the papers. He saw to it that the Congress appointed Lt. John Charles Fremont to head a federal exploring expedition to the Columbia, and report back again. Fremont was admirably suited — young, ambitious, a surveyor, geographer, and he had the finest of all possible qualifications: he was married to Jesse Benton Fremont, the senator's daughter.

Brady made this picture of John Charles Fremont, as he looked about 1856, when he lost Presidential election race.

Jesse Fremont, his wife, who also was the daughter of Sen. Thomas Hart Benton.

Fremont's reports, undoubtedly polished and illuminated by the brilliant Jesse, captivated the nation. Oregon was indeed as rich as it was said to be. It was easily reached by wagon, and a man might indeed find a better life out there. Then why, reasoned Tom Benton, should it not be given territorial status and protection by the government of the United States?

By 1844 the nation was polarized — not between Oregon proponents and Oregon detractors, but rather between those who thought with Henry Clay, that the U.S. ought to do everything she could within reason to win Oregon; and those who wanted Oregon all the way to 54°40', and right this very minute. Those people were aligned behind James K. Polk.

"James K. *Who?*" sneered the Whigs, but the national

conscience knew who. James K. Polk was elected, 1,337,243 to 1,299,068, and the single overpowering issue was expansionism. The people had spoken. Trouble was, they had spoken for Polk's slogan, "54° 40' or Fight!" and now that he was elected Polk didn't particularly want to put it that way. He told the British he would gladly settle for 49°(where it ended up), but John Bull wanted more, in the finest traditions of international negotiations.

Polk went back to 54°40', hoping the matter could be forgotten about, but sabres rattled in the senate and the British started caulking their bottoms for a long sea voyage. The temper of the British people, fortunately, was relaxed; with the fur trade nearly defunct there wasn't much reason to fight over Oregon. British occupation was only token anyhow. Americans were there in great numbers. The British came down to 49° and Polk snapped it up. Screams went up from the warhawks in the senate, and true westerners looked upon their President as treasonous. Senator Benton, more than happy with the compromise, supplied the necessary grease and the measure passed through Congress.

Benton would carry the guidon of expansionist leadership just once more. In 1848, when the senate was locked in debate over the Oregon territorial bill, he made a dramatic 11th hour appeal and Oregon officially became a territory.

All this political activity was accomplished with reams of publicity. The young nation gobbled up every printed word about the mysterious West and demanded more. Millions dreamed of making the great trek across the mountains. Only a fraction realized that dream.

Few men contributed more to the Oregon propaganda mill in the days prior to the great emigration than a young Boston schoolmaster named Hall Jackson Kelley. Kelley could write. He couldn't think very well but he could write. He formed some ideas about Oregon and wrote about them, and the eager Eastern press grabbed them and ran.

Kelley's interest began about 1815; he started writing about Oregon for publication in 1818; began a campaign for colonization in 1824; and formed the American Society for Encouraging the Settlement of the Oregon Territory (which really didn't have territorial status yet) in 1832. He published a circular in 1831 giving directions to the land he had never seen. He had a lot of things in mind — mostly he felt a burning need to Christianize those heathen Indians.

Kelley found a few converts. So unsettled, so disturbed was this early 19th century American society that almost anyone with any kind of "ism" to offer, no matter how nutty, could find converts. A few of Kelley's people went west in the 1830s, probably no more than a dozen. Kelley went west too. He missed a chance with Nat Wyeth and waited until 1833. After all his pamphlets, lectures, and bombastic mass meetings about the Oregon Trail, Hall Kelley for some reason chose to go through Mexico, alone. He picked up nine converts there, eight of them wanted for horse stealing, and moved northwest. He contracted malaria and his life was saved by Michel la Framboise, brigade leader of the very organization Kelley had used as a focus of his hatred, the Hudson's Bay Company. He was carried across the Columbia to Fort Vancouver. The good Dr. John McLoughlin didn't throw him in jail, although he could have, since he was traveling with some rotten company. He regained his health and disappeared. So Hall Jackson Kelley, once the national spokesman for western expansion, went down in ignominy.

The Kelley rumblings in the 1820s were but a preview of what was to come in the following decade. The 1830s would bring to the Oregon question fervent religious zeal, particularly on the part of the Protestants. Never mind that the need for Christianizing the Pacific Coast savages was questionable; and never mind that some of the Westering clergy were inept bluenoses unequipped to bring religion to their next door neighbor, let alone the primitive American Indian. The point is they had a massive impact on the colonization of the Oregon country, and that makes them important.

The Nez Perce Indians, a particularly intelligent and at least semi-civilized group, occupied regions of what is now Oregon and Washington. The Flatheads, just as advanced, were in western Montana. Both maintained considerable intercourse with first the Northwest Company, and after the merger of 1821, the Hudsons Bay Company.

Through this business traffic the Indians came to admire and envy the white man, and through the 1820s, they noted the gradual shift of the trade away from the British, whom they liked, to the Americans, whom they liked a lot more. They noticed the Americans possessed the same creature comforts as the British. The white man had great power — "medicine", they called it — and this resulted in his possession of the kind of goods the Indian coveted. How could the Indian get the sort of medicine that would give him the same way of life as the white man?

The Indian understood that the white man's medicine centered on his religion, as was the case with the Indian also. Since the white man had more of the world's goods, it followed that his medicine — his religion — must be more powerful.

The Nez Perces get credit for the idea. They would journey all the way to St. Louis and talk with Gen. Clark, the man they met in 1805 and 1806; the man who could help them find this religion.

The Nez Perces conferred with the Flatheads, and they bought the idea too. So four Nez Perces and three Flatheads left for St. Louis, probably with the great trader Lucien Fontenelle, in the summer of 1831. Down the Platte they came, out of the clean, thin air of the high mountains and into the muggy August heat of the lowlands. Three turned back. Four made it to St. Louis, probably around the first of October. One was a Flathead, Man of the Morning. The three Nez Perces were Black Eagle, No Horns on His Head, and Rabbit Skin Leggings.

The first problem they faced was one of communication. The four were the first transmontane Indians to come to St. Louis. There evidently were no traders in town at the time who had learned their language. Even Clark, the Red Headed Chief himself, couldn't understand their questions. After some weeks the conversants got to the point where they could communicate in sign language. Bernard DeVoto states that they wanted, principally, amulets, incantations and instructions in magic. Clark interpreted this as religious instruction and, perhaps, it was.

Certainly, until somebody learned somebody else's language, there could be no instruction as such. Nevertheless, the Protestant Clark took the braves across what is now the Third Street Expressway, past the huge limestone pile where teams of mules — human and equine — were dragging the big stones onto the walls that would soon encase the New Cathedral (now the Old Cathedral on the downtown St. Louis riverfront.) The next door to the east was the brick building which housed the St. Louis College, the predecessor of St. Louis University of today, if a point may be stretched a little.

There they met Rev. Edmund Saulnier and Bishop Joseph Rosati. Clark advanced the suggestion that they wanted a missionary to live with them, and that probably is true. Rosati could give little hope for this. The diocese already was pitifully short of both manpower and fiscal resources.

But the Indians lingered on in St. Louis anyway, filled with wonderment at the white man's accomplishments. The humidity got to Chief Black Eagle, and he died on Oct. 31, 1831. Saulnier baptized him on the way out, and the cortege wound out to the new Catholic cemetery at what is now 7th and Franklin. At that time it was out in the country, considerably past the limits of the burgeoning little town. Soon after, Man of the Morning died, fortified with the last rites administered by Fr. Joseph A. Lutz.

The early western artist, George Catlin, met Rabbit Skin Leggings and No Horns on His Head on the steamer *Yellowstone*, bound for the Upper Missouri country, in the spring of 1832. No Horns on His Head died near Ft. Union, at the mouth of the Yellowstone River, and Rabbit Skin Leggings was the only survivor to greet his people. He told his story to the Nez Perces he met on a hunt east of the divide, but on the way home he lost his scalp to a band of Blackfeet.

That, evidently, was what really happened. What really happened and what was said to have happened were two entirely different things.

In those days Methodists in the United States received a journal called *Christian Advocate*. (They still do.) The issue dated March 1, 1833, carried a letter to the editor on page one, sent in by a New York businessman named G. P. Disoway. The letter actually contained another letter, one of those seeming pieces of inconsequentiality which change the course of history.

The letter-within-a-letter came from William Walker, a Wyandot breed who had learned to write, and who happened to be in St. Louis. Not only had the white man taught him to write, he also had learned to tell one whopping lie after another, and although his motives aren't exactly clear, presumably he felt that if the lie were properly structured, there might be some way that the reaction could pay off for Walker.

Rabbit Skin Leggings was painted in 1831 by George Catlin, when both were aboard the Yellowstone on the Upper Missouri.

Walkers sketch from the Christian Advocate, *showing erroneous notion of how Flatheads deformed themselves.*

At any rate, the letter to Disoway said that Gen.

Clark had introduced him (Walker) to three Flatheads at Clark's house. He drew their picture, showing how their heads had been deformed — compressed to a point by a board worn in infancy. The Indians, Walker said, had come to St. Louis in search of the white man's book of heaven. Now listen to the anti-papist Walker quoting Indians who couldn't speak a word that anybody could understand, and whom he had never seen:

"My people sent me to get the White Man's Book of Heaven. You took me to where you allow your women to dance, and the book was not there. You took me to where they worship the Great Spirit with candles and the book was not there. You showed me images of the good spirits and the picture of the good land beyond, but the book was not among them to tell the way. I am going back the long and sad trail to my people in the dark land. You make my feet heavy with gifts and my moccasins will grow old carrying them, yet the book is not among them." Et cetera.

Disoway, in his covering letter, jumped on this with both feet. "Let the Church awake from her slumbers and go forth in her strength to the salvation of those wandering sons of our native forests!" was his pontification.

Disoway evidently was one fat cat, and when he howled the Mission Board listened. He had financed before, he would finance again. And so it came to pass that a big, awkward schoolteacher from a Methodist emplacement in Stanstead, Quebec, came to the West, toting the White Man's Book of Heaven. Jason Lee, an ordained Methodist minister, heard the call. He was able to hook up with Nat Wyeth on his tremendous scheme for exploitation of the West, and they headed for Independence.

Jason Lee did the best he could to ignore the hell raising, crap shooting, whiskey drinking, whore mongering town of Independence and finally, on April 28, 1834, the agony ended. Evil was left behind; Jason Lee and his nephew Daniel Lee followed Nat Wyeth down the Santa Fe Trail for a day, then headed up toward the Platte and a bright tomorrow.

On July 4, 1834, Jason
Lee saw his beloved Flat-
heads at Hams Fork of the
Green. He noted that their
heads were not flat at all.
(The name actually was
derived from the sign
language they used to
designate themselves —
hands flat with fingertips
touching over the high
part of the forehead.)
William Walker, who had
never seen a Flathead in
his life, had them confused
with the few degenerate
Chinooks of the coast,
who still practiced the
ancient custom of com-
pressing the heads of their
infants with flat boards.

*Jason Lee, the first of
the missionaries to go to
Oregon, hooked up with
Nat Wyeth in 1834 and
landed on the Willamette.*

But he never saw a Chinook either.

Jason Lee, to his dying day, never said why, on that
Fourth of July, he gave the order to continue on, on to
the Willamette and away from the Flatheads. He had
collected thousands of dollars in the East on the strength
of his intent to establish a mission among, and Christianize, the Flatheads. The Mission Board had given him
many thousands more for the same purpose.

DeVoto feels Lee must have concluded that before
the Indian could be Christianized he first had to be
civilized. Therefore, the Methodist Mission was duly
established on the banks of the Willamette, where the
red man could learn to farm the land, use soap, curse,
raise hell, shoot craps, drink whiskey and monger
whores. Only then would he be be sufficiently prepared to
accept the White Mans' Book of Heaven. Lee was right.
He could look reality square in the face and see reality.
After Marcus Whitman, Lee comes down to us known as
the best Protestant missionary of the early West.

The Mission Board shot the cash out to Lee, as much
as he could use. He returned in 1838 with two Indians

and three half-breed children; went on a lecture tour of the East. There were too few Indians coming in for the Christianizing process, he told the Easterners. He needed men and he needed money. He got more of both — several men and $42,000 in cash. The pious were ready to share their piety and their money. Lee was not attracting missionary activity with his talks about his marvelous farm; he was attracting white settlement. He was writing the book on Protestant activity on the Willamette — *How To Save Indians For Fun And Profit.* His reputation today is that of an honest, hard-working man of God an an enormous influence on the settlement of the West. He was a good man.

The press knew a story when they saw one, and Jason Lee was hot copy from the minute he left Independence. There was another man who would be hotter copy — he, in fact, would stand a nation on its collective ear. His name was Marcus Whitman, M.D. Whitman was first a man, second a physician, third a Presbyterian missionary. But first a man; the West would never forget that.

Whitman was a genuinely honest, religious man, who above all else sought to impress his own religion on the Indian, not because of any rewards he or his church would reap from the added membership, or even because conversion would lessen the Indian desire to speed the white man to the happy hunting ground. Rather, Whitman wanted to Presbyterianize the Indians because he honestly felt the Indians would be happier with that faith.

Whitman and Samuel Parker, a 56-year-old Congregational minister from an Ithaca school, left from Liberty (across the Missouri River from Independence) on May 15, 1835, with the annual fur caravan headed by Lucien Fontenelle. The American Board of Commissioners for Foreign Missions had financed their exploring expedition to the West, to see if the time was right for the establishment of Christian outposts far beyond the frontier. In the company were 60 men, 200 animals, and six wagons — bound for the rendezvous on the Upper Green River.

Fontenelle was a hard driver and the arrival at Ft. Laramie, then only a year old, was celebrated with a roaring drunk for all hands. Sam Parker frowned on this; Whitman's reaction was not recorded.

When they hit the Green they met the Flatheads and Nez Perces. There was rejoicing, and Whitman found the main thing he had come to find — that Walker in one respect had been right, the Nez Perces and the Flatheads genuinely wanted the religion of the white man. Parker went on to find some mission sites; Whitman high-tailed back to the states, determined to get an outfit together in time to establish a mission the following year.

Parker moved into Ft. Walla Walla, where the river of that name surged into the Columbia; then down to Ft. Vancouver where Dr. John McLoughlin, the Hudsons Bay Company "King of Oregon", held absolute and benevolent power over the Pacific Northwest. Parker kept moving, down the Columbia to the Coast and then up to the Lees' fabulous outpost of Methodism on the Willamette. The old bones were getting creaky with all that walking and riding and Sam Parker jumped at a chance to go home. McLoughlin put him on a barque for the East, via the Sandwich Islands (Hawaii of today). He floated into New London on May 17th, 1837; another good man who could call them as he saw them and he saw them as they were. Sam Parker suspected that Oregon missionary activities would not be very successful. He respected the Indian, he detested the white who would take advantage of him, debase him, torture him and kill him. He got out, and wrote one of the best of the Oregon guide books. That was copy the farmers wanted. They read. They dreamed.

Whitman came back to Missouri the following spring (1836) with the outfit he needed. He had two things with him that would alter the destiny of the nation. One was a wagon. It gave out on the lower Snake, but it got further than any wagon had gone before, and with a little better craftsmanship it would have made it all the way.

The other was the first real sign that the West was about to open for colonization — a woman, the delightful, articulate, lovely Narcissa Prentiss Whitman. Well-born, devout, and infinitely loving, she took her honeymoon on the Oregon Trail. All along the way she wrote letters; letters which somehow got delivered to her parents in the East and, somehow, they gained publication.

Also in the outfit were the two Nez Perce boys Whitman had taken from the rendezvous the year before, to help propagandize the East, plus another picked up in Liberty. And — dour Henry H. Spalding, a Presbyterian minister who had loved Narcissa for years, and who, after she had rejected his proposal of marriage, took a second-rate second choice, Eliza Spalding. Rev. Spalding, the guilt-ridden son of unmarried parents, was what he was in more than one sense of the word.

Also in the entourage — William H. Gray, a lay assistant, easily one of the least popular men who ever moved over the Oregon Trail.

They were late getting to Liberty, found that their outfit already had moved out; went up to Bellevue, just south of present day Omaha, and after a furious drive caught up with the fur brigade a week or so out on the north bank of the lower Platte.

In charge: the great Tom Fitzpartick, the old Opposition partisan of the defunct Rocky Mountain Fur Co., and his sidekick, Moses (Black) Harris. Milton Sublette (brother of the famous Bill), whose amputation put him on crutches and soon would put him in the Ft. Laramie cemetery; and Sir William Drummond Stewart, the Scottish nobleman who had a ton of money and knew how to have an exciting time with it.

Narcissa Whitman by this time must have known she was pregnant — she was some six weeks along and probably was feeling rather queasy by the time they hit Ft. Hall on the Snake. She rejoiced in her letters when the axle broke, meaning they could now make better time without the encumbrance of a balky wagon. Dr. Whitman had another idea, the wagon had another axle, and the wagon became a cart. The abandonment was postponed until Ft. Boise was reached, but Narcissa's letters got the point across to the East — the Oregon Trail would be receptive to wagons properly built. That is what Whitman wanted to prove.

Spalding and Whitman wisely separated; the former

going to his Lapwai mission among the Nez Perces, some 10 miles up the Clearwater from present day Lewiston, Idaho. Whitman picked a spot on the Walla Walla River, 25 miles up from its mouth, called Waiilatpu, "Place of the Rye Grass." He tried to Christianize the Cayuse, and that was a mistake that would cost him his life.

On Narcissa's 29th birthday, March 14, 1837, Alice Clarissa Whitman came onto this earth, to stay but two years before the waters of the Walla Walla would fill her lungs and snuff out her life. Both her birth and her death startled the nation.

Whitman returned to the U.S. in 1842. Greeley of the *Tribune* espoused his cause and, after a tedious lecture circuit with attendent publicity, the good doctor was able to return to Waiilatpu with a little more backing than he had before.

Finally, the world learned of the brutal massacre of Dr. Whitman and Narcissa on Nov. 29, 1847. Eleven others were chopped up by the Cayuse; and most of the rest of the mission population were taken as hostages. Joe Meek, one of the great, legendary mountain men and guides, lately big gun in the Oregon provisional government, saddled up and rode over the national spine in the dead of winter to carry the somber message to Congress — a message that was to do more than anything else to give official territorial status — and federal protection — to Oregon.

There were other missionaries. Rev. Cushing and Myra Eells, who weren't bad; Asa and Sarah Smith, who weren't bad either but who were next to worthless; Elkanah and Mary Walker, both of whom could have used a good physic; and William and (get this) Mary Gray. That William Gray took or was given a bride is the only evidence the world has that anyone on this earth had any fondness for him whatever, and that is only circumstantial.

Yet all were consequential to the development of the land. All were communicators, and wherever there was dissatisfaction with one's lot in life, there was a reader of their communication. They had something to say and there were a lot of unhappy midwesterners ready to listen.

Back in St. Louis something peculiar was happening. In 1835, at the same time the American Board was responding to the early plea of the four unfortunate pilgrims to St. Louis, and one year after Jason Lee's arrival in Oregon; a Flathead chief named Old Ignace and two of his sons showed up in St. Louis, renewing the earlier request for a minister to their people. Again, Clark did what he could, and again, they went home without promises. Didn't they know about Whitman and Parker?

They had to know about them in 1837, and again, Old Ignace, three more Flatheads and a chief of the Nez Perces turned up in St. Louis. By this time the message was beginning to come across. They didn't like the magic they were getting. The white man's Book of Heaven was not what they wanted. They wanted the real medicine — the beads, the amulets, the incantations. They wanted a Black Robe.

On the way back from their second trip, they passed through Ash Hollow. The Sioux were waiting there and they hadn't had a Flathead scalp in ages. They got Old Ignace's.

Back came another delegation in 1839 — Young Ignace and another Flathead. This time Rosati gave them a promise. There was a man on Rosati's farm in Florissant who was about ready for ordination. In the spring of 1840 the young priest would leave for the Flathead country. His name: Pierre-Jean DeSmet.

The Protestant press printed nothing of this, if, indeed, they even knew of it. DeVoto knew of it but for some reason chose not to mention it. The stocky little Jesuit, brusk, affable, sympathetic and intensely honest, did more for the Flatheads and Nez Perces — more for all the Indians of the West — than all the Protestants lumped together, and that even includes the great Dr. Whitman.

DeSmet established one mission after another, somehow managed to get other Jesuits to the West to man them, with concentration on teaching. DeSmet would cross the Atlantic time after monotonous time, doing a job he hated but which he could do better than anybody else, raising vast sums for the Jesuit missions. He would move from Europe, to St. Stanislaus Seminary in old Florissant, to the Rocky Mountains and back again. He continued this work until old age stopped him, then forced his stiffening fingers to write appeals for more help for his beloved Flatheads, up until a few days before death claimed him. He saved more American lives than any other man, through his soothing of Indian nations seething with rage at a demoniac white man possessed of neither ethics nor morals. He did it time and again, only to see the young and unprincipled nation break its word, time and again.

Catholics were in cities, and city people were aware that there was little opportunity for them in the West. It was the farmer who identified with the West, the Protestant farmer, the anti-Catholic farmer. It was the Protestant missionaries who got the play in the press. No question about it, it was the Black Robes who did the job they were sent out to do.

The American press was in high gear. National stories appeared constantly. What really was electrifying, however, was when the guy from your own township sold out his farm, threw everything in a wagon and moved over the trail to Oregon or California. Neighbors were fascinated and envious. If he made it, why couldn't they?

Then the letters to the home town paper started coming back; maybe three or four in one mail. Letters posted at strange sounding places like Independence, Westport, Ash Hollow, Ft. Laramie, Ft. Bridger. Letters full of wonderment at the prairies, the Indians, the buffalo, the deserts, and even the other emigrants. At a whole new life as different as a life could be without detachment from the planet itself.

Missouri and Iowa farmers, comfortable and secure, their farms paid for, their ground all broken and fertile, read these letters. The old thoughts welled up, the same thoughts that drove them to Iowa and Missouri in the first place. They had something to prove, and they proved it. Challenge was gone now. Neighbors coming in, working a section or two away from their farms. Maybe

a fence dispute now and then. Howling north winds in
January, working a half hour every morning to cut four
inches of ice out of the creek for the stock. Summer
heat so stinking a person couldn't go near the barn. The
paradise of 1830 was improved immeasurably, but in the
minds of the farmers it had become the hell of 1840.

Back in New York, John L. O'Sullivan had another
issue of the *Democratic Review* staring him in the face.
His job was to write the editorials, and he hadn't
especially distinguished himself until this particular
summer morning in 1845. He was a little disenchanted
with Polk's pullback from his warlike slogans that won
him the presidency in 1844. Like all editorialists then
and now, he chose to exercise his personal responsibility
to save humanity by dishing out free advice to presidents
and kings. In the course of his journalism of the moment
he wrote two words that were picked up by one editor
after another, and which, to this day, are being used to
title chapters of the American history of the 1840s. The
words: "Manifest Destiny." The national bird was
soaring high, every tailfeather in place and talons
sharpened. Right up there with God, whom everyone
knew was on our side too. Oregon was this nation's
Manifest Destiny. It would take a tremendous colonization to overcome the power of Britain's unquestioned
right of prior occupancy.

Men in the mid-19th century felt a deeply personal
sense of belonging to the United States and its federal
government; significantly moreso than they do today.
John Doe felt his duty was to his country then, almost
as much as it was to his family. He was getting together
with other men he scarcely knew, to found emigration
societies. He would do his part to lock up Oregon for the
U.S., and quite incidentally better himself in the process.
Wherever there was a town of more than a few hundred
people, a society was either in existence or was being
formed. They met regularly to pore over the latest
literature, swap guide books, talk about the military
unity they must form if they were to get to Oregon
efficiently and in one piece.

They would discuss their crops and farm prices —

both of produce and the land. Somehow they had to compress everything they owned into the cubic footage that would fit into a wagon (plus a few cattle and a saddle horse or two.) They would come home through the snow shaking with excitement, conjuring dreams of the Indians, the endless prairies, the stark deserts, the towering Rockies and always the unbelievably fertile Willamette Valley.

So stand back, world. When spring comes . . .

Spring came, the spring of 1842, and a total of 112 persons left Independence that year. They headed down the Santa Fe Trail from the square at Independence on May 14, with 18 wagons, plus horses, mules and cattle. Included in the group was Dr. Elijah White and a particularly odious PR man named Lansford W. Hastings; the same Hastings who wanted to be King of California so badly that he put out a guide book advocating a route he had never seen. George Donner bought a copy and swore by it . . .

The smaller Bidwell-Bartleson party, California bound, had left the year before, in the company of Tom Fitzpatrick and, again, Fr. DeSmet. Half the group left the Oregon Trail at the Soda Springs, but the rest went to the Columbia and the Willamette.

In 1843 the emigration was up to 1,000 people, principally Jesse Applegate's famed party. It consisted of 120 wagons and several thousand loose cattle and horses. The group was promoted by Dr. Whitman and included Peter Burnett, destined to become California's first governor. A couple of weeks behind them came the hunting party of Sir William Drummond Stewart, with Bill Sublette as a guide and Baptiste Charbonneau as a driver. Charbonneau, 38, was the son of Sacajawea. He was born while she was in the service of Lewis and Clark.

1844 was a wet year and the emigration was down; but it topped 3,000 in 1845.

In 1846 the emigration was down again, probably due to the impending trouble with England and Mexico. Somewhere between 2,000 and 2,500 Americans took the leap. The next year, with the international troubles ended, the emigration doubled, and by 1848 there were more than 12,000 people in Oregon; probably one in every four born in Missouri.

It kept up that way, on and off, even through the horrible years when the Indians were at open war with the whites. It didn't stop until the turn of the century, when the railroad fares were down so a man could afford them. By then at least 300,000 had moved along that trail, and 90 per cent of them made it. It follows that the other 10 per cent didn't. They were buried along, and generally in, the Oregon Trail, where the wagons would obscure the grave, dispersing the scent so the wolves couldn't find it; obscuring the evidence so the Indians couldn't cheat and bring home a free scalp.

BILL OF SALE

Having sold my farm and am leaving for Oregon Territory by ox team, will offer on March 1, 1849, all of my personal property to wit:

All ox teams, except two teams, Buck and Ben and Tom and Jerry. 2 milch cows; 1 gray mare and colt; 2 ox carts; 1 iron plow with wood mold board; 800 feet of poplar weather boards; 1,000 three-foot clapboards; 1,500 feet fence rails; one 60-gallon soap kettle; 85 sugar troughs, made of white ash timber; 10 gallons of maple syrup; 2 spinning wheels; 30 pounds of mutton tallow; 20 pounds of beef tallow; 1 large broom made by Jerry Wilson; 300 poles, 100 split hoops; 100 empty barrels; 1 32-gallon barrel of Johnson-Miller whiskey, 7 years old; 20 gallons apple brandy; one 40-gallon copper still; four sides of oak tanned leather; 1 dozen real hooks; 2 handle hooks, 3 scythes and cradles; 1 dozen wooden pitchforks; one-half interest in tanyard; 7 32-calibre rifles; bullet molds and powder horn; rifle made by Ben Miller; 50 gallons of soft soap; hams, bacon and lard; 40 gallons of sorghum molassas; six head of fox hounds, all soft mouthed except one.

At the same time I will sell my six negro slaves — 2 men, 35 and 50 years old; 2 boys, 12 and 18 years old; 2 mulatto wenches, 40 and 30 years old; Will sell all together to same party as will not separate them. Terms of sale, cash in hand, or note to draw 4 per cent interest with Bob McConnell as Security. My home is on McConn's Ferry Pike. Sale will begin at 8 o'clock a.m. Plenty to drink and eat.

It was happening all over the Middle West but this particular sale bill came from Kentucky. Men were compressing all they had to the maximum portability, preferably cash. They were ready to go; ready to cash in and move to Independence or Westport or St. Joe. Those who went first wrote back, and in the course of so doing they wrote reams of advice to their former neighbors, via the home town paper. Not so much on the advantages of any particular route, although that was ususally included, but mostly on what to bring. Heading the list, of course, were the wagons and the means of moving them.

Chester Ingersoll cashed in in 1847 and took deck passage on the Illinois River from Peru (midway between Joliet and Peoria) to St. Louis for $5. A cabin cost $11 and he didn't think he could afford that. Ingersoll went on to Independence and wrote nine letters to the *Joliet Sentinel* between May 1 and Nov. 20 of that year.

Ingersoll's advice led off with the wagon. It should, he said, be made on a wide track, with a box between 22 and 24 inches high, and about eleven feet long. Forget the covering; you can get that at Independence. You can get the cattle there too, at $30 to $60 a yoke. (Oxen frequently were referred to as cattle in those days.) Cows were from $12 to $16 a head, Independence. Flour, bacon and bread were actually cheaper in Independence than they were in St. Louis, at $2.12, $5 and $3.50 per hundredweight, respectively. He told his friends that the flour, bread, rice, sugar and other staples must be stored in highest quality sacking, as there should be no barrels.

Ingersoll advised that the "whoops" be no more than five feet from the bottom of the wagon box, that the covers be of two thicknesses, the outside being of "heavy drilling." And he said that if cattle were purchased in Missouri to go ahead and get the yokes too, with good bows and irons, as those things couldn't be obtained in Independence. Get 100 feet of one-inch rope for each five wagons, he counseled, so the wagons could be lowered into the ravines. Stay away from blooded cattle — get good sized, trim built ones from four to eight years old. It is better, he said, to yoke the animals and drive them as a team than it is to herd them (presumably because yoked oxen would be more reluctant to stampede). Start from St. Joe instead of Independence, and there will be no necessity to cross the Kansas River, said Ingersoll. The Papin boys at the ferry in Topeka evidently had gotten to him good.

Old Ezra Meeker, who went out as a teenager in 1852, left Eddyville, Iowa, with just one wagon, his wife and child, two yoke of four-year-old steers, one yoke of cows, and one extra cow. In writing about his trail experiences, Meeker advised packing the butter in the center of the flour in double sacks; packing the eggs in cornmeal or flour; carrying plenty of dried fruit, dried pumpkins, and jerked beef; and taking a tin reflector for baking bread. There was no place for the heavy cast iron stoves on the Oregon Trail — the remains of thousands of them probably are still out there.

Ezra Meeker went West as a young man in 1852 and returned along the Oregon Trail with an ox team in 1906, promoting monuments all along the way.

An exhibition wagon in use today. Motive power is two Mexican dogging steers trained to pull. Rig is owned by Lovell Turner, Burley, Idaho.

Meeker described oxen simply as steers trained to work. Steers, of course, are castrated bulls. They will weigh in at about 1,500 to 2,500 pounds apiece, and were shod two shoes to the hoof.

Narcissa Whitman had done her homework well. She packed beans, bacon, rice, coffee, tea, sugar, flour, pickles and vinegar. They carried their own milk cows, so there was always fresh milk, cream and butter. She would mix flour, warm water, soda and salt in a tin basin, doing her best to keep out the mosquitoes and the sand. She would knead the mix, flatten to one inch in thickness, grease her dutch oven and bury it in coals. The trick in baking bread was in temperature and timing — to bake it through without cremating the outside. There never was a shortage of food in the Whitman entourage.

Joseph E. Ware, in a good guide book, *Emigrant's Guide to California*, said that the bill of materials for four persons ought to be: six mules, a wagon, three sets of harness, a painted wagon cover, 824 lbs. of flour, 725 lbs. of bacon, 75 lbs. of coffee, 160 lbs. of sugar, 200 lbs. of lard and suet, 200 lbs. of beans, 135 lbs. of peaches and apples, 25 lbs. of salt, some pepper, and "saleratus." (That was bicarbonate of soda.) Take along tin plates and spoons, a coffee pot, a camp kettle, and knives. If the wagon and teams are sold on the Willamette, the total cost for four would be, according to Ware, $220.78.

They didn't always give good advice. Ware said to rest on the sabbath; and if one did he would get to California 20 days sooner. That was baloney and the experienced guide knew it. There was no earthly reason not to travel on Sunday; the animals and men were able to get all the rest they had to have at night. There usually was a two or three day layover at Ft. Laramie, considered the mid-point of the trip (it wasn't.) That was enough. Those who would lay by on Sundays in fact probably would get to the Willamette or San Francisco 20 days late, and if those 20 days happened to be in October and one was in the Blues or the Sierra, one would be well advised to do his praying every minute of every day instead of just on Sunday.

This is believed to be Meeker's 1906 wagon, on exhibit near depot in Baker, Ore.

DeVoto described the emigrant wagons as being considerably lighter than the freighters used in the Santa Fe trade, and they ought to be. The declivities on the Oregon Trail were frightening, and viewers today have a hard time imagining how they could have been negotiated at all. The Santa Fe Trail, for the most part, was less treacherous.

Capt. Randolph B. Marcy, author of a later guide book, said that the emigrant should make sure his wagon wheels were constructed of Osage orange, to minimize shrinkage in the high climate of the upper Platte. The next best wood would be white oak. The wagon tongue should be jointed, since a rigid tongue would break when wheels slammed into deep holes. The pins connecting the running gear to the wagon box should be removable, as frequently, in fording major streams, the box had to be caulked, the gear removed and stored in the bed, and the whole rig floated across. All other connections should be riveted, not bolted.

Marcy called for a supply of pemmican to be collected enroute; a great treat for Indian or mountain man, something less for the more domesticated emigrant. Pemmican was dried buffalo meat beaten until it was pulverized, placed in a hide bag, and covered with grease. When served, it was mixed with flour and boiled. The mixture, the emigrant found, tasted a lot better than it sounded, kept for months, and was highly nutritious. He also recommended pinole, which is flour mixed with ground corn, sugar, cinnamon or molasses. It was served with water only. Pinole didn't require a fire for palatability; a fact that would be comforting if hostile Indians were in the vicinity.

Thomas J. Farnham, author of a popular guide book, recommended a stock of oil cloths, to be used as ground cloths if sleeping on the ground. They would keep moisture from the earth from seeping up into the bedding. The sheeting also would literally keep the powder dry, and would come in handy as a poncho when driving during a rainstorm.

Joel Palmer, who made the western trip in 1845 and in 1846, returned to write one of the best guide books of all; and advice that was given then rings true to everything known in retrospect about the trail.

The book was distributed heavily to the emigrants. His style is simple and direct, rarely admitting to any problems on the trail if only the directions are followed.

To show what an encouragement this might be to a man wrestling with the idea of whether or not to sell out and go West, we reprint in its entirety the section from the guide book concerned with outfitting for the trip:

For burthen wagons, light four-horse or heavy two-horse wagons are the size commonly used. They should be made of the best material, well-seasoned, and should in all cases have falling tongues. The tires should not be less than 1¾" wide, but may be advantageously used three inches; two inches, however, is the most common width. In fastening on the tire, bolts should be used instead of nails. It should be at least 5/8" or ¾" thick. Hub boxes for the hubs should be about four inches. The skeins should be well-steeled. The Mormon-fashioned wagon bed is the best. They are usually made straight, with wide boards about 16" wide, and a projection outward of four inches on each side, and then another sideboard of 10" or 12"; in this last, set the bows for covers, which should always be

Typical of smaller wagons used on Oregon Trail, this one is on exhibit at new Ft. Walla Walla, Wash.

doubled. Boxes for carrying effects should be so constructed as to correspond in height with the offset in the wagon bed, as this gives a smooth surface to sleep upon.

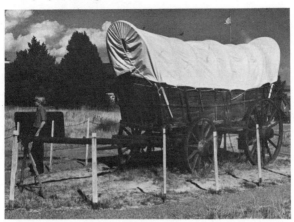

The great Conestoga wagon of Pennsylvania manufacture — the Cadillac of the Oregon Trail. This one is at Scotts Bluff National Monument.

Ox teams are more extensively used than any others. Oxen stand the trip much better and are not so liable to be stolen by the Indians, and are much less trouble. Cattle are generally allowed to go at large when not hitched to the wagons; whilst horses and mules must always be staked up at night. Oxen can procure food in many places that horses cannot. Cattle that have been raised in Illinois or Missouri stand the trip better than those that have been raised in Indiana or Ohio; as they have been accustomed to eating the prairie grass, upon which they must wholly rely while on the road. Great care should be taken in selection of cattle; they should be from four to six years old, tight and heavy made.

For those who set out with one wagon, it is not safe to set out with less than four yoke of oxen, as they are liable to get lame, get sore necks, or stray away. One team thus fitted up may start from Missouri with 2,500 pounds and as each days rations makes the load that much lighter, before they reach any rough road their loading is much reduced. Persons should recollect that everything in the outfit should be as light as required strength will permit; no useless trumpery should be taken. The loading should consist of provisions and apparel, a necessary supply of cooking fixtures, a few tools, etc. No great speculation can be made in buying cattle and driving them through to sell; but as the prices of oxen and cows are much higher in Oregon than in the United States, nothing is lost in having a good supply of them which will enable the emigrant to wagon through many articles that are difficult to be obtained in Oregon. Each family should have a few cows, as the milk cow can be used the entire route, and they are often convenient to put to the wagons to relieve the oxen. They should be so selected so that portions of them would come in fresh upon the road. Sheep can also be advantageously driven. American horses and mares always command high prices and with careful usage can be taken through; but if used to wagons or carriages, their loading should be light. Each family should be provided with a sheet iron stove with boiler; a platform can easily be constructed for carrying it at the hind end of the wagon; and as it is frequently quite windy and there is often a scarcity of wood, the stove is very convenient. Each family should be provided with a tent, and to which should be attached good strong cords to fasten it down.

Cooking fixtures generally used are sheet iron; a dutch oven and skillet of cast metal are very essential. Plates, cups, etc. should be of tinware, as queensware is much heavier and liable to break, and consumes much time in packing up. A reflector is sometimes very useful. Families should each have two churns, one for carrying sweet and one for sour milk. They should also have one eight- or 10-gallon keg for carrying water, one ax, one shovel, two or three augers, one hand saw, and if a farmer he should be provided with one crosscut saw and a few plow moulds, as it is difficult getting such articles. When I left the country plows cost from $25 to $40 each. A good supply of ropes for tying up horses and catching cattle should also be taken. Every person should be well supplied with boots and shoes, and in fact with every kind of clothing. It is also well to be supplied with at least one feather bed and a good assortment of bedding. There are no tame geese in the country, but an abundance of wild ones; yet it is difficult procuring a sufficient quantity of feathers for a bed. The muscovie is the only tame duck in the country.

Each male person should have at least one rifle gun and a shotgun is also useful for wild fowl and small game, of which there is an abundance. The best size calibre for the mountains is from 52 to 56 to the pound; but one of from 60 to 80, or even less, is best when in the lower settlements. The buffalo seldom range beyond the South Pass, and never west of Green River. The larger game are elk, deer, antelope, mountain sheep or bighorn, and bear. The small game are hare, rabbit, grouse, sage hen, pheasant, quail, etc. A good supply of ammunition is essential.

In laying in a supply of provisions for the journey, persons will always be governed in some degree by their means; but there are a few essentials that all will require.

For each adult there should be 200 pounds of flour, 300 pounds of pilot bread, 75 pounds of bacon, 10 pounds of rice, five pounds of coffee, two pounds of tea, 25 pounds of sugar, half a bushel of dried beans, one bushel of dried fruit, two pounds of saleratus, 10 pounds of salt, half a bushel of corn meal; and it is well to have half a bushel of corn, parched and ground; a small keg of vinegar should also be taken. To the above may be added as many good things as the means of the person will enable him to carry; for whatever is good at home is none the less so on the road. The above will be ample for the journey, but should an additional quantity be taken it can readily be disposed of in the mountains and at good prices; not for cash, but for robes, dressed skins, buckskin pants, mocassins, etc. It is also well for families to be provided with medicines. It is seldom, however, that emigrants are sick, but sometimes eating too frequently of fresh buffalo meat causes diarrhoea, and unless it be checked soon prostrates the individual and leaves him a fit subject for disease.

The time usually occupied in making the trip from Missouri to Oregon City [just above present day Portland, on the Willamette] is about five months; but with the aid of a person who has traveled the route with an emigrating company, the trip can be performed in about four months. Much injury is done to teams in racing them, endeavoring to pass each other. Emigrants should make an everyday business of traveling — resting upon the same ground two nights is not good policy, as the teams are likely to ramble too far. Getting into large companies should be avoided, as they are necessarily compelled to move more tardily. From 10 to 25 wagons is a sufficient number to travel with safety. The advance and rear companies should not be less than 20, but between it may be safe to go with six. The Indians are very annoying on account of their thieving propensities, but if well watched they would seldom put them into practice. Persons should always avoid rambling far from camp unarmed, or in too small parties. Indians will sometimes seek such opportunities to rob a man of what little effects he has about him, and if he attempts to get away from them with his property they will sometimes shoot him.

There are several points along the Missouri where emigrants have been in the practice of fitting out. Of these Independence, St. Joseph, and Council Bluffs are the most noted. For those emigrating from Ohio, Indiana, Illinois and Northern Missouri, Iowa and Michigan, I think St. Joseph the best point; as by taking that route the crossing of several streams (which at the early season we travel are sometimes very high) is avoided. Outfits may be had at this point as readily as at any other along the river. Work cattle can be bought in this vicinity for from $25 to $30 per yoke; cows, horses, etc. equally cheap.

Emigrants should endeavor to arrive at St. Joseph early in April, so as to be in readiness to take up the line of march by the middle of April. Companies, however, have often started as late as the 10th of May; but in such cases they seldom arrive in Oregon until after the rainy season commences in the Cascade range of mountains.

Those residing in northern Ohio, Indiana, Illinois Michigan, etc., who contemplate traveling by land to the place of rendezvous, should start in time to give their teams at least 10 days rest. Ox teams, after traveling 400 to 500 miles in the states at that season of the year, would be unfit to perform a journey across the mountains, but doubtless they might be exchanged for others, at or near the rendezvous.

Farmers would do well to take along a good supply of horse gears. Mechanics should take such tools as are easily carried; as there are but few in the country, and those are held at exhorbitant prices. Every family should lay in a good supply of school books for their children.

In case of an emergency, flour can be bought at Ft. Hall and at Ft. Bois, two trading posts of the Hudsons Bay Company, at $20 per hundred; and by forwarding word to Spalding's mission on the Kooskooskee, they will pack out flour to Ft. Bois at $10 per hundred, and to the Grand Round at $8, and will take in exchange dry goods, groceries, etc.; but at Fts. Hall and Bois, the company will take nothing in payment except cash or cattle. At Dr. Whitman's station, flour can be bought at $5 per hundred, corn meal at $4, beef at six and seven cents per pound, potatoes at 50 cents a bushel. It is proper to observe that the flour at Spalding's and Whitman's stations will be unbolted. Emigrants, however, should be cautious and lay in a sufficient supply to last them through.

Between the time the family divested itself of its land and those livestock that wouldn't make the Oregon trek, countless hours were spent poring over the guidebooks and making agonizing decisions as to what heirlooms could go and which had to be auctioned off or given to relatives. Wagons frequently were bought in the Midwest, and gradually the beds would be stocked to a traveling configuration. After one last round of goodbyes with friends and relatives (they knew they were seeing most of them for the last time), they would yoke up and move out, generally to the nearest river port.

If they were from Southern Illinois or Central Missouri, that would be St. Louis. One way or another, most of the emigrants from the 1840s funneled in to the home city of the Chouteaus. Their frightened and bewildered teams would labor along Wharf St. to the line offices, where passage would be bought on the next steamer up the Missouri. Wagons were rolled aboard, usually the running gear was removed and placed atop the boxes, and the family would eagerly walk up the cobbled streets to get their first close-up look at a big city.

The individual traveling family usually would make no attempt to hook up with a wagon train in St. Louis — those arrangements invariably were made in Independence. The emigrating societies, however, usually would produce a sufficient number of families each year that they could afford to send an advance man to the cities, or at least write ahead, to secure reservations aboard the boats.

Marcus and Narcissa Whitman came to St. Louis via the Ohio River. They arrived on Tuesday, March 28, 1836, and left three days later. Both had plenty of time to see the town, and Narcissa, a devout Protestant, spent an hour of meditation in the Old Cathedral (then the new cathedral — it was only two years old.) They visited Elijah Lovejoy, the editor of the *Observer*, who published their marriage notice in his paper. This was before the martyred abolitionist's fatal move from St. Louis to Alton.

On March 31, just six days short of a year after Whitman and Parker moved west out of St. Louis, the Whitman-Spalding steamer backed away from the St. Louis levee and nosed up the Mississippi River. This is exerpted from Narcissa Whitman's diary entry for that day:

"Twilight had nearly gone when we entered the waters of the great Missouri, but the moon shown in her brightness. It was a beautiful evening. My husband and I went up on the top of the boat to get a more commanding view of the scenery. How majestic, how grand was the scene, the meeting of two such great waters."

Three or four days up the Missouri, dodging bars, snags and sawyers the entire way, and the boats would nudge up against the Independence or Westport landings. Running gear would be re-attached and the wagons would be rolled down the plank to the wharf. Added to the cacophony of the boat itself were the bellows of the goaded oxen and the whinnies of the whipped mules.

Little kids would gawk in absolute amazement and complete silence. The scene at Independence Landing would be remembered the rest of their lives.

The noise and bluster didn't end at the landing — it continued along the three-mile ridge of the River Road, down to the square in Independence. There the sounds of the boats were replaced with the ring of the anvils, as the smiths worked long hours trying to meet the deadlines of the departing caravans. The roar went on into the night as the saloons did their work. The emigrants who had elected to do their buying in Independence put up at the hotels; those who didn't moved their wagons out as far as they had to in order to find good grass and water, then rode horses back to the action. When they went home to their wagons in the evening, provided their vision wasn't too blurred, they would see thousands of earthly stars, pinpoints of campfires for miles around.

The hookup with a train generally took a few days. In the early 1840s all emigrants left at once in one train, but the traffic had so increased by the end of the decade that trains were leaving daily from the last week in April almost through the month of May.

There was more than human action. The storms of the east, even eastern Missouri, somehow didn't come across with the violence that western storms could, and still do. All the way from Independence to Ft. Laramie, the thunderstorms of the spring would deafen the emigrants and stampede their stock. It was a spectacle that awed them all.

One such storm caught young Francis Parkman leading a pair of mules to the Westport Landing: "Such sharp and incessant flashes of lightning, such stunning and continuous thunder I had never known before. The woods were completely obscured by the diagonal sheets of rain that fell with a heavy roar, and rose in spray from the ground, and the streams swelled so rapidly that we could hardly ford them. At length, looming through the rain, we saw the log house of Colonel Chick, who received us with his usual bland hospitality."

Parkman had another encounter with a storm, this one near the town of Marysville, in northeastern Kansas:

"At last, towards evening, the old familiar black heads of thunder-clouds rose fast about the horizon, and the same deep muttering of distant thunder that had become the ordinary accompaniment of our afternoon's journey began to roll hoarsely over the prairie. Only a few minutes elapsed before the whole sky was densely shrouded, and the prairie and some clusters of woods in front assumed a purple hue beneath the inky shadows. Suddenly from the densest fold of the cloud the flash leaped out, quivering again and again down to the edge of the prairie; and at the same instant came the sharp burst and the long rolling peal of the thunder. A cool wind, filled with the smell of rain, just then overtook us, leveling the tall grass by the side of the path . . .

National Park Service

On-site sketch by William H. Jackson of violent prairie thunderstorm along the Platte, probably mid-1860s.

". . . just as the storm broke, we were prepared to receive it. It came upon us almost with the darkness of night; the trees, which were close at hand, were completely shrouded by the roaring torrents of rain . . .

"Our tent was none of the best defense against such a cataract. The rain could not enter bodily, but it beat through the canvas in a fine drizzle, that wetted us just as effectually. We sat upon our saddles with faces of the utmost surliness, while the water dropped from the vizors of our caps, and trickled down our cheeks. My india-rubber cloak conducted twenty little rapid streamlets to the ground; and Shaw's blanket coat was saturated like a sponge . . .

"Toward sunset, however, the storm ceased as suddenly as it began. A bright streak of clear red sky appeared above the western verge of the prairie, the horizontal rays of the sinking sun streamed through it, and glittered in a thousand prismatic colors upon the dripping groves and the prostrate grass . . .

"Scarcely had night set in when the tumult broke forth anew. The thunder here is not like the tame thunder of the Atlantic coast. Bursting with a terrific crash above our heads, it roared over the boundless waste of prairie, seeming to roll around the whole circle of the firmament with a peculiar and awful reverberation. The lightning flashed all night, playing with its livid glare upon the neighboring trees, revealing the vast expanse of the plain, and then leaving us shut in as if by a palpable wall of darkness.

"It did not disturb us much. Now and then a peal awakened us, and made us conscious of the electric battle that was raging, and of the floods that dashed upon the stanch canvas over our heads."

Ezra Meeker was struck with the suddenness of the storms of the Platte Valley. "Storms would wet the skin in less time than it takes to write this sentence. The cattle traveled so fast it was difficult to keep up with them. I have always thought of this as a cloudburst. Anyway, there was not a dry thread left on me in an incredibly short time. My boots were as full of water as if I had been wading over boot top deep, and the water ran through my hat as if it was in a sieve, almost blinding me in the fury of wind and water. Many tents were leveled, and in fact such occurences as fallen tents were not uncommon. One of our neighboring trains suffered no inconsiderable loss by the sheets of water on the ground floating their camp equippage, ox yokes and all loose articles away, and they only narrowly escaped having a wagon engulfed in the raging torrent that came so unexpectedly upon them."

It took all kinds, and Parkman wrote of a late-May or early-June storm on the Platte, east of Ft. Laramie. He described the morning as being close and sultry, with an oppressive heat, when a sudden darkness appeared in the west, followed by a "furious blast of sleet and hail, full in our faces, icy cold, a storm of needles."

There are very few places where the Oregon Trail today is like it was in the 1840s. Now, where it appears at all, it is seen as a single pair of ruts. This gradually evolved as the single, most used, or easiest traveled, trail. On some areas of the plains the trail was literally 10 to 20 miles wide, with all its detours. As the old saying went, better to be a mile wide than a mile deep.

DeSmet wrote this in 1851: "Our Indian companions, who had never seen but the narrow hunting paths by which they transport themselves and their lodges, were filled with admiration on seeing this noble highway which is as smooth as a barn floor swept by the winds, and not a blade of grass can shoot up on it on account of the continual passing. They conceived a high idea of the countless White Nation, as they expressed it. They fancied that all had gone over that road, and that an immense void must exist in the land of the rising sun. Their countenances testified evident incredulity when I told them that the exit was in no wise perceived in the land of the whites. They styled the route the Great Medicine Road of the Whites."

At that time DeSmet and his Indian companions were at the Red Buttes, a few miles southwest of present Casper, Wyoming.

This great width was due largely to the need for relief from the dust. The companies usually operated under a code of military discipline, which provided for position rotation from day to day. Yet, when there was no physical reason to follow another wagon and eat his dust, the traveler often would move to the side. Thus, at times a train a mile long and one wagon wide could become a mile wide and one wagon long.

The dust was bad wherever it was, but it was worst of all in the deserts west of Ft. Laramie. There it was a caustic powder, and even the teetotaling emigrants looked like they had spent the whole weekend in a saloon. Eyes were perpetually red and itching. The alkali would drive into the skin, and cheeks would peel, lips actually would split wide open. Mosquitos and gnats were a pain in the neck, but the alkali was even worse. The traditional remedy for irritated eyes was a zinc sulphate compound, but boric acid would have been better.

The diaries mentioned these ailments but they rarely dwelled on them. The travelers had trouble feeling sorry for themselves when every few hundred yards they saw a recent grave.

Few were the diarists who did not at one time mention having to discard some object of great importance to them, to lighten the chore of their draft animals. Many a traveler refused to believe the insistent advice of the guide books, to take plenty of staples and leave the furniture at home or ship it around the Horn. Some felt they could live on the plentiful game and wild berries, ignorant of the fact that for nearly half the length of the Oregon Trail game was scarce, indeed, for the amateur hunter.

Parkman had something to say about this: "It is worth noticing that on the Platte one may sometimes see the shattered wrecks of ancient claw-footed tables, well waxed and rubbed, or massive bureaus of carved oak. These, some of them no doubt the relics of ancestral prosperity in the colonial time, must have encountered strange vicissitudes. Brought, perhaps, originally from England; then, with the declining fortunes of their owners, borne across the Alleghenies to the wilderness of Ohio or Kentucky; then to Illinois or Missouri; and now at last fondly stowed away in the family wagon for the interminable journey to Oregon. But the stern privations of the way are little anticipated. The cherished relic is soon flung out to scorch and crack upon the hot prairie."

The eastern hauteur and contempt of the emigrants permeates Parkman's brilliant narrative. One cannot help wondering what his response would have been had he known that, only two weeks away from him, George Donner had $40,000 in cash strapped to his belly.

The throwaways caught up with Narcissa Whitman on the Snake. This is excerpted from a letter she wrote to a friend on Aug. 12, 1836: "Dear Harriett, The little trunk you gave me has come with me so far, and now I must leave it alone. Poor little trunk, I am sorry to leave thee. Thou must abide here alone, and no more by they presence remind me of my dear Harriett. 20 miles below the [American] Falls on Snake River, this shall be thy place of rest . . . The hills are so steep and rocky that husband thought it best to lighten the wagon as much as possible and take nothing but the wheels, leaving the box, with my trunk. If I were to make the journey again I would make quite different preparations. To pack and unpack so many times, and cross so many streams where the packs frequently get wet, requires no small amount of labor, besides the injury to the articles."

Death and westward expansion walked hand in hand. George H. Himes, an Oregon pioneer and former curator of the state historical society, estimated that 30,000 persons died on the Oregon Trail up to 1859, and that would be nearly one in 10 who made the trip. His estimate was that at least 5,000 died in 1852 alone, and that would mean a fresh grave every 700 yards, from Independence to Portland. In total, there is one grave for every 80 yards of the trail, from the Missouri River to the Willamette.

It has been said that the biggest killer was cholera, but this is not true. The prime killer was carelessness. People handling firearms in jolting wagons took a frightening toll. The diarists were a gory bunch, and more than one told of how youngsters would get jounced out of a wagon, take one last pop-eyed look at their mothers as a great wheel rolled right over their middles. Ornery cattle sometimes took human lives. Indians were down at the bottom of the list — they rarely killed until the 1860s.

The pervading fear in the trail years was the cholera. It took thousands of lives, more probably than all other diseases put together, but not as many as is usually stated.

Cholera was a plague of world wide dimensions. It festered in India in the early 1800s, then suddenly burst out and traveled across Europe like a grassfire. It came to Canada in the bowels of wretching Irish emigrants in 1832, and the following year it had reached St. Louis. In the early years it fluttered on and off, and finally in 1849 it slammed into the filthy city like a tidal wave, carrying away upwards of 10 percent of the population. It didn't stop at the city limits — it went out a hundred miles past Ft. Laramie before it was killed, either by the altitude or by the cleansing action of swifter streams.

The travelers didn't worry about accidents. They could be avoided with care. But cholera, the "Unseen Destroyer," could creep into the lungs on a spring breeze, or linger on the lip of a drinking cup, or come into the body via a goodnight kiss of a child. People who yoked up in good spirits after breakfast were gripped with agonizing stomach pains by noon and were cold in their graves by sundown.

The disease usually incubated in filthy surroundings, and Lord knows there were plenty of those on the Oregon Trail. Emigrants weren't careful with their garbage or their excrement. Why should they be — they would never be back there again. But another train would come to their campground the next day and camp right in the very same filth.

Wells frequently were dug within a few yards of latrines, and seepage would have been inevitable. Dr. Whitman knew (or guessed) the relationship between filth and cholera, but few emigrants did.

The disease hits like a ton of bricks. The first symptom invariably is a stomach ache. The pain goes from zero to intense in a matter of two or three minutes. This is accompanied by diarrhea and vomiting. Not even assumption of the fetal position can bring relief. The dehydration becomes evident within hours, and the skin draws in, wrinkles, and glazes. Cheeks sink in and eyes bug out, and a slight bluish cast covers the entire body, especially the fingernails. There is little middle ground. Things either got better after a few hours (a day or two at the most) or death occurred.

In the peak cholera year, 1849, the year of the gold rush, bachelors by the thousands headed for the American Fork. When one of them took the cholera, he was prostrated alone by the side of the road with his mule and his pack. If he managed to turn the corner, he might catch up with the train. There was no trouble with Indians; they knew very well what the problem was and they steered a wide berth.

Families would stick by their own, and when a death occurred the body was usually toted along until the end of the day. Then a shallow grave would be opened at the head of the trail, the body wrapped in an old comforter and lowered to rest. The earth was packed back into the hole. After breakfast the wagons would roll over the grave, one after another, to obliterate the scent of the grave. Too many times the emigrants had seen trailside graves torn up, covered with wolf tracks, and parts of a human body strewn around.

Once in awhile the grave would be violated by a lone Indian, hardup for a coup. He would come into his village, waving the scalp and displaying the hacked up genitals of the deceased to one and all, as he bragged about his victory in mortal combat.

Thus the trains were showing kindness when they rolled over a fresh grave. This is why, of the 30,000 to 45,000 graves along the trail, only about 200 have been located today, and almost all of those are unidentified. Those are the few who were not buried in the trail itself, but whose graves somehow escaped violation.

Many of the deaths supposedly caused by cholera actually were not. There is a good chance, in fact, that most were caused by alkali dysentery, and probably none died of cholera beyond present day Casper. Sometimes shallow wells would be drilled in the sands of the Platte valley and seepage from surface or underground alkali pools would penetrate the drinking supply. The symptoms were usually the same as cholera, except not as violent. The combination of bad water, sapped strength, an all-meat diet, hot days and cool nights probably produced a far higher fatality rate than cholera alone.

It is probably totally impossible for the man of the late 20th century to empathize with the Oregon emigrant of the 1840s. At no time before or since has a society experienced such a complete, multi-dimensional environmental change. Even the lunar explorations pale in contrast to the western movement.

The emigrant never before had seen a western sunset, never before had experienced a western thunderstorm, never before had seen a mountain, nor a desert, nor an Indian in his native habitat. Few had seen waterfalls. None had seen infinite prairies. Few had traveled for more than two or three days at a time; none certainly had traveled four or five months without respite. None had faced death on a day to day basis with such studied nonchalance or such determined fatalism. Few of those rugged individualists ever thought they would willingly subject themselves to the military discipline and sometimes despotism that had to prevail in the ranks of the wagon trains.

And none, certainly ever would get over the most startling phenomenon of all — the buffalo, American bison, the "buffler" of the mountain man. It was something the midwestern farmer had heard about and read about, but it was simply incomprehensible until it was seen.

John Bidwell, who was in the first large train, in 1841, left this recollection: "I have seen the plain black with them for several days' journey, as far as the eye could reach. They seemed to be coming northward continually from the distant plains to the Platte, to get water, and would plunge in and swim across by thousands — so numerous were they that they changed not only the color of the water but its taste, until it was unfit to drink. But we had to use it."

William M. Case, who journeyed west three years later, described a buffalo stampede along the Platte: "As the two divisions were moving along deliberately at ox speed in the usual parallel columns, the drivers were startled by a low sound to the north, as a distant thunder. There was no appearance of a storm, however, in that or any other direction. And the noise grew louder and louder, and was steady and uninterrupted. It soon

became clear that there was a herd of buffalos
approaching and on the run. Scouring anxiously the line
of hills rimming the edge of the valley, the dark brown
outline of the herd was at length descried, and was
distinctly made out with a telescope as buffalos in
violent motion and making directly for the train. The
front of the line was, perhaps, half a mile long, and the
animals were several columns deep, coming like a
tornado. They had, probably, been stampeded by
hunters and would stop at nothing. The only apparent
chance of safety was to drive ahead and get out of the
range of the herd. The oxen were consequently urged
into a run, and the train itself had the appearance of a
stampede. Neither were they too quick, for the flying
herds of the buffalos passed but a few yards to the rear
of the last wagon, and were going at such a rate that to
be struck by them would have been like the shock of
rolling boulders of a ton's weight."

The bulls in fact often weighed a ton — great shaggy
monsters with protruding eyes the diameter of a teacup.
There can be little question that when they did
stampede the earth really did shake — diaries by the
dozens testify to this in no uncertain terms. All equated
the sound to distant thunder. The fixation of the
observer was almost hypnotic.

Despite their formidable aspect, the buffalo provided
a great deal to the emigrant. The most important
contribution was meat, and, although some travelers
described it as sometimes tough and stringy, it was
generally credited with being more tasty than beef;
particularly the hump rib, prized by the mountain man.
The animal upon occasion helped to allay thirst. Some
travelers were known to plunge a knife into the paunch
of a recently killed animal, thus freeing liquid. To get to
the water, the surgeon first had to remove the green,
gelatinous juices floating on top. Sometimes, even the
blood was consumed.

The buffalo also provided warmth. There is no record
of an emigrant employing this technique but mountain
men on the high plains in the dead of winter sometimes
would knock off a big bull, remove his entrails and climb
into the cavity to pass the night, snug as if in mother's

arms. The hides served as warm robes and attained solid market value as such after the fur trade petered out.

The buffalo contributed to the "bone express" of the trail. Bleached bones generally were found along the trail all the way from southern Nebraska to Casper. Passing emigrants would use them to scribble messages. A skull would inform John that Mary was now well; a shoulder blade informed Polly that James now was taking the California Road, and where to find wood and water nearby. (The bone piles left by buffalo hunters in later years provided the nucleus for a brief bonanza in the 1880s.)

One of the least palatable aspects of trail life to the little farm wife back in Iowa or Missouri was the need to use the "buffalo chip" when the wood ran out north of the Alcove Spring. The *bois de vache* of the mountain man would save many emigrant lives, but it was with a shudder that the girls read about this in the guide books.

So, along the Little Blue, the girls would lay up a comfortable supply of firewood, but by the time they reached the Platte it was gone, and there was no choice if they wanted warm food and coffee. So dad would go out and collect a mess of the chips — dried buffalo droppings — at first picking them up off the plains gingerly, with the tips of two fingers. Before long the kids were sailing them into camp like Frisbees.

And, before long, the mothers came to regard the chips with more respect than cottonwood. They would burn hotter than charcoal, last longer than wood, and, strangely, they would burn with no odor at all and practically no smoke.

Probably the most fascinating prairie sport was the buffalo hunt — not even the most experienced Eastern hunter could describe the buffalo kill in any but the most incredulous terms. A hunter sometimes could walk to within a few yards of an animal — alone or as part of a herd. Unless the buffalo caught the man-scent the hunter could pour round after round into the 10-foot-long goliath and get little more response than a casual loaf away, just before he dropped dead.

Frederick Ruxton leaves a vivid description of the

death of a typical bull. "The buffalo invariably evinces the greatest repugnance to lie down when mortally wounded, apparently conscious that, when once touching mother earth, there is no hope left him. A bull, shot through the heart or lungs, with blood streaming from his mouth, and protruding tongue, his eyes rolling, blood-shot, and glazed with death, braces himself on his legs, swaying from side to side, stamps impatiently at his growing weakness, or lifts his rugged and matted head and helplessly bellows out his conscious impotence. To the last, however, he endeavors to stand upright and plants his limbs farther apart, but to no purpose. As the body rolls like a ship at sea, his head slowly turns from side to side, looking about, as it were, for the unseen and treacherous enemy who has brought him, the lord of the plains, to such a pass. Gouts of purple blood spurt from his mouth and nostrils, and gradually the failing limbs refuse longer to support the ponderous carcass; more heavily rolls the body from side to side until suddenly, for a brief instant, it becomes rigid and still; a convulsive tremor siezes it and, with a low, sobbing gasp, the huge animal falls over on his side, the limbs extended stark and stiff, and the mountain of flesh without life or motion."

Francis Parkman, out on the Platte, describes a kill by a hunter, probably Henri Chatillon: "As he sits upon the sand, his knee is raised, and his elbow rests upon it, that he may level his heavy weapon with a steadier aim. The stock is at his shoulder; his eye ranges along the barrel. Still he is in no haste to fire. The bull, with slow deliberation, begins his march over the sands to the other side. He advances his foreleg, and exposes to view a small spot, denuded of hair, just behind the point of his shoulder; upon this the hunter brings the sight of his rifle to bear; lightly and delicately his finger presses the hair-trigger. The spiteful crack of the rifle responds to his touch, and instantly in the middle of the bare spot appears a small red dot. The buffalo shivers; death has overtaken him, he cannot tell from whence; still he does not fall, but walks heavily forward, as if nothing happened. Yet before he has gone far out upon the sand you see him stop; he totters; his knees bend under him, and his head sinks forward to the ground. Then his whole vast bulk sways to one side; he rolls over on the sand, and dies with a scarcely preceptible struggle."

The hunt transpired on an almost daily basis. The scouts would lead the column by several miles, and a half hour behind them would ride the hunting detail. As time wore on and boldness increased, they would sometimes charge into the flank of a stampeding herd, aiming for the brisket or the trick shot that severs the spine. They usually shot more than they needed, but at times the shortage of buffalo would be acute, particularly beyond Ft. Laramie.

Even the hides came in handy. Some of the men would cure them as time permitted, and gradually build a store of robes to give added comfort to the old featherbed mattress. Sometimes, when crossing western streams high in their banks, they would lighten the wagon loads and pass some of their possessions across in bull boats. To make a bull boat the emigrant would thrust the butt ends of several willow branches in the ground in a circle, and gather their tops in a bow. Then they would lace willow twigs into the framework to provide a coarse, screenlike frame. Hides would be trimmed to fit and stretched over the frame. A slow fire would be kindled inside the enclosure, and this would warm the skins, make them pliable again, and at the same time tend to drive out the remaining moisture. Finally they would melt buffalo tallow, mix it with ashes, and daub the mixture into all the seams and kill the fire, to allow the whole to become rigid. The boat then would float like a leaf on the water. It could carry several hundred pounds of weight, without much steerability, but with great buoyancy.

The streams along the trail were aggravating and causes for delay, but rarely more than that. Only the great rivers caused difficulty and danger. These included the Kansas; rarely the South Platte at the Lower California Crossing; sometimes the North Platte at Bessemer Bend; always the Snake, both at Three Island Crossing and Ft. Boise; frequently the John Day and the Deschutes.

It was at those dangerous rivers that the wagons truly became prairie schooners. Oakum or rags would be jammed into the cracks of the wagon beds, then smeared with pitch or buffalo tallow. Running gear would be dismantled and thrown atop the beds. Oxen and men would drag the box into the water, while men on the other bank would lash the cordelle around a tree trunk or rock, and haul on the long line until the wagon was beached on the far bank. The stock swam across.

Marcus and Narcissa Whitman and the Spaldings were accompanied west in 1836 by two Indian boys that Marcus had used to attract attention to the Western missionary activity the year before. Mrs. Whitman reveals how those youngsters helped get their cattle across the streams:

"Our two Indian boys, Richard and John, have had the chief management of driving them [the cattle] all the way, and are to be commended for the patience they have manifested. They have had some one or two to help usually, but none so steady drivers as themselves. When a stream is to be crossed where it is necessary for the animals to swim, Richard comes to my husband and asks if he may go over with his horse . . . and then come back after the cows. After obtaining permission he rides over, accompanied by his fellow drivers, all stripped to the shirt. Then they return with their horses if the stream is wide and difficult. If not they leave their horses, tie their shirts over their heads, swim back, collect the cows, and drive them through, all swimming after them. If the stream is fairly wide and they return with their horses, they drive them swimming the river twice. They love to swim, as they love to eat, and by doing so have saved me many an anxious feeling, for the relief it has given my husband many times. In this case, all the horses and mules were driven across likewise. Usually the best Indian swimmer was selected and mounted the horse that was good for leading, to go before the animals as a guide, while many others swam after them to drive them over. When once under way such a snorting and halloa-ing you have never heard. At the same time you may see nothing save so many heads floating above the water. Soon they gain the opposite shore and triumphantly ascend its banks, shake themselves, and retire to their accustomed employment."

The various commercial ferries were vastly profitable, but some of the emigrants simply didn't have the cash to use them. Leander Loomis of the Birmingham (Iowa) Emigrating Company in 1850 found such a situation at the west end of the Sublette Cutoff in western Wyoming. There the Green was 330 feet wide, fairly fast and deep. The ferry operator was getting $7 a wagon and $1 a head for livestock. Loomis did the job himself for nothing, but he lost 12 hours of the several days he had saved by avoiding Ft. Bridger.

The Indians had a nasty habit of burning prairies to channel game into an ambush, and this was a painful circumstance for the oxen. Joel Palmer's guide book left a remedy for the sore hooves which was used extensively on the trail: "Burnt prairie leaves dry, sharp stubs of grass that irritate feet of cattle. Foot becomes dry, feverish and cracks. Into this opening grass and dirt collect and foot festers. Wash foot with strong soap suds, scrape or cut away diseased flesh, pour boiling pitch or tar upon the sore. Should the heel become worn out, apply tar or pitch and singe with a hot iron." This was considered a good remedy by everybody but the oxen.

There was a nine-year-old boy in the great emigration of 1843, Jesse A. Applegate, who had one hell of a memory, and in his later years he delivered it to the Oregon Pioneer Association in the form of a paper. That 1843 emigration of 1,000 persons, credited by many as being the real start of the permanent Oregon settlement, had a built in problem: a herd of 5,000 cattle. They traveled much slower than the rest of the column, which felt it was being imposed upon by having to travel less miles per day or travel longer hours. Thus, the decision was made to relegate the so-called cow column to the back of the line. The rest of the train would advance at its own speed and stop when and where it felt like it. If the cow column wished to keep up, it would have to drive an extra hour or so a day. If not — well, that was cow biz. Jesse's book described the typical day.

The day would start at 4 a.m., when the last shift of sentinels would discharge their rifles. Upwards of 60 herdsmen would then check the cattle to make sure none strayed away, and then move them back toward the encampment. All 5,000 were in a small circle by 5 a.m.

Breakfast then was enjoyed from 6 to 7 a.m. in the damp, sparkling air. They ate inside the circle formed by their 60 wagons where there was a forest of tents. As the hour of seven neared, the tents would start coming down. The hired pilot then moved out onto the trail with a cluster of hunters behind him, ready to search out the buffalo or antelope. Chains were removed that linked the wagons together, wheel to wheel, in a circle 100 yards in diameter. The lead wagon for the day moved out of the encampment and into the line of march. The rest fell into place, one by one.

If the nature of the terrain permitted it, the sea of grey-topped wagons fanned out into horizontal lines — otherwise the traditional line was maintained. The guide books often pointed out nooning places as well as night campgrounds, generally selected for wood, water, and/or grass. In Applegate's day, however, no such books were yet in print, and the train was dependent upon the experience of the pilot.

The guide usually was at the nooning place an hour before the train would arrive. The teams were brought in, unhitched from their wagons but not unyoked. The wagons stopped where they were comfortable, in shade if there was any, and there usually wasn't. There was no corral at noon.

It was at this noon rest that disputes which couldn't wait were settled by the elected council, which held both legislative and judicial powers. By 1 p.m. the bugle sounded and the line of march was resumed again.

The travelers would watch the desert lose its carpet of flowers, and see the tough, short buffalo grass come into predominance. Out by the rocks of the Wildcat Hills the yucca would send up slender spikes topped with cascades of opalescent blooms.

Milk from the family cow, which trailed along behind the wagon, was eagerly consumed at breakfast time, and the leftover was placed in a container tied to one of the wagon bows. Usually, by the noon stop, it was butter, and that meant delicious buttermilk for all.

Sometimes, women would drive the oxen, giving the men a chance to rest and stretch their legs. It generally was preferred to walk rather than sustain the constant jolting of the spring-less wagons.

There was always bickering along the line of march; the council frequently was charged with favoritism, certain cliques would form in loosely-organized trains and reserve the best campsites by arriving early, some would alter the line of march without permission, etc. When the problem got too severe it sometimes was solved by changing leaders.

When the sun was low in the west the pilot arrived at his chosen campsite and staked out another 100-yard circle. He conducted the lead wagon around the circumference, halting it when it had traveled almost the complete distance. The wagon behind headed in slightly, so its left front wheel was opposite the right rear wheel of the lead wagon. And so it went all around the circle. Teams were unhitched and unyoked, then driven out the last remaining opening and the hindmost wagon was moved into position to close the corral.

The kids then bounded out on the prairie and collected wood or buffalo chips. Men lowered campstoves from the rear of the wagons, and pitched the tents. Hunters had brought their game in and butchered it before the wagons had arrived. Free steaks for all! Women rounded up the utensils and started the evening meal. Within 45 minutes to an hour, grace was being said over 60 different fires and the ravished families dug in joyfully.

By 7 p.m. the kids were out on the prairie playing, climbing on rocks, doing whatever exhuberent kids can do to have the time of their lives. Some of the younger ones were playing games; those in their teens were dancing to the music of the fiddle, the harmonica or the flute. *Oh Suzanna, Arkansas Traveler, Hand Me Down My Walkin' Cane, She'll Be Comin' Round the Mountain, Old Black Joe, I Dream of Jeannie, De Camptown Races* – all were great favorites.

There was frequently a preacher in the trains, and if a

couple of youngsters found themselves in absolute misery, the wedding rites could be performed, and when this happened it was a cause for great celebration. This happened twice in the Bidwell-Bartleson party of 1841, and there were only 69 people in the entire train.

Out on the Bear River, Jesse Applegate and some friends went over to see some of the Soda Springs. They found the Steamboat Spring the most fascinating of all, as did most emigrants. There was a hole in the cone four or five inches across, some 10 feet from the top. Whenever the spring went into convulsions water and hot steam gushed out of that hole. It made a noise like that of the escape pipe of the boiler of a steamboat. Boys will be boys so they packed the hole with sod and grass. It was, of course, blown out with a roar, and this doubled the guys up with laughter.

One boy took off his wool hat with a floppy brim, placed it over the hole and braced the brim with his hands and knees. When the puff came the hat crown stretched, swelled like a balloon, and burst at the top. More fun.

When they were around the great rocks, they would walk or ride over, often with their parents, and carve their names in the soft stone or clay. It was a great life.

Finally, by 9 p.m., the feather beds and buffalo robes were out and everyone bedded down for the night. All men capable of bearing arms were formed into guard companies and each man drew guard duty every third night. There were four two-hour watches between 8 p.m. and the 4 a.m. reveille. By Applegate's time the Indians hadn't come to expect the spring migration — that was only the third year. Therefore, it was rare when a sentry was really needed.

There was a time, early in the 20th century, when it was a misfortune to be a grandchild of persons who went west in covered wagons. The conditioned response was to hightail it when grandad was seen wobbling your way with a nostalgic glint in his eye, ready to narrate his tale of hardship and privation on the Oregon Trail for the umpteenth time.

Contemporary kids with a knowledge of history could put the old coot down hard. With some exceptions the five-month excursion was the time of their lives, and there probably is no experience available today which could in any way dish up comparable thrills over such an extended period of time.

Hugh Cosgrove, who moved his family west in 1847, owned up to it. He recalled it as one of the most pleasant instances in his life. It was one long picnic; the changing scenes of the journey, the animals of the prairie, the Indians, the mountain men, the seasonal changes. There was always danger, of course, but rarely did danger materialize into catastrophe. There was sickness too, but there was a lot more cholera in the big cities than there was on the Oregon Trail.

American citizens then and now owe those pioneers an enormous debt of gratitude. Their great journey welded a nation together. It took a lot of guts. By and large, however, the passage was made primarily for self-betterment, and, it is a fact, that few of the Oregon emigrants failed to better themselves through the trip. In later years, few of the pioneers rejected the mantle of heroism when, in fact, they merely took advantage of an opportunity to have themselves a helluva good time.

CHAPTER 2   GENERAL ROUTE OF THE TRAIL

Part 2 of this work consists of a body of detailed directions on reaching the route of the old Oregon Trail, from Independence, Mo. to Oregon City, Ore. It should be understood that there was more than one Oregon Trail — in fact the road sustained minor changes every year, major changes every few years. Part 2 concerns only one route — that leading from Independence in the year 1845.

The trail starts not at Independence, but at Independence Landing, some three miles north of the square in downtown Independence. In the year 1845 the emigrant could go two ways. He could have headed south from the square, then west out over the old Santa Fe Trail. Or, he could have headed almost due west to the thriving little town of Westport, some 40 blocks south of the Missouri River and just east of the state line. From there he could have gone southwest through the Shawnee Missions and Olathe to hit the Santa Fe Trail, or, most likely, he would have traveled straight south over what is now Wornall Rd., to intersect the old Santa Fe Trail at the now-extinct town of New Santa Fe.

Possibly the traveler would not have chosen Independence at all — many did not. He might have proceeded right to the Westport Landing — not in old Westport at all but at the foot of Grand Ave., in what is now the old downtown of Kansas City. From there he would have proceeded almost due south to Westport itself, and then either to New Santa Fe or Olathe.

At any rate, it is safe to say that most of the travelers

of the late 1840s left the United States at New Santa Fe, or about where 122nd St. is today. They headed out onto the boundless Kansas prairies to the Lone Elm campground, and then to a point two or three miles southwest of the little town of Gardner, Kansas. There the two trails split — the older one leading southwest to the old Spanish town of Santa Fe; the other shooting to the northwest and the valley of the Willamette River.

From Johnson Co., Kansas, the trail moved up toward the crossing of the Wakarusa, then north into the college town of Lawrence, and west to Topeka. Southeast of Topeka the trail branched; one route going to the Presbyterian mission west of Topeka and the other crossing the Kansas (or Kaw) River in the heart of Topeka.

The trail then angled northwestward to cross the Red Vermillion, then the Black Vermillion, and finally reached the banks of the Big Blue at the sylvan Alcove Spring, south of Marysville.

After crossing the Big Blue, the Oregon Trail moved to the valley of the Little Blue and followed it into Nebraska. Without ever crossing that stream, it moved northwest for 100 miles, and as the Little Blue abruptly bent to the south the trail continued northwest over the arid hills to the great broad valley of the Platte River.

In 1848 the U.S. Government moved Ft. Kearny from the Missouri River to the Platte; a partial reconstruction is in a state park just a few miles west of the point where the trail struck the river. From there the emigrants continued up the south side, past the forks at present North Platte, then a few miles up the South Platte River. Just past today's Brule, Nebraska, was the great Lower California Crossing, where the emigration forded the shallow South Platte, hauled up steep California Hill and out onto the parched plateau between the forks.

Less than a day away was delightful Ash Hollow and the North Platte River, to be reached only after a hazardous descent down steep Windlass Hill. The trail now followed the south bank of the North Platte to the great rocks — Courthouse and Chimney — to the eastern extremity of the Wildcat Hills.

On west of there, into the deep sandhill country of extreme western Nebraska, the trail came to the massive obstruction of Scotts Bluff. Travelers of 1845 skirted to the south where they spotted Laramie Peak 120 miles to the west, after they had pulled up over the Robidoux Pass. From 1851 on, almost all of them would move through the great cleft in the bluff itself, now known as Mitchell Pass.

The trail crossed Horse Creek and the Wyoming line at the site of the greatest Indian treaty conference ever held, then moved up to Laramie's Fork and into old Ft. Laramie. (Ft. William in 1845, then Ft. John, but always unofficially known as Ft. Laramie.)

The travelers usually stayed at the fort a few days· to replenish their strength and that of their oxen. Then they would strike out west. They would pause beneath Register Cliff to add their names to the hundreds already there, cross the deepening gouges in the sandstone south of Guernsey, and find the warm spring where they could do their laundry al fresco. Then, following the shadowy form of Laramie Peak, they would cross the deserts connecting the bulges of the North Platte, and arrive at the site of present Casper, Wyoming. There, from 1847, the Mormons operated a ferry across the river and the trail went into the alkali deserts to the west at that point. Later the Platte bridge carried the traffic over. But in 1845 there was no crossing there at all — the trail continued up the south bank for 10 more miles to the vivid Red Buttes, then turned sharply west to cross the river and leave it forever at Bessemer Bend.

Thence southwest through the antelope herds to the Sweetwater River and old Independence Rock. Sometimes the Sweetwater was crossed east of the great bulbous mass, sometimes at the rock itself, and sometimes it went to the south of the rock and crossed west of it. Six miles further it came to the terrifying Devils Gate and skirted it to the south. On across the baked land, following the sight line of Split Rock in the Rattlesnake Range.

In the mid-1840s the trail pulled through deep sand on the south bank of the Sweetwater for several miles; later in the decade a route was found through the solid, rocky bed of the river itself, called the Three Crossings Route. It crossed the Sweetwater three times in a mile and a half.

The trail then passed the Ice Slough, where the emigrants excavated sheets of last winter's ice from the insulation of the peat bog; up into the mile-high country and finally, often without realizing it, over the continental divide at fabled South Pass, south of Lander.

Within two miles the trail passed near the Pacific Springs — today a totally inaccessible bog, where the first waters destined for the Pacific Ocean rose out of the divide. Within a day's travel the decision had to be made whether to move nonstop for 50 miles to the Green River, with neither wood nor grass nor water; or whether to stay with the wood, grass and water, heading temporarily away from Oregon, toward Ft. Bridger. Many took the Sublette Cutoff; most took the extra three days and headed down the Sandy to Ft. Bridger, east of present Evanston.

The trail headed due north out of Ft. Bridger to Carter, then northwest to the Bear River valley south of present Sage Junction, then north along U.S. 30N to the Idaho border.

The trail followed the same highway and the Bear River closely into Idaho, to Montpelier and Soda Springs; then the Bear turned for the Great Salt Lake while the trail sliced across the desert to the Portneuf, following it north, near Pocatello and into Ft. Hall, on the Snake.

The trail headed southwest into the American Falls reservoir from Ft. Hall, generally following the route of I-15W along the south bank of the Snake River, then 80N and back to U.S. 30 into Twin Falls. The emigrants, awed by the angry Snake at Twin Falls and Shoshone Falls, found it being fed by an underground river at Thousand Springs. Past the upper Salmon Falls the trail struck out across the desert to the Three Island Crossing at present Glenns Ferry. It left the Snake there, to head north to the Boise River, striking it just east of Boise.

It followed along the south bank of the Boise, forded it in present Caldwell, and stayed close to (or beneath)

U.S. Highways 20 and 26 to Parma. There it struck out all alone to Ft. Boise, of which not a trace remains today, and the final crossing of the Snake, just below the mouth of the Boise River.

The trail moved into the dryness of southeastern Oregon, northwest from Kingman to the crossing of the Malheur at Vale. From Vale it went due north to a final view of the Snake, at Farewell Bend, across the river from Weiser, Idaho. Then northwest along 80N to Ruckles Flat and Flagstaff Hill, overlooking the broad Baker Valley and the Powder River. Following I-80 north of North Powder, the trail entered the dreaded Blue Mountains, over the ragged rim of the great natural saucer, 20 miles in diameter, called the Grande Ronde by the French mountain men a generation before. The town of La Grande lays in that saucer, and past it the trail of 1845 either went due north to the Whitman Mission or northwest down the Umatilla to the Columbia, or west from Echo to the mouth of the Deschutes.

This narrative includes a visit to the Whitman Mission at Walla Walla as a side trip, takes the main trail northwest from La Grande through Meacham and out of the Grande Ronde toward Pendleton, following I-80N most of the way.

The trail took the 21 miles between Pendleton and Echo south of I-80N, and at Echo the trail moved due west through the utter desolation below the Columbia. The snowy cone of Mt. Hood materializes as a blue shadow, barely discernible on the horizon, as the trail moves through the alkali deserts to Wasco, then northwest through Mud Spring Canyon to strike the broad Columbia 15 miles east of The Dalles. It followed the south bank of the river for about five miles, crossed the mouth of the Deschutes, pulled up a monstrous hill for another five miles, then came into The Dalles from the southeast. Here it followed the river again down to the Rowena Bluffs, about six miles northwest of The Dalles, and from there could go no further.

At that point the emigrants frequently boarded rafts to float, and portage, down to Ft. Vancouver. After a brief rest, they would board other rafts and float across the Columbia, into the mouth of the Willamette River, and up to the falls at Oregon City. There they would wait out the months of October through January, and late in February they would start moving up the valley to stake their claims. That was the end of the Oregon Trail.

And that is the trail which has been selected as the subject of Part 2, where detailed directions are supplied to route the present day traveler to the old trail. There are, however, a number of ganglia at each end of the trail which should not go unnoticed. Three were seen in Jackson Co., Mo. alone — the original Santa Fe Trail to Gardner, Kansas; the Independence-Westport road, thence south to the Santa Fe Trail; and the same road southwest through the Shawnee Mission and Olathe, down to Gardner.

There was still another, across the Missouri from Kansas City, at Liberty. This was used chiefly by some of the fur traders, but some emigrants elected to land on the north bank of the Missouri, and move north a considerable distance, preferring to ford a narrower Missouri rather than the Kansas River.

Other attempts were made by emigrants who preferred to stay on the steamers until they docked at the Army's Ft. Leavenworth. Some emigrants who left from Liberty, and others who moved in their wagons from their homes in north-central Missouri, came to Weston, Mo., and ferried across to Ft. Leavenworth. Ft. Leavenworth was important, but it never carried the traffic of the major jumping off places.

The biggest threat to Independence was St. Joseph and, in fact, from the days of the gold rush on, it eclipsed Independence in the volume of traffic headed west. The village was only two years old in 1845, but by 1849 it was a bustling city of more than 1,500 people.

The road from St. Joe moved due west through Hiawatha to Marysville, where it crosses the Big Blue five or six miles north of the Alcove Spring. It joined the Independence road just west of Marysville.

The Ft. Leavenworth road moved northwest through Lancaster and Seneca, joining the road from St. Joe just east of Marysville.

Further north, on the west side of the Missouri, is Nebraska City, and at one time this carried a sizeable emigrant trade, for until 1848 this was the location of the decrepit old blockhouse, the first Ft. Kearny.

The old Ft. Kearny route shot directly northwest to hit the Platte about midway between Fremont and Columbus.

Then there was Plattsmouth, a relatively inconsequential port also on the west bank. Of more importance was Bellevue, about where the south limits of the City of Omaha is today. Of equal importance must be the road from Council Bluffs, Iowa, and Florence, Nebraska — the route of the Mormon emigration of 1847.

The road from Bellevue followed the north bank of the Platte literally, but the road from Winter Quarters (Florence) was due west across the Elkhorn River to the Platte, just below Fremont. From there the Mormons stayed on the north bank of the river, all the way to Ft. Laramie and sometimes beyond. Usually they crossed the North Platte there, however, and melded with the Oregon Trail. This is usually referred to as the Mormon Trail, but, in fact, it was quite heavily traveled by "gentiles" — including the Whitmans and Spaldings — long before the exodus. The Mormons didn't leave the Oregon Trail again until they hit Ft. Bridger. From there they moved down into the Wasatch Range to cross over into the Promised Land.

Ever since there was an Oregon Trail the emigrants tried to find a way to bypass the irritating opposite-direction dip to Ft. Bridger, enroute from the South Pass up to Ft. Hall. Old Caleb Greenwood came up with the best answer, but it was far from a good one. Just past the South Pass, at the crossing of the Sandy, wagons could head west for fifty parched miles to the Green River over what was to become known as the Sublette Cutoff. This had to be done in one jump, for there was absolutely no water nor grass nor wood along the entire route.

The U.S. Government for some reason thought they had a better way. They hacked out a road, the Lander Cutoff, which led from the last crossing of the Sweetwater, southeast of Atlantic City, over the divide at Sioux Pass, into the old rendezvous country of the mountain man, and joined the Oregon Trail fifteen miles east of Ft. Hall. The engineering of the Lander Cutoff was completed in 1859; yet few of the subsequent emigrants took the cutoff.

The two most important western ganglia were the California Road and the Hudspeth Cutoff to that road. The California Road actually started where the Oregon Trail crosses the Raft River, west of Pocatello, Idaho. From there it shot to the southwest, crossed the Raft three times and hit Goose Creek at the state line. It moved to the Humboldt River near Wells, Nevada, and followed it until it sunk into the burning sands east of Reno. The California Road then went across the California line between Donner Lake and Lake Tahoe, down the Bear to the Sacramento, and on up the American Fork to the mines.

The Hudspeth Cutoff started at Sheep Rock, four miles west of Soda Springs. The Bidwell party of 1841 followed the Bear all the way down to the Great Salt Lake, but Hudspeth moved west, rather than south, and simply cut out the northern probe to Ft. Hall. He struck the trail just after it left the Raft River, near Malta.

Some emigrants who didn't like the idea of fording the Snake at the Three Island Crossing, elected to move among the great rocks along the south bank all the way up to the Ft. Boise crossing. They generally made the trek safely, but the road down the Boise always was considered the better of the two.

Finally, there was the Barlow Road. The emigrants had been paying through the nose all along the Oregon Trail, from the Papin Crossing of the Kansas in Topeka, to the last crossing of the Snake. From the late 1840s on, ferries were established wherever there might be trouble, and an emigrant would rather pay $1 or $2 to get his wagon across, rather than unload it, caulk and tallow it and remove the running gear for a float across. Furthermore, it was faster, generally, than preparing his own wagon or building a raft.

By the time the emigrants hit The Dalles, however, when land travel further west was thought to be

Harold Warp Pioneer Village
*Barlow Cutoff, over south shoulder of Mt. Hood,
eliminated tolls charged by gougers on lower Columbia,
but as Jackson's painting shows, it was worth the effort
only if the emigrant was flat broke.*

impossible, many found they had very little money left
and none coming in for nearly a year. These people
bitterly resented the outrageous prices charged by the
ferry operators to float the emigrant wagons down the
Columbia to Ft. Vancouver. In 1845 Sam Barlow did
something about it.

Sam found the gougers hard at work at The Dalles
and stomped off in a huff. He mounted his company
and, wagons and all, they headed south out of town,
over Five Mile Creek, Eight Mile Creek, and Fifteen Mile
Creek to Tygh Valley. From there he took one look at
the great towering cone of Mt. Hood and headed right
for it. He passed on the south shoulder, near the town of
Government Camp today, then down the dizzying
slopes, hacking his way through the timber to the Zigzag
River and then the Sandy. From there it was relatively
smooth going into Oregon City from due east. The
Barlow wagons were left behind, but they were picked
up the next spring and rolled into Oregon City. Then
Sam, who a few months before had been so disgusted

with the toll-charging system on the Columbia, decided that his ox no longer was being gored and set up a toll system on the road himself; and that toll road continued in existence until 1912.

The trail was considered at an end in Oregon City. Emigrants first settled primarily to the south, along the Willamette, and in the later years of the century they fanned out all over the state.

The total distance from Independence to Oregon City was variable, depending upon whose odometer was being used and exactly which alternates were being taken, but the figure of 2,020 miles seems to be a good average. The time of travel ranged from four months for mule-drawn wagons in a good dry year, to five months with oxen in a wet year.

Part 2

CHAPTER 1   ADVICE TO TRAVELERS

This book is intended not just to acquaint the casual reader with one of the greatest dramas of world history, but to give him personal physical identification with it. It will take him west if he wants to go, and stand him precisely in the Oregon Trail in literally hundreds of locations. It will take about four weeks to savor the complete experience, seeing what ought to be seen without rushing. Those who cannot spare the time in one chunk are advised to break it into two or three sections.

Those in a hurry to do it all at once will find a passage in the back of this book just for them — a special speed trip that will take them from one end of the trail to the other and include the high spots, all in 10 days, and all referenced back into the text of Part 2. While this is a rewarding experience it doesn't yield the gut feel of history, and empathy with the emigrant of the mid-19th century may be harder to come by.

No one will return from either trip a nervous wreck. They will come back with a new and more intense feeling for American History. Hopefully they will have been helped, through this new proximity to the footsteps of the men who broke the West, to gain a new feeling of the past.

Since little physical exertion will be involved, it is

likely to get more interesting with each mile to the west, and, unlike the emigrants (who had it a little tougher), this interest should not flag at all until the traveler is in Oregon City.

A traveler can make this trip and sleep comfortably every night in a fairly decent motel. He doesn't have to plan his entire trip ahead of time and write for reservations, because most of the top motels and all of the lesser ones along these highways usually have vacancies at least until early evening.

We preferred to carry our motel with us. Our new Holiday Rambler trailer proved to be comfortable for a family of five. The self-contained features were especially helpful because full campgrounds usually will accept any self-contained rig. It requires only space — no utilities.

What to Read

There are seven books which ought to be read before the traveler takes this trip. One may be obtained at any public library — *Across the Wide Missouri* by Bernard DeVoto. This will give the reader the flavor of the West that awaited the great emigration. Irene D. Paden's *Wake of the Prairie Schooner* (now marketed by The Patrice Press), is a delightful work by a lady who in the 1930s and 1940s did what was done here in the 1970s, except that she did not attempt to locate the trail precisely for the traveler.

Signet Classics (New American Library) publishes Francis Parkman's *The Oregon Trail*. It is as superb a work today as it was when first published in 1847. The man was a fine journalist.

There is the splendid work of Merrill J. Mattes, *The Great Platte River Road*, marketed by The Patrice Press. Although Mattes does not relate the old trail to today's highways, he gives a splendid history of it, from the several jumping-off places to Fort Laramie.

The Patrice Press also offers three other books about the trail: Aubrey Haines's classic, *Historic Sites Along the*

Oregon Trail; my *Maps of the Oregon Trail;* and Stanley B. Kimball's marvelously edited version of William Clayton's *The Latter-day Saints' Emigrants' Guide.*

What to Drive

A pickup truck with a four-wheel drive is as much a part of the American West as cowboy boots or sage. Little old ladies drive them to church and undertakers use them for hearses. The field work for this book, however, was performed in a series of Ford Country Sedan station wagons. The effect was like bounding over a rock pile on a beach ball.

The Fords were taken for the same reason Marcus Whitman took a wagon to Waiilatpu (almost) — he wanted to show that it was feasible to do it.

Only once was a stretch attempted that simply was impassable with the Fords, and this would have been impassable in a Sherman tank. In all other cases it was obvious that the car shouldn't be tested to that degree, so it wasn't tried; if it was tried the goal was attained with a minimum of trouble.

The point is, the family car may indeed be driven on this trip. Whatever is taken, air conditioning is a must. There will be roads so incredibly dusty that the residue will build on the side windows so thick that vision will be obstructed completely. Rather than rolling the window down and letting some of it blow in, the inside of the glass should be tapped with a hard object, and the dust should come cascading down. Even with a brand new, tight automobile, the dust will somehow manage to seep in and cover everything inside with an irritating powder.

This is the same sort of stuff the emigrants were exposed to day after day. It was wind driven and the alkali in it caused eyes to burn bright red and lips to split like an overcooked hot dog. Persons who do not have air conditioning are advised to take the speed trip, as outlined at the end of this book.

Travelers who elect to tow a trailer will find the trip less expensive than staying in motels. The savings in room rates will be substantial, but the savings on food will be enormous. There is a problem though, in that a trailer should be pulled ahead and tied up in a campground, after which the traveler may double back as much as 100 miles, work past the campground, and then return at the end of the day. This will have the effect of doubling the mileage but added gas expense will be more than compensated for by the savings in food and lodging.

A folding tent trailer can go anywhere a car can go, but it should be extraordinarily tight, to keep the dust out. A pickup camper will make some of the roads — not all. The driver is advised to check the local sources to see about road conditions and bridge capacities and clearances on each leg involving back roads.

Be prepared for rain. In the first field trip, a series of real doozies was encountered, from Marysville all the way to the Sweetwater, almost every night in July. It is a strange thing though, that since the fall of 1970, after more than 20,000 miles of travel on this project, not a drop of rain fell. Only once, in Johnson Co., Kansas, some two hours before the end of a field trip in January, 1971, was there any precipitation — a snowstorm. But the traveler is reminded that this aridity is most unusual in Kansas and Nebraska. Be ready for some real pyrotechnics.

Some roads were encountered that had been dampened about 24 hours before, and only by great luck was a ditching avoided. The traveler is urged to read ahead on every stretch, and also to inquire locally as to road conditions should there be any doubt. To ignore this advice could be very serious — some of the stretches are long and lonely, and many are untraveled for weeks at a time. The traveler on such a road is advised to constantly keep in mind the point of no return. A storm can come up in a hurry and travel at 35 m.p.h., and should the traveler be short of his midpoint with a cloud between him and his destination, he is well advised to turn around and get the hell out of there. There already is an average of one dead person every 80 yards on the Oregon Trail.

Some of the routings in Part 2 lead over canal access roads. These are right on the banks of irrigation canals, separated from the water only by a low earthen levee.

Extreme caution is urged when driving these poorly-maintained roads. The canals sometimes carry the whole body of water of a river — the stream is deep and fast, and the banks are steep and slippery and devoid of hand holds.

All the routes described in this book actually have been driven by the author, and tape recordings and map notations were made on the spot. Within 24 hours of the actual field trip the first draft of the narrative for that day's activity was complete.

What to Bring

Prior to leaving it is suggested that the traveler run down a vacation check list — a good one is located in the Texaco Touring Atlas.

This book has been written so the average vacationer can have a lot of fun just following the text and his state maps, to find the trail. However, there are some conflicts between the book and the road or street maps published by the oil companies. When this happens, follow the book. Every one of these directions has been tested and holds up, or at least they did in the year of publication. The Kansas City street map, on the other hand, is all fouled up in many of the very areas where the traveler will be. It is to be used as a basic supplement and where there is conflict the book alone is to be used.

More determined students will take other measures. It is suggested that county maps be obtained from the highway departments of the states of Kansas, Nebraska, Wyoming, Idaho and Oregon. This could involve an expenditure of upwards of $100, but the county maps will locate the little gravel roads that the state maps can't, and thus give the historian and geographer a better sense of where he is in relation to the trail and the nearest paved highway.

The highway departments, their addresses, the county map names and numbers, and the city maps, respectively, are listed here:

Missouri Highway Department, Jefferson City, Mo. 65101; Jackson Co. and the City of Kansas City, plus the city of Independence.

Kansas Highway Department, Topeka, Kansas 66612;

Johnson, Douglas, Shawnee, Pottawatomie, Marshall, and Washington Counties, plus the City of Topeka.

Department of Roads, State of Nebraska, P.O. Box 94759, Lincoln, Nebraska 68509; Adams, Clay, Dawson, Deuel, Gage, Garden (south only), Gosper, Jefferson, Kearney, Keith, Lincoln (both maps), Morrill (south only), Nuckolls, Phelps, Scotts Bluff, and Thayer Counties.

Wyoming Highway Department, P.O. Box 1708, Cheyenne, Wyoming 82201; Goshen (1 & 2), Platte (2 only) Converse (1 & 4), Natrona (4 & 5), Fremont (1 & 2), Sweetwater (4, 8 & 9), Sublette (1 only), Uinta (1 only), and Lincoln (2 & 3) Counties, plus the City of Casper.

Idaho Department of Highways, P.O. Box 7129, Boise, Idaho 83701; Bear Lake, Caribou (1 & 2), Bannock (1 only), Bingham (2 only), Power (1 & 2), Cassia (1 & 2), Twin Falls (1 & 2), Elmore (1, 3 & 4), Ada (1 only), and Canyon Counties, plus the cities of Boise and Twin Falls. Also request the free booklet, Route of the Oregon Trail in Idaho. This is a series of strip maps in booklet form, but unfortunately it shows only major highways, not always the public roadways nearest the trail.

Oregon State Highway Commission, Room 17, State Highway Building, Salem, Oregon 97310; Malheur (2 & 4), Baker (1 & 4), Union (2 & 3), Umatilla (1, 2 & 3), Morrow (1 only), Gilliam (1 only), Sherman (1 only), and Wasco (1 only) Counties. Oregon also has a fine little booklet of strip maps of the trail in Oregon, which is free.

The most comfortable scale to work with in the field is ½":1 mile; and those maps also are the least expensive, ranging from 25 cents to $2 each from the various highway departments.

The Oregon Trail is indicated on the official state road maps of Nebraska, Wyoming, Idaho and Oregon, so ask also for several copies of each — they're free.

In all cases they are inaccurate, not because of poor research but because the present roadways must be indicated many times actual scale size, and it would be impossible to lay the track of the Oregon Trail atop those printed lines without causing a lot of confusion.

The route of the trail in Kansas may be transferred to the county maps only by visiting the microfilm room of the Kansas Historical Society in Topeka, where the U.S. Surveys are on file, or in the archives of the State Historical Societies of Nebraska (Lincoln) or Wyoming (Cheyenne), where the maps of Paul Henderson are housed.

Henderson's maps are the finest by far and despite years of research by many other trail historians, his scholarship remains unchallenged. With a little practice his lines may be transferred to the contemporary county maps with an accuracy of 100 yards or so, plus or minus.

In many cases it is impossible to guide the traveler with accuracy without a magnetic compass, so many directions are given in terms of degrees of bearing. The best instrument to use is the Boy Scout Polaris compass, Model 1070, available at department stores with official scout departments for about $2.95. Persons who recoil at this suggestion are reminded that about 800,000 11-year-old Tenderfoot scouts cope very successfully with this compass every year.

The base of the Polaris compass is a flat sheet of clear plastic. Onto this is mounted a liquid-filled circular housing containing a magnetic needle. To obtain a bearing of, say, 300°, the outer ring of the circular housing is turned to the figure 300. Then the entire instrument is rotated so that the red needle floating in the liquid-filled housing is lined up with the red arrow etched in the bottom of that housing — it will always point north if the instrument is held level, away from magnetic influences such as an automobile, pocket knife, metal buttons, etc. When the needle and the arrow are aligned the main body of the compass will then be pointing to 300°.

When the instruction is to walk so many yards in that direction, some object on the horizon should be selected which is aligned with the 300° bearing. The compass should be put away and the required distance toward that object should be paced off. To return, the compass should be held pointing toward the user, with the floating needle again aligned with the red arrow etched in the base. An object on the opposite horizon then should be selected, and the required distance paced off again.

Sometimes there is no possibility of finding a visual landmark, such as when the traveler is in a grove of trees. The compass then should be held at waist level, the arrows aligned, and followed in the direction in which the compass points.

The traveler again is reminded that the trail in most places wasn't just the width of the wagons. Out on the prairies it was a mile wide. Rarely was it less than 10 yards wide in the flats — there was no sense eating any more dust than you had to. So a few degrees of error in compass heading still will get the traveler where he needs to go, to the exact location of the Oregon Trail.

It is also a good idea to equip the automobile with a compass, calibrated to compensate for the magnetic influences of the car's metals.

All but extremely short distances are given in yards. Most adult males can pace a yard with comfort. Pacing distances are rarely given for more than 300 yards, and an error of an inch a pace over that distance would amount to only eight yards of overall error. Anybody who couldn't find the Oregon Trail when he is eight yards from it ought to stay home anyway.

At any rate it might be worthwhile for the traveler to get an idea of the feel of a pace of exactly one yard. The best way to do this is to walk between the yard markers of a high school football field, and try to measure the degree of "stretch" to make a pace of exactly one yard. (A half yard for small persons is a more comfortable stride.) The pace should be adjusted to one of the two by striding down the measured length of the field, crossing the yard lines.

The traveler should take a pair of binoculars and a camera with at least one long lens. People should appear in the photos as means of determining scale, not as photographic subjects in themselves.

When to Leave

The journey could not be taken in complete time synchronization with the emigrants unless it was walked,

Long, dead grasses from preceding season hold down new growth on virgin prairies until May 1. Only then could the trains depart, for only then would there be sufficient grass to nourish the livestock. This is Tucker Prairie, on south side of I-70 15 miles east of Columbia, Mo., on April 15, 1971. Ground has never been broken.

and walked slowly. Even a man walking at a normal pace would make a mile or two more a day than the laboring oxen of the 1840s. The trip took about five months then. The traveler today can depart from Independence any time from the first of May, when the prairie greens up, to the first of September, and somewhere along the line the time of the wagon train would be synchronous with the contemporary calendar and the 20th century traveler.

Those leaving Missouri on June 20, for example, should find themselves at Independence Rock on July 4, when most of the emigrants passed there. Those leaving May 1 will overtake the ghost train the first few days out. If the traveler wants maximum benefit from the experience, and minimum discomfort, he should start on May 15; not from Independence but from the Tucker Prairie, along the south side of I-70, 15 miles east of Columbia, Mo., or one mile east of the Hatton (M-HH) exit. There he can see the virgin prairie exactly as the emigrant saw it when he poked his oxen across the border of the United States (now the Kansas-Missouri line) in 1845. This would put the vacationer in the deserts during early June, and by June 10 he should be in Oregon City, giving him time to return home before the four weeks are over.

What to Wear

Persons familiar with the diaries of the western travelers will note continual references to the great heat, even on the high plains of the Platte. This situation has not changed, and even in the spring the mercury can move up toward 100 degrees. It follows that an abundance of light clothing should be carried. Travelers are reminded too of Francis Parkman's quote of the storm on the Platte, which describes the stinging sleet and hail of June. This admittedly is unusual, but it can happen today. So a good sweater or sweatshirt is advisable.

Finally, those planning some light hiking ought to have a pair of boondockers. The weeds of the West are an aggravating lot — their seed pods assume all sorts of weird configurations, from naval mines to spirochetes, and all designed not just to penetrate the socks, but to actually become part of them.

Boondockers also come far enough over the ankle to minimize danger from rattlesnakes. It will be an unusual trip if no rattlers are spotted somewhere along the trail. Finally, strong leather boondockers give far better ankle support than lower desert boots, and this will be most welcome when picking through fields of rocks.

Nothing anyone can spray on seems to be completely effective agains the ticks of the West. After hiking along the trail persons should examine exposed skin and scalp areas carefully for these pests. Don't pull them from the skin. Apply a lighted cigarette to the tick's rear end and get him to back out by himself. Otherwise his head will break away from his body and remain beneath the skin surface, probably resulting in infection.

Sometime during the compilation of this phase of the book the text came to be called the "begats." It is, hopefully, a little more exciting than that, but explicit directions must be given for those who actually make the trip and this can tend to be boring to anyone else. Therefore, passages which are solely directional in nature have been identified just as this paragraph has; placed between horizontal rules and set with a little less line spacing.

CHAPTER 2   FINDING THE TRAIL IN MISSOURI

In the earliest days the Oregon Trail, and in fact all trails to the West, originated in St. Louis — on the downtown riverfront, just below the Gateway Arch. Anybody who was anybody in the American West until the 1840s came through, or, from there. The Smith-Sublette-Jackson caravan, the first to take wagons up to the east slope of the continental divide, went out the old St. Charles Rock Rd., now St. Charles St., Franklin Ave., Easton Ave., and the present St. Charles Rock Rd. Lewis and Clark, in fact, outfitted there, although they assembled across the Mississippi from north St. Louis, at the mouth of Wood River. They would have made their rendezvous in St. Louis except they got a running jump on the transfer of power resulting from the Louisiana Purchase. The western bank of the Mississippi still was under Spanish control at the time the assembly outfitted.

The Chouteaus lived there and conducted their vast fur operations from the downtown riverfront. Manuel Lisa had a warehouse there which was torn down in the 1960s, in one of St. Louis' great acts of official vandalism. Robert Campbell, an Ashley lieutenant and later a principal in the outfitting firm of Sublette and Campbell, lived the life of a proper fur baron in his town house at 1508 Locust St. The house still stands, essentially as he left it a hundred years ago — same linens, same furniture, same curtains, same china. It is open to the public.

Despite the fact that Independence was founded in 1827, St. Louis remained the gateway to the West until the late 1830s, with most of the purchasing being done there. Stretching the imagination a little, it might be called the gateway during most of the 19th century, because it was from St. Louis that the steamboats departed, bearing the wagons, the livestock, the money — all earthly possessions of the families bound for the West.

The word "trail," however, implies land, since it is difficult to leave a trail on water. The origin of the land trail to Oregon centered in Independence sometime in the 1830s, then shifted to Westport and St. Joseph sometime in the late 1840s and early 1850s.

There were almost as many Oregon Trails as there were people who took it. Each year the route changed; sometimes only slightly, sometimes drastically. This book would have to be 10 times as thick as it is if all the major routes were covered. The year 1845 has been isolated, for no particular reason, and the trail pinned down in that year as closely as possible.

Detailed routes are not supplied for St. Joseph, Bellevue, Council Bluffs, Ft. Leavenworth or any of the other feeder routes that eventually merged into the route from Independence. Only the trail from Independence and Westport has been pinned down, and no others, because that was the origin of most of the emigration of the 1840s.

Our narrative will take the vacationer up to the Independence Landing on the Missouri River. That's where it all began for upwards of 100,000 emigrants. Their excited steps will be traced up the tortuous hill and down into the bustling square at Independence. Then directions will be given for the Independence-Westport road, to get to the old town on the state line.

Then straight south, following the rolling hills, to an intercept with the old Santa Fe Trail, and follow that famous old road into the now-vanished town of New Santa Fe, where the traveler leaves Missouri and, in our year of 1845, the United States.

Those who want to see it all will be directed back up north to the site of the Westport (or Kanzas) Landing, the birthplace of Kansas City; the first Chouteau

Landing (1821), and then the 1826 Chouteau Landing. All three landings are now close to downtown Kansas City, or actually in it. The old trappers' route will be taken out to Westport. Then back east to Independence and the original Santa Fe Trail down to the southwest, back to New Santa Fe.

To Reach The Independence Landing

There were two landings, at least, serving Independence. One was the Blue Mills Landing, which was subject to repeated flooding and thus was short lived. It was established in 1832. The landing that endured, and became known as the Independence Landing, was at Wayne City, about 3½ miles due north of the square at Independence.

From I-70 take State 291 northbound. About 5½ miles north, intercept U.S. 24 and take it westbound. This is one branch of the Oregon-Santa Fe Trail. It is beneath the concrete of U.S. 24. This is the very early portion of the trail which led both from Ft. Osage and later from the old Blue Mills Landing. It will leave this route at College Ave., about 1½ miles southwest. Continue on U.S. 24 to River Rd., about 2¾ miles from U.S. 24. Turn north, or right. About 1.5 miles north of U.S. 24 jog slightly to the left. About two miles north of U.S. 24 is Kentucky Rd., cutting across River Rd. at an angle. This is a very dangerous intersection — cross Kentucky Rd. with caution.

The overview of the Independence Landing is about .2 mile from Kentucky Rd. Continue on the River Rd. about a block past Kentucky Rd. to a fork. The road to the right is marked with a "Road Closed" sign. An arrow points to the left, for the Kansas City plant of the Missouri Portland Cement Co. Follow the road to the left about a block, to a white chat area on the left, at a sharp curve to the right. Park there. Walk straight ahead to the embankment.

Now use the compass for the first time. Turn the dial to 360 degrees. Position the red end of the floating needle over the red plastic arrow inside the housing. Then sight over the arrow on the outside of the dial, to look true north.

If one could throw a rock 2,000 feet in the direction of the compass, it should land right in the middle of what was once Water St., and the blocks of buildings that once stood there. That is the old Independence Landing.

Unfortunately, the landing most likely will be viewed in the summertime when the trees are in full leaf. One can see the river and that is about all. Note that the bank falls away steeply from the observation point.

The road up from the landing, described in almost every diary as tortuous, evidently is under the road that comes up from the cement plant, and which is closed to the public. It came down very steeply to the upstream side of the buildings that once were there, and ran between them and the water.

Now head back down the River Rd. for a closer look at the landing. At that dangerous intersection with Kentucky Rd., turn half right and follow Kentucky Rd. west for exactly one mile. Pass a steel oil storage tank on the right and then enter the refinery of the American Oil Co., at Vermont Ave. Turn right onto Vermont and follow it down to the levee. Just before reaching the

Old Independence Landing today; Cement City Rd. in foreground and plant of Missouri Portland Cement Co. at right.

small Sugar Creek railroad station turn to the right again.
This improved road, the Cement City Rd., runs between
the cliff, the first observation point, and the Missouri
River.

Cross the railroad tracks, once the Pacific Railroad.
When abreast a signal bridge over the tracks, proceed
.9 mile further and stop.

On the right is the building complex of the cement
company. The south bank of the Missouri River in the
year 1845 was about where the car is now. Stand facing
the cliff and look up. With only a little imagination one
can see a row of brick and wood buildings for two blocks
to the left — steamboats in back, the ferry a block downstream and crudely dressed men trying to hitch recal-
citrant mules to the whiffletrees of the wagons, which
had yet to be fitted out with bows and covers. It was a
study in sometimes frenetic activity.

The levee itself was packed solid with boxes, crates,
confused cattle and people. Black stevedores with
muscles like steel bands would wrestle barrels and kegs.
Children who had scarcely stopped babbling since their
first day on earth suddenly were silent; their eyes filled
with only a beginning of the wonderment they would
feel in the ensuing months. This is where the greatest
American adventure began for so many.

W. W. Phelps, the Mormon chronicler, wrote a description of the landing on Feb. 27, 1834: ". . . and on
the 23rd [Feb.] about twelve o'clock we were on the
bank, opposite Everit's ferry, where we found Captain
Atchison's company of 'Liberty Blues.' . . . About
twenty-five men crossed over to effect a landing in
safety, and when they came near the ware house . . ."
Thus, by this date there was an operating ferry, and
there evidently was at least one warehouse in operation
at Wayne City.

Retrace the route back through the refinery, back to
the left on Kentucky Rd. for the River Rd. Turn hard
right onto River Rd. This now is the trail itself.

Independence merchants saw a lot of their trade
bleeding away to Westport. Many an emigrant wrote his

hometown paper to tell them of the insufferable mud from Independence Landing to the square, and when the new Kanzas Landing became better known, more emigrants landed there, bypassing Independence.

To counter this the merchants macadamized the road and then installed a railroad from the levee to the square. This was a mule-powered contrivance, with cars riding on steel-topped rails. Probably it kept things alive for a little while but it didn't work long. Westport and St. Joseph both took their tolls, and Independence was the loser.

There are no vestiges of the trail left in this or any other part of the metropolitan area save one, the west bank of the Big Blue River at the crossing of the Independence-Westport Road. Here on the River Road, as in many other places, the paving was laid directly over the old trail.

Along this route one may find some of the major clues of locating trails. In this locale there are a lot of defiles and ridges. Wherever there is a line of ridges in the supposed location of the trail, pointing in approximately the same direction, it is a good bet that the trail itself ran atop or near the top of those ridges. The River Road is along the crest of one such ridge, running almost all the way into the square at Independence.

Retrace the route down the River Road. Travel two blocks past U.S. 24 to the first stop sign, which is College Avenue. The trail turned east (left) along and under College. Turn east. Proceed six blocks to McCoy Parkway and turn right. Follow it to the traffic circle and turn right onto Spring. It was at this point that the trail fanned out, heading in several southerly directions to the square. Turn right on Spring, follow it for three blocks. Turn east (left) again on Truman Road for three more blocks to Main Street. This formed the east boundary of the square and is one-way to the right, or south. Turn to the right, park in the public lot on the corner, and walk south.

On the east side of Main, a couple of doors south of Truman Road, is a handsome building remaining from the 1850s — the Marshal's House and, in an areaway to the east, the Old Jail. These buildings date to 1859. The structures are under the auspices of the Jackson County Historical Society and are open daily, closed on Mondays only except in June, July and August. The Old Jail houses one of the best small museums in the country and is well worth inspection. The building is well furnished and there is a good representation of regional history.

The next street south, Maple, forms the northern boundary of the square. On the northwest corner of Main and Maple is the greatly altered tavern and inn of Col. Smallwood Noland. It was a popular hostelry in the days of the trail, particularly for the emigrants who chose to purchase their entire outfits — wagons, livestock and all — in Independence, rather than pay steamer fare from the East on all that weight. Here they would stay while the dickering progressed in April and the early days of May. Parkman tells about it:

"Being at leisure one day [in 1846] I rode over to Independence. The town was crowded. A multitude of shops had sprung up to furnish the emigrants and Santa Fe traders with necessaries for their journey; and there was an incessant hammering and banging from a dozen blacksmiths' sheds, where the heavy wagons were being repaired, and the horse and oxen shod. The streets were thronged with men, horses, and mules. While I was in the town, a train of emigrant wagons from Illinois passed through to join the camp on the prairie, and stopped in the principal street. A multitude of healthy children's faces were peeping out from under the covers of the wagons. Here and there a buxom damsel was seated on horseback, holding over her sunburnt face an old umbrella or a parasol, once gaudy enough but now miserably faded. The men, very sober looking countrymen, stood about their oxen; and as I passed I noticed three old fellows, who, with their long whips in their hands, were zealously discussing the doctrine of regeneration.

"The emigrants, however, are not all of this stamp. Among them are some of the vilest outcasts in the country. I have often perplexed myself to divine the various motives that give impulse to this strange

Portions of Smallwood Noland's original hotel, ca. 1846, are believed to be inside this building at Main and Maple, on the square at Independence.

migration; but whatever they may be, whether an insane hope of a better condition in life, or a desire of shaking off restraints of law and society, or mere restlessness, certain it is that multitudes bitterly repent and journey, and after they have reached the land of promise are happy enough to escape from it."

While Kansas City and Westport both have strong ties to the fur trade, Independence seems to have evolved from its very beginnings more as a transportation center.

The softening of attitudes of the Spanish toward the American traders gave birth to the Santa Fe trade, and the old towns of Franklin (long since fallen into the Missouri River), and Arrow Rock, kicked the trade off with a bang. Soon the eastern terminus of what became the Santa Fe Trail moved to the west. By 1827, perhaps a year or two earlier, there was a motley little collection of huts southeast of where the Missouri makes its great bend to the north, and that became Independence and the eastern end of the Santa Fe Trail.

There were other reasons for Independence. The Federal government had pushed the Indians across the western line of Missouri and out of the United States. They were giving the red man some hefty annuities, and some of the entrepreneurs back in the states wanted another look at the money. Independence was a convenient place to work out of — only a morning's ride from the territory.

Back in 1830, when the town was about three years old, the famous caravan of wagons, dearborns and carts was assembled by Jedediah Smith, Dave Jackson and Bill Sublette; fought the sloughs of the lower Missouri River and became the first of innumerable wagon trains bound for the middle Rockies to pass through Independence.

When the steamboats came in, in the early 1830s, that obviated the need to fight the 300 miles of bottoms from St. Louis. In three or four days, without any effort, the emigrant could be in Independence, fresh and ready for the trek across the plains.

Phelps described the area near Independence on July 23, 1831:

''The prairies are beautiful beyond description, yielding prairie grass, wild sun flowers, small flowers in great variety and color, and continually presenting, or 'keeping up appearances' of a highly cultivated country without inhabitants. Meadow peeps o'er meadow, and prairie on prairies rise like the rolling waves on the ocean. Prairie pluvers, prairie hens, wild turkies, rabbits, gray squirrels, prairie dogs, wolves, rattlesnakes (the big breed), prairie rattlesnakes, copperheads, panthers, deer, etc., go when they have a mind to and come when they please.''

Joseph Smith himself, the target of all the misery suffered by the LDS at the hands of the Jackson County settlers, visited Independence in the summers of 1831 and 1832, wrote this in 1842, two years before his murder near Nauvoo:

"But as we could not associate with our neighbors (who were many of them of the basest of men and had fled from the face of civilized society, to the frontier country to escape the hand of justice) in their midnight revels, their sabbath breaking, horseracing, and gambling, they commenced at first ridicule, then to persecute . . ."

In 1832 the celebrated writer Washington Irving, accompanied by the Britisher Charles Latrobe, passed through Independence. Latrobe's description:

"The town of Independence was full of promise, like

most of the innumerable towns springing up in the midst of the forests in the West, many of which, though dignified by high-sounding epithets, consist of nothing but a ragged congeries of five or six rough log huts, two or three clapboard houses, two or three so-called hotels, alias grogshops; a few stores, a bank, printing office, and barn-looking church. It lacked at the time I commemorate, the three last edifices, but was nevertheless a thriving and aspiring place . . ."

The first issue of the *Evening and Morning Star*, the Jackson County Mormon newspaper, carried a June, 1832 dateline, and in it appeared these paragraphs:

"Early in May, Capt. Bonaville's Company (150) under the command of Capt. Walker passed this town, on its way to the Rocky Mountains, to trap and hunt for fur in the vast country of the Black Feet Indians. About the middle of May, Capt. Soublett's Company (70) passed, for the Rocky Mountains, on the same business. At which time, also, Capt. Wythe [Wyeth] of Mass. with a Company of 30, passed for the mouth of Oregon [Willamette] River, to prepare (as it is said) for settling a territory. During the month of May there also passed one Company bound to Santa Fe.

"About the 8th or 9th of this month Capt. Blackwell's Company (60 or 70) passed this place, for the Rocky Mountains, in addition."

Five months later, the paper carried these observations:

"On the 19th of September Capt. Sublett's Fur company returned from the Rocky mountains with 168 packs of fur, valued at about $80,000. The company was attacked at Piers Hole, on the 12th of July last, by the Black feet Indians, and lost in killed of their own men, 6, & 4 wounded, among whom was Capt. S; and of the friendly Nepersee [Nez Perce] Indians, 7 killed, and 6 wounded. On the 17th, five were again attacked by these Indians at Jackson's hole, near the Three Tetons, and 3 of them were killed. We learn that the Black feet Indians, said to be numerous, are becoming more and more warlike towards the mountain hunters' so much so, that some of the hunters returned, say, they will hardly be able to hunt two years longer, in the engagement in

Piers Hole, there were, of Capt. S's Fur company, Capt. Wythe's Oregon company, &c. about 250; of the Nepersee Indians 50, making a force of 300 against from 30 to 100 Black feet, Indians, and yet the action lasted some time. In about a year 28 trappers have been killed, the remainder is said to be healthy."

In 1832 a wagon manufacturer set up shop, and Independence was on its way. Two years later the noted ornithologist John Townsend, attached to the expedition of Nathaniel J. Wyeth, left his impressions of Independence:

"The site of the town is beautiful, and very well selected, standing on a high point of land, and overlooking the surrounding country, but the town itself is very indifferent. The houses (about fifty) are very much scattered, composed of logs and clay, and are low and inconvenient. There are six or eight stores here, two taverns, and a few tippling houses. As we did not fancy the town, nor the society that we saw there, we concluded to take up our residence at the house on the landing until the time of starting on our journey."

In 1831 Ezra Booth, an apostacized Mormon, wrote this description of the frontier in a letter back to Ohio:

"Independence . . . is a new town, containing a courthouse built of brick, two or three merchant stores, and fifteen or twenty dwelling houses, built mostly of logs hewed on both sides; and is situated on a handsome rise of ground, about three miles south of the Missouri River, and about twelve miles east of the dividing line between the U.S. and the Indian Reserve, and is the county seat of Jackson County."

Josiah Gregg, the prolific chronicler of the Santa Fe trade, pulled out of Independence on his first trip to New Mexico on May 15, 1831.

The American Fur Company outfit left Independence each year, laden with the goods of trade for the great mountain fairs. Lucien Fontenelle, the brilliant partisan, broke precedent and left from Liberty, across the Missouri from Independence, on May 15, 1835, and the Company did it again the following year. In 1837 Tom (Broken Hand) Fitzpatrick and Moses (Black) Harris stopped that nonsense and the trade reverted to Independence until the price of beaver plummeted and the business evaporated.

Nat Wyeth's Columbia River Fishing and Trading Company pulled out of Independence on April 4, 1834, on one of the most incredible business schemes of the age. The venture was so ludicrous that it might have succeeded in the 20th century, but it couldn't in the 19th.

Wyeth's scheme was to transport, under contract, trade goods for the annual rendezvous, wherein trading companies rewarded Indians and free trappers with whatever it took to separate them from their year's catch of peltry. While he was headed overland his ship would round the Horn and cross the bar of the Columbia, loaded with additional goods for trading. Proceeding down the Columbia, Wyeth would contract for the salmon catch, process it, and load the ship for the Eastern trade. It wasn't his fault, but the scheme failed miserably.

In addition to the scholarly Townsend, the Wyeth expedition included the botanist Thomas Nuttall and the celebrated diarist, Osborne Russell. The expedition had even more going for it than that — on board were the Rev. Jason Lee and his nephew, Daniel Lee. The expedition consisted of 58 men, including six free trappers, and 80 horses. In the 1830s it was important to Independence, but in the 1840s they would have been considered stragglers, so great was the volume of humanity through this western outpost.

There was trouble with mud at the Blue Mills Landing, and trouble with sand bars, and distance from the settlement of Independence. Somebody — his name is lost to history — found a better landing some three miles due north of town. Aside from the fact that it was one devil of a pull up from the levee to the top of the bluff, the landing had everything, including an unbroken ridgeline with no creeks to cross all the way down to the square. This became the Independence Landing, and by 1847 it was at least important enough to have a plat filed, under the name of Wayne City. It shows 32 lots, two north-south streets and an east-west street.

The old log courthouse, now at 107 Kansas, was built at Lynn and Lexington for $150 in 1827. It is often written that it served little more than a decade and then was replaced with a fine brick building on a square set aside for that purpose.

Mrs. Pauline Fowler, archivist of the Jackson County Historical Society, has uncovered evidence that the brick structure was started about the same time as the log building. The log structure evidently was erected to serve only until the brick building could go into service. Booth's quote, above, bears this out.

There was some static from the west. People in the little settlement of Westport, built almost on the state line, were having a lot of fun trading with the Indians. No matter — Independence had all she could handle by the late 1830s anyway. But then somebody opened a route to Westport from Independence in 1837, and a few emigrants decided to leave from Westport, passing right through Independence, to do their outfitting on the border.

Myra Eells and her missionary husband, Rev. Cushing Eells, left for Westport on April 20, 1838. They and three other missionary couples — each more picayunish than the other — were in the outfit guided west by the celebrated mountain man, Andrew Drips. It was Drips who probably pointed out the easiest ford across the Big Blue to Westport, and the way south to the intersection with the Santa Fe road. (Drips is buried in Mt. St. Mary's Cemetery, 23rd and Jackson, Kansas City.)

The way was being made a little easier. Steamboat passage from St. Louis now was down to $6 cabin, or $4 deck. The route was negotiated in 3½ days in the 1840s, instead of two to three weeks by land.

The months of April and May, from about 1842 on through 1853, saw growing volumes of wagons coming from the landing to the square.

J. Quinn Thornton, headed for Oregon in 1846, described the town as being full of "African slaves, indolent dark-skinned Spaniards, profane and dust-laden bullwhackers going to . . . Santa Fe . . . , and emigrant families bound for the Pacific."

DeVoto wrote of the heavy rains of 1846, how in

May the wagons had bogged to the hubs, and perhaps that sort of thing as much as competition from Westport caused the paving of the River Rd. After all, the merchants had to use it too, to bring their freight in from the landing.

By 1846 there were a dozen blacksmith shops near the square and one of them, Robert Weston's, survived for more than a century. Col. Smallwood Noland's inn was packed every night with more than 400 guests, two to a bed and no cheating. The predecessor hotel had burned Feb. 19, 1845, and he had erected his new Merchants Hotel on the same site. The building had a large porch on the east and on the west a livery stable facing the square. (It was remodeled in 1907 and called the Clinton Block, but Mrs. Fowler is satisfied that elements of the 1846 building remain within the structure today.)

Freight jammed the landings, wretched Kansas Indians wandered over from the territory to cadge a drink or two. Mexicans, bearded and smelly mountain men, the monstrous bullwhackers who would beat their way to Santa Fe and back two or three times a year, slaves, rivermen, soldiers, emigrants — all were thrown together in this melange of humanity.

Blacksmiths worked 14 hours a day at their forges, gouging the emigrants for every dime they could get. Not because they needed the money, but that they were tired and wanted some rest and wanted to get even with the people who were keeping them from it.

Clusters of buildings ringed the square and clusters of tents ringed the buildings. By late May the grass would be gone for five miles in every direction, and every day more wagons would be hoisted ashore at Wayne City. Cattle by the thousands would poke down the road, prodded on by men and dogs.

Here the emigrants would call on other emigrants, trying to get together 50 wagons or so — enough for a train to travel in safety. All feared the Indians; Indians who in those days would steal for social acceptance but who couldn't care less for white scalps. The travelers were less concerned with the infinitely more cruel killer, cholera. There would be meetings attended by the hundreds, and out and out political campaigns for leadership of the train. Campaign committees would go into action in opposite camps for their own candidates, and finally, on election day, the candidates themselves would stand alone. At a signal, their supporters would line up behind them. Whoever had the longest line behind him was the captain — at least until they hit the Kaw, a week or more out on the prairies.

The nights were something else. Out there the campfires glowed merrily until the wee hours. What the hell, who had to get up anyway? There was no law said a cow couldn't be milked in daylight. They would get stoned on the Independence whiskey at night, bought with the heavy money they got for their old farm in Missouri or Kentucky or Illinois. And by day they would marvel at the sounds and sights and smells of spring. Oregon could wait a day or two.

The smart ones, the men destined for leadership positions of the caravans, men like Black Harris, Andrew Drips, Jim Bridger — these men could see the snow falling on the Blues in southeastern Oregon. They could see the wagons straining up out of the Grande Ronde, emaciated oxen pulling for the Willamette and Oregon City before the blizzards killed them all. Never mind about the guides, they could survive anywhere in the winter. But not the inexperienced men, women and children. Many a guide had to throw ultimatums at the greenhorns to get them moving by mid-May.

By 1847 all necessary supplies could be purchased in Independence, and competition had driven the price down to reasonable levels on about everything but wagons. They were described as poorly ironed, heavily wooded, and costing upwards of $100 each. The permanent population numbered about 1,000, but they serviced five or six times as many persons in April or May of the later years.

Henry Page, moving west in 1849, stopped in Independence long enough to describe the courthouse which, with its fanlight over the door and its cupola, made him think of the college chapel at Middlebury, Conn. He noted that the green grass of the square was kept from the livestock of the emigrants by a rail fence.

Page was in Independence when two pieces of important news arrived: the U.S. Army had purchased Ft. Laramie; and the government was going to establish a new Ft. Kearny, on the Platte just above the junction of the roads from Nebraska City and Independence.

Westport and St. Joe and Kansas City finally took all the business by the late 1850s, after Wayne City clogged up with sand. But Independence had her moment in the sun, and she served destiny well.

The first "temporary" courthouse for Jackson Co. still is in use, now at 107 Kansas, a block south of the square.

Walk south on Main one block past Lexington, the southern boundary of the square, to Kansas Avenue. On the southwest corner of the intersection is the vacated city hall. The building to the west, at 107 Kansas Ave., is the original courthouse. Those logs, original but with fresh chinking, were laid in 1827. Continue west to the next corner, Liberty and Kansas. On the southwest corner of the intersection is the site of the old Weston blacksmith shop, active during the 1840s. It is now a parking lot.

Turn to the left and walk one block south to Walnut Street. Turn left again, or east, for 2½ blocks. On the right, at 131 E. Walnut Street, is the original site of one of the oldest buildings in Jackson County. The rickety log cabin which was there is believed to date from 1836. It

The Brady or Younger cabin, standing at 131 E. Walnut Street in 1971. It dates back to 1836 and stands today at Truman and Dodgion roads.

was built by a man named Younger or a Mike Brady.

Return to the south side of the square, along Lexington. This, according to Mrs. Fowler, is the location of the famous drawing of the square at Independence, showing the courthouse of the 1840s. Mrs. Fowler admits to being in the minority in this opinion, but she feels that the painting could have been made from no other place.

It was Mrs. Fowler who discovered only in 1971, the substantial evidence that the courthouse shown in that old drawing is the third courthouse, and not the second, as historians had believed. The second is thought to have been razed and the third built on at least part of the original foundation, which still is in evidence in the basement of the present building. The third courthouse, shown in the picture, is inside the fourth, and the fourth is inside the fifth and present courthouse.

It was on Liberty Street, the west boundary of the square, that the vast caravans started forming, headed south. They would be moved to the Old Jail if they tried it today, for it is now only open to pedestrians. The trains stretched down along Liberty, turning west along Lexington if they were headed for Westport.

The building on the northeast corner of the intersection of Maple and Liberty now houses the remains of the Hotel

Jackson Co. Historical Archives, Harry S Truman Library
*The courthouse known to the emigrants, as it
appeared about 1846.*

Independence, and that land use on that part of the block
never has changed. A hotel was built there about 1834;
later Lewis Jones built the Nebraska house on the same
site, probably in 1849. An addition was built on the east
side in 1851. The optical store on the corner once was
the saloon for the hotel. The hostelry was closed in the
mid-1970s, and the addition has since been razed.

Walk east along Maple to Main Street, then north on
Main a half block to the parking lot. Leave the lot on
Truman Road and head east about four blocks. Just past
Noland Road turn right onto Dodgion Street and park near
the old Younger cabin, which was relocated from Walnut
Street in the 1970s. Just past it is the open-air stone
garden. Stairs lead down to a sunken space, and at the bottom is a stone wall, out of which flows a stream of water.
This is said to be one of two principal springs which supplied water to the families moving west. It is said that
without those springs, Independence could not have survived.
The spring originally rose in the berm just west of the
present location. At one time Independence had three
other springs of major size. But this spring? Totally
phony. It's city water.

Continue through the park area on Dodgion, proceed
two blocks south to Kansas. Turn right, or west, for one
block to Noland, then right (north) a block to Lexington.
Turn left on Lexington and proceed west. Two blocks past

Jackson Co. courthouse today, containing elements of earlier structures in foundation.

the courthouse is Osage, and one more block is Spring. Turn left on Spring. Frequently the trains were this long. The wagons stood on that very ground, teams impatient in their new harness, awaiting the command to move on down the trail to the campgrounds and Westport.

It was at this point that the trails split. The original Santa Fe Trail headed south, sometimes on Spring, sometimes on the streets nearer the courthouse. The Independence-Westport Road, developed first in 1837, continued west on Lexington.

The Independence-Westport Road

The Independence-Westport Road probably has more claim to the title of the Oregon Trail than the original Santa Fe Trail moving south out of Independence, if numbers of travelers is any criterion.

By 1845 travel was extremely heavy over this road. It had been surveyed and made 40 feet wide in 1841-42. Movement over the Santa Fe Trail was down to a trickle, due to the normal reluctance of the traders to launch even the most elemental enterprise when the nations at either end could well be at war with one another before the trade was completed. Spanish silver and gold were attractive enough, but would be of little good to the bearer if he were dead on the Cimarron.

Head west on Lexington from the square at Independence. The old trail is directly beneath the road, and on either side for the next two or three miles were endless campgrounds. From the early spring right up to the first of June there would be whitetops almost as far as the eye could see. The area is laced with springs — campgrounds were not hard to find.

Further down Lexington a former service station stands between the forks in the road. The road to the left is Crysler Boulevard. Bear to the right.

About 1.4 miles from the square, between Procter and Vassar streets, a boulevard starts and the street name changes to Winner Road. Here the trail started to veer off to the left at 245 degrees.

Continue another block on Winner and on the southwest corner of Winner and North is a home believed to have been built by Smallwood Noland in 1845. The original portion is built of brick fired in a backyard kiln.

Continue on Winner abour seven more blocks to Sterling Avenue and turn south (left). Two more blocks on Sterling is 20th Street. The trail cut right through the intersection and now heads 235 degrees. It cut through the block to pick up the eastern end of the Westport Road. Turn right (west) on 20th, from Sterling, for just one block to Harvard, then left (south) a short block. Westport Road angles in from the right. Take it, half right, and check the odometer reading.

The trail once again is beneath the road and the evidence of this is abundant. Note how it winds, with no proper respect for the sensibilities of the surveyor. It's riding the crest of a great ridge — see how the land drops off sharply to either side. This ridge continues unbroken for about two miles. By now one should be getting the real feel of the trail. Although the emigrant road wasn't used extensively until 1837, it had been used by Indians

The Independence-Westport Rd. southwest of 23rd St. in Independence.

for probably thousands of years before. That, incidentally, is the case with almost all variants of the Oregon Trail, including the famed opening at South Pass.

The name of the road changes to Blue Ridge Cutoff at 30th Street.

Exactly two miles from Harvard Avenue is Pitcher Boulevard, a short cutoff to U.S. 40. Pitcher dead ends into Westport Road from the right, opposite a water tower on the left. Turn right onto Pitcher. Two blocks away is U.S. 40. (The Blue Ridge Cutoff continues south and merges with the main Santa Fe Trail at 66th Street, just before hitting the Blue Ridge Parkway.)

About 1.5 miles along Highway 40 the trail and road cross above a complex of railroad tracks. At the bottom of the hill is a steel bridge over the Big Blue. Just before reaching it is the driveway of a used car lot. Turn right and drive through the lot to a driveway between the hangars of a private aviation service. Park, facing the river. Take a bearing of 296 degrees.

(Review: set the compass ring at 296 degrees. Turn the entire compass until the red floating needle is lined up with the red north arrow inside the ring. Then sight along the body of the compass.)

A tall transmission tower is a few blocks away on the horizon to the left, and the compass should be pointing directly at a squat brick stack to the right of this tower.

This sightline is exactly over the route of the trail for nearly a mile — it takes a beeline across the Big Blue River.

There is a landing strip there. Follow the sightline on foot across the flat, muddy field, recently graded, then climb up a steep 10-foot embankment. Cross over an old roadbed and look down — this time to the Big Blue itself. There are the stone piers for a long-gone bridge, probably built before the turn of the century. No trace of the trail remains since the land has been built up with about 20 feet of earth fill.

Old bridge abutments flank Big Blue River at trail crossing along Independence-Westport Rd. This view is to the west.

Vestiges of trail remain on pull uphill from Big Blue to 27th and Topping in Kansas City.

Return to U.S. 40 and continue west. Turn onto I-70 and then exit at the very next interchange, which is the Van Brunt cutoff. Take it to the right (north). Continue north for seven short blocks to 27th Street (not 27th Terrace). Turn right, or east, back toward the Big Blue. Four more blocks and the road passes the Askew School on the left. Continue across the next street, Topping, and park. On the southeast corner of 27th and Topping is a small park. At that corner is a small stone marker identifying the little path cutting diagonally away from the intersection as the link between Independence and Westport.

Start walking into the park. Note the ground has been graded, but at the edge of the woods the land has its original integrity. The path is the original Oregon Trail. Until recent years the ruts originally cut by the wagons still were visible, but they are no longer. It is the trail all the same. The road maps give it a grey line, but it is doubtful if a passenger motor vehicle ever was on this path. Certainly it never was paved. Up this declivity strained tens of thousands of oxen, hauling creaking wagons still so new the axles were binding and the harness leather was a light tan.

Along the path down to the Blue are little springs, just as they were 125 years ago. At the base, where the path stops, is a huge concrete sewer pipe. Here the trail fans into several footpaths. Take one the few remaining feet down the bank.

The Blue isn't very wide here, and not especially deep either. When approached for the first time in any season, the men would stop their wagons and cross the stream several times with their horses. When they found a ford where the water didn't come up past the horse's belly, they would start digging a ramp from the water's edge back up the bank — on each side of the stream. Then, one by one, the white topped wagons would be eased into the water and hauled up the other side. It was a process that inevitably brought minor mishaps, cursing and some livestock with mighty sore behinds. The Big Blue was easy. Four months later the Snake could very well claim some human lives.

To those over 40 the hike back to the car may seem like half an hour, but it really is only eight minutes.

Drive north on Topping, past the front of the school, where there is a large stone marker identifying the trail. The trail itself extended along this ridge, between the roadway and the front of the school building. It gradually veered along the crest of the bluff toward the middle of the block, but stay on Topping to 24th, then turn west (left) there. Two short blocks and the street intersects Oakley Avenue and then is over the trail. The old trace generally follows 24th Street for the next mile. Note the ridge falling away on either side of the road. One block past Jackson is Norton, and from here the road makes one of those aggravating diagonals that is almost impossible to follow on the city's grid pattern of streets. It leaves the pavement at 24th and Norton following a bearing of 235 degrees. Return a block to Jackson and turn south for .9 mile, going under the I-70 overpass, to 31st Street. Head west (right) for four blocks to Cleveland. Turn right (north) on Cleveland for six blocks to the overpass over I-70. The trail came under this overpass, about under I-70 at this point, headed 240 degrees, and hit Benton Avenue at Victor Street. The street just before the overpass is 26th — turn left on it for one block, left on Monroe for one more block, then right (west) for three blocks to 27th and Indiana. The trail cut through that intersection.

Continue another five blocks to Benton and head south (left) three blocks to Victor. Again the trail cut through that intersection. Two more blocks south on Benton is 30th Street; turn west (right) there for a short block to Chestnut. The trail cut across this intersection, still heading southwest.

Continue on 30th two more blocks to Prospect, which also is U.S. Highway 71. Turn south (left) on Prospect. A few yards before reaching the next intersection, which is 31st, is another trail intercept. Stay on Prospect for one more block, past the east side of St. Joseph Hospital. The street running along the front of the hospital is Linwood — take it west (right) for five blocks to Garfield. The trail came through this intersection headed 250 degrees. Six more short blocks along Linwood and turn south (left) on Wayne. A few yards before the next corner, which is 33rd Street, the trail intersected, now headed 210 degrees. Turn west (right) on 33rd, going just two blocks to The Paseo. Turn left (south) on The Paseo for two blocks to Armour Boulevard. The trail intersected here, headed 230 degrees — by now more or less on a beeline for old Westport.

Turn west (right) five blocks on Armour, or one block past Troost, and then turn left (south) on Harrison Boulevard. Two more blocks and the road splits, with Harrison Parkway angling off to the right. Take it, and again the pavement is over the old road. This is where it comes in from the intersection of Armour and The Paseo.

A half-mile through the delightful Brush Creek Park will bring the traveler to Gillham Avenue, where the old road leaves the street again, angling to the southwest, while Gillham turns north. There is a stone marker in the center of the boulevard strip. This marks the exact location of the trail, which at this point cuts directly across Gillham headed 260 degrees, or straight across the road at that point. It would go adjacent to the north wall of the school building on the west side of the street.

Continue north on Gillham, but turn west (left) at the next corner, which is 38th Street. Go just four blocks on 38th to Main Street. Turn south (left) two blocks to Westport Road. Once again this is the trail, now on the eastern edge of the old town of Westport.

A Tour of Old Westport

Looming ahead, in the inside of the wedge formed by the junction of Westport and Main, is an Osco drugstore. For many years the Harris home (ca. 1855) stood here. Turn right (west) on Westport and continue only for a half-block and look over to the left. There is the big

Col. Jack Harris's house still stands at 4000 Baltimore in old Westport. It was moved here from a half-block away in 1922. Today it serves as the headquarters for the Westport Historical Society.

Harris home, now at 4000 Baltimore Street, where it was moved in 1922. The Westport Historical Society has acquired the building and has restored it as its headquarters. The society has furnished some of the rooms in the style of the times when John (Jack) Harris lived there. Other areas will house a tearoom, gift shop, and offices of the society.

Continue down Westport to Pennsylvania. It is a good idea to park at this point, as parking places in old Westport are at a premium. Westport is as charming today as it must have been riotous in the 19th century. It is a shopping and dining mecca.

On the northeast corner of Penn and Westport is a vacant lot. A marker identifies it as the site of the Harris House hotel. The first Harris house, a log building, was acquired by Jack Harris in 1846. It burned shortly after. Harris rebuilt with brick in 1852 and ran the three-story building until 1864. It was demolished in 1922. (A plaque in front of the site, indicating the razing took place in 1912, is in error.)

Across Penn to the west stands the swinging Kelly's saloon. A plaque just outside the door on the east wall gives credit for its erection to a Capt. Joseph Parks, a wealthy half-Shawnee.

Not true. William A. Goff, the leading Westport historian and scholar, has established that George W. and William G. Ewing, of Logansport, Ind., erected the structure for their Indian trade in 1851. Albert Gallatin Boone, a grandson of Daniel Boone, bought it in January 1854, the year the Indian trade died. A. G. Boone came to Westport in 1838 and probably moved into a building one door west about 1843, when he went into partnership with his brother-in-law, James Hamilton. The corner building housing Kelly's was modernized about 1892.

The two-story building next door, housing Stanford & Son restaurant, is the most important building in Westport. It was built in January 1850 by Cyprien Chouteau, a member of the fur trading dynasty of St. Louis. Here was published the *Border Star,* and here, in 1866, came Jim Bridger, the king of the mountain men. He bought the building then and opened a grocery. Thought to be long

Building at left, shown in 1971, once was owned by Jim Bridger. At right is Kelly's saloon, in a building which dates back to 1851.

gone, the original structure was found hiding behind a pressed brick front, in 1974. Before remodeling it had 16 fireplaces, later converted to coal stove flues.

Turn to the right on Penn and walk just past the alley. On the left is the site of Vogel's dram shop — the street number was 4054. It was the oldest building in Westport when it was demolished in 1907. The site now is occupied by the Manor Bakery.

It was there, in 1846, that haughty young Francis Parkman got the word about his jumping-off place:

"Returning on the next day to Westport, we received a message from the captain, who had ridden back to deliver it in person, but finding that we were in Kansas [really Westport Landing, in downtown Kansas City today] had intrusted it with an acquaintance named Vogel, who kept a small grocery and liquor shop. Whiskey, by the way, circulates more freely in Westport than is altogether safe in a place where every man carries a loaded pistol in his pocket. As we passed the establishment, we saw Vogel's broad German face and knavish-looking eyes thrust from his door. He said he had something to tell us, and to take a dram. Neither his liquor nor his message was very palatable. The captain

Westport Historical Society

Old Vogel Dram Shop, just before it was demolished in 1907. Here is where Francis Parkman got word that he would leave for the West from Ft. Leavenworth, and not via Santa Fe Trail. Address was 4054 Pennsylvania.

Plant of Manor Bakery now stands where Vogel building once was.

had returned to give us notice that R., who assumed the direction of his party, had determined upon another route from that agreed upon between us; and instead of taking the course of the traders, to pass northward by Ft. Leavenworth, and follow the path marked out by the dragoons in their expedition of last summer."

Return to Westport Road and proceed right, or west, past the next intersection. On the right is the new Quarterage Hotel, numbered 560 Westport Road. In back of this building, facing Westport Road, is the site of Daniel Yoacham's tavern, the first hostelry of the trail west of Independence. It started out in 1833 to be a one-story log building, but business was such that another story had to be added in 1840.

Just north of the tavern site is Big Spring, now underground, the source of the Mill Creek. The creek flowed beneath Westport Road between the hotel building and a rail spur to the southeast. Westport Road bridged the creek in trail days. The creek is underground now, covered by progress for nearly a century.

Francis Parkman had spent nearly six months away from here, about a third of the way west on the Oregon Trail, and his observations upon his return are interesting:

"At length, for the first time during about half a year, we saw the roof of a white man's dwelling between the opening trees. A few moments after, we were riding over the miserable log bridge that leads into the center of Westport [across Mill Creek, at this spot]. Westport had beheld strange scenes, but a rougher looking troop than ours, with our work equipments and broken-down horses, was never seen there. We passed the well-remembered tavern, Boone's grocery and old Vogel's dram shop, and encamped on a meadow beyond. Here we were soon visited by a number of people who came to purchase our horses and equipage."

Westport got off to a slow start. While Independence was booming mightily within ten years after the first cluster of log huts was erected, Westport didn't really roar until the early 1850s. It started out as early as 1825, according to Bill Goff, and was described by Jim Clyman in 1846 as "a small ordinary village." Rev. Isaac McCoy was an early settler, although the woods were full of itinerant French fur traders. Free trappers rarely were literate, so they could leave no printed word behind them. McCoy had a son, John Calvin McCoy, who was as talented as his father, and he, generally, is credited with the founding of Westport as an outfitting center. It was he who platted the town in 1834, and the same man is believed to have built the trading post on the site of the old Harris House hotel. The town, located some four miles south of the Missouri River and twelve miles west of Independence, became sort of a last chance settlement for the emigrants.

Habitation extended to about 43rd Street on the south, Main on the east, the border on the west, and 39th Street on the north.

The splendid new statuary group of Jim Bridger, Alexander Majors, and John Calvin McCoy, a project of the Westport Historical Society and the Native Sons of Kansas City, has been installed in Pioneer Park at Broadway and Westport Road. It is well worth a visit, as is the colorful map of the western trails cast in terrazzo near the statues.

McCoy wasn't the first white man in the area — that honor probably goes to Daniel Morgan Boone. He is believed to have been trapping in the area since before the turn of the century. He lived to see Westport's beginning, but he died of cholera in 1839, leaving most of the excitement to folks like John Calvin McCoy. D. M. Boone is buried near 63rd and The Paseo, in a remnant of the old Boone-Hays Cemetery.

Soon McCoy was the leading trader in Westport, trading anything the Indians wanted in exchange for that good old U.S. government money. That was the major early stimulus to Westport; the emigration of the 1840s was merely the frosting on the cake.

Westport was beginning to roar by 1845. Local workshops were turning out wagons, harnesses, saddles, tents, wagon covers, yokes and bows for oxen, candles for the trail, and other assorted items. The local merchants found that the emigrants had the same color money as the Indians, only a lot more of it.

As is the case with Independence, the big names of the West were in Westport. Jim Bridger, the greatest name of them all, lived here; Tom Fitzpatrick and Louis ("Ole Vaskiss") Vasquez, Jim's partner, too. Jason Lee, the talented Methodist missionary, was in Westport in 1838, rounding up reinforcements for his mission on the Willamette. He was just across the line, at the Shawnee Mission (Mission Road at 51st Street) when Paul Richardson brought word that his wife back in Oregon had died in childbirth. In Westport, the missionary wives Myra Eells and Mary Gray fixed tents preparatory for their long journey, while their husbands, Cushing and William, tried to out-dour each other.

By 1850, there were a number of fine farms carved out of the prairies around Westport, and the merchants had done their job well. Available for more-or-less reasonable prices were wagons, mules, cattle, ponies, grain, groceries, and other provisions needed for the long haul west.

Pierre-Jean DeSmet, the Jesuit who became the West's leading missionary, propagandist and fund raiser, left St. Louis on March 27, 1840, with Young Ignace, the Flathead brave sent across the mountains to get a Blackrobe. In 10 days they were in Westport, where they waited three weeks for a guide who knew how to get them to the transmontane West.

They found a good one — Drips. Also in the party: Joel Walker, Henry Fraeb, and Jim Bridger. They left Westport at dawn on April 30. Drips returned from the Green later that year. He was appointed Special Indian Agent for the Upper Missouri in 1842, a job he held until 1846, when he returned to the payroll of Pierre Chouteau Jr. & Co. (Some say he never left it.) He maintained his activity in the fur and hide trade until his death in 1860.

The following April 24, DeSmet was back again, and left on May 10, 1841 with the Bidwell-Bartleson party. He fought the cholera for 30 years; became the most traveled minister to the Western Indians and one of the few of any denomination who were completely honest. He wanted only the soul of the Indian. His superiors sent him to Europe time and again to hustle several fortunes for the order's missionary activity.

Westport was the incubator for something even bigger. A young, desperate man who had fled his native Swit-

zerland just a step ahead of the debtor's prison, hung a
shingle over a general store in Westport. The year was
1837. The man was posing as a member of the Swiss
Guards. His name: Johann Augustus Sutter. He signed
on with Drips the next year and headed west. He would do a
little better on the South Fork of the American River ten
years later.

Westport was thriving then and it thrives today, after
a century in the doldrums. It still is filled with quaint
shops — more highly contrived, perhaps. But it is still a great
place to spend an hour or two if one is in no big toot.

The Road to New Santa Fe

Back in the mid-19th century there was a little town
ten miles south of Westport on the Missouri state line,
then the western border of the United States, at about
where 122nd Street is today. The land to the west was
Indian territory, and that litle town of New Santa Fe
was the last civilized settlement the emigrants would see
until they hit the valley of the Willamette and the last
the Santa Fe traders would see until they hit Council
Grove. In Indian territory booze officially was a no-no.
Hence, a lively cluster of saloons sprang up and the town
of New Santa Fe was born.

The original land patents were dated in December
1844. A few years back there was nothing there but the
old frame church, built about 1895, and the more ancient
graveyard behind (north of) it. The church was razed in
1971 and a new church erected to the east of the site. En-
croaching clusters of fine new homes are moving in, having
closed to within a block of the heart of the long-disappeared
little town.

Proceed south of Westport Road, two blocks on Pennsylvania, and then go west (right) a few yards on 42nd
Street. Angle to the south (left) again on Wornall Road.

This is the road leading from Westport to New Santa Fe,
which by the mid-1840s had to be considered the main
line of the Oregon Trail. The old ox road, generally, is

beneath Wornall Road today. It ran due south out of Westport directly to the intersection with Santa Fe Road, just
east of the state line, and crossed Brush Creek, Dyche's
Branch and Indian Creek. The road was in regular use by
1834; and traffic was substantial enough that the County
Court ordered it widened to 33 feet in 1846.

About two blocks to the south is a marker on the east
(left) side of Wornall, in the 4300 block. This identifies the
site of the first home of Rev. Isaac McCoy, called ''Locust
Hill.'' McCoy was appointed Indian agent in 1830 to assist
several tribes in migration to the western lands.

Wornall slants off to the right in the 4600 block and ends
at 47th. This is in the heart of one of the world's most
famous examples of urban planning — Country Club
Plaza. Proceed west two blocks to Pennsylvania, turn left
for one block to Nichols, then one block east to Broadway
and turn right. Now the trail is following along about a
half-block to the east. Proceed south on Broadway and
cross Ward Parkway, and then the name of the street
changes back to Wornall Road.

Two miles south of Westport is 55th Street, along the
south side of Jacob L. Loose Memorial Park. Turn west
(right) and proceed to 1032 55th Street, about a half-mile
west of Wornall and two doors east of Sunset Boulevard,
on the north side of the street.

The house in front is the former home of Seth Ward.
It was in the center of a 400-acre farm; much of this
today is Loose Park. Ward was a highly successful Indian
trader in the Rockies and won the sutler's concession at
Ft. Laramie in 1854. He held the post until he retired to
Kansas City in 1870. He built this house two years later.
The itinerary of this book will lead the traveler to his old
store in Ft. Laramie in a few days, to see it as he knew it.

The house just behind it is the former home of William
Bent. Bent joined up with a St. Louisan, the great Ceran
St. Vrain. They formed the partnership of Bent and
St. Vrain. They built a fort (really a trading post) near
present La Junta, Colorado, in 1833. The emplacement
has been restored and now is open to the public. Bent's
Fort served the voluminous Santa Fe trade. Unlike his

contemporaries further to the northwest, Bent was a fair and honorable businessman. He wasn't out to take the Indians and they respected him for it.

According to Bill Goff, Bent owned property in Jackson County and Westport, but his main concern was the Fort. He commuted between Westport and the Fort, accompanying trains to there and cargoes back to St. Louis. He reluctantly became an Indian agent in 1859, and in resigning the following year he recommended A. G. Boone as his successor. He fought Uncle Sam for the next nine years for the back rent on his fort. He is buried on his ranch at Big Timbers, on the Arkansas River in Colorado.

Boone, on the other hand, was only too happy to get out of Westport. Like many of his neighbors he was a states-rightist and a pro-slavery man. The Federals put the squeeze on Westport and, as Goff says. "it was dead, dead, dead until way after the war. Boone was only one of a great number of merchants who were to sell out before they were burned out."

Go around the block to the right to return to Wornall Road over 55th.

About .8 mile further south on Wornall is West 61st

Wornall Home, restored by Jackson Co. Historical Society and now open to the public. House was built in 1858.

Terrace, and on the northeast corner of that intersection is the old Wornall homestead, once the central building of a 499-acre farm (The marker says 640 acres -- it's wrong.) It was occupied in 1858 by its builder, John Wornall. The property has been restored by the Jackson County Historical Society and now is open to the public.

This general area is the location of the famed Battle of Westport during the Civil War. The fighting was done mainly on the bluffs south of Brush Creek and on the pastures and cornfields of present Loose Park. Lt. Collins' four-gun battery of Joseph Shelby's brigade, facing north, had been successful in battering back one Union counter-charge after another. A civilian by the name of George Thoman, who was the victim of some uncivil treatment by the Confederate forces, lived nearby. On Oct. 23, 1864, he wandered down the hill, got his evens in a five-minute conference with the Union brass. The northern forces followed his suggestions quietly, circled around the west flank and came roaring in from the west to catch the Rebels by surprise. Gen. Price called a retreat, one that didn't stop until he was in Texas.

Three miles further south on Wornall is the I-435 overpass. Jim Bridger's farm started about here, on the right (west) side of Wornall. It extended all the way over to State Line Boulevard. The farm ran all the way down to about 112th Street. Jim's house was about across Wornall from the entrance to Notre Dame de Sion High School. Nothing there but woods in 1971, but the subdivisions are closing in fast.

Jim Bridger was a Kit Carson, Buffalo Bill, Wild Bill Hickok and John Colter all rolled into one. Six feet tall, grey eyes, clean shaven and a skin like untanned leather. He could speak English, Spanish and French but he couldn't read or write a word of any language. But how he could read sign! He could look at a moccasin track and tell the age, weight, sex and tribe of the maker. He had a fantastic memory — etched on his brain was a topographic map of the American West.

This was the most celebrated of all hunters, trappers, traders and guides. Bridger was at least the codiscoverer of the Great Salt Lake (1824). He was one of the first white men to traverse South Pass. He tramped the Yellowstone country in 1830, visiting Yellowstone Lake, the geysers, the boiling mud lakes. He let the soldiery on the Indian campaigns from 1856 to 1866.

From the age of 18 and for almost the remainder of his life, winters and all, he was a man of the western mountains. He took a pair of Blackfoot arrows in his back on the Green. A partner pulled out one; the other stayed there for three years.

His daughter, Mary Ann, from his first marriage to a daughter of a Flathead chief, was with Marcus and Narcissa Whitman in 1847 at Waiilatpu when the Cayuse killed the missionaries. Mary Ann became one of the hostages, and she herself died of illness shortly after.

In 1839, when the bottom fell out of the fur trade, Bridger returned to St. Louis. He couldn't take much of that and soon it was back to the mountains for him. Four years later, as he watched the emigrant migration to Oregon, he built the celebrated Ft. Bridger, which is on the itinerary of this book.

Six years after the horror of the Whitman massacre Jim came to Westport. He bought the old Thatcher farm, which ran south from Indian Creek almost to New Santa Fe and from Wornall Road to the boundary of the United States. He helped erect some of the log buildings in the booming town of New Santa Fe.

Jim built his two-story house on his farm, with huge chimneys at either end and galleries off both floors. He wanted to retire; his restless spirit wouldn't let him.

From May of 1859 until the fall of 1862 Bridger was on almost constant duty as a guide to the U.S. Army. He served first with Capt. W. F. Raynolds, then Capt. Berthoud, and finally Capt. W. O. Collins. In 1862 he wintered at Ft. Laramie and in 1864 he resigned because the government refused to ante up his back pay.

Gen. Granville M. Dodge was able to coax him back to the mountains as a guide for his Powder River expedition, which took place during 1865.

On Feb. 20, 1866, he signed the papers for that two-story building which is now Stanford & Sons Restaurant, in old Westport. (Actually, he signed with an ''X''.)

Jim Bridger — Old Gabe, the Blanket Chief. Shown in his last years.

The Santa Fe Trail (about 120th St.), looking west from Wornall Rd.

Bridger took title from Cyprien and Nancy Chouteau.

He was back guiding for the military in 1867 and 1868, so there couldn't have been much time to tend the Westport store. Goff feels that much of this duty was taken over by Bridger's son-in-law, Capt. Albert Wachsmann.

Bridger worked with Dodge in the preliminary surveys for the Union Pacific, and it was Bridger, more than any other man, who dictated the route of America's first transcontinental railroad.

Jim Bridger went through a lot of money. He didn't pretend to be a businessman, and left few records. He lost his Ft. Bridger but he was never there anyway. Old Gabe couldn't stay very long in any one place.

It was in the late 1860s, when he was back in Westport for good, that Jim's eyes started to give out. He is quoted as saying, "I wish I war back thar among the mountains again. A man kin see so much farther in that country." The last few years of his life were spent in complete blackness, and on July 17, 1881, it was all over for Jim. They buried him away from the great house, up on a knoll a half-mile north of Indian Creek. The house was demolished in 1908.

Gen. Dodge paid off an old debt to the man who helped make him a national hero. On Dec. 10, 1904,

Dodge had Bridger's remains moved from the humble grave to Mt. Washington Cemetery, and marked with a suitable monument. Bridger's daughter, Virginia Bridger Wachsmann-Hahn, noted that the original coffin had disintegrated and only a few bones and his skull remained for reburial.

At 120th St. is the intercept with the original Santa Fe Trail. As tens of thousands of emigrant wagons did, turn west here. One can tell immediately from the looks and the feel that this is the original trail, winding and twisting to follow the ridge. Just .8 mile further on is the old townsite of New Santa Fe, the last civilization in the "states," the last the emigrants would see of a tavern, a church, a bona fide cemetery until they reached the storied land of the Willamette. Most of them would wish, before they were through with that trail, that they were near a peaceful little cemetery like that, for few trains were able to go the distance without the loss of life.

The trail continues on through the site of the old theater, but the landowner would just as soon the travelers wouldn't. Turn south on State Line Rd. for a half block, then turn west again. The traveler now is in Kansas, and if it is May, perhaps he can feel something of what the emigrants felt 134 years ago as his groaning wagon creaked out of his United States and onto the stupendous infinity of the Western prairies.

The vacationer now has accomplished in a few hours what it took the emigrants several days to do. One may proceed on into Kansas satisfied that he has covered the trail today in Missouri as most of the emigrants covered it in 1845. But there are more things to see if one wishes to see them, requiring another half day. Return to New Santa Fe.

The Westport Landing

From New Santa Fe, proceed straight north on State Line Blvd. to the 8200 block. At 8201, on the right, is the old Alexander Majors house, ca. 1856.

Majors was a partner in the great freighting combine of Russell, Majors and Waddell, which operated both

The Westport Landing today, just upstream from A.S.B. Bridge. This, not Westport, is the birthplace of Kansas City.

Harold Warp Pioneer Village

William H. Jackson thought the landing looked like this in the late 1840s. He didn't see it himself until it had become a bustling city, in the early 1860s.

commercially and under contract along the Santa Fe and Oregon Trails. They maintained thousands of head of livestock and thousands of wagons. They were the originators of the Pony Express; the first and only bad business deal the company made. The combine grazed its stock here for as far as the eye could see.

This is the area which, right after the California gold

This print shows Westport Landing in 1853. It was a quiet day indeed — the landing was a beehive of activity during the months of April and May.

discovery, looked like the campground of a massive army. Thousands and thousands of wagons, their owners champing at the bit, waited here for the prairies to green up so they could be on their way to the South Fork of the American River and, of course, untold wealth.

Continue all the way downtown to Southwest Boulevard and take it headed northeast. Proceed under the I-70 overpass and just past 21st Street turn left (north) on Broadway. The street maps are confused here — follow the book. Odd numbered streets in this section are one-way westbound and even numbers are one-way eastbound. Turn right, or east, on 8th Street. Go about eight short blocks east and turn north (left) onto Grand Avenue. Proceed another eight blocks and a viaduct will branch to the left, with another road going down the right side of the viaduct. Take the viaduct, known as Grand Viaduct, across the railroad tracks and the traveler then is at the Westport Landing.

There is a small boat ride concession on the landing and an office trailer for the operators. Looming high overhead to the east is the A.S.B. Bridge. Not very auspicious but this is where Kansas City began.

Kansas City didn't grow out of either Westport or Independence. Kansas City grew out of the Westport Landing, at the foot of Grand, Walnut, Main and Delaware, and gobbled up Westport. It never gobbled up Independence — there is about as much chance of it gobbling up Seattle.

There were white people on the Westport Landing site long before either town was founded. Francois Chouteau had his houses beneath the Randolph Bluffs in 1821; and as has been said before, Daniel Morgan Boone led a more or less nomadic life all over the area at the turn of the century. The Chouteaus — Francois was joined by his brothers Cyprien and Frederick — moved on upstream to a point near the original landing, but their second post couldn't survive the Flood of 1844.

The legal claims of Francois Chouteau date to Nov. 10, 1831, with additions in 1833 and 1836. Pierre Chouteau is shown with a tract in 1853; and Cyprien Chouteau in 1833. The Westport Landing, however, was developed on land claimed by Gabriel Prudhomme on Oct. 18, 1830.

From the very beginning the landing was in the service of the merchants of Westport. In the woods above the Chouteau house, about where the observer is standing, the first deposit was made on what later became the Kansas City levee — a cargo of freight for J. C. McCoy's new store at the crossroads, put ashore in 1834 by the steamer *John Hancock*. By 1838 the commercial trade there had been supplemented by all the French fur trade.

Westport Landing was described by John Hudgins, in May 1848, as a fine ledge of rock five or six feet out of the river. (Hudgins mentioned that it was littered with a lot of clothing, discarded by emigrants because it was infected with cholera.)

The city itself developed out of the Prudhomme tract, tied up in a sticky legal snarl for a dozen years. It was broken open in 1846 by John Calvin McCoy, and from that time onward it radiated to the south of the river (It's still radiating.) By the late 1860s the landing had stretched all the way from the foot of Broadway to Gillis, and there was a good seven blocks of intensive development all the way behind it.

A ferry was in operation in the 1830s, owned by Pierre Roi (Peter Roy) and operated by his son, Louis. John Calvin McCoy won a license to operate a ferry at the end of present Broadway in February 1839. William Chick built a log house at Walnut and Second streets. Jessie Fremont, daughter of Sen. Benton and wife of Lt. John C. Fremont, stayed in that house during one of her husband's western expeditions.

The end of the Mexican trouble in 1846, and the resultant jump in the trade with Santa Fe, caused the landing to boom. Early in the year the population was about 300. Before the end of the year it was 700, and the name of the settlement had been changed legally to Town of Kanzas.

Parkman landed here in 1846 and repaired immediately to Chick's house. (Being fresh out of Harvard he knew all the best people.) From there he took a wagon to Westport to buy his horses and mules.

Parkman left a delightful description of his departure from the West that fall:

". . . we hired a wagon and drove to Kanzas landing. Here we were again received under the hospitable roof of our old friend, Colonel Chick, and seated under his porch we looked down once more on the eddies of the Missouri."

Parkman's friends at the landing wanted to have a ball celebrating his return, and even hired the old trapper, Antoine Lajeunesse, to play the fiddle. But the steamboat came before the affair could get cranked up and Parkman took off for St. Louis, the Planters House, and immortality.

In two years a visitor wrote that the town had four brickyards and a steam mill. There were 10 stores, three saloons and a livery stable.

In two more years the town had what was described as the best steamboat landing on the Missouri River, with the entire riverfront being a natural wharf. There were four big warehouses patronized by the booming town of Westport. There were several grist and sawmills, blacksmith shops, wagonmakers shops, grocery and provision stores and, to show that civilization had come to stay, there was a 46-room hotel, the Troost House.

The Old Road To Westport

There wasn't much point in having a fine landing unless there was a good road from the landing to somewhere. Chouteau had to build a road from his landing to the old fur road that dated back almost to the turn of the century. It undoubtedly was an Indian trail for countless centuries before then. The trail led from the interior of Missouri along the south side of the river, swung near the landing, and then angled off through the heart of what is now downtown Kansas City, out to the West, along the south bank of the Kaw and toward the fur country, after crossing the trace which later led to Westport.

Chouteau cut a road from his 1826 landing to hit this older trace. It took a much shorter road to run from the first building on the Westport landing — a 20′ x 40′ warehouse built about 1838 — to the Chouteau road, and then on down to Westport.

The route of the Chouteau road is obscure from the probable landing site — about where an extension of Olive Street would hit the river — to a point at about 15th and Grand. Here it angled to about 17th and Broadway; then to Summit and Southwest Boulevard; and then down to 39th and Broadway and on into old Westport. In those days (1826) there was no Westport of course, and the old Chouteau fur road continued along the old Indian trace onto the prairies and eventually the Rocky Mountains, via what later became the Oregon Trail. Jed Smith and Robert Campbell probably used that trace on their way west in 1825. Smith, Sublette and Jackson probably used it with their wagons, on the way to the 1830 rendezvous.

The roads cut by John Calvin McCoy and Louis Roy are believed to have headed due east to clear the bluff, then sharply southwest at Grand, to Sixth and Delaware, then south to about 18th and Main, where they picked up the old road to Westport.

Go back over the viaduct — the original road is directly beneath it. At the first stop sign, 3rd Street, there is a wedge. Take the left fork, which is Grand. By 1850 fencing had forced all emigration traffic onto what is Grand Avenue today, but until then the old McCoy-Roy road generally followed Main Street. At 5th Street turn right (west) for three blocks to Delaware. Turn left to another viaduct. Go over it. At the near approach the old trail came beneath the street.

On the south side of the viaduct is Main Street. Continue southward to one block past Truman Road (16th Street.) The trail continued on under Main for another half block before intersecting the old trail from Chouteau's warehouse, headed west. Continue south on Main.

Drive all the way past Penn Valley Park to Linwood, which is 3200 South. The trail is essentially beneath Main Street. Turn right on Linwood, as the trail did, and proceed four blocks south to Broadway. Turn left on Broadway, then right, or south, on 34th Street. Two blocks to the west is Pennsylvania. Turn left, or south, and proceed into Westport over the same route the emigrants took.

To The Chouteau Landings

Turn right (west) from Broadway onto Westport Road to the Southwest Trafficway, just before reaching State Line Boulevard. Turn right (north) and watch the speed — the police are alert. Follow the signs to I-35 North, then to I-70 East.

Continue about six miles east on I-70 to I-435 North. Proceed another six miles north and cross the Missouri River. The most probably site of the 1821 trading post established by Francois Chouteau is on the north bank of the Missouri River, only a few yards downstream (east) of the north abutment. Exit at Highway 210 eastbound and turn immediately back to the south on Randolph Road.

Proceed to the south end of Randolph but don't turn left onto Birmingham Road. Continue ahead to crest the levee on a poor dirt road. Park at this point. Somewhere in that vicinity was the 1821 Chouteau Landing.

The late John Edward Hicks, a noted Kansas City history buff and former member of the Landmarks Commission, believed that the original 1821 Chouteau landing was, possibly, on both banks of the river as well as on an island in the stream, but about three miles west of here. But old Frederick Chouteau, who worked there as a boy,

This is the probable site of the 1821 Chouteau Landing, on the north bank of the Missouri River just downstream from the I-435 bridge (background). The trading post washed away in the great flood of 1826.

lived long enough to be interviewed in 1880, and he testified that the landing was "at Randolph." This is the place known as Randolph.

Return to I-435 southbound. Exit at Highway 24, headed west. Proceed about 3.3 miles to Chestnut Trafficway. Turn right on Chestnut and proceed over the railroad viaduct, then continue north to Nicholson Avenue. Turn left on Nicholson for about four blocks, then half-left when the street ends. Proceed southwest a block and turn right onto Olive Street. Continue across River Front Drive, to the river bank, mount the levee, and stop. This is the probable location of the 1826 Chouteau Landing.

This landing survived until the great flood of 1844. The Westport Landing was better from many points of view, so in all probability the Chouteau warehouse would not have survived much longer under the economic onslaught than it did before the wall of water.

A Visit To Old Gabe

Return to Chestnut Trafficway, follow it south (right) to Independence Avenue (Highway 24) and turn left. Continue east to the 5400 block, Hardesty Avenue. Turn right, or south, for nearly a mile to Truman Road. Turn left on Truman Road and continue east toward Independence, for about two miles. Pass beneath a stone arch across the road. A half mile ahead on the left is the en-

trance to Mt. Washington Cemetery, which is open between 8 a.m. and 5 p.m. Turn left into the cemetery.

Proceed about two blocks straight into the cemetery,
pass over a small bridge, to a large stone on the right
located alone in a triangular plot of ground. This is the
grave of the greatest mountain man of them all, Jim
Bridger — Old Gabe, the Blanket Chief. There is his
monument, just as it was erected by Gen. Dodge.

The Old Santa Fe Trail

Return to Truman Road. Continue east for about three
more miles to Delaware. The big white house on the south
side of the street is the residence of the 33rd president
of the United States, Harry S Truman. Two blocks further,
turn south onto Spring St. and proceed south one block to
Maple. Turn left and go east for three long blocks to Lynn
(behind the Sears store.) Turn south for two blocks to Kansas Ave. and turn right for two more blocks to Liberty.
Then turn left, or south. This is where the trains formed,
heading south. Independence has done a fine job marking
the Santa Fe Road from this point to the city limit at

*Grave of Jim Bridger in
Mt. Washington Cemetery,
Kansas City. Monument
was erected by his friend,
Gen. Granville M. Dodge.*

*The 3100 block of
Santa Fe Rd., built over
the old trail south of the
square in Independence.*

Highway 40.

Proceed two blocks south to Pacific and turn right. Two blocks ahead is Spring Avenue and another route taken by those great freighters which broke the way to Santa Fe when Oregon was largely a rumor. In the early years, before Westport came into existence and for a few years after, the emigrants to the Pacific Northwest used this old trail too.

Some of the Santa Fe trains continued on Lexington two blocks to Spring; some continued south on Liberty two blocks to Walnut Street, then two blocks west to Spring. At Spring and Walnut the trail continued due south to the corner of Spring and Pacific, where Spring dead-ends today. On the east side of Spring, just north of Pacific, is an old emigrant spring — the other important spring that kept Independence supplied with an abundance of fresh water during the heyday of the trail. The site has been partially filled with construction debris.

Mrs. Fowler is convinced that there was no set way of getting out of Independence. The length of the trains, the number of different trains, the choice of major routes, the time of the year, who came first — all had something to do with the routing out of Independence. There were springs and grass and timber all over. They went out the best way they could under a varied set of circumstances.

On the northwest corner of Spring and Pacific is a small saloon. It once was the bottom half of the office building of the Waggoner & Gates grain mill. The mill itself — one of the town's earliest industries — is across Spring from the office. The residential buildings of the Waggoner family are on the large tract on the south side of Pacific. George Caleb Bingham, the celebrated artist, once owned the main house. The street to the east of that property, Osage, wasn't there during the trail days. In fact, one of the Waggoners petitioned the Jackson County Court to stop those damned emigrants from cutting through his property at that point. That in itself is sound evidence that the trains weren't limited to any one route from the square to New Santa Fe. In fact, Mrs. Fowler is at a loss to explain why they indeed wouldn't have utilized the high ground all the way south on Main Street to Southside

Boulevard. The topography indicates it would have been the logical thing to do.

The trains turned west onto Pacific at Spring, moved just a block, and then south again, on Pleasant. In about 1833, Lilburn Boggs, governor of Missouri during the unpleasantness with the Mormons in Jackson County, built a small house up from the northwest corner of Pleasant and Pacific. It has been gone for decades. Boggs went West too, his every step taken in fear of the Mormon travelers on the north bank of the Platte.

The trail continued south about three blocks, cutting diagonally toward the street from the left and hitting Pleasant at South Avenue. Pleasant jogs to the right there, but continue on west about a block to McCoy, and then south again. Now continue on south — the trail is just off to the right a few yards.

McCoy becomes Santa Fe Road at the railroad crossing, about .5 mile south. Stay on it nearly to 28th Street and turn left into Santa Fe Trail Park.

Proceed into the park nearly .2 mile, to a point about 30 yards before reaching a widening in the pavement. The car should be opposite a grove of trees in a depression down to the right. There are the remains of a ramp leading out of the creek. Mrs. Fowler believes this is a vestige from a very early trail, one which even predates what is known today as Santa Fe Road. It might be the one surveyed by George Sibley even before Independence was founded.

Return to Santa Fe Trail Road, the route of the trail in later years, and turn left, or south. Just past 31st Street there is a wedge in the road. Angle to the right for two more blocks, to 33rd Street. The trail wandered a little to the left here.

Mrs. Fowler says that in years past, in the middle of the summer, one could sight over the high ground and a few yards east of the road it could be noticed that the plants were not quite as high in one spot as elsewhere. That is more physical evidence of the trail in Jackson County — where the soil never has quite recovered from the thousands of steel-rimmed wagon wheels which compressed it into hard pan.

Turn right on 33rd Street for two short blocks to Crysler; here turn left, or south. At this point the trail will start heading toward Crysler, making the intercept at 35th Street. It continued a little to the west, then turned south to parallel Crysler.

Continue on Crysler past 37th Street. The second door on the right past the intersection is the old farmhouse of the Redford farm — dating back to the heavy trail days. The trail itself was just west of the house, headed 220 degrees.

Continue south to 39th Street and turn right (west). Four or five blocks away is Blue Ridge Boulevard. The old trail intersected Blue Ridge about 40th Terrace, so turn left (south) onto Blue Ridge and follow it. When approaching Raytown be continually observant of traffic regulations.

The trail followed beneath Blue Ridge all the way into the heart of Raytown, where it turned due west, as the traveler should, on the 63rd Street Trafficway. These beelines are not unusual because Raytown had been surveyed and was being fenced and developed when the trail traffic was at its peak. The caravans had to make those section line turns regardless of topography or be hauled in for trespassing.

Unlike the Independence-Westport Road, this trail was not dotted with encampments for some distance from the square in Independence. People headed out the Santa Fe Road either for the Southwest or for Oregon ordinarily didn't camp along this trail during their outfitting days. They outfitted quickly in Independence proper and left as soon as possible. By the time they reached Raytown they were well on their way.

About a half mile to the west of Blue Ridge Boulevard, along the 63rd Street Trafficway at a point just past the Regency East Apartments, there will be a Y in the road to the left. There is a "No Left Turn" sign. Continue past it one block to Elm, turn left for a short block, and right again and the traveler will be on Blue Ridge Boulevard and the Santa Fe Trail once more.

Within the next half mile the road starts a gradual curve due south. Just before completing that curve a traffic island is reached. Veer to the right past this triangular island and prepare to enter Blue Ridge Cutoff, headed south, or left.

This is the same road coming down from the Independence-Westport Road cutoff onto Pitcher Avenue and Highway 40. Proceed due south and again the trail is beneath the road. This is where all the alternates to the Santa Fe Trail came together.

Observe the left side of the road after making the turn, and shortly a granite marker will come into view. About a half-block past there at approximately number 6615 and also on the left is Aunt Sophie's Cabin, erected in the 1830s. She was a slave of the Rice family, and this was one of a number of cabins ringing the main house, which stands nearby, a well-restored structure. Aunt Sophie was there, possibly, when the cabin was built, and spent all but her last few years in it. She died at age 77 in 1896.

Continue to E. 87th Street, the north boundary of a shopping center. Turn to the right, past a small traffic island in E. 87th, which is only a few yards long. At the end of it turn south (left) again onto what would appear to be a small access road behind the shopping center. This, in fact, is the original Santa Fe Trail. Now the traveler is really out in the woods.

Aunt Sophie's cabin, one of the oldest buildings on the Santa Fe Trail, is about 6615 Blue Ridge Cutoff, southwest of Raytown. It was erected in the 1830s.

About .3 mile ahead the trail turns to the right — turn with it. It's primitive, so be careful. It makes a left soon. The trail continued southwest but unfortunately the road doesn't. Continue due south for a block or so and just past the Palestine Cemetery turn right onto 93rd Street.

Proceed over a railroad overpass and the original trail knifed in from the right about 200 yards ahead, headed southwest. Continue on to the next intersection, which is Hillcrest, and turn south, or left.

The high point on Hillcrest, just before reaching the electric signal at Bannister Road, is where the trail crossed, still headed southwest. Continue on past Bannister on Hillcrest to 103rd Street. The trail actually is paralleling I-435 about 50 yards south of it. Turn right, or west, on 103rd.

Just .4 mile ahead take an extremly hard left on Hickman Mills Road, before reaching U.S. 71 and I-435, and proceed all the way down to Red Bridge Road, or about 110th Street. Turn hard right and pass beneath U.S. 71. Proceed across the railroad tracks, and at the next stop sign turn to the left, or south, on Grandview Avenue for one block, and then to the right again on Red Bridge Road at about 111th Street.

The trail itself passed beneath the U.S. 71 and I-435 interchange, headed generally southwest, but there is no way to drive along it comfortably today. About 1.4 miles west of Grandview on Red Bridge Road, or about one block east of where Wabash comes in from the north, the Santa Fe Trail neared the Red Bridge Road, paralleling it about 50 yards to the north. At the bridge over the Big Blue it was some 300 yards to the north.

Soon after crossing the Big Blue the street passes over a railroad track and the trail crossed Red Bridge Road at this point too. It headed diagonally through the William E. Minor Park, which is on the left, and there is a very decided declivity showing there, along with a red gr nite marker, about 100 yards into the park.

Continue on to the next electric signal, which is Holmes Road, the western boundary of the park. Turn south (left) on Holmes.

Proceed down Holmes with the trail closing in from the left. The street makes a short jog to the left. The trail will make its intercept a couple of blocks past 117th Street at Santa Fe Road. Turn right, or southwest, and again the emigrant road is beneath the street, and again there will be no question about it. The intersection with Wornall

The Wayne City Landing, 3.5 miles north of the square in Independence, as it might have looked on an April evening in 1842. Full color prints of this 1978 painting by John Stobart are available at the Old Jail in Independence.

Road out of Westport is only a half mile further west, and the traveler soon will be headed into the West for keeps. Go straight across Wornall, through the site of New Santa Fe, and left onto State Line Boulevard.

CHAPTER 3   FINDING THE TRAIL IN KANSAS

The first eight miles of the route south from Independence were rocky, and after that, or about two-thirds of the way to New Santa Fe, the trail seemed to smooth out. But it wasn't really prairie, and the emigrants still didn't feel that they were out of civilization. The road south from Westport was a smooth one almost all the way, but it bisected a vast range of domesticated animals and campgrounds.

There was only a political boundary on the west edge of New Santa Fe. Sure, it couldn't be seen, but it had a sledgehammer impact on the Oregon emigrant. He had been born and raised in a society of law and order and now there was none. He achieved his adulthood through acquisition and ownership of property, and now there was none to be owned. Further, he was a trespasser — without feeling of guilt, perhaps, but a trespasser none the less. The nation had not yet grown so large that he hadn't considered himself an integral, vital part of it. And suddenly, he was no more a part of it. For he no longer was in the United States.

Perhaps this caused some measure of depression; if so there is no record of it. Political considerations were repressed, shoved into the background by as startling a view as he had ever seen. People of these United States, particularly those from Kansas, think of that state's topography as dull and monotonous. Think again, stranger. This emigrant, this man of the land, who had seen much of it by now, suddenly was dumbfounded by the grandeur of it all. Sure it was May, and his troubles had yet to begin. His juices were running and so were the land's. It had to be a stupendous sight.

Hear it from Edwin Bryant, an 1846 California emigrant, who knew a thing or two about the King's English:

"As we approached what is called the . . . prairie, the road became much drier and less difficult. The vast prairie itself soon opened before us in all its grandeur and beauty. I had never before beheld extensive scenery of this kind. The many descriptions of the prairies of the West had forestalled in some measure the first impressions produced by the magnificent landscape spread out before me as far as the eye could reach, bounded alone by the blue wall of the sky. No description, however, which I have read of these scenes, or which can be written, can convey more than a faint impression to the imagination of their effects upon the eye. The view of the illimitable succession of green undulations and flowery slopes, of every gentle and graceful configuration, stretching away and away, until they fade from the sight in the dim distance, creates a wild and scarcely controllable ecstacy of admiration. I felt, I doubt not, some of the emotions natural to the aboriginal inhabitants of these boundless and picturesque plains, when roving with unrestrained freedom over them; and careless alike of the past and the future, luxuriating in the blooming wilderness of sweets which the Great Spirit had created for their enjoyment, and placed at their disposal."

William Kelly, a '49er, likened the prairie to the "huge, lazy swell of the Atlantic."

Border to Topeka

Proceed west through the old townsite of New Santa Fe and note that Santa Fe Rd. terminates at State Line Blvd. Turn left, or south, to the first gravel road and turn west (right) again on 123rd St. About .1 mile down the road into Kansas is where the road abruptly turned to the southwest and crossed 123rd St. of today. Return to State Line Blvd. and turn south (right)1.5 miles. Turn back west on Kansas Highway 150, the Martin City Rd., or 135th St., which is the south boundary of the State Line Airport.

At 1.2 miles a gravel road comes up from the south, and about .2 miles further on the trail crossed, headed about 235. Proceed on west another two miles to the U.S. Highway 69 interchange. Take 69 southbound. About 1.5 miles from Highway 150 will be another trail intercept, just at the beginning of the exit ramp for Stanley Rd., or 151st St. Take that ramp down and to the west just one mile. At this point there is a large water tower on the north side of the road. The old Santa Fe Trail cut across Stanley Rd. just east of the tower. Continue on another 1.7 miles to Quivira Rd., and turn south a half mile to the little town of Morse (two dozen buildings.)

The trail cut through the center of Morse, now angling a little north of west. Return to Stanley Rd. and turn back west, or left. Proceed one mile and pass the Johnson County Airport. The old trail cut through the airport, headed northwest, and crossed Stanley Rd. just past the west boundary of the airport property. It proceeded some 50 yards north of Stanley Rd., turned west to parallel it, then turned back southwest to cross

Lone Elm Campground today, a few miles west of Kansas-Missouri line.

Stanley again at the next intersection, which is Black Bob Rd.

Continue one more mile on Stanley (151st) to MurLen Rd., which is graveled, and turn south, or left. The trail makes an intercept three-fourths of a mile from that corner. Continue to the next corner, which is 159th St., and turn west, or right, for another mile. The trail parallels the road here, about 100 yards to the north, but about .1 mile before the corner of Ridgeview Rd. it bends to the south and crosses 159th. Turn south on Ridgeview, and the trail will cross the road another .2 mile down the road. Continue to the next corner, 167th St., and turn back west, or right. One mile west of the corner is a railroad track, and then U.S. 169, also known as Craig Rd. Proceed .4 mile past the highway and the trail crosses 167th St. The next corner is Lone Elm; turn back south here. There is a marker on the southeast corner of that intersection.

On that corner, behind the marker, is the famous Lone Elm Campground, generally reached by the emigrants the first night out from Westport. The campground was a large one — it extended back along 167th for perhaps a quarter of a mile, and down Lone Elm for another quarter of a mile.

For many years the campground was called Elm Grove or Round Grove (not to be confused with Council Grove, further southwest in Kansas on the Santa Fe Trail). David Lavender writes that by 1843 only one large and one small tree were found there.

But here the emigrants were, the first day out, with plenty of grass, water, strong men, strong livestock, and strong equipment. It had been a relatively easy day for those who had come down from Westport. Few made it all the way here from Independence in less than two days (25 miles) so it had been easy going for them too.

Here, for the first time, they locked into that familiar formation that would be repeated every night for the next five months. They were some distance from the Pawnees, but from their first step out of New Santa Fe they were in Indian Territory, by decree of their own United States. The wagons locked in their circle, rear hub chained to the front hub of the next wagon.

Here for the first time, the children would bound from the wagons into the corral which they formed. Stock would be hobbled, tents would be pitched, fires would be started, latrines would be dug. An exciting adventure today; and within two weeks a dull routine.

John Charles Fremont stopped here — he had moved out the Kaw from the Missouri River for a look at Cyprien Chouteau's post, about opposite Muncie, and then dropped down through Olathe to Lone Elm in 1842.

Thomas J. Farnham moved to this campground on his first day out from Independence. Although it was customary to elect permanent officers for each caravan a few miles on down the line, Farnham broke precedent and did it right here, at the campground. On June 3, 1843, he reported the prairie grass was still only four inches high, but enough to keep the livestock healthy.

The Lone Elm itself was about three feet thick at the trunk, but by 1844 it was nearly stripped of its branches and bark. The emigrants needed firewood and they took it wherever they could find it. By the close of the decade they had burned the whole tree.

Proceed about .6 mile down Lone Elm Rd. to an intercept with the trail, which crosses the road bearing 240°.

Continue south on Lone Elm Rd. to the next corner, which is 175th St. Turn west (right) for one mile to the next intersection, and 25 yards before arriving there the trail crossed, bearing 255°. Continue another mile on 175th to Clare Rd. The trail has been angling away from the road to the south, and at Clare it is near the grove of trees visible about a quarter of a mile south of 175th.

Cross over I-35 in the next mile down 175th St., and then the next section line road. At that latter point the trail is a half mile south, but it is rapidly changing course and .7 mile down 175th it will cross the road again. It makes a sharp bend about 50 yards north of the following section line road, and .3 mile further west it crosses 175th (by this time also U.S. 56 and Main St.) for one last time, once again headed southwest. It crosses the railroad tracks and finally heads down toward that most famous of all 19th century intersections, towards the Road to Oregon.

Proceed the balance of that mile into the heart of Gardner, Kansas, on Center St. Turn left, on the viaduct over the tracks, for .7 mile south of Main St. The trail crossed there, by this time headed due west, only two miles away from the junction with the road coming down from Olathe.

Continue south to the next intersection and turn right (west) onto Cherokee. The trail at this point runs through a subdivision just north of Cherokee, but parallels that street for the next two miles. Proceed 1.1 miles and up over the Santa Fe Railroad. A half mile further, cross another railroad, and then immediately cross U.S. Highway 56. There is a small roadside park on the other side of the highway, with a marker describing the famous junction of the Oregon and Santa Fe Trails. Proceed on .1 mile to a fence row on the right, and park.

Walk north along the east side of that row of trees for

Bovine skull is on fence post in back of tree farm, where Oregon Trail left Santa Fe Trail, southwest of Gardner, Kansas. Junction was here in 1857.

.2 mile, or 350 strong paces. This will put the traveler within a few feet of the intersection of the Santa Fe Trail and the Oregon Trail. As recently as 1971 the area to the right served as a tree nursery. Rows of coniferous seedlings could be seen off to the right, but no longer. This was a bit ironic anyway. In the days of the pioneers nothing grew here but wild grasses from the unbroken prairie.

The road to Oregon left this spot headed due west. The road to Santa Fe headed 240°, or southwest. And here, perhaps, stood the little sign, "Road to Oregon." Says old Hiram Martin Chittenden, "Surely so unostentatious a sign never before nor since announced so long a journey."

Earlier emigrants evidently made the junction a mile to the southwest. Irene Paden reports that the trails — from Olathe and from Independence — converged for just one mile before branching for Oregon and Santa Fe. The only place they could join logically — and the one showing on the 1857 U.S. Survey — is here. Paden then goes on to describe an old codger in Gardner who says he stood in the wagon road himself and saw that same old sign just a block west of the schoolyard in Gardner.

It sounds like baloney but there may be something to it. This land is about as flat as land can get. There was no reason why the later emigrants moving west out of Westport, toward Olathe, shouldn't have turned back up northwest in Olathe.

But Applegate puts the junction a mile on down the Santa Fe Trail, by 1843, and he was there. He doesn't turn away from the Santa Fe Trail until he crosses Bull Creek. Unless he was mistaken about the creek, that is a mile on down the line. Arch Hulbert, as prolific a writer on the subject as there ever was, puts it there too, but in his famed Crown Collection of Maps, he shows the junction right there on the tree farm.

The late Dr. Margaret Long made a trip along the trail in 1940 and wrote a book about it. She places the junction about a mile and a half southwest of the historical sign, but she doesn't cite her sources for this conclusion.

Lower ford over Bull Creek, a mile from tree farm, has smooth rock bottom; banks of creek on either side are sheer, sometimes five feet high.

To look at the Bull Creek site, continue on down to the next intersection. The Santa Fe Trail crossed here, headed southwest. Proceed a half mile to the first little bridge. That is Bull Creek. Park 100 yards to the west of the bridge and start hoofing.

From the fence on the east edge of the field on the south side of the road, take a bearing of 190° toward a rather dark spot in a row of trees about 250 yards away. There actually are two dark spots — head for the one on the left. Possibly, the owner of that ground would not want anyone walking down his fence rows, but there is no way the author could stop anyone who would want to do so. The dark spot is over a rock-based ford over Bull Creek. Many old diaries mention that the trails separated on the "other" side of Bull Creek, and, in this case, that could be the northeast side, since the creek loops around at this point. Exploration of the creek for

many yards in either direction reveals that the banks
were earthen, up to eight feet high, and sheer. This ford
could have been cut by the farmers. On the other hand,
it could be The Ford. It is doubtful that anyone really
knows or could be able to find out.

Mrs. Fowler noticed a continuous serpentine
depression in the center of the field, which easily could
be a natural contour. Except it terminates exactly at
that ford, and wends its way back out to cross the road
before petering out. Could that be a part of the Oregon
Trail? It doesn't show on the U.S. Surveys of the 1850s,
so, possibly, it was largely invisible as a roadway even by
that early date.

The junction up on the tree farm was strong enough
on the face of the earth to make the 1857 surveys, and
obviously still was being used by several thousand
emigrants each spring, despite the growing pressure from
the Indians. The other traces evidently had grown to
such disuse by then that the surveyors didn't see them,
or felt they weren't significant enough to warrant
notation on the charts.

Return from the Bull Creek bridge to the next
intersection to the east, and turn left, or north, on
Corners Rd. At .3 mile the Oregon Trail crosses. Park
here and take a bearing of 276.° That's the direction the
trail took and if the time is just right, one might notice a
pair of parallel swales through the wheat field. That
marks the course of the trail leading to the second Bull
Creek crossing. On closer examination, one may see that
the swales, 12 inches wide, are actually quite flat, but
there is nothing growing there but an occasional stunted
weed. Maybe they are the remains of the old Oregon
Trail. Maybe they are a seldom used tractor path.
Probably they are both.

There is no trace of the crossing at that point of Bull
Creek; just an occasional narrow stock path down one
steep bank and up the other. Plenty of nice flat areas on
the other side that could have been the site of the
campgrounds, however.

Jesse Applegate reports that in 1843 he camped on
the other side of Bull Creek, where the trails separated.
But he doesn't indicate that this was the place.

The U.S. Survey shows the Santa Fe Trail bending in a bow shape to the southwest from the tree farm. Then, suddenly, about a mile due west of the lower Bull Creek crossing, it takes a sharp 90 dip to the southwest for no apparent reason. By drawing a line from that sharp curve up to the upper Bull Creek crossing it may be seen that the trail from that crossing, for many miles to the southwest over the known portions of the Santa Fe Trail, is straight as an arrow. Therefore, one could easily conclude that the ford and junction mentioned by so many emigrants in their diaries is not that slick little rock passage to the southwest, but the now-disappeared ford across the wheat field due west of the tree farm. The lower dip shown on the survey could have taken place in later years, due to a depleted supply of grass on the prairie, a rutted road, or both.

In the course of just one mile from the Upper Bull Creek Crossing, the Oregon Trail veered northwest, then southwest, and finally headed northwest again. Continue north on Corners Rd. to the next intersection, which is Santa Fe Trail Rd. out of Gardner. Turn west, or left. Proceed exactly 2.5 miles. The trail will be paralleling the route for the first 1.5 miles about a half mile south, or left. Then it will make another turn to the northwest and intercept at the junction with Edgerton Rd., where there is a stop sign. The trail actually crossed Edgerton about 50 yards south (left) of the intersection, headed northwest, and crossed Santa Fe Trail Rd. about 50 yards on past the intersection.

In other words, it would have passed approximately through the green building on the southeast corner of that intersection. The Oregon Trail then turned due north, to parallel Edgerton Rd. just beyond the farm buildings on the left. It follows the road about the line of the second fence row on the left, out into the fields. At the end of the first mile it starts to veer gently away to the west. At the end of the second mile it is about 400 yards to the left. It continues, heading almost due north to the third mile, and then starts to veer to the west again, so by the time Edgerton Rd. ends, four miles north of the last turn, it is a half mile to the left.

Turn left, or west, onto Prairie Center Rd. A half mile ahead (to the west) is a row of trees on the left. The trail crossed at that point, headed due north. The emigrants were stalling now, following Captain Creek north to a better ford. Cross the creek .5 mile west of the intercept. The emigrants would skirt an eminence 1.5 miles north of there.

Proceed west 1.5 miles from that intercept and turn north (right) along the Douglas County line. Turn back east (right) just one mile to the north, onto a well-graded gravel road, and proceed for one more mile to a point just past some old farm buildings on the right. Turn north (left) and at this point the emigrants were still .5 mile east, heading north, and getting ready to make a sweeping curve around Coon Point and cross the creek headed due west. Many an emigrant succumbed to temptation there and climbed the hill to get a good close look at infinity.

One cannot get to that crossing easily. Proceed .6 mile due north to the point where the trail crossed the road, headed due west at this point. Go on north .4 mile more but don't follow the banked turn to the left — turn right, or east, instead. This is a seldom used gravel road, but quite passable it would seem. Proceed one half mile into a right turn, just past a steel bridge over Captain Creek. A half mile to the south and on the right is the tranquil little Prairie Center Cemetery. The road turns into the cemetery. Two parallel ruts proceed on into the wilderness toward the emigrant route. Don't try this with a regular car. About 200 yards to the southeast the emigrants made their big turn and proceeded west along the section line just south of the little cemetery.

It was here, probably, that Myra Eells wrote: "Encamped on a small creek, crossed one creek. Scenery, delightful. The creeks are studded with timber, the plains are covered with grass and flowers of every color." The date was April 30, 1838.

Backtrack by making a loop inside the cemetery and proceed back a half mile north (left, from the cemetery exit); make a left turn again at the corner and re-cross the little bridge over Captain Creek headed west again. The trail is now a half mile to the left, and paralleling the route. One more mile from that intersection is the Douglas County Line Rd., but continue on past that intersection for .6 mile. At that point the trail, which changed direction to about 310 degrees at the county line, crosses the road.

There is a stop sign at the next intersection and at that point the trail is nearly a half mile to the north. Continue on west one more mile and turn right, or north, onto a macadam road. Proceed north .4 mile to a little bridge, and the trail crossed at that point, headed a little north of west. There is a gravel road on the left just past the bridge, but continue on ahead another half mile to a good gravel road, and turn west (left) for three miles. The trail intersects 1.8 miles from that corner, headed northwest, but it turns due west again shortly after, about the time the second mile is reached.

At the end of the third mile turn south, or left; the trail is only .2 mile to the right, and slanting back toward the southwest again. Continue south on this gravel road; which is Douglas County Rd. 1057, for another .5 mile. Turn west, or right, on a very obscure gravel road at that point. Proceed west for about a mile and then make a rather substantial jog to the right. These are roads that should not be traveled within a few days after a rain.

About .4 mile on west of the point where the road straightens out again is another intercept, with the trail crossing the road heading a little south of west through a broad meadow. It was in such meadows as this that the emigrants found delicious strawberries growing wild. Chester Ingersoll reports there were plenty left even in 1849.

Blue Mound, six miles southeast of Lawrence, often was climbed by skylarking emigrants. Fremont used it as signal mound in 1842.

Now, looming dead ahead is the famed Blue Mound — about a mile long, and now used as a ski slope. This great bump on the plain was a favorite spot for skylarking emigrants, and many of them climbed to the top for the big view. (Fremont used it in 1843 as a signal mound.)

The gawking tourist was a constant source of irritation to the experienced pilot. He would roar at the greenhorns at Coon Point and roar still more at the Blue Mound. "How miny mile to the Blues?" 1,744. "An how miny days to do her in, afore the snow flies?" 123. "An how miny mile a day that make?" 14. "At's right boy. Fourteen mile a day and ever god damn day so git yore ass off'n that 'ere hill and git the hell t'goin'!"

Proceed another .1 mile to the next left turn and take it, headed south. The Blue Mound now will be on the right. Just after making the turn the trail crosses again. Continue on south .5 mile and turn right, or west, onto a very narrow gravel road.

Just .5 mile from that corner the trail will be .2 mile to the right, now nearly paralleling the road. There is a rather substantial jog to the left in this road; then proceed onto a wood-floored bridge over a branch of the celebrated Wakarusa River. The emigrants crossed this branch about .2 mile to the right. The traveler today will soon be at a gravel road which is 1.5 miles from the last turn, and now at this point the trail is still .2 miles to the right, ready to face the inevitable crossing of the Wakarusa itself.

One mile from this point, at Douglas County Rd. 1055, the trail is about .7 mile north and starting to head west again. Proceed one more mile, or a total of 3.5 miles from the last turn and turn right. Drive north .9 mile to the new concrete bridge over the Wakarusa. It was erected in 1978.

The emigrant crossing is about .2 mile due east of the bridge. There the emigrants turned north to make their perilous ford.

Jesse Applegate, who would later achieve lasting fame with his *A Day With The Cow Column In 1843,* described the crossing. They let their wagons down the steep banks with ropes, there being too much excavation required to build the usual ramps. In the spring of 1846 James Pratt noted that there was a Shawnee nearby who was making a nice living pulling wagons out of the mud of the Wakarusa.

Continue on north into Lawrence. The trail is about .2 mile off to the right and exactly paralleling the road, which soon is identified as Louisiana Street.

Pass a new junior high and the Broken Arrow Elementary School on the right (east) side of Louisiana Street and three miles from the last turn, turn right (east) onto Kansas Highway 10, also known as 23rd Street. Two blocks away is Tennessee Street. The trail ran beneath it, but don't take it — it leads to a labrynth of one-way streets in the campus of the University of Kansas. Go on two more blocks to Massachusetts and save a lot of trouble.

Turn left, or north, on Massachusetts, to 11th St., and turn left again, or west. The trail is to the left at this point, angling to the northwest and an intercept with 11th Street. Cross Tennessee and note the big hill to the left. The trail was .2 mile up there, following the ridge. It crosses 11th between Louisiana and Indiana. Turn right, or north, on Indiana for just two blocks, to 9th. Turn west again, or left, for about a mile. The trail crossed 9th just west of U.S. 59, but turn right (north) onto 59, which also is known as Iowa Street. U.S. Highway 40 is just a few blocks ahead. Turn left or west on 40 and proceed exactly one mile. At that point the Oregon Trail comes into Highway 40 and continues beneath it. The location is just two blocks east of a large water tower on the right.

Exactly 2.5 miles from the junction with U.S.40 is a gravel road coming in from the left. At this point the trail started veering to the right of the highway. Another half mile further west is a blacktop road, and the trail crossed that road about 300 yards to the right, paralleling Highway 40.

Proceed another .8 mile west. The trail crossed the highway here, headed southwest. Another .2 mile is a blacktop road, and the trail is .2 mile to the left, by now headed due west again.

Ahead and to the left, along the south side of U.S. 40, is a standpipe and a radar tower. The trail passed directly beneath that tower, headed due west. One and a half miles west of that intersection on the right is the old Kanwaka Hall. The Oregon Trail turned to cross the highway just past the hall, headed exactly 330°. Another half mile to the west, Highway 40 turns right, or north; turn with it. One more mile and it starts a gentle turn back to the west, and it is at this point that the trail again comes beneath it. There is, however, no evidence of the old trail in the surrounding grasslands to the left.

Mrs. Eells was probably close to here on May 1, 1838, when she wrote: "Scenery delightful. Meet Indians at every encampment, some of them entirely naked, especially the children."

About .7 mile from the junction of the present and the old roads, the trail briefly leaves Highway 40, splits off to the left for about a half mile and then comes back beneath the highway about a half mile further west. Halfway between the point where the trail leaves 40 and re-joins it there is a small safety rest area.

In that area is a marker stating that the Coon Point campground on the Old Oregon Trail was three miles north, and this is true. This was an early variant of the trail which passed along the south bank of the Kansas River. The campground was on the west edge of present Lecompton.

It is five more miles out Highway 40 — the trail generally following beneath the road all the way — to the little town of Big Springs. On the east edge of town, on the north (right) side of the highway, is a buff brick Methodist church. A half block on west there is a small gravel road coming in from the south.

It is at this point that the new and the old trails split, with the new trail staying generally under the highway and the old branching off to the left to pass south of

Topeka, and to make the crossing of the Kansas River
south of Rossville. The two trails met again on the eastern
city limits of that town.

The new trail continued one more mile under U.S. 40,
through Big Springs and to a right curve just prior to
reaching the Shawnee County line. At that point the
trail continued northwest, while the highway turns north
to cross beneath I-70. Stay on the highway, and after
one mile it turns back to the west, or left, again. The
trail itself took a beeline from the first curve to the north,
on the county line, to the second, about two miles northwest. So about a mile from the place where the highway
turns due west, it curves almost due north again, and
that is where the trail once again comes beneath the
concrete.

About three miles further northwest on 40, Du Pont
Road will be passed on the left, and it is at that point that
the trail begins a gentle split to the right of the highway.
The trail passes south of the little town of Tecumseh,
about a block north, or to the right, of U.S. 40.

About 2.5 miles west of Tecumseh Road is Rodgers
Street, in Topeka. Turn right, or north, for two blocks to
Fourth Street. Behind the houses on the left is the emigrant crossing of Deer Creek. There is no trace of that
crossing there today. Retrace to Highway 40, or Sixth
Street. Turn right, or west. At Tefft Street, about two
blocks away, turn right, or north, for three blocks to E.
Third Street, and then turn west, or left. This is an oiled
road, and the Oregon Trail is through or just behind the
houses on the right side of the street. It proceeds west for
another mile. At the next street, Woodland, turn left and
return to Highway 40. Turn right again, or west.

Proceed west another eight blocks to California Street
and turn right, or north. (Highway 40 splits off to the
right in that stretch — split with it, please.) Two blocks
north is Fourth Street and the trail crossed California
Street headed due west about 30 yards north of that intersection. Turn left, or west. At Leland it crossed the intersection, then ran alongside the left side of Fourth. Continue three more blocks and cross a little bridge at Lawrence Street. This bridge is over Shunganunga Creek.
As nearly as can be determined, the old emigrant road
passed beneath this bridge too, and just after making the
ford it turned to the northwest. Proceed straight ahead

on Fourth St. Cross the Santa Fe tracks and proceed
three more blocks west to Madison St., just east of I-70.
Turn right but do not go up the entrance ramp to the
interstate — continue on past it to First St. The railroad
goes down the First St. median, so cross it before turning
west, or left. The trail is beneath the street now, having
passed through the Santa Fe railroad shops to the east.

The Oregon Trail followed beneath First St. for six
more blocks to Harrison St., where it turned north or
right. Go only one more block, to Crane St., where the
way is blocked by an earthen levee on the south bank of
the Kansas River.

This is the location of the ferry which was operated
for many years, perhaps, as early as 1842, by two
half-breed brothers named Papin.

Make a U turn to return to First St. and turn left, or
east, for three blocks to Kansas Ave. Turn right, or
south, for five blocks to Sixth St., or Highway 40, and
turn right again, or west. Four blocks ahead is Topeka
Ave., or U.S. 75. Take it right, or north. Cross the

*U.S. Highway 75 spans Kansas (Kaw) River in
downtown Topeka, and a half block downstream is site
of Papin's Ferry, where emigrants crossed in 1840s and
'50s.*

Kansas River now, just one block upstream (or west) of
Papin's Ferry.

There is nothing at the site now but a well-manicured
levee, but there was a lot of action there in the 1840s
and 1850s. Few emigrant diaries contain any words of
praise for the two breeds, Joseph and Lewis Papin, but,
unlike other ferry operators further west, there did not
seem to be open hatred of them either. The travelers
evidently regarded them as a necessary evil and were
quite willing to pay the price of $1 a wagon rather than
ford a river which had claimed entirely too many lives
already. By this time they already were bickering
extensively among themselves and perhaps didn't feel
like cutting strangers in on the maliciousness. The Papins
made a lot of money at that spot. The ferry boat in
1843 consisted of three dugout canoes supporting a
single deck.

If the breeds were on duty here on June 14, 1842,
John Charles Fremont doesn't mention it, He described
the ford as being 230 yards wide, with a "swollen, angry
yellow turbid current." The emigrant road was described
as being unusually fine, well beaten and level. The
expedition's coffee was lost in the process of crossing
the river, and this was bemoaned all the way West.

Fremont leaves an interesting quote at this place. "In
the steep bank of the river here, were nests of
innumerable swallows, into one of which a large prairie
snake had got about half his body, and was occupied in
eating the young birds. The old ones were flying about
in great distress, darting at him, and vainly endeavoring
to drive him off. A shot wounded him, and, being killed,
he was cut open, and eighteen young swallows were
found in his body."

The 35-year-old Joel Palmer, leader of the emigration
of 1845, crossed on the Papin's flatboat. Bennett C.
Clark, consumed with the gold fever, had left Cooper
Co., Mo. for the American Fork, and crossed on the
Papin ferry on May 8, 1849. He noted that the rate was
$1 a wagon, an indication that the breeds hadn't yet
heard of the inflation of that spring. He noted that two

boats were in operation, each capable of holding two wagons.

Chester Ingersoll wrote to the *Joliet Sentinel* that the Kansas ferry was eight days out of Independence. He made the trek in 1847, as part of a 78-wagon caravan.

Later in 1849, the tariff had jumped to $4 a wagon, two bits a mule and a dime a man. But the buyer got more service then, too. The operators had advanced to lowering the wagons to the water themselves with a rope secured to a tree. Double teams hauled the wagons out and across the spongy sands to the north.

James Clyman, the veteran mountain man who was guiding the Ford party of 1844, was approaching the crossing when he made one of his typical warm observations in his famous diary:

". . . and here let me say there was one young Lady which showed herself worthy of the bravest undaunted poieneer of west for after having kneaded her dough she watched and nursed the fire and held an umbrella over the fire and her skillit with the greatest composure for near 2 hours and baked bread enough to give us a verry plentifull supper . . ."

The Bidwell-Bartleson party, which had left Independence May 12, 1841, started a custom at the Kansas Crossing which would continue through the next two or three decades. The shakedown part of the cruise was over at this point, and the temporary leadership had been tested. Here, at the crossing, the caravan was reorganized, with Bartleson elected captain. Tom Fitzpatrick, another veteran mountain man and trapper, was hired as the guide on a formal basis. Also, in the caravan were DeSmet and the recently rediscovered Nicholas Point, a Jesuit artist.

From then on the Kansas Crossing became the reorganization point, the signal for the tightening of military discipline, the re-forming of the companies that would spend nearly five more months together with varying degrees of incompatibility.

It was near here, in 1843, that young Jesse Applegate observed the election of officers of his company. At a given signal the vote-seekers would march across the prairie. The general mass of people would break and run after them, so that behind each candidate would be a long tail of people. The man with the longest tail was elected the leader, and in that case it happened to be Peter Burnett, destined to become the first governor of California.

The Burnett Company had no intention of using the ferry, if, indeed, there was a ferry there by 1843. They built two canoes, bridged a space between them with a pole platform, and then towed each of the 120 wagons across with ropes. The livestock swam across, but the people took the catamaran. The operation took five days.

Topeka to Nebraska Border

After leaving the north bank the emigrant road headed northwest, passing under the bridge approach about where the Union Pacific tracks are today. Proceed ahead to Grant and turn due west, or hard left. Proceed four blocks to Taylor St. and turn right, or north. At this point the trail is a block to the south and heading northwest.

Proceed north to Silver Lake Rd. and turn left, or west, for four short blocks. The trail crossed that street just past Winter, still headed 330 degrees. Continue ahead about .4 mile to Vail Ave. and turn right, or north. About a block south of Lyman St. the trail crossed the road, still headed northwest. Continue on a block past Lyman to U.S. Highway 24, and get on it, headed west.

About a quarter of a mile from the point where the entrance ramp joins Highway 24 the trail crossed again, headed northwest. Ahead is U.S. 75, running north and south. The trail crossed that highway about a quarter of a mile north of U.S. 24, then turned abruptly to the southwest and crossed Highway 24 again about where the westernmost of the State Highway 4 access ramps leaves Highway 24.

As the traveler proceeds west the trail continues its dip back toward the river. About 3.4 miles west of U.S. 75 is the antenna of KSTB-TV, on the south, or left side of the highway. Turn left, or south, at the next corner, which is Huxman Rd., and proceed 1.5 miles down toward the Kansas River. There are two stone farm buildings on the east side of the road; the trail passed just to the south of them, headed back northwest by this time. Turn west (right) at the next corner, which is Northwest 13th St., and proceed a mile to the next road. Turn back north again, or right. Go exactly .7 mile to another trail intercept; then go to the next corner, and turn left, or west onto Northwest 21st St. A half mile ahead is another intercept, where the trail comes angling through a set of farm buildings on the left and crosses the road headed northwest. Go another half mile to the next corner and turn right, or north, onto North Hodges Rd. At .3 mile is another intercept, and the next corner is U.S. 24 again. Turn left, or west. About .4 mile ahead the trail made another intercept with the highway, and headed almost due northwest into the little town of Silver Lake. The highway must follow the section lines. Stay on 24 and make a right turn to go north to Silver Lake, and then make a full left. At that left turn, in Silver Lake, the main line of the Union Pacific is only a few yards north of the highway. That is where the trail came in. It stays beneath the UP roadbed for the next two miles, with U.S. 24 paralleling it a few yards to the south.

Two miles from Silver Lake there is a tree farm on the north side of the railroad tracks. It was at this point that the trail branched off to the north slightly, to avoid difficult crossings of two creeks the highway is about to bridge. Continue ahead for 2.4 miles past this point and note a narrow gravel road coming across the tracks from the right. This is Carter Rd. Take it north, or right, and shortly after crossing the tracks jog to the left at Northwest 46th St. Continue north, and .3 mile from the last jog the trail comes in from the right. Another tenth of a mile is Northwest 50th St.; turn left, or west, at that point. At .3 mile past that corner the trail comes into the present road and continues beneath it another half mile, into the little town of Rossville. Remember, it is at the east city limits where the two trails came together — the one from Topeka and the one from the upper Kansas crossing.

In Rossville turn to the left on Main St. and cross the UP tracks. The Oregon Trail made its intercept with those tracks dead ahead and continued beneath them to the northwest. Turn right onto U.S. 24 again, and the road once more will parallel the emigrant trail, which continues beneath the tracks. The Pottawatomie Co. line is 5.5 miles west of Rossville.

This country is described in emigrant diaries as high rolling prairies, and in the middle of the last century it had little timber and even less water.

Proceed another two miles into the town of St. Marys. On the east edge of town, along the north (right) side of the road, is the site of the old St. Marys Catholic Mission, founded here by Belgian Jesuits from the Bishop's farm in Florissant, Mo., northwest of St. Louis. The missionaries came here in 1848 to Christianize the Potawatomie Indians — and succeeded. They had lived with the tribe in eastern Kansas since 1838, and moved here with them when the government forced them to locate to a new reservation. The original building of the U.S. Potawatomie Agency stood on the grounds until recent years.

All this distance the trail will be beneath the UP tracks along the north (right) side of the road. Past the heart of town is Eighth St.; turn right, or north. Cross the railroad tracks and proceed another three blocks to Durink St., and turn left, or west. At this point the Oregon Trail is beneath the road. Get ready now for a fascinating trip.

About 2.3 miles ahead is a jog — turn half right; make sure to turn back to the left before going over the hill ahead. The trail didn't make this jog; it kept heading west, passing immediately to the right of the farm buildings just past the turn to the right.

After completing the jog, the trail will be about .2 mile off to the south, or to the left. Cross a couple of small iron bridges with load limits of five tons. Pass a primitive road on the right, crest a steep hill and then look across a defile to the left and see Highway 24 about a third of a mile to the south. The trail was between the highway and a pond in the valley, soon will turn and once again come beneath this gravel road, .4 mile ahead, as it makes a gradual turn to the northwest.

This road is quite primitive, but passable, if a speed of 35 miles an hour is maintained. The rocks can shoot up against the underbelly of a car or trailer and cause rather

The Oregon Trail, about five miles northwest of St. Marys, Kans.

Grave of the Pottawatomie chief, Louis Vieux.

serious damage at higher speeds. About two miles past the point where the trail rejoined the gravel road is another five-ton bridge, and the emigrant ford, evidently, was at that exact spot. Continue on across the road to Belvue, headed northwest. A mile and a half further is a Y. Take the right branch, then immediately take another half left. The trail again is beneath the road. It is at this point, however, that the trail performs a paradox by taking a bee line of 290 degrees while the road starts into a series of gyrations. This condition continues for the next mile. Go another 1.5 miles, cross a paved road, and continue due west for .5 mile.

At a point where the road assumes a most primitive appearance, the trail crosses, following a fence row headed due west, and at that point turn due south for .1 mile and then turn right, or west again. The trail has proceeded west on the north side of an ancient cemetery; go west on the south side of it, with trail and road joining at the bridge across the Red Vermillion River.

The cemetery is about .2 mile from the turn to the west. By all means stop. There is a small loop up to an information area, resembling a crypt, carved into the hillside.

The dominant stone in this graveyard is that of Louis Vieux Sr. — business agent, interpreter, and, finally, chief of the Potawattomie Indians. He was born Nov. 30, 1809, at the site of present Milwaukee, and was given an allotment of land on the Red Vermillion in 1857. He bought the bridge over the Red Vermillion and charged a toll of $1 an outfit. He also supplied the emigrants with hay and grain. South of his stone is the grave of his first wife, Charlotte, mother of his children, who died April 13, 1857, age 37. North of him lies his second wife, Mary, who died April 11, 1859, also age 37. His third wife, Mary L., is buried in the Wamego cemetery, some four miles to the southwest.

The area is the site of one of the great tragedies of the trail. Late in May 1849, a huge outfit camped around the ford on the east bank of the river. Asiatic cholera took over and before the week was over many were dead. Some 50 emigrants are believed to be buried on the river bank.

The campground was a popular one, with good wood, water and grass. There would be all too few of these later on, and the people knew that very well.

Stand in the northwest corner of the graveyard (far left) and take a bearing of 250 degrees. The sightline is toward the latest of several successors to the Vieux bridge, and is in the same place. For a better look, follow the old stock trail down the hill.

This was the third major crossing faced by the emigrants, after the Wakarusa and the Kansas. Joseph

Old bridge over Red Vermillion was one of several successors to original Vieux bridge. It, too, has been replaced.

Ware forded here in 1848, mentioning steep banks and a
rapid current.

Continue down the road to the bridge. Instead of crossing, park and walk down the access road to the north,
along the east bank of the river. About 70 yards ahead on
the right is a chain link fence enclosing the graves of T. S.
Prather (May 27, 1849) and two unknown emigrants.

Cross the new bridge. Immediately on the left is America's
second-largest American Elm, 130 years old during the
gold rush. Here the trail veers sharply to the north to pass
diagonally through the townships toward the present town
of Westmoreland. Take a long jog to the left, or south, and
one mile from the point where the jog heads back west
again, at a stop sign, turn right, or north, for 1.5 miles.
Here the good gravel road goes into a banked turn to the
right, with an intercept just 500 feet to the east. Don't
take it. Turn to the left (west) instead and proceed two
miles on a primitive gravel road at about 35 mph.

This is the sort of terrain where the land use could have
allowed the traces of the trail to have remained visible
from the last century. Obviously the emigrants saw no
reason to eat one another's dust so they spread out. The
ruts weren't deep to begin with. Consequently, they are
gone today. The country now is beginning to pitch and
heave, but there are plenty of flat or gently rounded areas
where it made good sense to go to one side or another of
a given path.

Turn right on the paved road and proceed north for 1.6
miles, to an intercept of the trail, now headed northwest. About
.2 mile into the section it turns due north. Proceed north .4
mile to the next intersection and turn left on County Rd. 224,
a gravel road. Another intercept is just .2 miles west. The
emigrant route now turns to head directly toward
Westmoreland, paralleling Kansas Highway 99 about a mile
northwest of it.

Continue west for .8 miles and then turn right, or
north, for 1.5 miles. Just past a concrete bridge over a
dry wash is where the trail crossed the road, behind
a cluster of farm buildings on the left. This is a poor
gravel road, but passable safely at 35 mph. Continue .5 miles

north.

Turn to the left, or west, just past those farm buildings, and .2 mile down that road is another intercept. Go to the next corner, over a five-ton bridge, and the trail is nearly a mile to the north at this point. Continue another .8 mile west and turn right onto Kansas Highway 99. Proceed only a quarter of a mile and knife off to the right again, to head due north. One mile north there is a farmhouse on the right. The trail cut through it, and just past another farmhouse on the left side of the road. Continue ahead one more mile, then turn left, or west, a mile over a rocky, twisting gravel road to rejoin Highway 99. The trail hit the highway just east of the point where the road does, having come in from the left. It continues under or to either side of 99 to the heart of Westmoreland. Stop at the rest area on the left, a mile from the point where the highway was joined.

There is a historical marker in that rest area, a mile south of Westmoreland. It suffers from the ills of many of its brethren in that it presumes the traveler has a compass. It states that Scott Spring is "180 yards north." To find it, hike across the ditch across the road, climb the barbed wire fence and stay on the east side of the north-south fence. About 100 paces from the highway is a spring, now just a gurgle eminating from the base of a steep rock hill. The mound a few yards to the north is an emigrant grave. The marker says the stream still offers the "delicious cold water" of the emigrants' day. Don't believe it; the little pool is covered with green slime.

The trail crosses the highway about two blocks past the rest area, just under the bridge. Turn left into a small lane about one block south of the bridge, and park. Walk south 50 more yards to a gravestone just west of the highway. The unknown emigrant actually rests beneath the shoulder of the road. Continue 16 yards further south, then 20 yards west. There, friend, is another Scott Spring.

From the bridge the trail angles slightly off to the left, then turns to parallel the highway about a block to the west, all through the town of Westmoreland.

Three miles north of Westmoreland a decision must be made. If one is traveling in a normal car with a relatively light camper, and if it hasn't rained for a couple of days, and if his St. Christopher medal is shined up, he may want to try to find the trail off to the west of the highway. Otherwise, proceed four miles straight north to Blaine and pick up the narrative four paragraphs below.

The travelers with lots of guts will turn left, or west, on a poor gravel road. Just .8 mile from the highway will be an intercept of the trail, which had gradually been veering away from the highway north of Westmoreland. There is a great deal of earth in the composition of the road, giving it a slippery quality. At best it is a little spongy. Just .3 south of this point is the grave of an emigrant known only as "Marshall."

The trail crossed the little gravel road about .1 mile before the road turns to the right, or north. The trail is headed north of northwest, and hence, crosses the road about .2 mile from the corner. There is a nice set of ruts evident in the field on the west (left) side of the road about .4 mile from the corner, but there is no matching set in the grazing land along the right side of the road, so obviously those do not indicate the Oregon Trail. Proceed to the next corner and turn left, or west. It is possible to go straight ahead but the road is no more than two parallel ruts. At .2 mile is another intercept. Look quickly but keep the rig moving — this is no place to get stuck. Proceed to the next corner and slither around to the north, or right, for another mile, and then turn back east, or right again. Just .8 mile down this road the trail crosses, and again there is no evidence. This time it is headed just a shade east of true north. Turn left, or north, at the next corner, and another .8 mile down the road the trail will come knifing in through a pig lot on the left and go beneath the roadway.

If anyone wants to chicken out of the last two miles this is a grand place to do so. Just turn right onto Kansas Highway 16 and take it a mile and a half into Blaine. Otherwise, proceed straight ahead. The trail is directly beneath the road for the first two blocks or so, then veers gradually to the left. One mile ahead the trail is a quarter of a mile to the left. Before reaching that mile road a little stream must be forded, but it is only an inch or so deep. Turn to the right, or east, onto a fairly good gravel road. Just before hitting Highway 16 the road will angle to the right. Make a left onto 16. Proceed only about two blocks and then turn to the left again onto Kansas Highway 99, some seven miles north of Westmoreland. The road is headed due north at this point.

Proceeding north from Blaine, the Oregon Trail is paralleling the road about 1.5 miles to the west. Go north for three miles and turn left, or west, and proceed for 1.5 miles. This is where the Oregon Trail crossed the road. Fencerows are along the north-south half-section line on both sides of the road, then the trail crossed just west of those rows, angling a little west of true north. A dark swale may be seen in the field on the right, following the approximate line of the trail.

A half-mile to the west the road turns right, or north. Proceed for two more miles north and at the Marshall County line the trail will cross the road again, this time coming in from the right. Stop here and look to the right. There they are — ruts coming down the hill headed toward a little creek. The Oregon Trail crossed near the little bridge the road passes over. The road turns there and heads west for one mile along the county line. Take it, and then turn back north again into Marshall County.

The trail now is angling up toward the ford over the Black Vermillion River, one mile to the right, or east. Proceed north for 2.5 more miles. The trail has been closing in from the right, and at that point the trail cuts across the road from the southeast bearing about 320 degrees. There is a litle gate and an old entry into the fields on the left (west) side of the road — that, probably, is where the Oregon Trail crossed.

A little less than a mile down the road is an old abandoned country church on the right. At that point an obscure gravel road comes in from the left. Take it, headed west. A half-mile away is another primitive road, coming in from the south, and it is at this intersection that the Oregon Trail crossed again, through the trees on the southeast corner, and into the field across the road, still headed northwest. Because of loose gravel and rock this road should not be traveled at more than 35 mph.

Jog to the right, then turn north a half-mile farther down the road. About .6 miles ahead will be a T intersection; turn to the left, or west. At this point take a bearing of 273 degrees. A half-mile along that line is the famous ford over the Black Vermillion River.

There was no doubt about it in the minds of the emigrants now — they were in Indian country. Peter Burnett saw the Kansas Indians returning from a skirmish with the Pawness, laden with scalps. In fact, the Pawnees came by too, but in many pieces, all borne by the mutilating Kansas. Neither the Pawnees nor the Pottawatomies were any match for the bloodthirsty Kansas, who rejoiced in watching the application of hideous torture to their captives. One diary after another in the late 1840s mentions the cavalcades, but none records any damage of whites by the Indians.

About a mile west of the view of the ford over the Black Vermillion is an irregular four-way intersection. Turn right, or north. A little more than a half mile away is the bridge over the Black Vermillion. Sight to the right off the bridge toward the emigrant ford again, which is less than a half mile away by land, or five miles away by the stinking water. Note the steepness of the banks.

It was at the ford that the trail split. The earlier branch — up to about 1849, proceeded on an average bearing of 310 degrees to the Independence Crossing at the Alcove Spring. Later waves of emigrants crossed the Big Blue at Marysville, on a bearing of 330 degrees, along with the people leaving from St. Joe. This book follows the trail to the Alcove Spring.

Proceed north to a T intersection and turn left, or west, and at that point the trail will be .5 mile to the right. Continue west about .6 mile and turn right, or north. About 1.5 miles dead ahead is an intercept, but don't take this road within a day or so after a heavy rain. A substantial amount of clay in the base turns it into a quagmire. It is firm and solid in dry weather. The intercept is at the top of a hill, and another half mile ahead is Kansas Highway 9. Turn left there. A short distance on the left is a farm house — the trail cut through it, crossing the highway and into the fields just past another farm house on the north side of the road.

Continue for one mile past the next section line road

and turn north, or right, onto a gravel road. The Oregon Trail is 1.2 miles ahead, closing in from the right. There is no trace of the trail at this point. Proceed ahead another .8 mile to the next corner and turn left, or west. Proceed to the next intersection, a mile away, and stop.

In the northeast corner of that intersection, out in the field, a ridge runs from the road just traveled across the little gravel road leading north. The trail ran atop that ridge, but there is no trace of it there today. For the next two miles to the west the trail angles away to the north, and at that point — two miles away — turn north. The road parallels the east bank of Mosquito Creek. Take some nasty jogs in that mile and a half before crossing the creek at the same place the emigrants did. They had to ford but the traveler today gets a bridge. Look off this bridge and see that, even though the creek is small, the banks are extremely steep. The road paralleled this bridge. Just beyond it, the road turns left, and that is where the trail came in beneath it. Another tenth of a mile is a right turn; at that point the emigrant road went straight ahead. Continue north for about .6 mile and turn left, just after passing an old country cemetery on the right. After hauling over the ridge on the left as the traveler proceeds north, the trail turned left too, so, now, it is paralleling the road, headed due west.

The emigration now was heading toward the Big Blue, and they had read enough tour guides to know that their tour of the prairies was about at an end. The land already was writing the preamble to the struggle that lay ahead. There would yet be flowers, but they would spring from the spiney yucca on barren Scotts Bluff. There would be greenery but it would soon be the exception rather than the rule. Brilliant bursts of wild flowers on billowing swells of land would soon be behind them, with only some ugly heaves of earth to call this to mind.

Fremont noted the difference in the environment too, in 1842. "The night was cold, with a heavy dew; the thermometer at 10 p.m. standing at 46°." That was on June 19.

That same night his moody cartographer, Charles Preuss, made a much more subjective diary entry in his

Charles Preuss, melancholy artist and cartographer, accompanied Fremont on several trips west. He hated his boss and vented his feelings in a trunk full of letters that weren't translated until 1954, exactly 100 years after he hung himself.

native German. He was eternally contemptuous of his employer, who at times exhibited the traits of a martinet. "Our big chronometer has gone to sleep. That is what always happens when an egg wants to be wiser than the hen. So far I can't say that I have formed a very high opinion of Fremont's astronomical manipulations. We have started to botanize. I wish I had a drink."

Proceed only a half mile after the last turn to the west before turning north, or right, again. Go just a half mile and turn left, or west, at a full intersection and then a mile and a half ahead to the intersection with U.S. Highway 77, which leads into Marysville.

At this point note the swell about 100 yards to the left, the west side of 77. The trail came across that high ground headed northwest. Ahead is a gravel road leading up that same steep ridge. Again, the trail crowned this ridge. Just to the right of the road it turned due west, stayed on that bearing for perhaps a half mile, then angled down to the Alcove Spring and Independence Crossing of the Big Blue.

Proceed north, or right, for two miles, then turn west, or left, on a good gravel road for one mile, then left again, down the River Road for three miles to the Alcove Spring. This is private property owned by Mrs. Stella Hammett, 413 E. 5th St., Blue Rapids, KS 66411 (913) 226-7925. Please contact her for permission to visit.

The area is on the left, and it comes up fast. Turn at the steel gates, park, and enter the property. Note first the DAR monument to Mrs. Sarah Keyes. More about her later. Proceed down the footpath by the marker and across a broken footbridge over Alcove Spring Creek. The path will continue up a gentle incline. A sharp turn to the right and the path leads over a wood footbridge to the alcove itself. This is sort of an amphitheater, with a ledge of rock over the stage. In the spring, water trickles across the path and falls over the ledge, splashing down to the rocks 10 feet below.

Monument to Mrs. Sarah Keyes, who died at Alcove Spring in 1846. Grandma Keyes was one of more fortunate members of Donner Party — she died early.

Broken ledge is like proscenium over alcove. In springtime, water from hill cascades over it in a 10-foot fall. Spring itself is out of picture.

Walk down into the alcove. Cross a large boulder, and immediately to the right and directly beneath the wood footbridge is another spring. It gushes from a porous rock formation. It is as clear and cold as the emigrants said it was.

If one is watching the spring he is probably standing on a very large boulder in the path. Look at it carefully.

Engraved there is the legend "Alcove Spring." Edwin Bryant, traveling with the Donner Party to California in 1846, left this diary entry for May 26: "We continued to ascend elevated ridges until we reached the bluffs which overlook the Big Blue River. Descending from these, and ascertaining that from the late rains the stream was so much swollen as not to be fordable, we encamped on a slope of the prairie, at one o'clock P.M. The timber at this point is about half a mile in width, and is composed of oak, cotton wood, walnut, beach, and sycamore. A small spring branch empties into the main river, just above the ford. The waters of this branch are perfectly limpid, and with a lively and sparkling current bubble along over a clear bed of gravel and large flat rocks. In the banks and bed of this small stream are several springs of delicious cold water.

"May 27. This afternoon, accompanied by several of the party, I strolled up the small branch, which I have previously mentioned as emptying into the river above the ford. About three-fourths of a mile from our camp we found a large spring of water, as cold and pure as if it had just been melted from ice. It gushed from a ledge of rocks, which compose the bank of the stream, and falling some ten feet, its waters are received into a basin

This probably is not the rock Byron McKinstry carved on May 30, 1846. It bears the legend "Alcove Spring."

fifteen feet in length, ten in breadth, and three or four feet deep. A shelving rock projects over this basin, from which falls a beautiful cascade of water, some ten or twelve feet. The whole is buried in a variety of shrubbery of the richest verdure ... We named this 'Alcove Spring;' and future travelers will find the name graven on the rocks, and on the trunks of the trees surrounding it."

Many presume that Bryant himself did some of the engraving, and this may be true. Byron N. McKinstry, another member of the party, made this notation in his own notebook for May 30, 1846: "About a half mile from camp up the spring branch on the right hand fork is a most beautiful spring and a fall of water 12 feet. Mr. Bryant of our party has named it 'Alcove Spring." ... I this day cut the name of the spring in the rock on table at the top of the falls."

Possibly this boulder had at one time been above the spring; in fact, it would seem from the various emigrant notations that a wide protective shelf had been above the entire semicircular alcove.

Others, however, claim that the legend indeed appeared on the right edge of the overhanging cliff. The

This rock, believed to have been carved by James F. Reed on May 26, 1846, now lies at the water's edge of the pool of the Alcove Spring.

Dan Jacobson

A remarkably accurate depiction of the Alcove Spring, this painting shows "Alcove Spring" carved on edge of table rock at right side of proscenium.

rock supposedly broke and fell into the mud below.

Just before arriving at the big boulder there is a path leading off to the left, above the spring branch. Ten yards away is another boulder in which are incised the initials, "J.F.R.." the "R" probably being followed by "eed." Those letters have worn away in the past several decades. Reed was a survivor of the Donner tragedy. He also carved the date, "26 May, 1846."

James Frazier Reed was 46 and fairly wealthy. His wife Margaret was 32. Their family: Martha (Patty), 8; James, 5; Thomas, 3; Margaret's daughter from her first marriage, Virginia Backenstoe, 13; and Margaret's mother, Sarah Keyes. All Grandma Keyes wanted to do was live long enough to see her son, who had been in the 1844 emigration to Oregon.

Also in the party were George Donner, his brother, Jacob, and Tamsen Donner, George's third wife. The party was an efficient one and ordinarily wouldn't have camped any one place for three or four days but, as it happened, the Big Blue was bank full and indicated that it was going to stay that way for a good many more days. So the party finally concluded that the only way to cross that river was to raft it.

While the men busied themselves making the flotation gear, little Grandma Keyes gave up the ghost. Reed dug her grave and snipped a lock of her grey hair for little Patty before they laid her grandmother to rest. Then her name was carved on a small headstone and, for good measure, Reed also cut it in an oak tree located at the head of the grave. The grave is believed to be located about 100 yards north of the marker. When the Tuttle Creek Resevoir was being prepared, the River Road was routed to higher ground. The graders passed over the grave, taking the oak trees in the process. (Some remnants now are along the north edge of the property. The grave is under the near shoulder of the road.) But don't forget that lock of hair.

Retrace some steps to get to the foot of the hill above the alcove. A climb to the top reveals a lot of foot trails and the great swale of the Oregon Trail leading to the meadow below.

The emigrants came down this hill, maneuvering their awkward wagons to the intersection of the larger creek and, if there was room, camped there. If not, they would have crossed the creek to proceed to the old, pitifully broken parking lot to camp. That's probably where members of the Donner party stayed, or possibly across the gravel road. They indicated their campground was a half-mile downstream from the spring. This isn't, but emigrants had the habit of uniformly overestimating distances that were difficult to negotiate.

The creek crosses beneath the River Road in a concrete box culvert. Just opposite the steel gates, on the west side of the River Road, is a gravel road paralleling the Alcove Spring Creek a few yards to the north. Walk as far west as possible, and do not take the fork to the left. Stop at a locked gate.

One may wish to pass through the gate and hike 250 yards farther down the road onto private property. At an opening in the trees on the left take a bearing of 175 degrees and cut through the tall weeds down the bank; suddenly the Big Blue itself will pop into view. Trouble is, if one is there during the summer or a dry spell, the Big Blue isn't there anymore. The observer is looking at

*The Independence Crossing today is at mouth of
Alcove Spring creek. Big Blue often raged bank full in
spring, had to be rafted by emigrants.*

what once was an island, and the river flows now on the
other side. The bed of the old river now is a deeply
etched and cracked mud flat, brittle dry, and smelling to
high heaven from the pollution of man.

The Alcove Spring branch flows sluggishly into what
appears to be a stagnant arm of the Big Blue, which then
meanders out of sight around the island. It is extremely
hazardous to walk further near this stream or near the
old river bed. Without warning and with no evident
change in the composition of the earth, one can
suddenly find himself thigh-deep in soft mud and going
deeper. Should this happen, lie forward and gently dog
paddle toward more solid earth. Panic could force a
victim deeper into the ooze and induce suffocation.

There is no trace whatever of the old ford, the
Independence Crossing. In Bryant's May 26 notation he
observes that the confluence of the creek with the Big
Blue is just above the ford. The ford, therefore, would
be about where that stagnant pool is today.

The Donner Party wasn't the only one to find the Big
Blue a holy terror. Rev. Parrish left this entry for
June 19, 1844: "Preparing to move to Big Blue, in order
to cross. The morning is cloudy and it thunders.
Forenoon raining. Afternoon clear and warm. We landed
on the Big Blue a little past 1 o'clock with 11 wagons.

Prospect for fair weather is now flattering but we are waterbound again as the blue is still out of its banks.'' It was six days before Parrish would hit the other shore.

Myra Eells evidently was close to this spot on May 10, 1838: "Encamped on the Blue. Soil becoming more sandy as we camped in the Pawnee's country. Find a little calf so badly bitten by wolves that Mr. Walker and Smith thinks it best to kill it.''

Jesse Applegate got the word here. His cattle no longer would be allowed to hold up the great emigration of 1843. So they split — with Jesse's cow column required to move an additional two hours a day to keep up with the rest.

And Joe Meek swore that the emigrants lied about the mosquitoes around the Alcove Spring campgrounds — none were as big as turkeys. "Why," he said, "the biggest one I saw was no larger than a crow.''

John Minto, in the emigration of 1844, found the Big Blue a "raging torrent . . . with whirlpools.''

All the people who would come west from St. Joseph, and this would include most of the 49ers, crossed the Big Blue River at Marysville. B. C. Clark was one of them. On May 16, 1849, he wrote: "Beautiful stream about 50 yds wide and from 2 to three feet in depth we had a devil of a time getting our team over our leaders got turned around and all tangled up i had to plunge in and get wet all over got them stratened out at last and came through theare was two graves on the bank of the stream both made this year traveled on till two o'clock when we came to the place where the independence and St. Joseph road joined a few miles further we crossed a small creek.''

James Clyman doesn't mention the high water in 1827 when he crossed the Big Blue at the Alcove Spring, enroute to St. Louis. On the other hand, he had no wagons, only several hundred head of horses and mules.

Return to Highway 77 and proceed north into Marysville. Turn left on U.S. Highway 36, in the heart of town, and travel west for 3.4 miles to a good blacktop road. Turn left and proceed south for exactly five miles. At this point the Independence Crossing is exactly two miles away on a bearing of 126 degrees. The trail itself crosses the sightline a half mile south. Turn right. The trail crosses this road a half mile ahead.

Complete that mile to the west and turn right at the stop sign, onto a blacktop road. Just a half mile further is another intercept, with the trail headed due northwest. Complete that mile and turn left, or west, off the blacktop. This time the intercept is only .3 mile away. Continue ahead the balance of that mile and turn right. At the end of the first section the trail is off to the right .2 mile, but after it crosses that line it heads sharply to the west and will cross the gravel road just .1 mile from the section line. The trail turned to the right immediately after crossing the road and parallels the roadway about 100 yards to the left. It passed just behind the white house on the left.

At the next section line road look to the left — the trail passed through the farm buildings on the left side of that road about .2 mile west of the intersection. Do not turn; proceed on ahead for one more mile and turn left, or west.

Proceed only .4 mile, just past a small creek, and there is another intercept. Now the trail will change direction to the northwest; proceed on the rest of that mile and turn right to meet it, .7 mile on ahead. As is the case with all these intercepts, there is no trace; the cultivation of a century having erased all the evidence of that great migration. Continue ahead .3 mile and turn left onto U.S. 36.

Enjoy that pavement — all one mile of it. There is nothing at .4 mile west, but look anyway for there is another intercept. Continue the balance of that mile and get back on the blacktop with a right turn. About .8 mile ahead is another intercept, probably on top a gentle ridge, since it is running in the proper direction.

Continue the balance of that mile and turn left, or west, on a good gravel road. About .4 mile ahead are two farm houses on the right. The trail crossed the road just southeast of the first and passed in front of it. Then it passed just behind the second. Continue the balance of that mile to arrive at the Washington County line. Turn right, or north, and intercept the trail again just .5 mile ahead.

At that point the trail is headed northwest, but halfway into that section it turns rather sharply to the north, and as the next section line road is crossed the trail will be headed due north, about .7 mile west. Do not turn; continue ahead to the next mile road and turn left, or west.

An intercept is .7 mile ahead. On the right is a grassy swale and some ruts. The trail? Probably, with some help from a couple of generations of farm wagons. The trail there is headed due north but shortly after it enters that section it makes a broad curve to the left. Continue the .3 mile west and turn right, or north. A half mile ahead the trail crosses, headed due west now.

Continue .5 mile north and turn left, or west, on the section line road. Now the trail is starting a gradual curve, from its due west direction to northwest. This time the curve has not been influenced by a creek or a hill, but by the Little Blue River, which is still more than two miles away. The ancient road will follow the Little Blue out of Kansas, into Nebraska and almost to the Platte River. It will be a friendly river indeed.

Proceed ahead one mile. On the far corner of that intersection is the Hollenberg ranch house. It built about 1857 by Gerat H. Hollenberg, in order to capitalize on the Oregon-California trade, which passed the doorway. Three years later it became a Pony Express home station. It is believed to be the only such station on the entire trail which is neither altered nor moved from its original location. It is much as it was in the beginning — only older. Although it is not of consequence to the period covered by this book, it still is well worth a visit.

Circle through the driveway of the station and exit onto the gravel road in front of the building, headed north. Proceed to the next mile corner, turn left, travel west a little more than .5 mile and stop.

The car should be about 25 yards east of the crest of a hill. Climb to the fence row on the left and sight 120 degrees. There is the broad swale of the Oregon Trail, leading back toward the Hollenberg Station.

Continue to the next corner and turn right onto Kansas Highway 15E. Another intercept is .2 mile ahead. The trail cut through a house on the left, then passed behind a second house some .2 mile further down the road. Continue the balance of that mile. The trail crossed that section line road .3 mile to the left, or west, but do not turn. Continue on ahead two miles and turn left. In those two miles the trail has continued on a north-northwesterly course, gradually veering away from the highway. Proceed one mile west, cross the railroad tracks, and turn right.

Now the emigrant road turns to parallel the contemporary road, only about 150 yards to the left. Continue north for two more miles. At the end of the first mile the trail still is only 150 yards away, but by the time another mile is traversed it has angled sharply to the northwest and is exactly a mile away. Turn west at that second mile corner and proceed exactly one mile, to the next intersection. The trail cut right across the center of the intersection.

It had to be right along here where John Charles Fremont, on June 21, 1842, left this notation: "Evening closed over with rain and its usual attendant, hordes of musquitoes, with which we were annoyed for the first time."

And the next morning, he allowed something very human to creep into his *Report To Congress:* "Here a pack of cards, lying loose on the grass, marked an encampment of our Oregon emigrants."

Turn north now, or right, and proceed one mile to a T in the road. That is the end of the Oregon Trail in Kansas. This is the Nebraska state line. Turn left, or west, and the trail crosses into Nebraska just .6 mile ahead.

About .9 mile west of the T is the unique triangular-shaped tri-county marker which describes the old trail. Turn right at this point on a grass-grown dirt road and quit crabbing because there will be much worse before this trip is over. Ahead are some surviving examples of the splendid job the people of Jefferson County did in marking the trail through their county. Small signs on either side of most roadways crossed by the trail denoted not only the location of the intercept but the direction the trail took also. Vandals have taken their toll.

Continue north for exactly one mile — the trail crosses into Jefferson County at about .4 mile from the turn. After the trail crossed into Jefferson County it made a gradual turn to the right. Proceed to the gravel road a mile north of the state line, where the trail is headed due north a half mile to the west. Don't turn — continue ahead for one more mile.

At the end of the first mile of gravel the trail is still a half mile to the left, but in the middle of the next section it turns to the northwest again. Turn left at the end of the gravel road, when two miles into Nebraska, and proceed one mile. A half mile from the turn the trail crossed. Turn right and proceed north one mile. There is an Oregon Trail marker on the right, near the corner, but the trail was to the left, cutting diagonally across the roadway only a few yards west of the intersection. Turn left, to the west, for one mile. Just 1.2 miles from the turn is a small spring branch, crossing beneath the highway. The water is from the Fremont Spring, which is about .2 mile due north. Fremont, Kit Carson, Preuss and the other members of his company camped there in 1842. Continue west the balance of that mile and turn to the north, or right. Proceed .9 mile and there is another intercept. Continue the remaining .1 mile, turn left, or west, and the trail crosses the roadway headed northwest, just .1 mile to the west.

Proceed the remaining .9 mile of that section, note the marker ahead, and then turn right. The trail will make another intercept about .6 mile ahead. Continue north to the next section line corner and turn left, or west. The trail is .5 mile ahead and is marked perfectly. It is headed northwest. At the end of that section there is a T in the road — turn right. The markers are about .3 mile north of that corner — Henderson's map shows the intercept to be more than .4 mile. The difference isn't important — the evidence is long gone and chances are the trail went both ways at various times.

Continue the balance of that mile and turn west, or left. Paul Henderson's map shows the trail exactly one mile ahead, passing through the intersection. The county signs show the trail about .1 mile east of there, but close enough. Turn to the right in the intersection and head north again. The trail coursed due northwest, through the intersection where the turn was just made. Proceed north to the next road and turn west.

Go exactly one mile west. Both Henderson and the county signs agree that the old trail crossed right through the intersection, still headed northwest. Turn right again, or north. Go a full mile and turn left, or west. Proceed a mile in that direction and turn south. Then turn left into the West Rock Creek Pony Express Station site.

The Nebraska Game and Parks Commission has done a splendid job of restoring the Rock Creek Station. Sophisticated archaeological techniques were utilized to rebuild the structures, and a fine new visitor center is now open to the public. Markers direct visitors to deep swales of the trail.

Return to the main road, turn right, proceed to the corner and turn left. About 20 yards ahead is a Pony Express marker. That route crossed the road there, headed northwest, but Henderson's maps reveal that the route of the Oregon Trail of an earlier period held off until the intersection .1 mile ahead before it crossed. The two routes merged in the next section to the northwest.

Do not turn at the next corner. Proceed ahead another mile. Turn to the right, or north, at that intersection. The intercept is about .6 mile to the north, although the signs show it to be somewhat further ahead. Again, there is no visible evidence. Proceed to the next mile marker and turn left, or west.

At .9 mile to the west is another intercept, as the trail cuts across the cultivated fields headed northwest. Proceed the remaining .1 mile, turn right, and there is another pair of signs .2 mile to the north. Proceed the balance of that mile and turn left.

Follow the gravel road for one more mile to the District 39 School, no longer in use. The Oregon Trail crossed the road running to the east side of that school about .1 mile south, then passed about where the building is today. Continue west, past the school, for another mile, and then turn right, or north. The trail crossed just a mile away, again headed northwest, and again, right through the intersection. Here the signs are in variance with Henderson, for they show an intercept about .3 mile south of there. At the intersection turn left, or west. About .3 mile ahead is U.S. Highway 136. Cross over the tempting highway and continue on the gravel for another 1.1 miles. The Oregon Trail crossed the highway just about where the road does, and there is a marker to that effect in a rest area on the left, just before crossing the highway.

About 1.1 miles west of Highway 136, or abreast of the Fairbury water tower, turn to the right, or north. Don't go .1 mile too far to Highway 15. The road proceeds north for one mile to cross a section line road, and .2 mile further (according to Henderson and the county signs), the trail crossed, headed almost due west. There is a granite marker on the left, near the intercept. Continue ahead for another .8 mile to the next intersection. About .2 mile before reaching that intersection there is another pair of county markers. These indicate the route of the Virginia Cutoff, used by the Pony Express riders in 1860. Continue north to the corner and turn left, or west. This road leads only a half mile before it ends in a T. Turn right on the blacktop at the stop sign and go one mile to the north. Only .1 mile before reaching that intersection is another intercept of the Virginia Cutoff. The Oregon Trail itself has been paralleling the traveler nearly a mile to the south. Turn now to the left to meet it.

Just a few yards ahead is another intercept of the Virginia Cutoff. Continue a mile ahead. The Oregon Trail intercept is just .1 mile east of that intersection. Continue through the intersection .4 mile more to a farm gate in the fence to the right. You are now going to visit the grave of George Winslow, who died June 8, 1849. Turn right and don't forget to close the gate.

Original 1849 marker on grave of George Winslow has been mounted in granite obelisk in Jefferson Co., Neb., where trail buffs do everything right.

The granite obelisk is atop the gentle hill in the field. Winslow's sons found the original marker, imbedded it in the newer stone monument. The trail headed west to the grave, and from there headed southwest down toward the road, but turning again to the west before it hit the road.

In the west face of the monument is a bronze tablet in which is cast: "IN MEMORY OF GEORGE WINSLOW who died on this great highway June 8, 1849 and was buried here by his comrades, of the Boston and Newton Joint Stock Association. This tablet is affectionately placed by his sons, George Edward and Orrin Henry Winslow."

The marker also has this inscription put into the stone itself:

"Oregon Trail Marked By The State of Nebraska and the Sons of George Winslow, 1912."

The original marker, of extremely hard stone, evidently was cut right on the spot, probably on the date of

Winslow's death, and has since been imbedded into the monument. It reads "George Winslow. Newton, Ms. AE 25."

Retrace the way out of the field. (The gate Charlie — don't forget the gate.) Turn left .4 mile, then left again onto the gravel road to head north. Intercept that Virginia Cutoff route again about .8 mile ahead, go another .2 mile to the corner, turn left, or west, and proceed for three more miles. There will be another Virginia Cutoff intercept a few yards ahead. At the end of the second mile it is about ready to begin a substantial turn to the northwest, and after proceeding .6 of the third mile a final Virginia Cutoff intercept is made.

Proceed less than .2 mile to a marker denoting the site of the Little Sandy Pony Express station. This also is an intercept of the Oregon Trail. Go ahead another .1 mile or so to the next intersection. A marker denoting an Oregon Trail crossing is off to the right a few yards. Don't turn here. Continue on ahead another two miles. At the end of the first mile, the trail has looped to the north about .8 mile. At the end of the second mile it is still .8 mile to the north, so turn right, or north, to intercept it. There is a Pony Express marker at this point.

Continue the balance of that mile and turn left, or west, onto the shaft of a T intersection. Proceed west for three miles. The trail angles away from the roadway toward the southwest, about .2 mile away at the start of that stretch to one mile away at the end of it. Turn left, or south, and continue .9 mile. There is another intersection. On the left is the District 10 school, now being operated as a museum. Turn to the right at the intersection; there is a marker denoting an intercept, but Henderson's maps show the trail about 100 yards on the north side of the road, headed almost due west, so, perhaps, there shouldn't be an intercept at all. Proceed a half mile west, then jog 200 or 300 yards to the left. Another half mile is the Thayer Co. line.

Just a few yards across the county line the road makes a left jog of another 200 to 300 yards. Some .7 mile after the jog is over, the road makes a hard right turn onto a blacktop road. There is a stop sign there. Go another .7 mile to an intersection, with a Catholic cemetery on the far side of the road. The trail crossed the road on the north side of the cemetery, headed west. Turn left at the cemetery and proceed west for .7 mile. The trail will come south to touch the road, then veer away so that at the end of the first mile it will be nearly 100 yards to the north. Continue one more mile. At that second intersection the trail is about 300 yards to the right. There is a high tension transmission line paralleling the route over there also, and the trail was about half way from the road to the line. Turn left, or south, for one mile and then turn right, or west, again. Continue seven miles dead ahead before hitting the trail again. It takes that long to move to the south to effect an intercept; cutting right through the intersection, headed west-southwest.

Continue ahead for 4.5 miles — the trail at the end of that first mile, where U.S. Highway 81 is crossed, is about .3 mile to the south, even though there is a marker at this corner. At the end of the second mile it is .5 mile to the left, but turning to come up to meet the road. Three miles away it is a quarter-mile to the south, and at four miles just 200 yards into the field on the left. A half-mile ahead the trail passes in front of an old schoolhouse, headed northwest, exactly where the road turns to the right.

Both the traveler and the trail are now avoiding the banks of the Little Blue, which at that turn is only 300 yards to the left. Proceed north only .2 mile and turn back west, or left, again, and go a half mile to a T in the road. The trail came up just to the left of the T. Turn right, or north, for about .2 mile and cross a T — turn left, or west, down the shaft of the T and proceed one mile. The trail is nearly paralleling the road, about .3 mile to the left.

Turn left at the end of that mile, or south, where the intercept is just halfway from the last turn to where the road turns again — this time to the right, or west. The distance on that leg is about .2 mile.

Now the trail parallels the roadway, ranging from 50 to 100 yards off to the right. Proceed west one mile. There is a rutted dirt roadway going over the hill ahead. Don't take it — turn right instead and 50 yards ahead is another intercept. The trail will climb up that hill and intercept the little dirt road a half mile ahead, where it (the road) peters out. Proceed north .7 mile and make a left turn. Go west for three miles. At the end of the first mile the trail is about .8 mile to the left, but turning to meet the road. At the second mile it is a quarter-mile away, and just .4 mile into the third mile it crosses the roadway, headed northwest again.

Proceed west the balance of that mile. Turn right, or north. There will be another T in the road .5 mile ahead, but don't cross it — turn down the shaft and head west for three more miles. Here the trail meets the road and comes beneath it. It will stay beneath the road or just off to the right 20 yards or so for the full three-mile distance. At the end of that stretch the road jogs to the left, but of course the trail had no reason to do so. It moved gently to the left, but by the time that 100-yard jog to the left is completed the trail will be just .5 mile ahead, to the west.

At the end of the first mile after the jog there is an intersection; the trail is a few yards to the left, and the traveler now is in Nuckolls County. When reaching the county line the trail will be beneath the road again. Proceed ahead for another mile to a T intersection and turn left, or south. At that point Henderson shows the trail slanting away to the northwest, and this would not be logically inconsistant. However, it is suspected that a later variant continued just west-southwest from that corner.

Go to the banks of the Little Blue, about a half mile south, where the road turns right, or west. Proceed just one mile and arrive at a T intersection. Turn right there, completing a shallow U, and go ahead about .3 mile. There is an Oregon Trail marker on the right, and just past that marker turn left onto a winding road, on the right bank of the Little Blue. This is where that variant might have come; in fact it could be directly beneath the roadway for the next mile. Henderson's trail would be nearly a mile north at this point.

Just .9 mile from the last turn is a marked site of an Indian massacre, dated 1864 — added evidence that this is a later trail. Just .4 mile from the marker make a half-right turn, arrive at a stop sign, and cross a blacktop road. Do not turn onto the road. Continue across into the

town of Oak, about a half mile ahead. Now the two variants
are one, just a few yards to the right. In fact the trail would
seem to go right through Oak's delightful little city park.
Continue ahead almost to the railroad tracks and turn to
the right, or north. Cross the trail just .2 mile ahead.

Then the road turns to the left to cross the tracks. It
continues west for a half mile past those tracks; then it
turns to the right by the Little Blue, where the road and the
Oregon Trail coincide once more. The trail, however, will
continue due northwest, past "The Narrows," where the
space between the river bank and the bluff leaves only
enough room for a single wagon. The traveler is unable to
see this; proceed 1.5 miles north. Turn to the left, or west,
and start on an eight-step, left-right sequence of turns,
each a mile from the last, as the road and the trail proceed
in a northwesterly direction.

Continue west for the first mile to a T intersection, and
turn right. The trail is a quarter-mile to the southwest.
Then a mile to the north and turn left for another mile.
Just 50 yards before that intersection is an intercept, the
trail headed due north at this point, and it maintains that
distance for .6 mile. Turn right to parallel it. At .6 mile
the trail suddenly resumes the northwest direction and
crosses the roadway. Continue to the next corner and turn
left, or west, to intercept the trail just .3 mile ahead.

Continue the balance of that mile and turn right, or
north, and .9 mile ahead is another intercept. The trail
still maintains a northwest course. Proceed to the corner
and turn left, or west. There is another intercept just past
the bridge, less than .2 mile away. Continue the balance of
the mile and turn right, or north. Another .7 mile away is
another intercept. Continue to the corner and turn left,
proceeding for two miles. At .8 of the first mile there is
another intercept. Continue another 1.2 miles and turn
right, or north.

Note that this land is extremely flat, rather a plateau
between the rugged lands of northern Kansas and the
dunes along the Platte River. It was described by Joseph
Ware as being a well-timbered valley, with plenty of
water and grass. There was no reason for a constricted
traffic flow — Hulbert feels that the trail in Nuckolls Coun-

ty would range from 165 to 660 feet in width, although he doesn't say how he arrived at his figures.

From the turn proceed north .8 mile to another intercept, and at .2 mile further turn left. A half-mile west the trail crosses the road again, headed from left to right. At the first mile corner the old road is off to the right a tenth of a mile, but don't turn. Continue to the next mile corner and turn right, onto Nebraska Highway 4-14. (A detour on good highways must be made because the nearest roadways now are closed.)

The Little Blue, in this country at least, is merely a smaller version of the Big Blue; high banks, water of only medium cloudiness, and a fairly sprightly current.

Continue north and east 2.7 miles, toward Clay Center, and turn left at that point, onto Nebraska Highway S-18C, the road which leads to DeWeese. Meanwhile, the trail has continued to follow the valley of the Little Blue, on a north-westerly course. Four miles ahead the trail has closed toward the highway, and at that point is only 100 yards to the south. Continue ahead another .2 mile, where the blacktop turns south. Continue across the turn, still proceeding west, but now on a gravel road.

Another .2 mile ahead and the road will make a gentle half-right curve. In the middle of that curve the trail crosses the road, which now is only a few yards to the north of the Little Blue.

Go northwest another .3 mile and turn half right at the T, or north. An intercept is just .2 mile ahead but again — no trace. Continue for about 1.6 miles and turn to the left, or west. After proceeding for a mile turn right, or north, for a half mile, and then turn west again. The trail is off to the left, paralleling the Little Blue and very close to it, and again it is coming up to meet the road.

The traveler now is starting a three-mile westerly stretch. At the end of the second mile the trail is off to the left about .6 mile, headed northwest. It will make an intercept at .6 mile ahead.

Continue to the next mile marker, with the trail off to the right about a tenth of a mile, passing through a fine set of farm buildings. Turn north, or right, for about .1 mile and there is a trail marker on the right, at the intercept. Go ahead for another .2 mile and turn left, or west, on another gravel road. The trail is just a few yards to the left. A tenth of a mile ahead, at the bridge over Pawnee Creek, is where the emigrants also made their ford. There the trail moves over to the right side of the little road.

At the first opportunity turn to the right onto a gravel road, and jog only a few yards; then back to the northwest again. There is a marker on the left as that jog is made. About .2 mile further the road turns from northwest to due north, and just .1 mile further is another intercept. About .8 mile ahead is an intersection — turn left, or west. Just .8 mile ahead is another intercept, with the trail heading diagonally through that section of land. Don't turn at the next mile road. The trail is about .2 mile north of there and quickly turning to the west. Continue ahead another mile and at the T intersection turn right, or north, on the Adams Co. line.

Proceed north for a half mile to another intercept; then the balance of that mile to Nebraska Highway 74, a paved highway. There, at the stop sign, turn left, or west. Exactly two miles ahead the Oregon Trail passes diagonally through the intersection, headed northwest. Then it curves to the west as the road proceeds through the third mile, paralleling the trail a half mile to the north. Go another half mile and, just after the road crosses the railroad tracks, turn to the right, or north.

A half mile ahead is another intercept, and at the end of the first mile the trail is off to the left a half mile. Continue another mile ahead and the road makes a gently curving jog to the left. Just 3.3 miles from the turn (off Highway 74) turn to the left. That is about a mile north of the completion of the left jog.

All this time the trail has been taking the diagonal, and now the intercept is 2.4 miles ahead. That will be only .2 mile before arriving at the stop sign. There is an Oregon Trail marker on the far side of U.S. Highway 281.

Here the trail finally leaves the Little Blue River — the little stream that had been such a friendly provider for the emigrants. It had seen the emigration through some tough land and now was about to curve away and leave them, just as the Bear River would do so many miles further ahead, on the far side of the Continental Divide.

Cross U.S. 281 for one mile and then turn right, or north. Proceed ahead for about .4 mile and note the houses on both sides of the road. The trail crossed the properties on the north sides of both houses, only a few yards away from each, headed northwest. Off to the west .3 mile the trail forded Thirtytwo Mile Creek. Continue to the next corner and turn left, or west. Now, a half mile away, the traveler may see what the emigrants saw a quarter mile to the south, the ford over the creek. Thirtytwo Mile Creek is far from being the most serious challenge the emigrants faced. The banks are gentle and one wouldn't have to go far even today to find a natural ford.

At the next mile corner, just as the road turns right, or north, the trail nicks the corner, but there is no trace of it as it lines its way across the boundless plains to the northwest. By the time the traveler is a mile north of there it will be nearly a half mile west of the road. At the stop sign turn left, onto a good gravel road and proceed .4 mile west. It is at this point that the trail comes up to within 100 feet of the roadway, turns abruptly west, and parallels it for .3 mile. Then, less than .1 mile from the corner, it slants across the road. At the first mile corner it will be on the north side of the road, about .1 mile away and headed west. As the road continues west in the next mile, the trail is looping away from it toward the northwest. Two miles past the last corner, turn to the right, or north.

About .6 mile ahead the road will make a gradual half left curve, and at that spot the trail comes beneath the road from the southeast. Fifty yards before that turn, stop, and look over the right shoulder. There are some substantial earthen depressions — one of them undoubtedly is the trail, probably both. Cross the west branch of Thirtytwo Mile Creek exactly where the emigrants did.

Continue to the mile corner and turn left at the T intersection. About .3 mile west there is a dirt road leading off to the right of the road. Don't take it. The

Oregon Trail cut through that intersection. Another half mile ahead is a gravel road, and at that point the old trail is a half mile to the right. Proceed west another half mile and turn right, or north, on a good gravel road.

Continue north .8 mile where there is another intercept. Proceed to the mile marker and turn left, or west. About .2 mile ahead there is a dirt road coming out of the cornfield on the left. This is where the old emigrant road crossed the road, headed northwest. Continue another .3 mile and turn right, or north, just past a set of farm buildings on the left. Less than .3 mile ahead is another intercept, another invisible one. Continue to the next mile road and turn left, or west. Another intercept is .6 mile ahead. Turn right, or north, at the next mile road and another intercept will be just .5 mile ahead. Continue ahead for a half mile, and turn left on U.S. Highways 6 and 34. Go one full mile — the trail cut exactly across the intersection there. Then go another .3 mile to a fine historical marker — in a rest area on the north side of the highway. The marker commemorates the Oregon Trail and Pony Express. The trail actually ran behind the snow fence to the rear of the rest area.

Continue another .7 mile and turn right onto a gravel road. (Follow the arrow that shows Prosser to be eight miles away.) There is an intercept about .6 mile ahead. Turn left, or west, at the next corner. A half mile ahead make a final crossing of the west branch of Thirtytwo Mile Creek. The emigration crossed a quarter mile due south of the bridge. At this point it has dwindled to little more than a long mud puddle.

Just .1 mile before the next mile road the trail comes up to meet the roadway. It is beneath it at the section line road and for .2 mile past it. Then it slants away to the right, or northwest. Continue ahead for 3.5 miles from that last section line.

One mile ahead and the trail is off to the right .3 mile. One more mile and it is a half mile to the north. At the third mile it is .6 mile away, and a half mile further ahead turn to the right to a good blacktop road, Nebraska Highway 206, to go up to meet the trail.

About .9 mile north on Highway 206 there is a marker on the left. The trail came through here, crossed the road headed due west, then turned suddenly in that field and moved due north. Continue to the corner and turn left, proceeding only another tenth of a mile, and make another intercept. Go another .4 mile and turn to the right onto a good dirt road. Proceed another .4 mile to another trail crossing — it again is headed northwest.

Continue another .6 mile to the corner and turn left, or west, and a half mile ahead is another intercept — nothing is visible. Proceed a half mile more and turn right, or north. Go north for .3 mile and there the trail cuts across the road headed due west. Once into the field the trail will turn sharply to the right and parallel the roadway the rest of the way to the next mile, only 100 yards (or less) to the left.

At that next corner, turn left, and .1 mile west of there is another intercept — the trail is back to northwestering again. Go west the other .9 mile and turn north for one mile. Cross Nebraska Highway 206 there, and engage a weak, little, dirt road. About .2 mile ahead is an intercept, with no trace. Continue the balance of that mile and turn left, or west.

About .3 miles ahead start looking out into the fields on the right. Soon a lonely little grave will come into view — the last resting place of Susan O. Hail, buried some 50 yards off to the right on one of the sand hills. The lane to the grave is just a half mile from the last corner.

Mrs. Hail, so the story goes, drank from a spring poisoned by Indians on June 2, 1852, and the 34-year-old woman died with shocking suddenness. It is

Lonely grave of Susan Hail, in sand hills just before reaching broad valley of Platte River.

much more probable that she died from polluted water, either from a well too close to a campground or too close to a buffalo wallow. Dysentery or cholera could kill a person in a matter of an hour or two.

The griefstricken bridegroom had no intention of leaving the grave unmarked. It is said that he moved quickly back to St. Joseph after installing a temporary marker, had a fine marble headstone engraved, and moved it back to this point in a wheelbarrow. This may or may not be true. At any rate, Susan Hail's grave has become a landmark on the Oregon Trail. It is ironic that no one knows the location of her husband's grave, or even his first name. The stone over the grave today is not the original.

The trail is to the west of the grave, headed northwest toward the Platte River. Proceed a half mile to the next corner. At this point the trail is about .7 mile north, and turning to parallel the Platte at last.

Bonneville reported hitting the Platte, about 25 miles below the head of Grand Island, on June 2, 1832. He found it to be 2,200 yards from bank to bank — more than a mile wide — and three to six feet deep. Fremont got there on June 26, 1842: ''From the foot of the coast, a distance of two miles across the level bottom brought us to our encampment on the shore of the [Platte] River, about twenty miles below the head of Grand Island.''

Preuss, on the next day, added that there was a tree every few miles, and very little shrubbery for fires. This, of course, is an enormous contrast to today. The cottonwood, once started, is a self-proliferating species.

Rev. Parrish arrived at the Platte on July 7, 1844, but, by far the most moving description was by Francis Parkman. He described in detail the low, undulating sand hills overlooking the Platte, and how he rode 10 hours before entering the hollows and gorges of the gloomy little hills. He gained a summit somewhere and beheld the long-expected view of the valley of the Platte, with its plain as level as a lake. He described how the river divided into a dozen thread-like sluices and how, from every gorge and ravine, there were well-worn buffalo trails down to the water.

Joseph Ware warned that there was a 21-mile stretch without water before hitting the Platte. His guide book indicates it is 90 miles to the forks of the Platte (at North Platte, Nebraska). Ware found little wood, and the buffalo chip came in very handy as a form of fuel.

Rufus Sage hit the river on May 24, 1849, about a mile below Ft. Childs (renamed Ft. Kearny a few months later), and at a point exactly opposite the head of Grand Island. He found the river as muddy as the Missouri, with no wood on the banks but with islands heavily timbered. He found the river so shallow it could be forded at any place. One emigrant said that it flowed bottom side up.

Evidently, since the river plain was several thousand yards wide, the various trains came down to the water when they needed water; otherwise paralleled the river along a wide trail into Ft. Kearny.

At the Kearny County line, a half mile west of the Hail grave, proceed north, or right, for one mile. The trail makes an intercept .7 mile north of the turn. Turn west, or left, and .3 mile ahead is another intercept. The junction of the Independence road with the road out from Nebraska City is exactly .8 mile northwest of that intercept. Continue west to the next mile corner. The trail is .6 mile north of there. Proceed west for three more miles, with the trail laying midway between the road and the Platte River. Continue west another .7 mile, where the trail now cuts across the road, still paralleling the river. Turn left at the next corner; an intercept is .2 mile south. Proceed the balance of that mile and turn right.

Continue west for 3 miles and then turn left. At the end of the first mile the trail is still about .7 mile north; at the second mile it is about .3 mile north. Where a turn to the south becomes necessary at the end of that leg, the trail comes right through that turn, headed only slightly south of due west. Proceed one-half mile south and turn right for two more miles. At the end of the leg, where again a south turn is forced, the trail is still 300 yards north of the corner. Proceed south, but only for about a half mile, and then turn to right again. At the right turn the trail is

.7 mile north. Proceed for 4.7 miles to Ft. Kearny State
Historical Park. (Do not turn .7 mile too soon and enter
the Kearney Recreational Area, also on the right.)

Ft. Kearny to Ash Hollow

On the way into the old fort notice that what once
was described as grassy sand, no longer is. Modern
irrigation methods and powerful fertilizers have changed
the land into a garden. The ground is extraordinarily
productive.

*Cottonwoods planted
by Lt. Daniel Woodbury in
1848 now are giant senti-
nels around Ft. Kearny
parade ground.*

Ft. Kearny is well
worth a visit, more for the
archaeological work than
anything else. One build-
ing has been re-
constructed to simulate
adobe, but out of thin
cement-dirt bricks ve-
neered to concrete block
walls. The Nebraska His-
torical Society has done a
fine job of excavation,
locating the sites of the
original buildings. These
outlines are marked with
concrete slabs. The cottonwoods planted around the
parade ground by Lt.
Daniel Woodbury, founder
of the fort, still are there
— now monstrous in size.

The state also maintains a fine slide show in the little
auditorium, which is free.

Ft. Kearny was established in 1848, the year before
the United States bought Ft. Laramie from the
Chouteaus in St. Louis. It was the only fort established
in the early days of the Oregon Trail solely for the
protection of the emigrants. Jim Bridger's fort was built
for the emigration, but to fleece it, not protect it.

Capt. Stansbury described the fort as a number of
long, low buildings of adobe, with nearly flat roofs.

National Park Service
William H. Jackson, undoubtedly, saw Ft. Kearny many times. His view shows the trail ran between the river and the fort.

There was a large hospital tent, two or three workshops and a stable enclosed by canvas walls, one or two adobe stables with dirt roofs, and tents for the officers and men of two companies of infantry and one of dragoons. This was the 1852 configuration.

The fort was named in honor of Stephen Watts Kearny. An earlier Ft. Kearny stood near Nebraska City prior to the year 1848. That was only a blockhouse, and was removed when the new Ft. Kearny was built. There was very little traffic past the old site, but by the 24th of May in the new fort's first full year, 1849, 1,980 teams passed through.

There is mention of the specific area before the fort was moved there. Preuss, for example, was just west of the site on Sept. 17, 1842, enroute to St. Louis, when he wrote this about his employer: "This afternoon Fremont joined the buffalo hunt once more but again did not bag anything. 'I knocked down one, and that fellow will not get much further,' etc. That does not mean anything, my

dear lieutenant! You have to bring home the tongue —
the tongue!"

On May 11, 1850, the journal of Cornelius W. Smith
carried this entry: "Nine hundred wagons are reported as
having passed [so far] this spring." Two days later
another writer from another train reported 3,200
wagons ahead of his. On May 17 Lorenzo Sawyer said:
"The opposite bank is lined with emigrant trains on
Council Bluff road."

On May 26 of that year a traveler on the north side of
the Platte said, "The road on our side of the river for
miles ahead are lined with teams from our camp & from
the Missouri behind us is one continuous line of
wagons." It was just across the river from the site of Ft.
Kearny, incidentally, that in 1847 the Mormons rid
themselves of the tedious job of counting wheel
revolutions by coming up with an odometer.

Just before the Civil War, 800 wagons and 10,000
oxen passed through the old fort in a single day.

Ft. Kearny also sports a reconstructed stockade. This
was built atop earthworks constructed earlier as a
protection against Indian thieves. The stockade was built
in 1864, just seven years before the fort was abandoned.

Exit from Ft. Kearny to the right, or west. The trail
was somewhere to the north — anywhere to the north —
coursing through what once was nearly barren sand. It
was probably just a few yards to the right of the road.
Continue ahead for seven more miles from the section
line corner, with the trail paralleling on the right.

Two miles west of the fort is the historical marker for
"Dobytown," a cluster of up to 15 adobe buildings built
to house the retinue of camp followers, male and female,
that accompanies any military installation. Within two
years after the fort was abandoned, in 1871, so was
Dobytown. Two more miles and Nebraska Highway 44
will be crossed. Three miles further turn right, or north.

The trail, virtually beneath the road after Highway 44

is crossed, will be .7 mile to the north three miles west of there. There is no trace of that intercept. Proceed .3 mile further to a T in the road and turn left, or west, at the stop sign. The trail is to the left .3 mile away at that turn, and will close toward the road so that a mile to the west, it will touch the intersection.

The trail runs along the road for the next mile. At the Phelps Co. line it veers sharply to the southwest for a quarter mile, then resumes a northwest heading. Proceed to the next section line road and there the trail is just .1 mile south, or left. Do not turn. Continue ahead for a half mile. At that point the trail comes beneath the roadway and will stay beneath it for the next two miles.

Just 3.4 miles into Phelps Co. the old emigrant road leaves the present roadway and angles slightly to the right. At the end of that mile there is a stop sign, and at that point the road is only 100 yards to the right. Just 2.6 miles ahead is a four-point intersection, and the road is still 100 yards north. Two more miles west of there it comes down to meet the road again and travel beneath it.

One mile further the trail knifes off to the right, and one more mile is U.S. Highway 183. The trail is to the right .1 mile.

Continue across 183 (there will be plenty of pavement in Wyoming). A half mile ahead the trail dips down to touch the gravel road, then veers off to the north again. Seven miles west of U.S. 183 turn to the right. The trail has been paralleling the road all this way, ranging from 50 to 800 yards away. Proceed north for a half mile and turn west, or left. It is at that turn that the trail nicks the corner, headed slightly north of due west. It nearly parallels the roadway for the next mile to the west. Then turn right, or north, and .1 mile ahead is another intercept. Continue another .4 mile and turn left, or west, at a T in the road.

Proceed to the next section line road a mile to the west, and .3 mile past this the old trail crosses from left to right. By the time that mile is finished the trail will be right on the high bank of the river. Go another mile west.

A half mile to the right is the mouth of Plum Creek. It flows from the west into the Platte, which at that point is angling to the northwest. Continue another mile

to the cemetery in which are buried the victims of the
Plum Creek Massacre of 1864. There was a stage station
here, and on Aug. 7, 1864, the dozen or so people who
happened to be there wound up without their scalps.
There is a large monument to the murders in the cemetery.

There has been an abundance of wood along the south
bank of the Platte since the shores came into view east
of Ft. Kearny. In the trail days, however, Plum Creek
provided the first wood and water to be had by the emigrants since leaving the old fort.

Here, in 1850, John Wood found no enemy worse
than the dread cholera: "The sick and the dying are on
the right, on the left, in front and in the rear, and in our
midst. We ourselves are nearly all sick; I feel very weak
myself. Death is behind as well as before. Many are
stalking their way through pestilence unmoved, while
others view each step with perfect consternation."

Continue west one more mile and turn right, or north.
One mile ahead the road will be forced by the Platte
to turn left, and where it does it comes over the Oregon
Trail. Nowhere are there more typical views of the Platte,
as are encountered in the next mile. That's where Gosper
County begins.

Pass into Gosper County and the trail will move slightly
off to the left, only a few yards. Continue two miles
ahead. The trail is angling toward the road, and at that
second mile it passes through the intersection, headed
northwest. Continue one more mile and turn to the right,
or north. A half mile ahead on the left is a steam plant.
Just before reaching it there is a bridge over a small
canal, and it is at this canal where the emigrant route
crossed the road. Continue the balance of that mile and
turn left, or west. Ahead .8 mile is another intercept.
Proceed the balance of that mile and continue .6 mile
further and turn right, or north, on a gravel road. The
road now is in Dawson County.

Continue north for .6 mile and the emigrant road
crosses the contemporary road, still headed northwest.
There is a little stub of a dirt road on the right, coming
out of the fields. This could well be a remnant of the
trail. Continue .4 mile more to the T in the road and
turn left. Go west a mile to the blacktop road. The trail

Platte River once was devoid of trees except on islands. Some said it flowed upside down, others termed it a mile wide and a foot deep.

is just .2 mile to the left. Continue across, go .6 mile more, and the trail crosses the road, following the Platte on the same general northwesterly course it will maintain all the way to Casper, Wyoming. Continue west another 1.4 miles to U.S. Highway 283. At that point the trail is a mile to the right. Go one more mile west and turn right, or north. Proceed another mile and turn to the left, or west, on a blacktop road. At that point the trail is about 300 yards to the right.

Continue west for a mile to a T in the road; turn right, or north. Note how the land now is no longer flat — to the south of the Platte a few miles are great hills of sand. But the valley itself — flat as a pond.

Proceed north for .9 mile and the trail will intercept, just a short distance from the point where the road makes a left turn; a tenth of a mile to the west and it will cut across the road again. It will pass to the rear of the group of farm buildings on the right side of the road. Continue west for two miles — the trail will angle sharply away to the right. At the end of that second section (there is no road at the first section) the road makes a right turn. Continue north for exactly 1.8 miles to a white house on the right. Across the road, on the left, and buried in the weeds at the edge of a cornfield, is a grey granite marker. That is the intercept. Continue ahead for .2 mile more and turn left, or west, at a T in the road, and proceed west on Nebraska Highway 3. Ahead .4 mile is a shallow swale used by the cattle, and this could well have been the route of the trail. It is rather muddy at all times due to the high water table in the river bottom. It should be remembered, however, that the trail would have fanned out considerably on land such as this.

Continue ahead for four miles from the last turn; the trail is moving sharply to the northwest now, and at the end of that stretch, just where the pavement ends, turn right, or north, for two miles. When that stretch is completed the road turns left, and at that point the trail nicks the corner, still headed northwest.

Go a mile to the west and turn right, or north. Just .5 mile ahead is another intercept, where the old trail runs through a house on the right side of the road.

Continue the balance of that mile and turn to the left, or west. A half mile ahead on the left are two sets of farm buildings. The Oregon Trail passed behind both, and .8 mile from the last turn it crossed the roadway at a shallow angle, then passed through the house on the corner of the section to the right. Continue another half mile west from the section line road and turn to the right at a T in the road.

Just .6 mile ahead the road takes a half left turn to parallel the Platte, and it is at this point that the trail comes beneath it. Ahead about .3 mile is the road leading to the bridge over the Platte at Cozad. In the center of a grassy spot, seemingly in the middle of the road, is a trail marker. Do not turn into Cozad. Continue northwest. Just one mile from where the trail was gained by the half left turn, leave it with another half left turn. Proceed west the balance of that section — about .6 mile, and then on west two more full miles before turning right, or north.

Go north one mile and make a left turn at the Platte. Here the trail nicks the turn. Continue west for three miles and turn right, or north, at the stop sign. A mile ahead the trail comes within 50 yards of nicking the turn. Make a left at the T and head west again for another mile, then north another mile. This time the trail does hit the corner, where the traveler turns to the west. Go a mile west, then turn right, or north, onto a dirt road with a lot of grass in the crown. About 30 miles an hour would be a safe speed for this road; some bumps come up awfully fast. At the end of the mile, the road is forced into a left turn in a farmstead. There is a long log building off to the east of the turn, next to the farmhouse. This is an original, unmoved Pony Express station; now painted white, with new chinking, and the original coarse landscape has been softened by an abundance of flowers, planted by someone who cares.

Proceed from the farmyard to the west, and at the mid-point of that mile the road takes a 100-yard jog to the right. Proceed the balance of the mile and turn right, or north, where the traveler will be rewarded with Nebraska Highway 47. Turn right, or north, and proceed .4 mile, where there is another intercept. No trace. Continue the balance of that mile and the paving turns to the left. Turn with it. Continue ahead two more miles from the intercept and turn to the right, or north, onto a gravel road. Now the road is riding the Lincoln County line.

To the north about .7 mile, or just past a farmhouse on the left, the trail crossed over the road. Proceed .3 mile and turn left. West of there a half mile, just before reaching a long string of cottonwood trees on the left, is where the trail comes up to meet the road, stays beneath it for .3 mile, then angles away to the right. Continue .2 mile to the next road, then another mile on to the west before turning right again. About .8 mile ahead (north) is another intercept; go the balance of that mile and turn left, and another intercept is .4 mile to the west. Continue the rest of the mile and turn right, where there is another intercept a half mile to the north.

Another half mile and the Platte forces the road into another turn to the west — go .8 mile more and the trail passes through the first of two farm buildings on the right. By the time the next section line road is crossed, just ahead, the trail is off to the right .2 mile. Proceed another mile onto the blacktop and turn right. Just .8 mile to the north is another intercept — go another .2 mile and turn left at a T in the road; this time the intercept is a half mile to the west. Continue ahead for another mile and a half and turn to the right, or north. About a half mile ahead is an irrigation ditch, and just .1 mile past that is where the trail crossed, headed northwest.

There is a T in the road at the end of that section — turn left. West of there .6 mile is another intercept. Continue .4 mile to the blacktop and turn right. North

.2 mile is another intercept. Turn left on the blacktop just short of the full mile; about .9 mile from the last corner.

Proceed two miles west on that blacktop. At that point the trail intercepted from left to right, passing on the far side of a building on the corner. Just 4.5 miles from the last turn a transmission line comes out of the hills on the left, down to touch the roadway. At that point make a half right turn. Proceed another .7 mile and complete the change of heading to the north. A half mile ahead the road turns left, and at that point the trail touches the corner. Proceed west a mile and hit some blacktop — then turn right. Proceed north .5 mile, where the road turns left, or west, as the trail nicks the corner of the intersection. Proceed west .5 mile and turn north, or right.

Just .1 mile ahead is an intercept. Continue for .4 mile more and turn left, or west. Proceed ahead 1.2 miles to a T in the road and turn right, or north. Just a half mile north is the Ft. McPherson Military Cemetery. Turn left, or west, just before reaching the cemetery. The old trail cut south of it and made an intercept about .7 mile to the west. Continue west a half mile past the intercept and turn right on a section line road. About .4 mile north the trail crossed, headed northwest. Continue .1 mile more and turn left onto a blacktop road and proceed west. The trail made an intercept .2 mile ahead.

Continue the balance of that mile and the road makes a half right turn. The turn will be completed at a T in the road a half mile further on. About .7 mile ahead is another intercept, right through the intersection. Turn left, or west.

About 1.3 miles ahead the road will make a gentle turn to the right, then at a T turn the rest of the angle to the right, or north. Follow the blacktop as it turns to the northwest, just .7 mile ahead. If one would go ahead another .1 mile, there is a farmer's gravel road that parallels this one — that is over the trail itself, and continues for about .5 mile, as does the good road. Then turn half left again; there is an Oregon Trail marker on the right, misplaced a few dozen yards to the south.

Just 1.5 miles due west the road makes a right turn, at the base of a huge hill. The Sioux Lookout Monument is atop the hill. Stop, get out of the car and make the climb. The view is well worth the exertion.

Proceed north one mile to a T in the road — turn left,

as the trail cuts squarely through the intersection, still headed northwest. Continue west for 1.9 miles and turn right, or north, still on the blacktop, for one mile. Then turn to the left. At that point the Oregon Trail is .3 mile north, just south of I-80.

Exactly 1.6 miles north, on the north side of Interstate 80, is the fork of the Platte. On July 3, 1842, Fremont made this notation: "As this was to be a point in our homeward journey, I made a *cache* . . . a barrel of pork. It was impossible to conceal such a proceeding from the sharp eyes of our Cheyenne companions, and I therefore told them to go and see what it was they were burying. They would otherwise have not failed to return and destroy our *cache,* in expection of some rich booty; but pork they dislike and never eat."

Fremont was camped in the tip of land between the forks. Some emigrants forded there, but not many. Sage crossed within the boundaries of the present city of North Platte, where he reported the river was a mile wide and a foot deep. Bonneville, however, found it impossible to ford there when he hit the forks on June 11, 1832.

Continue west for 4.8 miles and turn right on U.S. Highway 83. The trail makes an intercept .4 mile ahead, headed due west.

Continue north the balance of that mile and turn left on a blacktop road, headed west. The trail now is to the left .6 mile, but it soon will close to an intercept. At 2.4 miles from the corner there is a trail marker indicating the trail has come to a junction with the road. Then it bounces to the left for about 300 yards, and returns to make a positive intercept at the intersection 4.2 miles west of U.S 83.

Continue ahead 2.5 miles to a little country school, still in use, and in front of it is an Oregon Trail marker. It would seem that this marker actually is about .6 mile south of the trail. Continue the balance of that mile, then one more mile ahead on the gravel and turn right onto a good gravel road. Just .7 mile ahead is another intercept. Continue the balance of that mile and turn left beyond a grove of trees on the left. One mile to the west is another intercept, right through the intersection.

During the second mile west of the last turn the trail is off to the right .2 mile; the third mile, to the right .3 mile. Turn to the right at the fourth mile onto a blacktop road and the trail cuts across the road .7 mile to the north. There is a marker there. Turn left, or west, after going another .3 mile to the corner, and return to gravel again.

The trail is only .3 mile away at the corner, but it will take exactly 1.9 miles to make an intercept. This was the location of the Fremont Springs Home Station of the Pony Express. The trail was at the road in this spot, and will continue beneath it for the next 1.1 miles. There it turns south — the trail continues on, slanting slightly to the northwest.

The trail is moving toward the Platte, to pass O'Fallon's Bluff, the noted landmark of the mountain men. The bluff starts a mile to the west and extends to the vicinity of the northernmost bank of the Sutherland Reservoir. The trail moves northwest to touch I-80 about a mile west of the corner, then slants down toward the reservoir.

Turn left, or south for one mile; then 3.2 miles due west. At that point turn half right to go around the Sutherland Reservoir. Just 1.1 miles from there cross a gravel road. Thirty more yards and there is a stop sign and the black-topped Nebraska Highway 25. The trail dismounts the bluff about .2 mile north of there. Turn right onto Highway 25, proceed to I-80 and turn into the eastbound lane. About 1.5 miles east is a rest area right on the flank of O'Fallon's Bluff. Turn in and experience the wonderful interpretive facility installed by the Nebraska State Highway Department. Then backtrack to the Sutherland Reservoir and turn west about one mile south of I-80.

The trail, meanwhile, drives due west of its intercept of Highway 25 for a mile; comes up against a creek and slants southwest. Proceed 1.2 miles further southwest on Highway 25 and turn half right onto a blacktop road. The black-top lasts only about 10 yards, then the road becomes gravel. Sorry about that.

Travel one mile due west. There the trail is a half mile north. Proceed a second mile west and turn left, or south. The trail is about .2 mile north. Proceed south a mile and turn right, or west, for three miles, and the trail is slanting south, toward the road.

At the end of that three miles there will be a T in the

road — turn right for just .3 mile and then turn left again. At that point the trail is about .3 mile north, or about a third of the way up to the interstate highway.

The Keith County line is one mile west. At that line the trail is approaching the interstate, and, after the traveler drives one mile into the county, the trail is beneath the big highway. It will stay beneath it for two more miles.

Continue into Keith County for 4.5 miles, until stopped by a T in the road at an old cemetery. The interstate, just a few yards to the right, is halfway between the road and the trail. Turn left, or south, for .2 mile, and turn right after crossing the canal. Continue just 1.5 miles ahead. There the road makes a pronounced curve to the left, but disregard this and follow the faint track to the right, to cross a bridge over a canal. Immediately after crossing turn to the left, on the first of two parallel roads.

This is an access road on the right bank of an irrigation canal. The Oregon Trail is either down to the right a few yards or directly under the road, for the next two miles. At that point, turn to the left to cross the canal over another bridge, and proceed just .9 mile south. The trail doesn't do that — it continues on ahead, paralleling I-80 on the south side for the next three miles, then crosses to the north side of it for another 1.5 miles. The traveler will parallel it one mile to the south.

After proceeding that mile south from the canal, turn to the right and go west for three miles, then turn right again. Just .8 mile north the road curves half-left to parallel I-80, and the trail at that point crosses I-80 and turns along its north side for that 1.5 miles mentioned above. Two miles west of that last turn is the road leading to the bridge across I-80. This is to the right about .3 mile. The trail passed beneath this bridge too, headed for the road.

Three miles west of there, as a blacktop road is crossed, the trail is only 150 yards to the right, more or less paralleling the road. There it changes direction, to the northwest.

Continue due west for two more miles and there the trail once more changes its mind and heads southwest. Continue two more miles, or a total of nine miles from the last right turn. Go north just a half mile and turn left — the trail comes beneath the road at this point, headed due west. It will stay beneath the roadway for two miles, then slant away gently to the left. Continue ahead for another 1.3 miles and turn left on Nebraska Highway 61, leading away from Ogallala.

Just .3 mile ahead, after crossing a small bridge, the trail made an intercept, and a total of .5 mile away turn to the right, around a water tower. One mile to the west is another intercept — there is now only a culvert there. Follow the highway as it curves to the left about a half mile ahead. Go another .2 mile south and there is another intercept. Continue south the balance of that mile, then west for three more miles. The pavement ends two miles to the west. The trail will close in toward the road from the right down this stretch, making an intercept 2.5 miles from the last turn. It came through the farm property on the right and moved across the road just past the first of two hills to the west of the property. Turn left at the next corner, a T, and another intercept is just .2 mile away.

The trail crosses through the farmhouse on the right. Continue south the rest of that mile and follow the better gravel road as it banks to the right. Continue west for 4.3 miles. At this point cross the road leading over the I-80 and South Platte River bridges, to the town of Brule. The traveler will return here shortly, after a westerly probe to the Lower California Crossing.

Continue west another .7 mile, then one more full mile. For the past two miles the trail has been off to the right only 50 yards or so. It will cut through the turn as the blacktop heads south. (There the road changes to gravel again.) Proceed a half mile south, then one mile right, or west. There turn to the right, and in .3 mile or less a bridge will lead over I-80. Go atop the bridge, stop, and whip out the old compass.

Take a bearing of 290 degrees from the north end of the bridge. This will point directly to the old Lower California Crossing of the South Platte. One is not able to see a damned thing because of today's abundance of cottonwoods and the scarceness of water in the South Platte. But at one time, only a century ago, the river was a mile wide there, and not a tree in sight.

Now take a bearing of 305 degrees. This is the famed California Hill. The emigrants pulled hard at this one, knowing that ahead was a fine plateau all the way to Ash Hollow and the North Platte River. The scars from that day were so deep and pronounced that they are with us today.

National Park Service
William H. Jackson, a bullwhacker in his trail days, used Upper California Crossing of South Platte River, near Julesburg, but Lower California Crossing must have looked a great deal like it. Lower crossing is west of Brule, Nebr.

The emigration usually reached this point by mid-June. B.C. Clark, however, arrived on May 31, 1849, demonstrating how mule drawn wagons performed against oxen, and how the gold motivation of California was more compelling than the agriculture of Oregon. Clark found the river very wide and formidable looking, but very shallow and most easy to cross.

On May 27, 1852, Lodisa Frizzell saw a signboard there announcing that the ford of the South Platte was safe. She found the river two miles wide.

Francis Parkman reached the crossing at 11 a.m. June 8, 1846. He found the river channel almost level with the plain, a great sand bed but only a half mile wide. He reported the average depth to be 1½ feet. He watched with wonder as the oxen lugged the wagons down the bank, dragging slowly over the sand beds and the thin sheets of water.

Chester Ingersoll found the river to be a half mile

wide also, a year after Parkman's 1846 jaunt. When he arrived however, on June 13, he found a strong current.

Capt. Bonneville jumped the gun a little. After being rejected by the river at the forks he continued just two days upstream — and they must have been easy days — and then crossed. This time he did it with bull boats. Bonneville moved only nine miles to the North Platte, then followed it upstream for two more days before striking Ash Hollow.

Ware counseled his book buyers to incline downstream when entering the river at the Lower California Crossing — he didn't say why. Ware counted 22 miles over the high plateau before the descent into Ash Hollow was started.

Joel Palmer reached the crossing June 11, 1845. Palmer didn't, but a lot of other emigrants joked about the river being a mile wide and a foot deep, as they approached the crossing. When they finally got there they found it was no joke at all — that it was literally true.

The Lower California Crossing is some 440 miles from Independence, 35 miles from the forks of the Platte at the present city of North Platte, and 35 miles east of the Upper California Crossing, near Julesburg, Colorado. The upper crossing route joins the North Platte at Courthouse Rock. The lower route, which is the earlier one, hit the river at Ash Hollow.

Return to the bridge across the highway and river just south of Brule, and proceed 1.1 miles to U.S. Highway 30 in Brule. Turn left on 30 and proceed west for 3.8 miles, to a section line road. Ahead a half mile is an Oregon Trail marker, at the foot of California Hill. It cites the bearing of the California Crossing, which meshes with the data given above.

The emigration headed up the hill, their wagon wheels still tight from the swelling induced by the waters of the South Platte. They moved to the northwest, onto the broad, level plateau stretching between, and high above, the forks of the Platte.

A half mile west of the monument is an extremely poor dirt road. Proceed up the hill to the north exactly .7

mile and stop next to what would appear to be the high point of ground in the section of land to the left. Walk due west to the crest of the hill and look down to the west. There is a magnificent gouge of the Oregon Trail, etched deeply into the land. The ruts may be followed most of the way out of that section of land, and will include some in a sandstone formation.

Return to the car and continue to the corner, where a left turn is forced. Proceed for .7 mile, where the trail crosses out of the section, just to the west of a farmhouse. Continue the balance of that mile, plus two more miles, as the trail angles along a northwesterly course across the rolling ground. Turn north and proceed for three miles, where the trail makes a perfect intercept through the intersection and the farm buildings off to the right. There are more depressions in the cultivated ground northwest of this corner for more than a mile to the opposite intersection. Go one more mile and turn left. The intercept is just 100 yards short of another mile. Go on to the corner, which is the Deuel County line, and continue one more mile.

Charles Preuss, leading part of Fremont's detachment while he made a probe to visit the St. Vrain emplacement in Colorado, crossed the highland between the forks in only six hours — there were no wagons to hold him back.

Now the waters of the South Platte left the wagon wheels and the dry air took its toll. Tires rolled off, dry axles shrieked. Spokes pulled out of the hubs and brittle wagon tongues snapped.

There was little wood now — there would be some at Ash Hollow but no more for weeks after that. The emigration had still another reason to bless the American bison. Fuel from here on, for the most part, would be the *bois de vache* used by the mountain man.

Children wandered out into the sand hills — by now they had learned to laugh and mock the cry of the coyote. But when the eerie sound of the wailing wolf hit their ears they hightailed it for the corral.

Proceed west one more mile, into Deuel County, and turn right. Another intercept is 1.7 miles north. Continue the remainder of that mile and turn left. An intercept is just .3 mile to the west. Continue another .7 mile and turn right. Then 1.3 mile north is another intercept, where the trail came angling toward the road in a shallow angle from right to left. Proceed the balance of that mile, to the Garden County line.

Continue north into Garden County for one mile — the trail is off to the left from .2 to .5 mile. Turn left, or west, at the end of that mile and proceed a half mile. The Oregon Trail at this point is synonymous with a dirt farm road, just east of a steel grain storage bin. The trail is headed a little to the west of true north.

Retrace the half mile and turn to the left, or north. Ahead just .1 mile is U.S. Highway 26. Turn left and proceed ahead (northwest) for a couple of miles; the trail will be off to the left about .7 mile during that stretch. On the left side of the road is a historical sign marking the location of Windlass Hill.

Ash Hollow to Wyoming Border

Turn in, up to the loop drive, and park. The traveler is going to take a little walk.

Look straight up the hill, past the windmill. There is a faint set of ruts on the left, leading down from a stone monument atop the hill which is barely visible. To the right is an angry wash, coursing down this steep grade. This is the Oregon Trail. Wagon wheels cut into the turf, pulverized it, and the rains took it from there. The jagged scar is getting deeper.

Walk up the hill to the summit. Atop the hill the trail turns sharply to the left, and one may follow the ruts as far as he pleases. The swale ranges to two feet deep in places; and elsewhere there is only a faint trace of the wagon wheels. Return to the crest of Windlass Hill. Now it may be seen as the emigrants saw it — from the top. From the crest of the hill the level plain seems unbroken as far as the eye can see. The hills form a smooth line from left to right. Suddenly there is no foreground — the plain has given way. The horizon is still there but there is nothing between the observer and it but thin air. And one hell of a hill.

About 300 yards below is Ash Hollow — a level plain some six miles long, reaching all the way to the North Platte. Below is a delightful grove of cedars, and if the emigrant read the guide books he would know the best water on the Oregon Trail was only an hour or two away.

One Englishman wrote in 1849 that the descent was so breathtaking that no one spoke for two miles. That had to be an exaggeration — the hazardous part of the hill is less than a half mile long. Riders led their horses. Wheels were locked and chained, front wheel to back wheel. Two mules were crushed when one wagon escaped even those bonds.

The descent was described by one writer as breaking the monotony; also the legs of the horses, mules and oxen, and the arms of the teamsters. The ravines were filled with wagon wrecks. Wagon bows were smashed and no willow to replace them.

Much has been written about the "windlass" activity on Windlass Hill, but Paul Henderson is strongly skeptical of the use of long ropes here. "It is perhaps 300 yards from the brow of the hill to the level ground below. A manila rope strong enough to hold one of those wagons would have had to be an inch thick. It is inconceivable that a wagon would haul a bulk like this when space in the box was at such a premium. Nor do I think that several 100-foot ropes from several wagons were spliced together.

"In some cases pines would be cut, tied behind the wagons, and dragged down the hill top first. This was an effective brake. When diarists speak of lowering the wagons with ropes they meant relatively short lines — picket ropes, etc. They would attach as many ropes as they had people and let the wagons go, with the people sliding their feet and other parts on the ground to provide as much braking power as possible.

"I recall reading somewhere about a lady who was going down this way when she was confronted with a cactus, but that's another story."

B. C. Clark leaves this quote from 1849: "The road was steeper than any we have ever yet encountered. The scenery was really magnificent — the green hills for miles around presenting a picture varied in hight & shade rarely exceeded in beauty."

In making his descent, Clark reported that one wagon tongue broke and one mule broke a leg. He found the grass in the hollows to be sparse — not because of any

Deep, angry scar that once was Oregon Trail is at left in this view down precipitous Windlass Hill. Erosion cut the gash, once wagon wheels had erased ground cover. Area from base of hill to North Platte River is called Ash Hollow.

aridity but because of the tremendous emigrant and '49er traffic. They had to move until 10 p.m. to find a campground with grass.

This was accented by Capt. Howard Stansbury, who came west in the same year. He reached Ash Hollow July 3: "The traces of the great tide of emigration that had preceeded us were plainly visible in remains of camp-fires, in blazed trees covered with innumerable names carved and written on them; but more than all, in the total absense of all herbage. It was only by driving our animals to a ravine some distance from the camp, that a sufficiency for their subsistance could be obtained."

Joel Palmer, on June 14, 1845, evidently found the hill a little too much, for he recommended in his book that future travelers keep to the bluffs for 16 or 17 miles, to avoid the hill. On June 17 he wrote, "A quarter of a mile from the river is a fine spring and around it wood and grass in abundance."

Francis Parkman, unencumbered by wagons, took

one look at Windlass Hill and kept right on going, skirting
the hollow to the west.

Rufus Sage had no such luck but he found the weather
more disturbing than the grade. On June 5, 1849, he
wrote: "It had been very warm the first part of the day
when we struck ash hollow the wind has raised and blewe
very strong the sand blew in every direction."

There are two incidents that happened at Ash Hollow
that ought to be remembered now. Remember Old Ignace, the persistant Nez Perce who came to St. Louis in
search of the "White Man's Book of Heaven"? On his
return from the second St. Louis trip, in 1837, Ignace,
another Nez Perce and three Flathead companions were
ambushed and killed here by a band of Brule Sioux.

A few months earlier the companion (and noble post-
mortem friend) of Dr. Marcus Whitman, William Gray,
was escorting a band of a half dozen of his now-civilized
Indians back East, probably to put them on exhibit to
hustle some more loot for his failing missionary activity.
They came upon the Brule Sioux, possibly the same scalp-
hungry band. They announced through a white companion, a trader, that they wanted no white blood but they
were, as a matter of fact, somewhat behind quota on Flathead scalps. While Gray and the trader were talking it
over, according to Gray, the Sioux advanced on the praying Flatheads and solved their dandruff problems once and
for all. Gray's self-righteous diary notwithstanding,
the experienced men of the West knew damned well what
had happened. DeVoto called it the way it was — Gray
had traded Indian lives, the lives of his friends, converts
and parishioners, to save his own skin.

Contrary to popular belief, Ash Hollow is more than the
dish set below the hill. It is a long plain stretching all the
way from Windlass Hill to the North Platte River. The pull
down the hill is directed toward the east, paralleling the
river.

Before leaving that area take a loving look at the
handsome little sod house in the middle of the plain
below the hill. This is as typical as one will every find of
the soddies that once covered the whole of western

Nebraska. It is unoccupied. Old? It dates all the way back to 1968.

Return to Highway 26 and turn left, or north. Within a few yards is the bridge over Ash Hollow Creek. Water from here would sustain the caravans until they hit the spring.

Nearly 2.5 miles north is the old Ash Hollow Cemetery, originated by the grave of Rachel Pattison, and still in use today. Turn left into the cemetery. The Pattison grave is to the right of the far entrance, a stone obelisk with the original marker preserved behind the glass, recessed into the monument itself.

Gravestone of 18-year-old Rachel Pattison now is preserved beneath glass in a stone obelisk. Grave is first in Ash Hollow Cemetery, still in use.

Her stone, badly weathered but still readable, gives her name, her age (18) and June 18, 1849, the date of her death, probably from cholera. The spring mentioned in so many diaries is a half mile south of the grave, in a grove of trees now used as a campground.

Just past the cemetery, and just before the bridge over the North Platte, there is a gravel road turning west around the bluff. The Oregon Trail bisects the angle formed by that gravel road and U.S. 26. It skirts along the south bank of the North Platte to Oshkosh, but the roads would be a little destructive to the family automobile, so cross over the river, following the highway as it turns through Lewellen and parallels the North Platte along its north bank. The Oregon Trail will be on the left, ranging from one to three miles away as the traveler proceeds into Oshkosh.

Nebraska Highway 27 intersects U.S. 26 on the east side of Oshkosh International Airport — turn south there and proceed just .2 mile past the bridge over the North Platte, and turn right. Go just a half mile and the Oregon Trail will come beneath the road and stay beneath it for the next eight miles.

There are times when a semblance of a trail may be seen just to the right of the roadway, but generally the old Oregon Trail just was widened to make the present gravel road, which is a fine one. Suddenly, the country turns from irrigated lands under heavy cultivation to grazing land. Pastures stretch as far as the horizon.

Eight and one half miles from the entry on this road is a gentle left turn, forced by the North Platte, and at that point the trail continues on to the northwest while the gravel road follows a due-west section line. The trail stays generally to the right side of the road, but usually less than a half mile away. At 9.8 miles from the entry on the road there is a right turn past some farmhouses on the left, and .3 mile ahead is an intercept, the trail running from right to left across the gravel road. Just 3.6 miles past those farmhouses the trail comes back to the gravel road from the left, at a point a short distance past Rush Creek, or about .2 mile past a large cottonwood tree on the right. It will parallel the road 100 yards away for the next three miles, then cross to the left and parallel to the left a half mile away for the rest of the distance, to a small cemetery on the right.

Just past the cemetery there is a T in the road; turn right for .2 mile. There will be a three-way intersection there — turn to the left onto a blacktop road, then .1 mile further, to the right again on a gravel road, continuing to parallel the North Platte River. Less than a half mile ahead will be the Morrill County line.

Some 2.4 miles from the little cemetery, or about 1.5 miles into Morrill County, the Oregon Trail is quite visible some 20 yards to the left of the roadway. It will cross the road shortly, and 2.2 miles west of the county line it will come beneath the road, headed northwest. It will stay with the road for .7 mile, until the road turns to the right. At 4.7 miles into the county it crosses again as the road heads due west. Then the road enters into a series of twists and turns, emerging onto a straight due west course at a little cemetery on a hill to the right. At that point the odometer should indicate 8.4 miles since the last cemetery, back in Garden County, or 7.5 miles west of the Morrill County line.

Proceed one mile west from the cemetery, then turn

north. Just .8 mile ahead is an intercept, the trail coming from right to left. There is no trace of it there. Continue ahead another .7 mile and turn left. A mile and a half ahead there is a line of trees on the left side of the road. The Oregon Trail came to the site of the gravel road on the east end of those trees and stayed beneath the roadway for the next two miles.

Note that this is a most constricted passageway. The North Platte is immediately on the right, and immediately on the left is a line of hills. Shortly the hills will move out to the left, and the old trail went with them. But it stayed on the flat, and in this area there is cultivation so there goes the old trace. The roadway will end in a T 7.8 miles northwest of the cemetery. Turn to the right for only a few yards on a blacktop road, then turn to the left, just before the bridge over the North Platte to Broadwater, on Highway 92. The trail is now a half mile to the left, paralleling the roadway. Five miles northwest is an intercept of the trail. Proceed just one more mile and stop. About .3 mile out in the land to the north is the solitary headstone of Amanda Lamin, with the ruts of the Oregon Trail a few more yards north.

About .7 mile ahead 92 joins U.S. 385, northwest-bound, and two miles further ahead there is a grove of trees on the right.

The trail went through there, although there certainly were no trees there in the trail days. It is from about there that the emigrants caught their first good view of a landmark that they had been approaching for the past two days — Courthouse and Jail rocks. Look to the left of the roadway, on a bearing of about 250 degrees. The tiny shapes are six miles away.

About a mile ahead the trail comes beneath U.S. 385 and stays beneath it, or perhaps a few yards to the left, until about two miles east of Bridgeport, when it cuts due west, to pass through the fairgrounds. Continue on into Bridgeport and turn hard left, or due south, onto Nebraska Highway 88. Just 1.4 miles south of the corner is the intercept, right at the entrance to the fairgrounds. Continue south for a total of five miles from the corner and turn right, immediately past the two famous rocks. This gravel road will lead to a point just southeast of the rocks. Then turn right again and proceed to the base of

Biggest thrill of trail to date was emigrants' first view of Courthouse (right) and Jail Rocks, south of Bridgeport, Nebr.

the formations.

Note that the traveler has to leave the trail some four miles to do all this, and there were very few emigrants who didn't do the very same thing. After moving some 500 miles from Independence, another four miles was nothing, particularly when it could be negotiated either on horseback or afoot, without wagons. The trains arranged to make camp in the vicinity of the river — the last hours before dark invariably saw a swarm of 19th century tourists climbing the wondrous walls of the ancient formation.

Courthouse Rock, allegedly, was named by emigrants who fancied it resembled the courthouse in St. Louis, now a part of the Jefferson National Expansion Memorial on the downtown riverfront. Those familiar with that building might question the similarity, but it should be remembered that the courthouse known by the emigrants hadn't as yet been outfitted with its present tall, Italianate dome. In fact, the name came because the rock looked like a courthouse — any courthouse. The St. Louis building wasn't even started until 1845, and the formation was being called Courthouse Rock before that.

Sizes estimated by the emigrants ran the gamut, but the main rock is about 400 feet higher than the North Platte. They form the eastern terminus of the Wildcat Hills, which follow the trail all the way through Scotts Bluff. The lower parts are largely Brule clay, while topside are anchoring layers of Gering sandstone, alternating with the clay.

Samuel Parker, traveling with Dr. Marcus Whitman, left a vivid description of the formation when he passed in 1835: "It has . . . the appearance of an old enormous building, somewhat dilapidated; but still you see the standing walls, the roof, the turrets, embrasures, the dome, and almost the very windows; and the large guardhouses, standing some rods in front of the main building."

It is a rare diary that has no mention of the Courthouse, and almost all of them are glowing. The rock had a magnetic attraction, but few were the travelers who could judge its distance. Since it stood alone on the horizon, since the air was (and still is) perfectly clear and clean, it invariably looked considerably nearer than the four miles from the trail that it is. Some traveled for considerable periods of time in an attempt to visit the formation, only to give up because they erred so far on its distance from their camp.

The Courthouse probably had as many names carved into its soft stone as did Independence Rock or Register Cliff, but the chalk-like rock was entirely too soft to sustain the images more than a few years. There are only a few names left today, above the south walkway, although one emigrant wrote that there was no room left on the entire rock for him to carve his own name — so he didn't.

Visitors to the rocks today are urged to be alert to the danger of rattlesnakes. They have as much fear of man as man does of them, but, if they are cornered, they will strike back.

A view from the top to true north will show Bridgeport nearly five miles away, and the main trail is about a mile nearer the rock. Facing northeast, the trail from the Upper California Crossing at Julesburg passed from right to left about a half mile northeast of the rocks and would blend with the earlier trail about seven miles northwest of Bridgeport.

Courthouse and Jail rocks are Bridgeport's second most important attraction. The foremost, to serious trail people, is the monument to Paul Henderson.

Proceed back to Bridgeport and head west on U.S. Highway 26.

Just 2.5 miles west of Bridgeport there is a cemetery on the left. Right in front of that cemetery is a marker in memory of Paul Henderson, who is buried there: ". . . honored historian and mapmaker of the Oregon-California Trail which passed this way. With his wife, Helen, he explored and recorded trail remains and shared his knowledge with a legion of

The Oregon Trail's most familiar sight, Chimney Rock, as seen from the flats to the southeast.

trail followers."

In another .2 mile a gravel road slants off to the right — this is the old Oregon Trail. It may be traveled with a family car for about 1.3 miles. Return to the highway and continue west. The trail will be off to the right all the way to Chimney Rock, at distances varying from just a few yards to almost a mile.

About 14 miles west of Bridgeport there is a concrete divider in the middle of the highway, and about .1 mile past the point where the median ends there is a gravel road crossing the highway. Turn left on that gravel road.

There is an old school on the corner about .3 mile ahead.
Proceed on south one more mile, or a short distance past
Chimney Rock. Then turn right and continue west to
the loop at the end of the road, a half mile away.

From there it is about a 10-minute hike to the base of
the great rock, and the closer one gets the more
awe-inspiring it becomes.

Cross a fence and follow a foot trail across grazing
lands, perhaps, a quarter of a mile to the base of the
cone. The area isn't exactly infested with rattlers, but be
on guard — they are around. A number of deep, angry
defiles separate the parking lot from the cone, plus a few
fences. Scout the land and take the easiest of these trails
down through the cuts. By all means, do not give up.
This experience is a must for anyone trying to empathize
with the emigrants. At the base of the cone, on the
south side, is a marker, and this is as good a place as any
to begin the ascent. The cone is about as steep as the
roof of an average house. Take plenty of time — the fat
and 40s will make it about 10 minutes after the
teenagers. The base of the sandstone shaft is at the
summit of the cone, and there is no way to climb this —
the Brule clay is entirely too soft to support the weight
of a man.

That was the case with the emigrants too, and there is
no known instance of an emigrant reaching the top of
the spire, or even coming close. There is an Indian legend
which indicates a young brave made it, only to fall from
the spire to his death.

The clay is interlaid with volcanic ash and Arickaree
sandstone. Emigrants, seeing only the clay, predicted
that the column would be totally disintegrated within a
few years, but they didn't know of those reinforcing
rods holding it together. It is wearing to be sure, but
there is a lot left and chances are there will be some of
Chimney Rock standing many generations from now.

The first record of the name was in the journal of a
trapper, Joshua Pilcher, in 1827. Capt. Bonneville wrote
this in 1832: "At this place was a singular phenomenon,
which is among the curiosities of the country. It is called
the Chimney. The lower part is a conical mound rising

out of the naked plain; from the summit shoots up a shaft or column, about one hundred and twenty feet in height, from which it derives its name. The height of the whole . . . is a hundred and seventy-five yards . . . and may be seen at the distance of upwards of thirty miles."

Not bad. By actual measurement the pinnacle is now 160 yards above the North Platte. It certainly was higher then — perhaps at least another 15 yards. The vertical spire is 120 feet high, the tip being 325 feet above the base of the cone. The spire has a diameter at the base of about 40 feet.

Eroded tusk of Brule clay and sandstone towers nearly 500 feet above the North Platte River. Emigrants would climb as high as the base of the chimney and carve their names, which washed out within a few years.

Alfred Jacob Miller painted the noted landmark in his 1837 excursion with Sir William Drummond Stewart. His tower was considerably taller (or more slender) than the rock is today. Did he exaggerate? Certainly Miller tended to romanticize his human subjects, but, heretofore, not his landscapes. Others have indicated the spire looked taller than it seems today. From 1885 until today there has been an erosion of only 17 feet, by actual scientific measurement.

There is a rumor that a gang of soldiers lobbed off the top few feet with a small cannon, but it is extremely vague. There is a good chance that Miller did indeed exaggerate his view, not for the sake of exaggeration but simply to show how it might have appeared a few decades before. In so doing, he made the universal mistake of presuming that the erosion was a great deal more than it actually is.

DeSmet made this presumption too, in 1840: "A few

National Park Service

Jackson's painting shows a wagon train near Chimney Rock, forming into the familiar circle for protection against Indians. People will sleep inside ring in tents; stock is hobbled or staked outside, under guard.

years more and this great natural curiosity will crumble away and make only a little heap upon the plain; for when it is examined near at hand, an enormous crack appears in its top." The crack is still there.

The penchant of the emigrants to carve their names in rock never was more exercised than on the spire of the Chimney. Because of the soft nature of the rock, however, no historical names survive. But it was great sport at the time.

This is one traveler's account from 1850: "I went up it about 4 hundred feet then it became so steep that they was feet holts cut in so we could clime up about 25 feet further than we could see where some had cut noches and drove little sticks to clime about 20 feet further but did not venture up that I suppose that thare is not less than 2 thousand names riten in difrin plases."

James W. Evans, heading to California in 1850, said: ". . . I engraved my name and the name of my wife. There were several Ladies and Gentlemen on the rock with me; and after I had completed my name I looked to my left and there stood a young lady who had cut foot and handholes in the soft rock busily engaged in

Ezra Meeker during his sentimental journey of 1906 stopped at Chimney Rock with his two oxen.

inscribing her name about 2 feet higher than my own!"

Uniformly the emigrants, who had kept the noted landmark in their sights for several days, underestimated the distance to it just as they did with Courthouse Rock. This was partly because of a lack of other landmarks around it and partly because of the magnification properties of the atmosphere lying close to the earth.

One 1849 emigrant left the following account: "For eight miles I was trudging along ahead of the train, expecting every mile to be at its base — At last, I stood trembling with fatigue and excitement at the foot of this grand column — After a few moments of wonder and rest I began to wind my way up its steep sides till I came to where further progress was impossible — I cast my eyes down and the horses and men at the foot looked like pigmies. I turned my eyes aloft and looked at the upright shaft above me, till I was glad to take my way back down."

Nat Wyeth had less to say about the Chimney than he did of the conditions near it: "my face so swelled from the musquitoes and ghnats that I can scarce see out of my eyes and aches like the tooth ache." Wyeth, however, was no tourist. On that 7th day of June, 1832, he had in mind only the Rocky Mountain Fur Company, his ship which should have been rounding the Horn at about that time, and the salmon shooting up the Columbia.

It is a rare event when an emigrant doesn't mention Chimney Rock in the diary he is keeping. Rev. Eells' wife Myra was one of those exceptions. She missed Chimney Rock, Courthouse Rock and even Scotts Bluff. There is, however, plenty of crabbing about having to travel on Sunday.

Rev. Parrish interspersed only occasional references to the landscape in his narrative of self-pity: "A clear morning. My health not much improved. Preparing to start early. Made a good days drive without stopping at noon, which was hard on me. Camped near 'Chimney Mound.' We are now 80 mi. from Ft. Larimo."

Dr. Whitman made mention of the rock in his writings, but not nearly as extensively as Rev. Sam Parker, who described it at length. They were there July 22, 1835, in company of Lucien Fontenelle. It was here that they met Fitzpatrick's men on the way to the rendezvous.

Return to Nebraska Highway 92 and turn left. An overlook of the great rock is maintained by the Nebraska State Historical Society about .2 mile further west, together with a trailer full of historical items. Ten minutes spent there is a good investment. The trail is about 500 yards to the north, or halfway between the highway and the North Platte. Chimney Rock is now lighted in the evening.

About two miles west of the trailer is the Scotts Bluff County line. At that point the trail is only 50 yards or so

Scotts Bluff from a farm pond to the east, with the great gash of Mitchell Pass cutting it in two. The Robidoux Pass is to left of formation.

to the right of the highway, and about another 100 yards is the line of cottonwoods marking the bank of the North Platte. About 2.5 miles is the hamlet of McGrew, and 2.7 miles from there, about 300 feet south of Highway 92, are some substantial ruts of the Oregon Trail. To the rear is Chimney Rock, right down the center of the highway. Dead ahead looms the low, dark, forbidding line that is Scotts Bluff, the slash of Mitchell Pass clearly visible in the center. To the left, not unlike the Courthouse, is Castle Rock, only two miles due south of the highway. Just three miles ahead is the little town of Melbeta, and .8 mile more is a marker denoting the site of the old Ficklins Spring Pony Express station.

It is about at that point where the old trail came back to the highway from the left, and generally stayed beneath it for the next 2.3 miles, when again it moved off to the left.

Continue on into the town of Gering and turn right on Nebraska Highway 71, cross over the North Platte River and proceed toward the town of Scottsbluff. Just .1 mile from the river turn right (east) at the traffic island and onto East Beltline, the truck route of U.S. 26. Ahead is the grave of Rebecca Winters. Soon the road will be paralleling the Burlington Railroad, to the left, and the grave is on the north side of those tracks, but very difficult to see from the highway. Pass two radio antennas on the right. Cross a small bridge and proceed only .2 mile more to a "Speed Limit 35" sign and a "Sharp Curve Ahead" sign. This point is 2.1 miles from Nebraska Highway 71. Move ahead just 300 feet and pull into a small substation on the left. Park and walk 300 feet back to the west on the gravel road to the grave.

Rebecca Winters was born in New York State in 1802. She was a Mormon pioneer, having been baptised with her husband Hiram into that faith in June 1833. It was 19 years later when they joined a caravan to Utah. Cholera overtook their party somewhere west of Fort Kearny. On August 15 Rebecca succumbed to the wretching pain. She was laid to rest in this lonely grave after a simple ceremony. A family friend found an extra wagon tire, bent it, and

Grave of Rebecca Winters was found in 1902 by Burlington Railroad surveyors. They moved line 10 feet so grave would not be. disturbed. Note wagon tire by stone.

This is the wagon tire that marked the grave; bent and placed in the soft earth at the time of Mrs. Winters' death. It was engraved by a family friend.

imbedded the words, "Rebecca Winters, Age 50". The family continued on to settle in Pleasant Grove, Utah.

A half century later, Burlington surveyors were laying out the new route and came across the old grave. They petitioned the Denver office and won a slight change of routing, so the old grave would not have to be disturbed. The resultant publicity flushed out her relatives, still in Utah, and subsequently a new marker was erected, plus a protective fence around the grave. But for that old wagon tire, which still is there, the old grave would have been lost forever.

Return to Nebraska 71, turn left, and proceed south through Gering. Less than a half mile south of the intersection of Nebraska Highway 92, there is an intercept of the old wagon road to Mitchell Pass. About 2.2 miles from Highway 92 leave Highway 71 by making a right turn onto a gravel road, and proceed west through Robidoux Pass.

Four miles from the pavement is a jog to the right, about 100 yards. This is a good, solid, gravel road, but horribly afflicted with the same nuisance that plagued the emigrants — thick, white, choking dust.

The old Oregon Trail made its intersection with the gravel road exactly 2 miles west of the jog in the road. There is a gravel road coming up from the south, and the trail crossed on the near side of the road, to parallel now on the right side of the gravel road leading to the pass. Another 1.5 miles ahead is a half-right turn, and the gentle lift over the hump is started. Only .5 mile further on is a great boulder and a sign, on the left side of the road, marking the site of the Robidoux blacksmith shop. The trail looped in from the right to cross the road there, wound high up the hill to cross the arroyo, then back down to touch the road .6 mile from the boulder.

There is plenty of evidence to show that the post wasn't there at all, but rather some 2,500 feet north of there, at a bearing of 356°. This is the conclusion reached by both Merrill J. Mattes and Paul Henderson, both of whom have studied the matter thoroughly.

Robidoux was either Antoine Robidoux or Joseph Robidoux IV, or perhaps both. They were the nephew and son, respectively, of Joseph Robidoux III, founder of St. Joseph, and grandsons of Joseph Robidoux II, a founder of both St. Louis and Florissant, Mo.

No drawings of the old building(s?) survive, but most journals mention it as a terribly rundown establishment, the principal function of which was blacksmith work. Robidoux also handled a stock of trade goods, probably, more for the emigration than the Indian trade. Evidently the merchandise included whiskey, guns, tinware, stoves, clothing, powder and the like. Robidoux, singular or plural, evidently lived in the same building, with one or more squaw wives.

Proceed on up the gravel road for .2 mile more and turn to the right, down an extremely rutted dirt roadway with a crown of grass. Just .1 mile down that road is a small enclosure on the left, containing six nameless graves. The graves are about halfway between the granite marker and the actual location of the Robidoux buildings, and about .1 mile west of the sightline.

Continue on west on the good gravel road. Now look ahead and to the right. In the saddle between the great hills is the faint trace of the Oregon Trail, just as it was over a century ago. Just .8 mile from the graves a set of ruts slants away to the right. Walk over there perhaps a dozen yards or so, and there is a very deep swale — the Oregon Trail.

Down that swale came Ashley's cannon in 1827, the first wheels to penetrate the West. On that same road came Smith, Sublette and Jackson with their stock of trade goods for the rendezvous of 1830. And over that road came the young, observant, and terribly Ivy League Francis Parkman.

Continue up to the top of the hill for a truly magnificent view of the trail far below, leading up to Horse Creek. Then look due west — squint through the haze. Looming fairly large, but only a purple shadow in substance, is Laramie Peak — 120 miles away! Many emigrant journals noted this first view of the mountain that would guide them for another week or more, and many incorrectly identified it as part of the Rocky Mountains. The shape assumes more definition in the morning, but it may be discerned as late as two or three hours before sunset.

Return to Nebraska 71 but don't turn. Cross it and continue east on a good gravel road. Proceed for two miles — the trail leading up to the Robidoux Pass came through that intersection, from left to right. Continue ahead one more mile and turn left. North just .3 mile is another intercept of that trail. Proceed just .2 mile further and there is an intercept of the trail leading west to Mitchell Pass, the great visible cleft in the bluff. The split was right in the center of that mile-square section of land on the right. There is no evidence of either trail there today.

Continue north to intersect Nebraska Highway 92 about .7 mile ahead, and then turn left, or west, to proceed into Gering again. Continue through Gering, and three miles from Highway 71 is Scotts Bluff National Monument. Park in the lot at the Visitors Center and tour the museum; unquestionably one of the finest in

Dome Rock is on left flank of Mitchell Pass, one mile away.

the National Park Service.

Here in the museum is the mother lode of William H. Jackson paintings. This remarkable old bull whacker, who helped haul the freighters through Mitchell Pass in the 1860s, waited until he was into his 80s to commit his memories and site sketches to water colors; long after he had established his reputation as the finest photographer of the early American West.

Visitors now may mount to the 4,649-foot crest of the great bluff in the family automobile, and pass through three tunnels in the process. The skylarking emigrants, thoroughly enraptured with the place, did it the hard way. But they did it.

Walk the entire summit trail, and, particularly, sight out Chimney Rock, about 20 miles due east. It is harder to make out the Courthouse, but it is visible too, just to the left of the Chimney. Some 760 feet below is the North Platte and just at the base of the bluff, the grotesque badlands, inhospitable to man or beast. Across the river sparkles the clean little city of Scottsbluff. And looming 120 miles to the west, the great shadow of Laramie Peak.

The Scotts Bluff formation is almost identical to that of Chimney Rock and Courthouse Rock. A lot of Brule clay, reinforced with sandstone rods. It doesn't take

National Park Service
Jackson's view of a bull train moving through Mitchell Pass is most precise.

much looking to see what Alfred J. Miller saw in 1837: "At a distance as we approached it the appearance was that of an immense fortification with bastions, towers, battlements, embrazures, scarps and counterscarps."

Mitchell Pass, not known by that name until Ft. Mitchell was built a short distance to the west in 1864, came into use about 1851. William C. Lobenstine passed through there that year without difficulty, and felt he saved about eight miles. It is questionable if anybody really saved anything, because of the twisting nature of the Mitchell Pass roadway on its way to the junction with the Robidoux road.

The best way to return to the museum is to walk the delightful nature trail laid out by the National Park Service. One member of the party will have to drive the car down the road, however, from the summit parking lot.

From the museum parking lot take the asphalt walkway some 250 yards west to the junction with the great swale through Mitchell Pass. Visitors may easily walk the Oregon Trail from that point through the pass and on to the William H. Jackson campsite.

The swale through Mitchell Pass is cut into sandstone in many places; it is several feet deep most of the way. Visitors may walk about 1.5 miles along the trail if they wish.

The Oregon Trail was used through Mitchell Pass with such intensity that the ruts are sometimes as much as eight feet deep. One factor of the preservation is the soft nature of the rock roadbed — another is the fact that, once Mitchell Pass came into general use, it was taken by virtually all the wagons. Still another — there was room for one wagon through the pass — no more. Each passed over the track of the one in front. The traffic was incredible. More than 50,000 wagons moved over this road in 1852 alone.

From Mitchell Pass the trail fans down the slope toward the North Platte and Horse Creek.

Continue west from the parking lot, and the trail continues next to the roadway for about a mile. It is ranging through the gullies, and it will remain a mystery how the first wagon ever got that trail started. At 1.2 miles from the museum the road begins a left turn, and at that point the trail is off to the right a half mile.

Just 3.2 miles from the museum, where the trail is exactly a quarter of a mile to the right, the highway makes a left turn and heads west. The trail down from the Robidoux Pass intercepts the highway 13.6 miles west of the museum, or just before the bridge over Owl

Creek. Ahead .6 mile is the little unincorporated village of Stegal. Turn right and proceed due north for .8 mile to another intercept. At the end of that section, another .2 mile, turn left, and .2 mile to the west is another intercept. Continue just .7 mile further and turn right. Proceed north one mile, and again the route of the Robidoux Trail is crossed — this time right in the intersection. Continue another mile and turn left. West just .6 mile is another intercept. Continue to the end of that section, another .4 mile, and turn right. Proceed about 1.6 miles north, and in the great field off to the right, and all the way ahead to the North Platte, is the site of the great Horse Creek treaty grounds.

Early in September, 1851, DeSmet rode into Ft. Laramie on one of his quests for Indian souls. He was immediately perplexed by the fact that the fort seemed deserted. Always before there had been hundreds of Indian lodges on the plain surrounding the fort — now there were none. Once in the fort he was informed that a treaty conference had been called and resulted in such participation that the land around the fort could not sustain all in attendance. So the assemblage moved, bag and baggage, to the mouth of Horse Creek.

DeSmet accepted Robert Campbell's invitation to ride in his grand carriage, and at sunset on Sept. 11, 1851, they rode onto this broad plain. There were more

The great Horse Creek Treaty Grounds, where 10,000 Indians assembled in 1850 to smoke the peace pipe with DeSmet, Campbell, and others.

than 10,000 Indians on the north side of the river — Arapahoe, Cheyenne, Sioux and nine other nations. It was the largest council ever held, and the whites were mighty happy to see the stocky little Blackrobe come tooling in to help keep it all glued together. This Fr. DeSmet was glad to do. But of greater importance to him was his spiritual work. Here, in a few days, he was able to baptize 305 Arapahoe kids, 253 Cheyennes, 280 Sioux, and 60 to 80 mixed breeds (by that time he was losing count).

The council was held on the west side of Horse Creek and the south bank of the Platte River. The Indians agreed to cease their depredations on the trail and the whites agreed to respect the tribal boundaries and pay annual fees for crossing Indian lands. The Indians accepted the gifts from the Great White Father and went on home, actually believing the U.S. government was good for its word.

Continue across Horse Creek and the balance of that mile and turn left for another mile. The road is forced into a right turn at the end of that mile, continues a mile north and is forced into another left turn. Proceed west two miles from there and turn right. Just .4 mile north is an Oregon Trail marker, on the point where the Robidoux and Mitchell pass roads join once again. Proceed north for two more miles and cross the North Platte River into the little town of Henry.

It was along this stretch of the Oregon Trail that cholera took more of a toll than anywhere else. Oscar Hyde, in the edition of the *Frontier Guardian* dated May 2, 1850, said that he had counted as many as 500 graves along the North Platte east of Fort Laramie. "Sickness lasted usually but a day. Many with beds and blankets were abandoned by the roadside, and no man, not even an Indian, dared touch them, for fear of the unknown, unseen destroyer."

Turn left onto U.S. Highway 26 in Henry and proceed west into Wyoming.

CHAPTER 5   FINDING THE TRAIL IN WYOMING

Proceed northwest along U.S. 26 into Wyoming, with the Oregon Trail on the left, following generally the south bank of the North Platte River, two miles to the left. Right at the state line there are ruts about a mile long, nothing for the next mile, and then another mile of ruts. These are not easily reachable with a normal American automobile. Continue on into the city of Torrington and turn south on U.S. Highway 85. Exactly 2.4 miles south of U.S. 26 turn left, or east, following the directional sign to the town of Huntley. Go 1.4 miles to the east and south, and turn left, or east again, on a gravel road. Exactly one mile ahead is a poultry farm and a no trespassing gate. An original section of the trail is ahead a half mile, headed northwest, directly for Ft. Laramie.

Retrace the route one mile back to the blacktop, and follow the 1.4 more miles back to U.S. Highway 85. When that highway is reached the trail is beneath the road, intersecting it and now headed briefly southwest. It will make a great curve during the next mile, to head back northwest again. Curve to the right at the entrance to the highway and proceed ahead only .1 mile, then turn west again, or left. The trail now is making its curve a quarter of a mile away from the road, right at the base of the ridge on the left. About 1.2 miles west of U.S. 85 the pavement turns to the south, but continue straight west on a gravel road. Within .2 mile there will be a crossing of the creek, where the emigrant road crossed it;

this time it is headed northwest.

As the second mile of gravel is concluded, the trail is to the north one mile. Turn right at that corner, which is at the bottom of a steep hill. Go north one mile to the stop sign at the blacktop and turn left, or west. At that corner, the trail is off to the north just a few yards, but it doesn't quite touch the intersection. Again it is headed northwest. Proceed ahead for a mile, make a sweeping curve to avoid the canal, and head back north, or right, again. About .8 mile ahead is another intercept, with no visible trace of the trail. It passed through the third farmhouse on the right from the great curve, then through the farmhouse on the left just before reaching the gravel road which leads to the left, or west. Turn west at that point.

The intercept will be about .2 mile ahead. Again, no trace. The traveler is on the great Laramie Plain now, which at the time of the overland traverse did not seem to be anything but desert, suitable only for Indians and buffalo.

From the emergence onto the gravel road, proceed one mile to the west, turn north a half mile, then another mile to the west, and another half mile north. The first half mile of the second westerly mile is right on the trail. Then the emigrant road slants off to the right, and is .3 mile ahead when the second northerly half mile jog is made. The trail comes through the farmhouses on both sides of that road, in the same northwesterly direction. It is at the end of that stretch that the traveler comes out on a blacktop road; turn left, or west, at that point.

Just .2 mile west of the corner is another intercept. Continue the balance of that mile and make a gradual curve to the right, or north. Just .6 mile ahead is another intercept. Upon completion of that northerly mile there is a broad curve to the left, or west. After that turn is made three farmhouses will come into view on the left. The trail passed through the back of the first one and the front of the second, then crossed the roadway. At the end of that mile make a curve to the right, and just after pulling out of the curve is another intercept, about at the location of the 30 mph S Curve sign. Then comes a series of curves as the road heads up to the North

Platte and the town of Lingle. Just 50 yards before arriving at the bridge take a blacktop road to the left, to follow along the south bank of the river. A half mile ahead, or to the west, is another intercept. At this point the trail leaves the highway to the right in a most visible pair of ruts. This, however, is a canal access road, which follows on the man-made elevation along the north side of the canal for the next two miles. Thus, the trail itself is perhaps five feet or more beneath the access road. It is not easily traversable by the family car, so continue on ahead for a full mile past that point.

One mile past the intercept the pavement turns to the south. Continue on to the west, however, on a fair gravel road for another mile.

At the start of the gravel road the trail is off to the right about .7 mile. Continue on the gravel for one full mile and turn right, or north. Just 1.4 miles ahead is another intercept, but again, due to the cultivation of the area, no trace is visible. At the end of that two-mile northerly stretch is the pavement; turn left, or west.

Just .3 miles west is a monument commemorating the site of the Grattan Massacre, which occurred a half mile northwest of there.

The massacre took place some years after our period, but it is important to the understanding of the American Indian and his distrust of the whites. On Aug. 17, 1854, one of the few Mormon trains to use the south bank of the North Platte was passing here, where the marker stands. One man had a lame cow and was struggling along the rear of the column with her. Something frightened the animal and she ran, of all places, into a small Sioux village nearby. The Indians were friendly and it would have been quite safe for the emigrant to have followed his cow and reclaimed her. Of course, he didn't know this at the time, so he proceeded on into Fort Laramie and reported the incident.

Meanwhile, a brave who was visiting the village had a hankering for some roast beef, so there went the cow.

It was the nation's great misfortune to have its most strategic fort on that particular day in the charge of a young second lieutenant, John L. Grattan. He took 29 men, an interpreter, and a cannon out to unsully the national honor and in the process, get back some choice cuts from Old Bossy.

Grattan used some muscle on the chief, who was under a tribal oath not to reveal the name of the offender, who was not one of his own. Young Grattan did not feel he could go back to the fort without so much as a cube steak, so he leveled the three-pounder at the lodge of the suspected culprit and touched her off. This wounded one Indian but did not produce the brave who had killed the cow. So the detachment started firing at anything that moved in a general shoot-em-up.

The statement of the fort's civilian factor, Bordeaux, takes it from there: "Accordingly the chiefs that had gone with the soldiers to help make the arrest, ran, and in the fire they [the soldiers] wounded the Bear Chief of the Wazzazies; and as soon as the soldiers' fire was over the Indians in turn rushed on the soldiers and killed the lieutenant and five men by their cannon, and the balance of the soldiers took to flight and all were killed within one mile or so from the cannon."

The Indians knew the fat was in the fire then; that they would be denied their annuity from Uncle Sam because they had been bad boys. So they rushed the fort and took their annuity by force, plus more trade goods for good measure.

The national press knew a grabber when they saw one and played this for all it was worth. In the general blood cry the facts got a little garbled and it turned out that Lt. Grattan was a hero who was felled in the line of duty in attempting to protect the emigrants and their property, and nothing should stand in the way of Manifest Destiny now, should it? Thus, all the good that was done at Horse Creek now was undone, and the great bloodletting of the Indian Wars was now to proceed at its own pace, not to abate until the century was nearly over.

Continue west for the balance of that mile, and the trail made an intercept just .1 mile from the point where a gravel road comes in from the right. Continue for the balance of that mile and turn right, staying on pavement all the way. The intercept is exactly one mile north of there. Again, no trace. Continue another 2.3 miles, across the North Platte River to U.S. 26. Turn to the left there and proceed into the little town of Fort Laramie, some 4.5 miles to the northwest. The trail is continuing up the left bank of the North Platte, and is about as far south of the river as the road is north of it. For the first two miles the trail itself is on a poor farm road south of the river; then it wanders off to the left where no trace is visible, to head into Ft. Laramie.

Follow the signs in town to go to the Ft. Laramie National Historic Site — that road proceeds on west in the town of Ft. Laramie, when U.S. Highway 26 turns to the right. Just before crossing the North Platte River there is a historic sign identifying the old steel bridge on the left as one built by the U.S. Army in 1875. The present bridge is directly over the site of the original ford. Whitman crossed here in 1836, as did the Bidwell-Bartleson party. The Ft. Laramie officers established a ferry at that site in 1850. Cross the bridge and, immediately, turn left on a good blacktop road. The contemporary traveler is going to see Ft. Laramie as the emigrants first saw it, from the east.

Proceed just .7 mile, onto a gravel road and across a most ramshackle wood bridge spanning the Laramie River. Note how deep and fast it is. Just .1 mile past the bridge is a Y in the road; bear right. Now the road is headed due west — several of the traces are sometimes visible a few yards to the right of the road; but the main trail is coming up from the southwest to make an intercept with the road at a horseshoe bend to the left. Just as the curve is started look out to the right, or due west.

There she sits — old Ft. Laramie, the crown jewel of the National Park Service. One can see the so-called Old Guardhouse on the left, ca. 1866, and the New Guardhouse, built in 1876, on the right. The new guardhouse is built on the foundations of the earliest jail, which post-1850 emigrants could readily see.

Dominating the view of the 1840s, however, was old Ft. John, which was demolished in the 1860s, the last remaining vestige of the fort when it was owned by the American Fur Co. Ft. John was only a technical name; everybody called it Ft. Laramie.

National Park Service

Jackson's painting of Ft. John, the adobe emplacement which stood where the double officers' quarters building is today. It stood from 1841 to 1862.

In between the viewer and the buildings is the Laramie River — which once varied between a squalid stream and a raging torrent, nearly impossible to ford. Now it is somewhere in between, and completely stabilized by man.

Retrace the route to the Platte bridge and turn left, on the way to the fort. The National Park Service now has plans for a new and proper entrance to the site from the east, as the emigrants first saw the fort. The present entrance is from the west. About .2 mile from the bridge is a marker depicting the site of wretched old Ft. Platte, built in 1841 by the unsuccessful trader, Lancaster P. Lupton, 50 yards north of the marker. Proceed into Ft. Laramie and park in one of the lots.

There is a self-guided tour which explains the fort in the comprehensive manner of the National Park Service. The explanation is largely in the military period, however, and this doesn't include all the highlights of the years when the fort was owned by the American Fur Co., prior to its transfer to the U.S. Army.

The fort, evidently, was named for a little-known

*This magnificent painting by Alfred Jacob Miller
shows Old Ft. William (Laramie) as it looked in 1837.*

French trapper, Jacques LaRamee, who, supposedly,
camped on the river that now bears his name, in 1818.
The location of that camp now is lost to history. Both
the Laramie and North Platte Rivers have established
different beds since that time.

The exact first location of Ft. Laramie also is lost.
This was properly known as Ft. William. It could have
been built just to the south of the parade ground, where
the successor fort, Ft. John, stood. DeVoto feels it was
less than a mile away. Paul Henderson says it was a
quarter-mile south of the old iron bridge, and aligned
with the longitudinal axis of that bridge.

For all the mystery surrounding the location of Ft.
William, there is virtually none about the fort itself. It
not only has been described in minute detail, it has
been sketched by the most masterful of all the painters
of the early west, Alfred J. Miller.

Bonneville was at that mysterious first site on
May 26, 1832. Washington Irving leaves this quote about
him: "By an observation of Jupiter's satellites, with a
Dolland reflecting telescope, Captain Bonneville
ascertained the longitude to be 102°57′west of

Miller's painting of the interior shows the great double entry. Indians rarely were admitted into the quadrangle.

Greenwich." (Actually, that is many miles east of here, which illustrates the crude nature of the navigational instruments used in the mountains in those days.)

Nathanial J. Wyeth's journal puts the aggressive entrepreneur at the site on June 1, 1834: "At the crossing [of the Laramie River] we found 13 of [William] Sublette's men camped for the purpose of building a fort, he having gone ahead." In the same company were Jason and Daniel Lee, enroute to the Willamette and the first Protestant Christianizing attempts west of the Rockies. Jason Lee says the Sublette men were planting corn at the time. Sublette himself was there when the fort was started, as was his partner, Robert Campbell. They were enroute to the annual rendezvous.

Dr. F. A. Wislizenus, in 1839, left a fine description of the first fort: "It is on a slight elevation, and is built in a rectangle of about eighty by a hundred feet. The outside is made of cottonwood logs, about fifteen feet high, hewed off, and wedged closely together. On three sides there are little towers on the walls that seem designed for watch and defense. In the middle a strong gate, built of blocks, constitutes the entrance. Within, little buildings with flat roofs are plastered all around against the wall, like swallows' nests. One is a storehouse; another the smithy; the others are dwellings not unlike monks' cells. A special portion of the courtyard is occupied by the so-called horsepen, in which the horses are confined at night. The middle space is free, with a tall tree in it, on which the flag is raised on occasions of state."

The fort was named for William Sublette.

Within a year the old stockade was sold to Tom Fitzpatrick, Bill Sublette and Jim Bridger, and the following year it was purchased by the American Fur Co. They changed the name to Ft. John, in honor of John Sarpy, a St. Louisan, who was a powerful director in Astor's operations.

It was in 1835 that Lucien Fontenelle's company, with Dr. Whitman and Samuel Parker in tow, roared into the new fort. By this time the fur caravans were more than half-way to the rendezvous, dead tired, and in need of relaxation. Here were Siouan women, here was whiskey; here was their first taste of civilization since leaving the states at Independence or Liberty. So here hell was raised, and it was proved that the men of the cloth could not deter it one whit. There was a mass drunk lasting five days. When it came time to part company Whitman offered to pay for his escort service, but Fontenelle, knowing a truly great man when he saw one, absolutely refused.

A year later Narcissa Whitman described Ft. William as a comparison with Ft. Hall on the Snake River: "The buildings of Ft. William . . . are larger [than Ft. Hall] and more finished than here. Here we have stools to sit on. There we had very comfortable chairs bottomed with buffalo skin." White women never before had been seen at Ft. Laramie; Narcissa and Eliza Spalding could have had a throne had one been available.

Mrs. Myra Eells left this quote in her diary entry of June 2, 1838: "Leave here this morning, ride into Ft. William. It is a large, hewn log building with an opening in the center, partitions for various objects. It compares very well with the walls of the Connecticut State Prison."

It was about 1841 when the company, probably bedeviled with the flooding lowlands of the Laramie, decided to abandon the old structure and rebuild — this time of adobe. Archaeological excavation has determined that the front wall of this building was directly under the ridge of the building today known as the double officers quarters, located at the southeast corner of the parade ground. The walls were about four feet thick and of varying height, enclosing an area about 180 feet long and 120 feet wide. At the northwest and southwest corners were bastions commanding the approaches. Within were 12 buildings — an office, store, warehouse, meathouse, smiths shop, carpenter shop, kitchen and five dwellings. There was a yard for about 200 animals. Thirty men were employed in the enclosure, the outside of which was braced with log buttresses. The tab for the new fort was $10,000, and shortly after it was completed the original was destroyed.

The first party of bona fide emigrants, under the leadership of John Bidwell and Joseph Williams, stopped here in 1841.

Fremont, there in 1842 on his first exploration trip, cites old Ft. Platte, the rival and wholly unsuccessful establishment located near the first Ft. William. Then he arrived at Ft. John. Preuss, on July 20, left this typically melancholy quote: "Of course if I had known it I should not have come along. I see no honor in being murdered by this rabble. But all that is too late now."

Clayton, the celebrated Mormon journalist, described the ford at the fort as being 108 yards wide in 1847. Parkman was at the adobe structure in 1846, and, in fact, caught a glimpse of the Donner Party there — among the 3,000 whites in the area at the time. He found the prices exhorbitant — sugar at $2 a cup, 5-cent tobacco going for $1.50, bullets at 75 cents a pound. He found the American Fur Co. exceedingly disliked, but they were the law and had to be obeyed. Parkman found the walls to be 15 feet high, but surrounded by a palisade. He found the entrance protected with two gates, with a little square window in between. When the inner gate was closed, a man outside of it still could talk with those inside.

When Parkman crossed the Laramie it was swirling, and the water "boiled against our saddles." They crossed a little plain, descended a hollow, came up a steep bank before the gateway to the fort. "Numerous squaws, gaily bedizened, sat grouped in front of the rooms they occupied." Parkman's room was large but poorly furnished. There was a rough bedstead, but no bed; two chairs, a chest of drawers, a tin pail, and a board upon which tobacco was cut. The amenities were not forgotten — the white Anglo-Saxon Protestant found a crucifix on the wall and a recent scalp with hair over a yard long. Buffalo robes were brought in for a bed. His balcony overlooked the courtyard, which was surrounded by cubicles, mostly for the men and their squaws. "Old Vaskiss" [Louis Vasquez, the close friend of Parkman's hunter, Henri Chatillon], who greeted the Parkman entourage upon their arrival, was about to leave for the mountains in search of a diminishing supply of furs.

Shortly before arriving at the fort, Parkman decided to shave. A six-week growth of whiskers went floating down toward St. Louis, on water Parkman related as to a "cup of chocolate."

The next year, 1847, Chester Ingersoll found about 3,000 Sioux camped around the fort, waiting to tie into the Crows. There were only 40 whites stationed in the fort at the time.

DeSmet was probably the most frequent visitor to the fort, hitting it almost every year after his first arrival, June 4, 1840.

In the summer of 1848 the clamor for protection of the emigrants was heard all the way to Washington, and the U.S. Army authorized the purchase of the fort from the American Fur Co. Pierre Chouteau, sweating it out in St. Louis, probably would have given it away had anyone asked — the fur trade was that terrible that year. But Uncle Sam, as generous with the peoples' money then as he is now, paid hard cash and Chouteau was home free.

Lt. Daniel Woodbury, Corps of Engineers, who was the builder of Ft. Kearny, came in to Ft. Laramie to negotiate with Chouteau's lawyer, Bruce Husband. The deal was closed for $4,000 on June 26, 1849, and the same day two officers and 60 men occupied the garrison; 55 more men were moved into the garrison Aug. 12. Timber, what little there was, was being cut for Old Bedlam, and lime was being burned for mortar. New structures were being built as fast as men could do the job.

None too soon. By Aug. 14, 1850, the Army had counted 39,506 men, 2,421 women, 2,609 children and 9,927 wagons through the fort. They recorded 316 deaths enroute, but that was far too conservative. In 1851, there probably were 20,000 people past the fort.

Adobe portion of sutler's store, foregound, was built in 1849. Stone addition was erected in 1852. It has been restored and authentically stocked today by National Park Service.

Bill Goff of Westport says that, after the sale of Ft. Laramie, Andrew Drips, of the Chouteau firm, built a small post near the Robidoux Pass at Scotts Bluff, in order to intercept some of the emigrant trade. It was a failure.

A sutler's store was started at Ft. Laramie in 1849, and the store still stands. The adobe portion was raised first, and that original structure now houses a carefully assembled collection of trade goods which closely

"Old Bedlam," the white building in center, was started in 1849, and restored from near ruin when acquired by National Park Service in 1937. It stands amidst "officers' row."

resembles the original stock. A stone addition was made in 1852 — it, too, has been carefully appointed. But no reconstruction. The buildings are original.

Old Bedlam, started in 1849 and added to in succeeding years, was snatched from the brink of destruction by the National Park Service and restored painstakingly to the fine building it is today. It, too, is carefully furnished as the great emigrations would have seen it, ca. 1852-68. Up on the hill, where the hospital ruins now stand like a bombed out shell, is the old traders' cemetery, where Milton Sublette is believed to

Old Guardhouse at Ft. Laramie is restored to original appearance.

have been buried. Or, at least all of him but the foot that he amputated himself years earlier.

And finally, in 1862, the remains of old Ft. John were destroyed to make room for the new double officers' quarters still standing near the parade ground.

Ft. Laramie, never attacked, was in grave danger from the Sioux and Cheyenne in the late 1860s. The final bugle blew on March 2, 1890, when the fort was abandoned. It gradually decayed, but there was enough left in 1937 for a start back. A visit to Ft. Laramie is a unique experience — it deserves a day of any American's life.

In addition to the sutler's store and Old Bedlam, the visitor should try to envision old Ft. John. The front of the stockade was directly beneath the ridge of the roof of the double officers' quarters. Envision too the grave of Mini-Aku, posthumously known as "Fallen Leaf," the 17-year-old daughter of Spotted Tail. Enamored of the white culture, she asked for burial within sight of the fort. Permission was granted by the Army as a peace gesture. She preferred the traditional Sioux burial — the body was laid out, in March, 1866, on a scaffold out of

Ft. Laramie National Historic Site
The burial scaffold of Mini-Aku, daughter of the Sioux chieftain Spotted Tail. She asked for burial within sight of Ft. Laramie and got her wish.

the reach of wolves; but otherwise protected only by a red wood blanket. There the daughter of the old Sioux chief lay for several years. Paul Henderson has unearthed fragments of the coffin from the site, which now is on private land. It bears about 330°, about 1,100 yards distant from the visitors' center. Trespassers are not welcome on that land.

The travelers left the fort about the same way visitors do today. Instead of turning right on the pavement, continue on ahead on a gravel road. This is one of the principal branches of the Oregon Trail, headed due west. Go one mile to the point where the road turns to the left. There the Oregon Trail turns to the northwest again, toward Mexican Hill, three miles away. There is a farm road there now, which has been greatly improved over the original, but which is altered now by a canal. Return toward U.S. Highway 26.

This is sort of figuring things backwards, but .8 mile toward the fort from the bridge over the North Platte is a knife in the road. When driving toward Ft. Laramie, don't take the gradual turn the pavement makes; veer to the right instead, cross a cattle guard and head for Mary Homsley's grave. Proceed 1.2 miles over a poor gravel road which needs grading and has shoulders and crown of soft, deep sand. At that point, there is a modified T in the road — turn to the right, or north. There is a marker, indicating the Oregon Trail is here again. Cut through some deep sandstone. Go .2 mile more and turn to the left onto an extremely poor road; the Oregon Trail continued on down the swale. The reason the Homsley grave survived is because it is one of the few which wasn't directly in the trail. The grave is inside a loop road a few yards ahead. There the old stone has been preserved under glass, and mounted in a concrete obelisk; the whole protected with a board fence. The original legend, as carved by Mary's husband, still is clear and sharp:

MARY E HO
MSLEY

DIED JUNE
10.52
AGE 28

Gravestone of Mary E. Homsley, who died in 1852 at age 28, was carved by her husband.

Stone now is preserved beneath glass in this concrete monument, near Ft. Laramie.

The stone fragment was discovered in November, 1925. Mary Homsley's daughter, then age 76, was found, and she related how she had witnessed her mother's burial there at the age of 3.

Return to U.S. Highway 26 and head left, or northwest, toward Guernsey.

Proceed down the highway, with the trail on the other side of the North Platte River, paralleling the route. Sometimes little-used roads come into view — off to the left of the river about as far as the highway is to the right. It is quite possible these could be the Oregon Trail, or at least branches of it.

At 2.5 miles past the Platte County line, look to the left. There is the famed Register Cliff. Continue on into Guernsey and turn south, following the signs to Register Cliff. Just across the North Platte is a junction — follow the signs to the cliff, which is 1.4 miles from there. Proceed into the parking lot at the base of the cliff.

Just below the cliff is an iron fenced area, protecting the graves of three emigrants, now unknown. Walk to

Register Cliff, with swale of Oregon Trail running along left edge of photo.

the left, past the information sign. Just 120 yards ahead is a stone monument. Thirty more yards, look in the fenced area about two feet above grade. There, among hundreds of names carved in the trail days, are three names, now badly deteriorating. The top one is A. H. Unthank 1850. The center one, O. N. Unthank 1869. The bottom one, O. B. Unthank, 1931. The first is significant in that his grave is only a week away, near Glenrock. Alva Unthank is said to have died of cholera; his grave is marked July 2, 1850. He was from Wayne Co., Indiana. O. B. Unthank was his great-grandson; O. N. Unthank, a nephew.

The old trail is readily visible just a few yards below the cliff.

Return to the junction just on the south side of the North Platte. Turn to the left on the road toward the ruts. Park in another parking area and hike 100 yards or so to the top of Deep Rut Hill. There are ruts carved six feet deep in solid sandstone. They were made as countless wagons coursed over the knob. Follow them down a short distance and look toward the North Platte. There is a small concrete obelisk. This marks the grave of Lucindy Rollins, who died in 1849. Retrace the route to the last turn, into the parking area, and turn left there, instead of right toward the bridge. Less than a block away is a little gravel road leading up to the knoll where Lucindy lies. The monument is identical to Mary Homsley's, but the original gravestone, once encased in glass, is missing. Both glass and the original stone were recently destroyed by vandals.

Important carvings on Register Cliff (from top): A. H. Unthank, 1850; O. N. Unthank, 1869; and O. B. Unthank, 1931. A. H. Unthank lived only one more week — his grave is near Glenrock.

Enormous sandstone ruts southwest of Guernsey were cut deeply by wagon tires. This is called "Deep Rut Hill."

Proceed back to U.S. Highway 26 and head west, through Guernsey and out past the bridge over the North Platte River. (This is a hairy one — make sure the weather has been dry before trying it.) Turn left onto a good gravel road immediately past that bridge. Exactly a half mile away there is a Y in the road — bear to the right. The road now becomes fairly rutty. Pass a dry gulch a mile from the Y and in another .2 mile cross a T in the road. Do not take the road to the right; continue on ahead. One and a half miles from the first Y is another, where the good road seems to go to the right up a very steep hill. Don't take it. Continue to bear left. Now the road is down to a single pair of ruts. They will lead between two huge trees; a live one on the right and a dead one on the left. Continue ahead less than a block and there is a gate which does not bear a "No Trespassing" sign. There are cattle there; remember the responsibility of the visitor is to close the gate.

The warm spring, known as the Emigrants' Laundry Tub, is 250 more yards down the ruts, which gradually deteriorate into a cattle path. Or, by following a bearing of 230°, the traveler will come out at the same place. The spring flows from a rock pile into a cattle wallow. It would seem to have a temperature of about 70°, not warm at all, but certainly less cold than the mountain streams.

Joel Palmer, on June 28, 1845, found those springs, and found the water too warm to be palatable. He said it was a quarter of a mile below his road. Clayton said the water was warmer than river water at all seasons of the year.

Return toward U.S. 26; note a Y in the road at .6 mile from the closed gate, which would not have been noticed on the trip in. Do not veer to the right, as that road is a shortcut to the Lucindy Rollins grave that will mire a car axle-deep in loose sand. Continue to the left, hit U.S. 26, and proceed west exactly 2.2 miles.

At this point turn right, or north, onto a good gravel road, veer to the right past some farm buildings. This journey will be a probe into the "no-mans lands" through which the trail is cutting, in following the south bank of the North Platte River. Just before reaching the road there is a marker showing the location of the so-called Cold Spring branch of the Oregon Trail, a sometimes-used alternate.

Continue north on the gravel road some 4.2 miles. There a line of telephone poles marches up from the left flank to meet and parallel the road. The Oregon Trail was just to the right of those poles. It continues beneath the road from here to a point where one can go no further. At 2.2 miles down the road cross a railroad track, where there is an Oregon Trail marker. Continue ahead a block or so to a ramshackle bridge bearing a "Caution" sign; a substantial understatement. Don't try it. Return to U.S. 26 and head southwest to intersect I-25, and turn right there.

At this point take an emigrant's eye view of Laramie Peak, now bulking large to the southwest. The first sighting, remember, was considerably to the east, as the traveler was coming down from Mitchell or Robidoux Pass at Scotts Bluff.

Continue north on I-25 for 7.5 miles and turn right past the large radar relay tower onto Cassa Rd. This is a fine paved loop road that moves out into the pitching, heaving country that the trail is transversing. The point where the probe ended is exactly eight miles east of the entrance to the Cassa cutoff. From there the trail headed sharply northwest and the road now is moving almost due east. At a turn to the north the trail is only two miles east, headed northwest. Exactly six miles from the start of the cutoff a gravel road comes in from the right, and now the trail is only a mile away, headed due north. Just 4.1 more miles and the trail comes beneath the road from the right and stays beneath it for about 1,000 yards. Then it slants away on the right to follow the road's curve, about 300 yards to the right of the highway. Turn to enter I-25 again. Exactly one mile past that entry the trail crosses, and immediately heads in a due-westerly direction to cross a neck of land formed by a northward bulge of the North Platte River.

This area cannot be probed efficiently; one would have to penetrate many miles over poor roads to find so much as a mile of the trail, and it simply isn't worth it. Continue north on I-25 past the Glendo Reservoir, pass into Converse Co. and proceed to the North Platte bridge, a mile or so south of Orin.

Just before the bridge there is a monument on the left commemorating Jim Bridger's ferry. It was in the twilight of his career, in 1864, when Jim set up a ferry here for travelers on the Bozeman Trail. Cross the bridge and look to the left. Off in the distance the river curves to the right, and the ferry was located there. Like most of Jim's big deals, it was a flop.

Continue on I-25 past the south side of Douglas and turn off at the West Douglas exit. At the bottom of the exit ramp there will be a Phillips 66 station — turn right at that point and proceed due south, beneath I-25, on the Esterbrook Rd. Exactly 9.6 miles from the underpass is an Oregon Trail marker on the left. Stop

Harold Warp Pioneer Museum
*Jackson painted a wagon train approaching La Bonte
Creek, with great bulk of Laramie Peak in background.*

there and turn around. Retrace only 100 yards or so, to
where a gravel road knifes in from the left. Take it, to
the northwest, and this again is the Oregon Trail. It is an
ungraded gravel road now, but in fairly good shape.
There are some weeds in the crown.

About a mile ahead cross the bridge over Wagon
Hound Creek, at the same spot the emigrants did. The
Oregon Trail then turns to the west, but it can be
followed only a quarter of a mile or so. Retrace the
probe all the way back to I-25. Sheep Mountain is on the
left, and the trail is about half way over there.

Do not go beneath I-25. Just before hitting the
underpass turn to the left, following the arrow toward
the Cold Springs Rd. The trail is far to the south, making
the so-called Bow String Cutoff. The highway and the
North Platte are the bow, and the Oregon Trail was the
string. Since the land was no less hospitable along the
cutoff than along the North Platte, men like Bridger and
Harris and Drips encouraged this route to the west.

Three miles to the west will be the Cold Springs Rd.
itself — turn left, or south. Just 3.7 miles ahead is
another intercept and a large sandstone marker,
commemorating the junction of the Oregon Trail and
the road to old Ft. Fetterman, built several miles north

in 1867. The Oregon Trail continued northwest but the road doesn't. Return once more toward I-25. Turn to the left on the blacktop used to leave I-25, and hit the freeway again by proceeding west, going beneath it at the first opportunity, and turning left.

Proceed west again on I-25, with the Oregon Trail on the left some three miles to the south. It was near here that the moody Preuss, with Fremont's 1842 expedition, made this diary entry on Aug. 30: "A polecat! Last night a stinker was killed, and we ate it this morning for breakfast. I never thought such a foul-smelling beast could taste so good. During the attack it squirted right into Badeau's face; the fellow still smells of it . . . ''

About 13 miles south and east of Glenrock, Fremont broke the second of his three barometers, on July 25, 1842.

The trail is veering slowly toward the road from the south, and by the time the Natural Bridge road is crossed, some five miles from the point where the highway was last entered, the trail will be about 2.6 miles to the left.

The traveler may wish to leave the interstate highway here and proceed south for those 2.6 miles. Exactly one mile east-southeast of that point is the original grave of Joel Hembree. It will require permission from the next ranch to the south before a visit may be made.

In December 1961 the owner of that ranch started collecting rocks for a dam he was about to build. He came across one pile on the north bank of LaPrele Creek, and on turning over the largest of the dolomite boulders he no-noticed it had a flat face. Into that face had been chiseled "1843. J. Hembree." The "4" was reversed.

An article in a local newspaper about the find, and seeking information about the deceased, was sent to Paul Henderson in Bridgeport, who identified Hembree as a 9-year-old boy who became the first fatality of the famed Applegate migration. "He fell off waggon tung & both wheels run over him," reads the diary of one eyewitness. The youngster probably had been doing what many boys did on the trail — riding on the tongue between the animals, with a hand on the back of each.

The accident happened on July 18, and the company continued on into camp on LaPrele Creek with the unconscious boy. Joel died at 2 p.m. the next day, as the great company laid by. He was buried on the 20th and the company then continued its journey.

Henderson hurried to the site with a team of experts. The grave had to be moved. Machines removed the first three feet of earth. Hand tools continued the job until some decayed wood was reached. This turned out to be an old oak dresser drawer, covering the top part of the body. Branches had covered the lower part. They rested on ledges on either side of the excavation. The deepest part contained the perfectly preserved skeletal remains of Joel. The fracture of the base of his skull was most evident. Henderson reasoned that the skill of Dr. Whitman probably kept the lad alive that long. The bones were moved 1,625 feet due west to higher ground, placed in a new pine box, and reburied.

Alva Unthank, who carved his name on Register Cliff a week before, died from cholera July 2, 1850, near Glenrock, Wyo.

Return to the highway and turn west. About 2.4 miles past the Bixby interchange the trail has moved northward to the point where it is only about 200 yards to the left, now paralleling the road. Proceed to the next exit, where U.S. Highways 87, 20 and 26 leave the interstate, and leave the freeway. At the bottom of the ramp leave the U.S. highways by turning hard to the right. The trail crossed the interstate about at the point of exit, and generally follows on the right side (north) of the U.S. highways. The traveler now should be headed due east, however, on a blacktop service road. Proceed ahead just a half mile and some 50 yards out in the field to the right is a lonely grave, that of our old friend, A.H. Unthank.

Alva Unthank is supposed to have died of cholera, but more likely he succumbed to dysentery. He was laid to rest and Sol Woody, an artist with the company, carved the inscription on his stone: "A H Unthank   Wayne Co. Ind. Died July 2 1850" Unthank had carved his name on Register Cliff only a week before. His is one of the few graves on the Oregon Trail with a footstone also, containing the letters "A H U".

Proceed to Glenrock on the old highways and from the exit from I-25 the trail moves to the right, on the north side of the railroad, and then veers back in to follow the highway immediately to the right for the last couple of miles into Glenrock. In town, however, it veers out north of the railroad tracks again. In the center of town cross over Deer Creek — Ingersoll said the crossing was tolerable; that there was plenty of coal in the bluffs and banks of the stream.

Proceed two miles west of the center of town. The trail crosses the highway at a most gradual angle, parallels it for a mile and a half, then crosses again. Exactly 3.9 miles west of town is a narrow gravel road angling off to the right from the old highway. This is the old, old highway. Take it.

Go another 1.6 miles and on the right shoulder of the road, glowing with a bouquet of plastic flowers, is the pathetic little headstone of Ada Magill.

The grave of Ada Magill, age 6, who died July 3, 1864 from dysentery contracted near Ft. Laramie. Site is west of Glenrock.

The daughter of G. M. and M. C. Magill, little Ada became ill with dysentery at Ft. Laramie and had to lie in the jolting wagon during the long hard journey to Glenrock. During the night of July 2, 1864, her condition worsened, and when they hit this point, a popular nooning spot, it was all over. She was six years old. The grave was piled with stones, then surrounded with a crude wood fence to keep predators away.

Had old G. M. dug some 2,994 feet deeper when he buried little Ada he would have stayed right there. Those are the oil-bearing sands of the Big Muddy field, one of the richest deposits of black gold in the West.

Proceed on another .3 mile and turn to the left on a good gravel road, then another block or two and intersect the U.S. highways again. Turn to the right, toward Casper. The trail continues near or under the highway for the next several miles, and it is not until reaching the settlement of Big Muddy, 10 miles west of Glenrock, that the trail is as far as a half mile away — there it is to the right, or north.

At the Natrona Co. line the trail is off to the right, or north, .4 mile. It closes in to intersect the road just 2.4 miles from there, and will continue on the south side of the road for the next 2.4 miles, never more than 100 yards or so away. Neither intercept is visible today. Now the trail is snaking, first on one side of the highway and then on the other. At the point where the highway divides, the trail crosses from left to right, and will now stay on the north side of the roadway all the way through the City of Casper.

The trail passes through the huge Texaco refinery between Evansville and Casper. Follow the U.S. highways; do not get onto I-25. The trail still follows on the north side of the railroad track past the ramp down from the East Casper exit from I-25. Continue ahead on the U.S. highways; the name of the street soon changes to Yellowstone, East or West.

Proceed west on East Yellowstone to the Bryan Stock Trail. There, two blocks to the right, the trail finally crosses the railroad tracks, headed toward the route of the traveler. Continue on ahead several blocks to N. Fenway St. There another street knifes off to the right — take it. This is East C St. Drive due west to N. Melrose St. — that is where the trail finally crosses, headed southwest. Continue on west several more blocks to N. Grant St. Turn left, or south, there and proceed to the next corner, which will be East A St. Just before the corner the trail intersects, and just after turning right onto East A St., it intersects again.

Proceed west several blocks to N. Wolcott St. and turn left, or south, for one block, and turn to the right, or west, on E. First St. The trail cut through that intersection, right through the First National Bank. Two blocks to the west turn to the left, or south, on S. David St. A half block ahead is another intercept. Turn right at the next corner, Yellowstone again, and proceed past Oak St. There the trail intersected again at Oak St. Continue ahead for two more blocks and turn left onto S. Walnut St. Go south across the railroad tracks and turn half right onto W. Collins Dr. The trail now is passing through the rail yards to the right, generally paralleling the street, which turns a few blocks ahead on S. Cypress Rd. Turn left there and proceed to W. 13th St. Turn right and straight west is old Ft. Caspar.

Three or four blocks ahead this branch of the Oregon Trail turned to the southwest, at about Maple St. There was an important route, however, that continued on ahead to cross the North Platte River at the site of Ft. Caspar.

The name of the street soon changes to Ft. Caspar Rd. The gates are visible up ahead, down the leg of a Y to the right. Proceed to the gates and turn right into the parking lot.

Ft. Caspar to South Pass

Old Ft. Caspar is something else. There are so very many points of interest in the old West that are completely ignored by the community leaders. Here is one that is of little significance to our period, and really didn't figure prominently in the course of national Western history. It was built in 1858 and lasted just nine years. Yet, the city fathers at Casper, who seem to have been doing everything right since the first recorder spelled the name wrong and it stuck, have lavished so much care on the installation to force it into the front rank of things to see on a Western tour.

When they went to work on the site there was nothing there but some foundations and some regularly spaced mounds in the earth. Now there is a fine complex of log buildings which must have resembled the fort as it originally was built.

In front of the fort are two monuments — one commemorating the Platte Bridge, built by Louis Guinard in 1858 and 1859. Guinard erected the 1,000-foot-long span on 28 log cribs, each filled with stones. They were 30 feet apart, with the first one being

Wyoming Travel Commission
Reconstruction of old Ft. Caspar on the North Platte River at the site of the Platte Bridge.

just 30 yards from the marker. The bridge, 13 feet wide, was used by thousands and thousands of emigrants, usually at $1 a head, until it burned in 1867. After that the cribs gradually rotted away and earth mixed in with the ballast rock. Today there are 28 evenly spaced mounds of earth, marching over the field and across the North Platte River.

The other monument commemorates the earlier Mormon ferry, established in 1847 by Brigham Young, then on his way to Zion to build the City of the Great Salt Lake. He directed nine men to remain to operate the ferry, which was made of two large cottonwood canoes fastened together with crosspieces.

The precise location of the 1847 ferry is unknown but by 1849 the ferry definitely was about 4.5 miles down-

Old Ft. Caspar Commission
Jackson's painting of the Platte Bridge, which he probably used several times, shows the 28 log cribs, on 30-foot centers, which were rock filled. After the bridge burned in 1867, logs gradually rotted away leaving rocks to mix with earth. Today there are 28 mounds leading across North Platte River from Ft. Caspar, spaced 30 feet apart.

stream, about 125 feet east of where an extension of Melrose Street would intersect the North Platte River.

Both the ferry and bridge were used by those emigrants who chose to travel to the Sweetwater and South Pass via Emigrant Gap and the Poison Spider Creek. The route selected for this book goes beneath the Red Buttes and over the North Platte River at Bessemer Bend. This is not to discount the importance of the Platte crossing at old Ft. Caspar.

The 52-year-old Rev. Parrish chose this Bessemer Bend route in 1844: "We crosssed N. fork of the Platte & left it immediately. It was quite small. We saw it no more." Fremont crossed on July 28, 1842, describing the river as being 200 yards wide, with an average depth of three feet in the channel. At the Platte crossing at present Casper on June 25, 1846, James Clyman saw "one continual stream of Emigrants winding their long and Tedious march to oregon and california." Kit Carson was there in June 1850 at a time when the banks were covered with travelers who had been waiting up to a week for passage.

Just outside the gates of Old Ft. Caspar, turn to the right and proceed south to Wyoming Highway 220. Just before the road reaches the highway the trail crosses it. Turn right onto the highway. The trail now is off to the right, about two blocks to the north.

Just 3.2 miles ahead is a marker showing the site of the Red Buttes battle of July 26, 1865, across the river from the marker. There the trail crosses the highway, makes a loop to the left, and recrosses a half mile down the road. For the next .8 miles the trail is beneath the highway, then swings out to the left again.

Thus the trail continues down to the settlement of Goose Egg; first to the right, then to the left of the highway. At the Goose Egg junction the trail is off to the right a few yards. About a half mile past the Goose Egg road is a blacktop road to the right, the Bessemer Bend Road, and it is so marked. Take it as the highway turns away to the left. The trail is about 200 yards to the right of the road and parallels it perfectly. Now look to the south to see the famous Red Buttes.

Fremont arrived at the Red Buttes late in July 1842 and

The Red Buttes today. Here, at Bessemer Bend, the emigrants turned to cross the North Platte and leave it for good.

complained bitterly about the grasshoppers: "There had been no rain, and innumerable quantities of grasshoppers had destroyed the grass. This insect had been so numerous since leaving Ft. Laramie that the ground seemed alive with them; and in walking, a little moving cloud preceded our footsteps."

He described the buttes as ". . . a famous landmark in this country, whose geological composition is red sandstone, limestone and calcareous sandstone and pudding stone."

He said that the wagons passed the road once or twice a year, insufficient to break down the roots of the

Harold Warp Pioneer Village

One of Jackson's favorite subjects was the Red Buttes, just south of present Casper, Wyo. He painted it several times.

artemisia bushes. That condition wasn't to last much longer.

Preuss, who made little mention of a bad wreck on the waters of the North Platte on his return from the divide, wrote this on Aug. 26, 1842: "Today it was again an ordeal, the entire twenty miles in a trot. Oh, my poor arse!"

Ware says much of the ground of the trail was swampy with alkali water, and advises emigrants to avoid it and prevent the cattle from partaking of the water.

On June 18, 1849, B. C. Clark described this country as the most barren he had ever seen. About five weeks later Stansbury came through, reported he had seen eight oxen lying in a heap by the roadside; later in the same day he saw the relics of 17 wagons and the carcasses of 27 more dead oxen.

It was just about 80 miles south of here, a long way from the Oregon Trail, where Milton Sublette, Bill's brother, showed the incredible courage of the mountain man. A bullet from an Indian rifle had smashed through the ankle of his right foot, and he was alone. He knew gangrene was only hours away so he went to work. He hacked away the edge of his beaver knife until he had a saw. He sharpened another knife to a keen edge. Then he threw the plates of his beaver traps into a fire and went to work. After the foot was off the wound was seared with the red hot beaver plates. Then he rode back to St. Louis to have the stump worked over by a pro. Then back to the mountains to trap again.

Just 1.6 miles away turn to the right. Just before reaching the bridge over the North Platte River one could turn right onto a gravel road. A quarter of a mile to the northeast is about where Robert Stuart built his cabin in 1812, intending to winter there before the Indians changed his plans.

The original trail comes beneath the road about .2 mile before the bridge is reached.

Cross the bridge, which is about 10 feet from the ford. Look down to the right. Note the gentle slope down into the stream, and back out the other bank. That is the original ford. Bonneville, probably, crossed at this spot on July 12, 1832. He said the stream was 20 yards wide, four or five feet deep, and flowing between low banks over sandy soil. He must have hit it just after one hell of a rain.

On the far side of the bridge turn to the right onto a blacktop road that changes to gravel within a few yards. Follow it around to the left, or west. At that point the trail is off to the left about 250 yards. Exactly 3.8 miles ahead the good road turns to the left. Don't turn — continue ahead on a real stinker of a rutted road for about .6 mile and pass between a pair of fence posts. Then a quarter-mile loop to the left along an irrigation canal and the Oregon Trail Road is reached. To the right is a wood bridge that the road has just crossed. Turn to the left and take an odometer reading. All distances down to Wyoming 220 will be measured from that little bridge.

Proceed exactly one mile and the Oregon Trail will be off to the left about 200 yards. Just 1.5 miles further to the southwest the trail will cross from left to right and there is a concrete marker post at that point. The trail then will parallel the road, ranging from 10 to 50 yards to the right for the next four miles.

The road is friendly but the country certainly is hostile. Angry stone formations jut out of the earth in grotesque shapes. Cattle and antelope alike graze comfortably but God knows on what. The earth seems barren of life. Yet there was no reason to keep in a single trail in most places. So the wagons ranged far to the right and left, and that is why the trail is completely invisible in spots.

About six miles ahead is a little wood bridge. The trail now is off to the right just a few yards, going down through a grassy swale. Just .9 mile past that bridge the trail will cross again, this time from right to left. It will stay there for another 1.3 miles, when it will cross again.

From this point on one herd of antelope after another may be seen, bounding over the ridges and cutting down the swales. Cattle will try to stare the traveler down, defiently chewing their cuds as the car nears to pre-empt their bed in the soft dust of the roadway. A bird of prey reluctantly swoops away from a jack rabbit on the roadway, his neck opened for a fine dinner.

Here the road bed seems to be largely of dirt and, presumably, would not hold up at all in inclement weather. If there is any danger of rain the traveler should not attempt it. There are no better roads for miles around and once in, it would be most difficult to get out during a storm. About 15.9 miles from the point where the Oregon Trail Road was entered there is a beautiful example of the trail as it leaves the roadway to the left.

It is along this stretch that one may view an almost unbelievable desecration of the national heritage of the Oregon Trail. A pipeline was buried through here in the mid-1970s and mile after mile of ruts have been willfully destroyed. The kids who pulverized Lucindy Rollins' headstone are pikers compared to these boys.

Three miles on ahead the road goes between a pair of fence posts; there is a marker there, where the trail is just to the left. It has been knocked over and now lies in the sage. A little road comes in from the left — don't take it. Continue on ahead.

The trail continues virtually beneath the road for the next 1.2 miles, where the road makes a gentle left turn. A few yards further and a poor dirt road slants off to the right next to an Oregon Trail marker. The dirt road really is the Oregon Trail but the bridge is so raunchy looking that it couldn't be recommended. Wyoming Highway 220 is just 2.3 miles ahead — turn to the right there. The Oregon Trail Road emerges just 1.2 miles to the west; the trail itself off to the right about 50 yards all the way from where the traveler left it.

Ahead and on the left is the Steamboat Rock and, just opposite the point where the Oregon Trail Road comes into Highway 220, there is a farm road cutting to the south and west. This is not the Oregon Trail. Continue on another 50 yards or so and the trail will appear along the west side of an electrical transmission line which courses down the far side of Steamboat Rock. At this point the emigrants would be only hours away from the world's friendliest river — the Sweetwater.

Exactly 8.8 miles to the west is the first view of the noted Independence Rock. The highway has been making a

National Park Service

Jackson's view of Independence Rock shows a wide Sweetwater (it is now a creek), the south end of the rock, and a greatly exaggerated Devils Gate six miles to the west.

bow toward the northwest, but the trail from Steamboat to Independence Rock makes a beeline. In the center of the bow the highway is two miles northwest, but by the time the turtle-like rock comes into view the trail will be less than a mile to the left.

Orientation of the trail around Independence Rock may best be gained by driving to the parking area on the west side and climbing to the top. That, unfortunately, can no longer be done, as the public has been fenced out. Be most alert for rattlesnakes in the weeds at the base of the rock.

The rock is a long, narrow hunk of igneous origin, consisting of red and white feldspar and mica. The U.S. Geological and Geographical Survey of 1870 found it to be 1550 yards in circumference, 193 feet high at the north end and 167 feet at the south. It is less than a half mile long.

The rock is a great autograph collection of the Oregon Trail, and by far the most famous. DeSmet, in fact, called it the "Register of the desert" when he

Wyoming Travel Commission
Independence Rock resembles a great black scarred turtle shell bulging from the flat plain before the Antelope Hills.

visited here on July 5, 1841, and heaven knows how many other times.

Every famous name connected with the Oregon Trail is or was recorded here, including those of many who couldn't write but who could persuade others to make their personal engravings for them. Robert Stuart, on his way back to St. Louis from Astoria in 1812, camped on the south side of the Sweetwater on Oct. 30, and didn't mention the rock. After what he had been through it probably seemed to be pretty tame stuff.

The name of the rock is believed to have been given by Tom Fitzpatrick, at that time a new principal of the Rocky Mountain Fur Co., who cached his furs there July 4, 1824.

A dozen years later, on his way to his ill-starred venture, Nat Wyeth stopped to make an inscription, and in so doing noted the names of Bill and Milton Sublette, Bonneville, Fontenelle and others.

Alfred Jacob Miller paused here to make his famous sketch in the summer of 1837, and left this diary entry: "Selecting the best site & setting to work being completely absorbed, about half an hour transpired when suddenly I found my head violently forced down & held in such a manner that it was impossible to turn right or left. An impression ran immediately through my mind that this was an Indian and that I was lost. In five minutes, however, the hands were removed. It was our Commander [Sir William Drummond Stewart]. He said, 'Let this be a warning to you or else on some fine day you will be among the missing. You must have your eyes and wits about you.' "

And catch this note on the climate from Mrs. Myra Eells, dated June 14, 1838: "Rode 9 hours, 28 miles, encamped on the west side of Ind. Rock at the foot of the Rocky Mts., so cold that we need all our winter clothes. Saw a large number of buffalo."

Independence Rock may be climbed in 10 minutes by any novice. View is well worth it. Wyoming Highway 220 is below base of rock in this view to north.

Lansford Hastings, the man who led the Donners to their deaths, and A. L. Lovejoy lingered at the rock long enough in 1842 to carve their names and be captured by a band of Sioux. Unfortunately for history, they were traded back to their party, the Elijah White caravan, for a few twists of tobacco.

Preuss left a diary entry for July 31, 1842: "Just now we have reached Sweet Water [probably at a point now beneath the waters of the Pathfinder Reservoir], and tonight we shall camp at Independence Rock." His employer, Fremont, described the mound as 650 yards long and 40 yards in height. Fremont found a small depression on the summit, where a little soil supported a scanty growth of shrubs including one small dwarf pine. He said that within six or eight feet of the ground, and in some places 60 or 80 feet above, are enscribed the

DeSmet termed Independence Rock the "register of the desert." The granite surface is covered with thousands of names dating from trail days.

names of travelers.

Preuss found a bloody pair of trousers pierced by a bullet, with a pipe still in the pocket. He presumed that they belonged to a straggler who had been killed by the Indians.

The party remained at the rock until noon on Aug. 2, to dry meat. They were back again on Aug. 23, and at that point tried to put a boat in the Sweetwater (also under the Pathfinder Reservoir) later, but failed due to the shallowness of the water.

Fremont, on his return, committed an act which some say cost him the presidency of the United States. His much-circulated *Report to Congress* contains this quote: "Among the thickly engraved names I made on the hard granite the impression of a large cross, which I covered with a black preparation of India rubber, well calculated to resist the influence of wind and rain." That fanned the prejudices of a bigoted electorate, which considered this a Popish act. Dynamite took the cross away some years later, but it was too late.

By the time most emigrants hit Independence Rock they were starting to feel the great weariness and dejection of the long haul up the western plains. The diary entries still were abundant, however — particularly at such a legendary spot as Independence Rock. Consider this entry by Rev. Parrish, for Aug. 15, 1844: "A fine, clear morning. The country around is quite romantic, for the rocks, mts. and plains, the sun, with its native majesty, beautifying the whole. O, my soul, read in nature, nature's God. Soon after leaving camp passed Independence Rock, one of singular appearance."

Marcus Whitman and his party of 1843 stopped at the rock and left this inscription, now disappeared: "The Oregon Company arrived July 26, 1843." Joel Palmer resisted temptation and camped some two miles past the rock, on July 12, 1845.

The 20th century visitor finds that an entire day may be spent just looking at the old names, and it should be remembered that, while these names are all over the rock, that the parking lot is on the north end of the formation and the trail generally passed along the south end. The shallower south end has some excellent examples of the calligraphy of the 19th century, and should be examined by all means.

After mounting the summit from the parking lot, a feat which takes no more than 10 minutes but is guaranteed to leave anybody winded, take a bearing of 58°, out over Piaya Lake, with the Sweetwater sharply defined to the right. The trail comes down between the south shore of the lake and the north bank of the Sweetwater. One variant continued in this manner, but crossed the highway about a block north of the parking lot. The main trail cut sharply to the south at about the center of the south shore line of the lake and crossed the river, then continued on the south bank around the rock, crossed the highway just west of the bridge and paralleled the highway on its northwest side about 50 yards away for the next mile.

A second variant, and one used, probably, almost as much as the first, leaves the trace leading to the highway about half way between the lake and the rock, and is readily visible today as it loops to go around the south end of the rock. This variant crossed the Sweetwater about 50 yards due west of the Highway 220 bridge and joined the main trail at the pavement. This figures, for in Joseph Ware's guide book of 1849 he advises that if a ford of the Sweetwater could not be made at Independence Rock, the traveler should proceed another mile up the river and try again.

The campgrounds are all around — a visitor on the south hump probably has within his vision every possible campground that the emigrants used, with the exception of the grounds in the parking lot to the north. In years of the big emigrations, the entire plain would be aswarm with the whitetops, as far as the eye could see, and on any evening from late June to mid-July there would be thousands of emigrants, chisels in hand, ready to cut their own names and search for those of their friends. Old Ezra Meeker, who passed the rock in 1852, said that the trail was occupied by an unbroken column 500 miles long, that at 15 miles a day it would take one month for that column to pass this point.

It was a good place to stop for other reasons. Coming up was the continental divide, the long haul up either deep sand or white water of the Sweetwater, and the parched deserts beyond the South Pass. Here the oxen were twisted to the earth, their cracked hooves anointed with grease and gunpowder, or searing irons. In the heyday of the trail the area was strewn with anvils, bellows, plows, bar iron, stoves, kegs, axes and even extra wheels and axletrees. This probably was the last

Harold Warp Pioneer Village
Jackson saw the Devils Gate this way — very close to a literal interpretation.

The Sweetwater flows through the base of the gate, which is 30 feet wide at bottom. There is 300 feet of air between the walls at the top, 300 to 500 feet above the river.

big dumping ground of the trail, and an adventurer with a metal detector probably would find more worthless junk than he could carry in half an hour.

The view to the west will show a faint gash in the rocky ridge some five miles away. This is the Devils Gate, actually a spectacular cleavage in the stone worn by the Sweetwater, and one which prohibited passage by anyone without mountain climbing equipment.

Return to Wyoming 220 and turn left, or southwest. Note immediately after the bridge over the Sweetwater is crossed that the trail crosses the highway from left to right, then turns to parallel the highway for 1.2 miles. Look behind and see the stunning view of the rock that was used by most of the artists.

Exactly four miles from the bridge over the Sweetwater is a sign marking the entrance to the old Tom Sun Ranch. Turn right, off the highway, and proceed only a block or two to hit a good blacktop road which parallels Wyoming 220. This is the old highway, and the old highway was built right over the Oregon Trail. Turn to the left, or west, onto that highway, and do not turn at the next sign, which only will lead further into the Sun Ranch.

Continue one mile to the west on the old highway, to a point opposite the west end of the Devils Gate, but, like the emigrants, one will be unable to see much from there. Look to the left and see the reason why this pass is called "Graveyard Gap" — there, just a few yards off the highway, is the well kept grave of a little-known emigrant, T. P. Baker. The headstone is marked simply with his name and the year, 1864. Another .6 mile ahead there is a group of farm buildings on the right and a gravel road knifing away sharply from the left. On the far side of the gravel road is a group of unknown emigrant graves marked with a commemorative stone. Turn sharply to the left on this road toward a handsome new farmhouse; then look to the east. There, exposed in full view, is the awesome Devils Gate, and this is the best view it is possible to get from the Oregon Trail.

The emigrants left a multiplicity of dimensional estimates on the Devils Gate. It would seem to be from 300 to 500 feet deep, about 30 feet wide at the bottom, and 1,300 feet through the chasm, and, perhaps, 300 feet across at the top, at the widest part.

Clark Meeker, Ezra's brother, drowned near here in the Sweetwater in 1854, two years after Ezra made his passage. Ezra made attempts in succeeding years to find his brother's grave, none of them successful.

Go down to the old highway again and continue west .2 mile, to the bridge over Pete Creek. The Sweetwater is wandering through the flat on the right, the trail sometimes off to the left a few yards, more often than not directly under the road. Here, at the Pete Creek bridge, a good view may be obtained of a cleft in the Rattlesnake Range 1,000 feet above the trail and 13

Split Rock is another landmark on the trail, 13 miles west of Devil's Gate.

miles to the west — Split Rock. The emigrants often had the rock in sight for the better part of two days, always headed generally toward it. The highway may be blocked by a barbed wire gate. If so, make a hairpin turn to the south at the cluster of emigrant graves southwest of Devils Gate and seek permission to pass from the owners of the Tom Sun Ranch.

Two miles past Pete Creek is a fine Mormon marker — these carefully researched legends are among the best in stone along the Oregon Trail. The text: "Survivors of Captain Edward Martin's Handcart Company of Mormon Emigrants from England to Utah were rescued here in perishing condition about Nov. 12, 1856. Delayed in starting and hampered by inferior handcarts, it was overtaken by an early winter. Among the company of 376, including aged people and children, the fatalities numbered 145. Insufficient food and clothing and severe weather caused many deaths. Towards the end every camp ground became a graveyard. Some of the survivors found shelter in a stockade and mail station near Devil's Gate, where their property was stored for the winter. Earlier companies reached Utah safely."

On June 27, 1849, Rufus Sage passed more than 20 dead oxen between here and the Split Rock, victims of alkali poisoning from water in the holes.

Here, perhaps, more than any other place, the travelers would realize how delightful the Sweetwater was in comparison to the North Platte. The pull, generally, was easy. They must have known of some of the horrors up ahead, and this made the road up the Sweetwater all the sweeter.

Six miles past Pete Creek the old highway re-joins the new; continue another 6.8 miles to Muddy Gap Junction. Turn to the right onto U.S. Highway 287 and head back up toward Split Rock.

Today's traveler will not be able to see Split Rock at this time as the emigrants did, as they came directly toward the cleft from the east, instead of moving up from the southeast over the highways.

As the line into Fremont Co. is crossed the old trail once again is near — it will be less than a mile due north. Continue on into the county for about 2.3 miles to a cluster of buildings called Split Rock, about 100 yards to the right of the highway. The trail passed directly through there, as close as possible to the south bank of the Sweetwater. That was the only reliable water around — livestock would head for the closest water, and, therefore, it was a good idea to make sure that the closest water was fresh water.

The view to the east shows Split Rock now as the emigrants saw it — they would have it in view for still another day. About four miles into the county is a bridge over Cottonwood Creek. From the buildings at Split Rock to this point the trail is, generally, beneath U.S. 287, but at this point it begins to move into the desert, toward the historic Three Crossings.

It is this area, a narrow strip along the Sweetwater from Devils Gate to the South Pass, that Paul Henderson feels ought to be made into a national park, and few lovers of this era of American history could disagree. That, at least, ought to yield a passable roadway to this point — no passenger car can make it today without risk of mechanical damage.

Just 5.5 miles past Cottonwood Creek and 1.6 miles north the great trail split. Due west was the deep sand route. Emigrants whose animals were strong, rested and healthy generally preferred this route, although it meant many days of hard pulling through deep sand. Those not in that fortuitous circumstance slanted to the northwest and crossed the Sweetwater less than a mile away. They continued along the north bank of the river for another mile and a half, then cut sharply south to cross again, scarcely got onto the south bank before they had to pile back in, forced by the sheer walls of the canyon, and crossed again to the north side. That sounds pretty rough but actually it was somewhat preferable to the deep sand route. The bed of the Sweetwater was solid and it rarely was over a foot deep. The moisture served to swell the wheels and tighten the tires again, thus giving a little more life to the running gear.

Proceed another five miles into the little uranium town of Jeffrey City and gas up here — there is a lot of desert ahead. At Jeffrey City the trail may be probed but it is hardly worth it. A poor gravel road leads north of town. About 1.8 miles from U.S. Highway 287 the Deep Sand Route crosses, east to west. Another 1.2 miles, or a half mile past the bridge over the Sweetwater, the Three Crossings Route intercepts. The last of these river crossings is 1.5 miles to the east over the most primitive of roads.

Proceed west from Jeffrey City. Three miles out of town and the Deep Sand Route is only 200 yards to the right of the highway; the trail will continue to parallel U.S. 287 for several more miles. So does the Sweetwater, now reduced to a nutty little creek that can't make up its mind where to go. Now it is going to make a bow to the north, but it will be back in due course. Just 9.4 miles west of Jeffrey City is a historical marker denoting the Ice Slough. Ahead a few yards is the bridge over the slough itself.

The Ice Slough is one of those absolutely delightful interludes that somehow seemed to crop up just as the incessant beating of the route seemed to get the

Rushes poke through the peat bog beneath the bridge over the Ice Slough.

emigrant to the lowest of spirits. Keep in mind that for the last several days the route was through loose sand. Wheels had started falling apart and frequent stops had to be made to pull the tires, carve flexible arc shims and tie them to the wheel with wet rawhide bands. Then they had to build a large enough fire to heat the tires, slam them on the wheels red hot and then douse them before the shims caught afire. This was hard work, particularly when the mercury sometimes rose to 110° during the day. There was little game and no fish at all. This was tough country. And then came the Ice Slough.

Here is the diary reference by Granville Stuart, dated 1852: "Somewhere in this vicinity was a grassy swamp, where we dug down about 18 inches and came to a bed of solid clear ice. We dug up enough to put into water-kegs, and enjoyed the luxury of ice-water all that hot day, while we traveled through the famous 'South Pass' of the Rocky Mountains."

Orson Pratte found ice just below the surface in 1847, and '49ers William Kelly, Alonzo Delano and Maj. Osborne Cross all did the same. William Clayton in 1847 located the "Ice Springs" on a low swampy spot on the right side of the road, and that would be just where the bridge is now — the Oregon Trail evidently passed between the historical marker and the bridge, to cross the slough a few yards south of the bridge. The ice, however, could have been found anywhere in the vicinity. Clayton had to go only two feet down to find his.

All the circumstances found by the pioneers remain today — except the ice. Walk below the bridge — very carefully. At best the ground is spongy — a natural peat bog with resilience not unlike a stiff foam mattress. During the ancient winters the frost would extend down three or four feet below the surface, and the peat would act as an insulator, keeping the ice from melting through most of the summer.

Paul Henderson, however, has found ice at Ice Spring, 1.6 miles away on a bearing of 068 degrees, but not here. Possibly the winters are less severe now than they were then. Possibly the peat continued to develop so that it now works in reverse — keeping the cold away from the subterranean moisture in the winter, rather than keeping the heat away in the summer.

Adventurer and historian alike will not settle for this. Those with self-contained recreational vehicles (with showers) would be advised to don bathing suits and go below the bridge. Taking one step at a time, proceed to one of the little rivulets below the span. Lie down on the peat and plunge an arm straight down — there will be little resistance. Perhaps if one is there in the spring of the year, and with a little luck, he will feel a sheet of ice down about three feet. Even in the hot summer it is quite cold, but obviously not cold enough to sustain ice. When the arm is withdrawn it will dry with great rapidity, leaving an opaque coating of pale grey dirt that simply will not wipe off. Furthermore, it smells to high heaven. The only solution is a soap shower. Better to stop at a service station and buy some ice.

Just after crossing the slough, the trail turns to parallel the highway about 200 yards to the south, and continues along that route for two more miles. Then it turns west, while the highway continues generally in a northwesterly direction.

There is a bridge across the Sweetwater at the little cluster of buildings known as Sweetwater Station. At this point the trail is two miles to the south, but paralleling U.S. 287. Just 2.2 miles from the bridge over the Sweetwater turn left, or south, on a poor looking gravel road. (It isn't as bad as it looks.) At .8 mile there is a Y in the road; bear left, and at 2.5 miles from the highway the trail intercepts. It may be seen vaulting over the rolling hills toward the South Pass, still 40 miles away. The swale is grass grown now, with lots of hostile sage in the crown. Return to U.S. 287 and proceed west. That is as close as one can get to the Oregon Trail for a long time. It is going to cut through some incredibly mean country, the solitary blessing being the little Sweetwater.

The observer is probably looking at the location of a hanging; Ezra Meeker describes the justice and compassion of 1852:

"One incident well up on the Sweetwater will illustrate the spirit of determination of the sturdy old men — elderly, I should say, as no young men were allowed to sit in these councils — of the plains. While laboring under the stress of grave personal cares and with many personal bereavements, a murder had been committed, and it was clear the motive was robbery. The suspect had a large family and was traveling along with the moving column. Men had volunteered to search for the missing man, and, finally, found the proof pointing to the guilty man. A council of twelve men was called and deliberated until the second day, meanwhile holding the murderer safely within their grip. What were they to do? Here was a wife and four little children depending upon this man for their lives. What would become of this man's family if justice was meted out to him? Soon there came an undercurrent of what might be termed public opinion, that it was probably better to forego punishment than to endanger the lives of the family. But the council would not be swerved from their resolution, and at sundown of the third day the criminal was hung in the presence of the whole camp, including the family, but not until ample provisions had been made to insure the safety of the family, by providing a driver to finish the journey."

Now, wasn't that thoughtful?

Follow U.S. 287 for 37 miles up toward Lander, but, before arriving there, the highway will intersect Wyoming Highway 28. Turn left and head down toward South Pass. The traveler will probe into the approach to the pass, then return to the highway and probe again, this time over the pass itself — not the modern version but the rutted little rise traversed by the heroes of this book.

Proceed 20 miles south on Wyoming 28 and a directional sign will show the road to Atlantic City, and that has to carry the title of the goddamnedest road in all creation — not that there aren't worse on this trip, but this one is supposed to be better. It is a 20-mile-an-hour washboard for three miles, and it will jar fillings loose every inch of the way.

In Atlantic City the road takes a fork — the right branch leads to South Pass City, but don't take it. Turn left instead and head up the hills south of town. A half mile or so out and there will be another fork in the middle of a left curve — bear left on the better gravel road. There is another fork 3.9 more miles to the southeast; take the road to the left again.

At exactly four more miles take the left road of a Y again and cross over a wood bridge over Rock Creek. It was here that the Oregon Trail came beneath the road and stays beneath it for the next four miles. Then the trail meanders through the desert all the way east to Split Rock and the Sweetwater. Actually, the Sweetwater is still around, just three miles due south of the bridge over Rock Creek. One may proceed east for that four miles, but it will only deliver more of what is here, with the road getting gradually worse, wearing down to a pair of ruts.

It was here, at Rock Creek, that another stunning Mormon disaster occurred. James G. Willie organized a handcart company in 1856, bound for the City of the Great Salt Lake. They started late and winter came early, and by late October, when they arrived here, the snows were terribly deep and the food had run out. Relief parties from Salt Lake City found that 13 persons were frozen to death here in a single night and were buried in a common grave. Two others died the next day. Of the 404 who started the trip, 77 died before help could reach them. The rest arrived in Salt Lake City Nov. 9.

Return across the Rock Creek bridge and immediately after passing the bridge take a gravel road leading to the left. This is the Oregon Trail. Take it for two miles; it is no worse than any of the roads taken since leaving Highway 28, even though it has a grassy crown. Exactly two miles from the bridge turn right onto a fine gravel road and return to Atlantic City. The trail doesn't do that — it degenerates into a pair of rocky ruts and proceeds for five miles southwest to the Burnt Ranch. Burnt Ranch is important because this is where the last ford of the Sweetwater was made, with the famed South Pass a scant 10 miles ahead.

The Burnt Ranch also was the eastern end of the Lander Road, an ill-timed enterprise that finally resulted in a direct road to Ft. Hall that by-passed the great sweep south to Ft. Bridger. The road was built in 1857-59, and about 9,000 people used it the year it opened. By this time the emigration was tapering off; the Lander Cutoff never did gain the traffic that would have justified its construction.

Three miles ahead on the road back to Atlantic City is another Y — bear right. Upon re-entering town, just before reaching the only two-story building there, which is a sign-less hotel, turn left. The road signs are misleading here, so do not proceed into town again. After turning left, proceed five miles to intersect Highway 28. Turn left, or southwest, toward South Pass.

About 12 miles to the southwest is a bridge; take one last look at the Sweetwater. The emigrants got their last look at the Burnt Ranch, although they passed within a mile of the friendly little creek a couple of miles east of the pass. Exactly .7 mile past this bridge is a road leading to the right — the Big Sandy entrance to the Bridger

Harold Warp Pioneer Village
Jackson shows the South Pass -- wagons coursing over many trails as they cross the wide saddle over the continental divide.

Wilderness. Across the highway from that road is an unmarked road — take it, turning left, or southeast, off the highway. Proceed 2.7 miles to a railroad track. This is the line that closely follows the old trail through the South Pass. Continue exactly .4 mile more to a Y in the road. It's easy to get mixed up here, particularly if the official county maps are being used for reference. Disregard them — they are in error. Follow this book. Veer to the right at the Y, then immediately turn full right onto a fine pair of ruts. The pass isn't far so don't give up here.

Another .2 mile ahead is another Y in the road. Bear right. Another .6 mile is a cattle guard in a wood fence. Proceed just 50 yards ahead and the traveler will be halfway to Oregon. The road is a stinker at times — it might be a good idea to hike the last half mile or so.

Standing on the South Pass, straddling the continental divide, are a pair of markers — one devoted to Narcissa Whitman and Eliza Spalding, the first white women to traverse the pass. The other simply states, "Old Oregon Trail 1843-57." The ficticious dates are a product of old Ezra Meeker, who placed the granite there himself in 1906. He found the rock at the Pacific Spring, two miles west, lugged it here and cut it himself.

This is South Pass today. Meeker placed the marker on the right in 1906. The other, commemorating the first two white women over the pass, was placed by Capt. H. C. Nickerson.

Four decades later, when the U.S. Geological Survey engineers were surveying the divide, they found that the precise location of the divide had been missed by less than 50 feet.

Capt. H. C. Nickerson placed the other marker 10 years later. The trail here was more than a pair of ruts — it was 25 to 50 yards wide in the heyday.

The road goes from bad to worse here so return to Highway 28 for a splendid panoramic overlook. Turn left on 28 again and proceed for 4.2 miles, then turn left into a parking area and a historical marker. Here the National Park Service has provided an orientation board equating the landscape with a profile map, showing the location of the trail through the pass.

On the left, or north, is the end of the Wind River Range. To the right is Pacific Butte and the Antelope Hills. In between is the great saddle, 950 miles west of Independence and fully 29 miles across, through which coursed the tide of suffering humanity that wrote the most dramatic chapter in American history. Over that slope the threads all came together, forming an umbilical cord over the national spine to tie the West forever to the United States. A nation in its undying gratitude has marked it with two little rocks, neither of them so much as three feet high, and both placed by private citizens at their own expense. The USA has ignored it completely on its

The National Park Service erected this orientation board four miles west of South Pass, showing the flatness of the 29-mile-wide saddle.

highway maps and left access only to those who don't mind driving their cars over craggy sage and wretched roadways.

A cluster of decaying buildings far below marks the site of the Pacific Springs. Abandoned now, they once served as the farm buildings for the Pacific Ranch. They were built on the site of the old Pacific Springs Pony Express and stage stations. The trestle carrying the railroad over the spring branch is plainly visible. The branch itself comes beneath the observation hill; the trail over that hill just a few more yards on the road which brought the traveler to the parking lot. Since the overlook is a good four miles from the pass, the tiny markers are not visible from here.

The emigrants rarely stopped at the pass. They knew fresh water was only a couple of miles away at Pacific Springs, and they wanted to see what water looked like that was to flow into the Pacific Ocean. The springs now are in a bog. Irene Paden got within a hundred yards of them 30 years ago, but the literal pursuit hardly seems worthwhile today.

Robert Stuart discovered South Pass — his diary

leaves little doubt of this. He probably caught his first look at it from the very same overlook where the observer is now standing, since he was headed back to St. Louis from Astoria.

His diary entry for Oct. 22, 1812: "We set out at day light, and ascended about 3 miles, when we found a spring of excellent water, and breakfasted; 5 more brought us to the top of the mountain, which we call the big horn, it is in the midst of the principal chain; in scrambling up the acclivity and on the top, we discovered various shells, evidently the production of the sea, and which doubtless must have been deposited by the waters of the deluge . . ."Stuart had elected to climb the ridge due east of Pacific Spring, rather than swing northeast through the South Pass. Why? Because he had seen a fresh trail left by Crow Indians going over the pass.

It is doubtful that the significance of Stuart's discovery was apparent to him or anyone else until some years later. No white man came that way again until February, 1824, when the great Jed Smith, Jim Clyman, Jim Bridger, Tom Fitzpatrick, and seven other Ashley men made their way through, and all knew very well what they had found. Then Capt. Bonneville led a small wagon train over on July 24, 1832. Here came the Whitmans and the Spaldings in 1836, Dr. Whitman and Sam Parker having looked it over first the year before. And, in 1843, the great migration of 1,000 persons erased any doubt that the South Pass was anything but a friendly way to cross the continental divide.

John Charles Fremont passed on Aug. 7, 1842: "About 6 mi. from our encampment brought us to the summit. The ascent had been so gradual, that, with all the intimate knowledge possessed by [Kit] Carson, who had made this country his home for 17 years, we were obliged to watch very closely to find the place at which we had reached the culminating point. This was below two low hills, rising on either hand 50 or 60 feet. When I looked back at them, from the foot of the immediate slope on the western plain, their summits appeared to be about 120 feet above. From the impression on my mind at this time, and subsequently on our return, I should compare the elevation which we surmounted immediately at the Pass, to the ascent of the Capitol Hill from the avenue at Washington. Approaching it from the mouth of the Sweetwater, a sandy plain, 120 miles long, conducts by a gradual and regular ascent, to the summit, about 7,000 feet above the sea; and the traveler without being reminded of any change by toilsome ascents, suddenly finds himself on the waters which flow to the Pacific Ocean."

Preuss, crabbing as usual about his boss, wrote on the same day: "Today he said the air up here is too thin; that is the reason his daguerreotype was a failure. Old boy, you don't understand the thing, that is it."

Fremont returned 12 days later, and at 10 a.m. stood exactly on the divide "where the wagon road crosses."

Perhaps Preuss wasn't terribly wrong in his estimation of Fremont. In 1856, when Fremont's presidential candidacy was being touted, there was an attempt to credit the discovery of the South Pass to the candidate. The *Detroit Free Press* on June 28 ran a letter from Ramsay Crooks, correctly crediting Stuart with the discovery, and that took care of that.

Fremont's father-in-law, Tom Benton, made a speech in the Senate in 1850 crediting the discovery to Andrew Henry, who went up the Missouri in search of furs for Ashley. He wandered all over the interior before returning to St. Louis a wealthy man. He supposedly found it in 1811. Benton came up with no documentation then and there is none now; but it could have happened.

Lorenzo Sawyer crossed the pass in 1850 and left this narrative: "Most emigrants have a very erroneous idea of the South Pass, and their inquiries about it are often amusing enough. They suppose it to be a narrow defile in the Rocky Mountains walled in by perpendicular rocks hundreds of feet high. The passage at this point is somehow regarded as important, which causes a great rush to somehow get through the 'pass.' The fact is they are in the South Pass all the way up the Sweet Water. The 'pass' is a valley some 20 miles wide, with the Sweet Water mountains on one side and Rattlesnake Mountains and the Wind River range on the other . . . the summit of the whole range are buried in deep snow which extends far down their sides.''

And young Chester Ingersoll? All he could think to write was, he was now 1,500 miles from Joliet.

South Pass to Idaho Border

Return to Wyoming Highway 28 and proceed southwest (left) toward the Sublette County line. One branch of the trail follows along Pacific Creek almost a mile to the left; but the more heavily traveled trace veered up to the highway, and at the Sublette County line it is only a few yards to the left of the road.

Just 4.9 miles from the South Pass overlook, or .6 mile into Sublette County, the trail knifes across the highway from left to right and heads toward a concrete marker a tenth of a mile ahead and 50 yards out into the range on the right. This is supposed to be the famous ''Parting of the Ways,'' the place where the emigrant had to make up his mind whether to take the wet route down to Ft. Bridger and then down the Bear River, or the dry Sublette Cutoff, to shoot straight west to hit the Green and then the Bear at about the mouth of Smith's Fork.

The parting would seem to be almost directly in front of the marker. The trail to Ft. Bridger is obscure except at that point, but by looking into the hills across the highway to the left it may be seen easily. What is supposed to be the Sublette road is most visible straight ahead, then angling to the northwest and the mountains. In reality, that is the Oregon Trail. To the left is the old stage road to the Green River from South Pass City. This isn't the ''Parting of the Ways'' at all. Somebody goofed.

The trail continues westward, north of the highway, cutting into Sweetwater County a good five miles due west of where Highway 28 cuts in. At a point where North Pacific Creek is crossed, the trail and the cutoff are three miles northwest and quite inaccessible. The Sublette Cutoff then heads due west over the desert in an almost perfectly straight line (that is why it is so logical — there was no reason to turn, and a primitive road like this shows up on on the fine Wyoming county maps.)

Another good piece of evidence is contained in Ware's *Emigrant's Guide to California:* "When you cross the Dry, or Little, Sandy, instead of turning left, and following the river, strike out across to the Big Sandy, 12 miles. If you get to the river along through the day, camp till near night. From the Big Sandy to Green River, a distance of 35 miles, there is not a drop of water. By starting from the Sandy in the cool of the day, you can get across easily by morning. Cattle can travel as far again by night as they can during the day, from the fact that the air is cool, and, consequently, they do not need water." All this jibes. Except it was nearly 50 miles, and many an emigrant had blood in his eye for Ware before the jaunt was over. The 50 to 75 miles that was saved by avoiding Ft. Bridger wasn't worth it. Once at the Green they had to ford. B. C. Clark took the easy way on June 30, 1849: "After much difficulty & no little risk crossed our wagons & loads separately on a crazy mormon craft made of 5 canoes. Had to pay $1.50 pr wagon."

Exactly 14.5 miles into Sweetwater County cross over a canal. Three miles off to the right, or due north, the emigrants crossed the Little Sandy.

That is where Jim Bridger met Brigham Young, a man he was to detest to his dying day. Jim gave Young a rambling account of the area and the way to the Great Salt Lake, which he is credited with discovering in 1824. Jim generally discouraged the idea of farming that valley but Brigham insisted. So they went their separate ways — Jim holding a free pass for the Mormon ferry over the North Platte at Casper.

Fremont, on Aug. 8, 1842, found the Little Sandy 40 feet wide and two or three feet deep, clear water with a full swift current, over a sandy bed. That must have been after a heavy rain in the mountains. And there, finally, is where the Donner Party really formed up, after making the

decision to split from the main party to take that great
new route Lansford Hastings had found to California.

The trail is coming down toward the highway; the
traveler now will probe over to it, get aboard, and ride it
**all the way down the Sandys to the Lombard Ferry over
the Farson.**

Just 1.3 miles past the bridge over the canal, or 2.5
miles past the tall television relay tower on the south side
of the highway, turn half-right around an abandoned, un-
painted, lap-sided building onto what shortly will become
a dirt road. Just .2 miles away, due west, is the first of three
section-line roads, each a mile apart. About .6 miles more
cross over the Little Sandy River, something the emigrants
did four miles northwest of there. The trail passed just
beyond the intersection of the third section-line road,
which is about 2.2 miles from the highway. Proceed one
more mile, where the road turns south, or left. About .8
miles ahead is another intercept, but as a result of the avail-
ability of irrigation the land has been farmed and the trail
can rarely be seen. Continue south for another 1.4 miles,
intersect Wyoming Highway 28 again, and turn half-right,
or southwest. Proceed one more mile into the town of
Farson and turn right, or north, onto U.S. Highway 191.

On the northwest corner of the intersection of highways
28 and 191 are two historical markers — one for the Big
Sandy stage station and the other for the Litle
Sandy crossing of the Oregon Trail. The latter speaks of the
Bridger-Young discussion at the crossing ''near here.''
Actually it was eight miles northeast.

Less than a half mile north of that corner is the bridge
over the Big Sandy River. The emigration made its ford a
mile due north of here — from the looks of the river here
that would be no big deal. Anna Vanderburgh Clinkenbeard reported that in 1864 there was fresh grass, willows,
and friendly flowers in profusion along the banks of the
Big Sandy. While DeVoto claims the trouble with the
Indians virtually vanished at the South Pass in the era of
the mountain man, in the late 1850s and all through the 1860s
this was certainly not the case. Clinkenbeard reported
one train utterly wiped out by Indians, probably up on

the Sublette Cutoff, with only two survivors out of 300. She also added that fresh graves were being passed daily. The second part of the claim may be believed; the first impugns her credibility.

The trail cut through the northwest corner of Farson and joins Highway 28 at its intersection with U.S. 191. The trail essentially is dead ahead, following the new Farson-Fontenelle road to the new bridge over the Green River. The Wyoming State Highway Department realized they were on sensitive earth when they laid out the new highway and worked diligently to take as little of the wagon road as possible — probably less than a mile of ruts in the entire twenty-five mile stretch.

In fact, it is difficult to say where the original wagon road was. Ranchers have been using it since pioneer settlement days. Whenever things got a little boggy they would deviate from the trail a short distance to bypass the problem. Sometimes the bypasses would be permanent, sometimes not. Before siting the highway in 1981, the WSHD used photogrammetry to determine as accurately as possible the route of the trail, and that is the basis of the following directions.

About one mile southwest on the Farson-Fontenelle highway, where the highway makes a gentle curve to the left, the trail slants away to the right. For the next 8 or so miles, the trail shadows the highway, at times running just underneath or alongside it, at other points deviating to the left or right a few yards. At 9.5 miles from Farson is Simpson's Hollow, where **Brigham's "Destroying Angels" burned the supply train of** the troops sent to wipe him out during the Mormon War. About a half mile to the left are several unidentified graves. At 11.7 miles from Farson, the trail slants across the highway from right to left and will stay on the south side of the road for the next 6.2 miles. At that point, about 18 miles from Farson, the Slate Creek Cutoff begins, slanting off to the northwest. The trail remains a few yards south of the highway as it begins its sweeping curve to the left to enter the bitter Little Colorado Desert. At 21.8 miles from Farson the trail makes one last crossing of the highway, following it off to the right a few yards as the approach to the Green is made. The trail and the highway join again at the east bridge approach. The Lombard Ferry was located at this site during the last years of the trail.

The highway department built the turnouts and provided

for the hiking segments and historical markers along this tremendously important section of the trail. Cross the bridge and turn left about a half mile ahead, on the first road to the left. This is right over the trail. Follow it south a little more than a mile, to the point where it makes a half-right turn. At that point the trail proceeds straight ahead (due south), cutting across another patch of perfect desolation, down toward Granger, the lovely Blacks Fork, and Fort Bridger. Don't try to follow it. Turn half-right, proceed almost two miles to Highway 372 and turn to the left. At that point the Green is off to the left only two miles, and because most automobiles are not equipped for primitive desert travel, today's traveler must follow the highway for 23 miles down the Green to I-80, then due west for 16.5 miles to U.S. 30N, and up 30N into Granger. Only then will the vicinity of the trail be reached again. The emigrants did all this with a fairly routine, but dry, 18-mile effort.

Chester Ingersoll found that the Green, placid as it might look today, had a strong current in 1847. He crossed on a raft, probably at the Lombard Ferry, but it took four days to do it. Joel Palmer made his crossing on July 21, 1845, and to do so he had to raise his wagon beds six inches to keep from soaking the contents. He described it as a beautiful, clear stream, 100 yards wide and with a gravelly bottom.

Continue up 30N for exactly 4.8 miles to the bridge over Blacks Fork. Go another 1.8 miles. An intercept of the trail is another .2 miles ahead, but turn left there on a solid but rough road leading to the Texaco oil fields.

Proceed south 1.1 miles and turn right, and .7 miles from there the road leads over the Union Pacific tracks. Do not cross. Park there and walk 20 yards down the tracks to the right to a railroad bridge across Hams Fork. The emigrations crossed this friendly little stream less than a half mile to the northwest, and this is as close as one can get to that ford.

Thomas Farnham hit that ford across Hams Fork on Aug. 22, 1839, and found the water to be 16½ feet across and between three and four inches in depth.

Return to the last corner and turn right onto the oiled road again. Just before reaching the tracks turn to the left to cross over the tracks into Granger. That will be .8 miles from the last turn.

After crossing the tracks, immediately turn right onto First Street, a blacktop road, and follow it out to Spruce, the third street over, where the traveler turns left. Proceed across a bridge over Blacks Fork. The emigrant ford is 2.4 miles west — they had to ford this stream just 1.5 miles past the Hams Fork ford.

Ware's *Emigrants Guide* notes that there will be three more crossings of the Black's Fork in the next 17 miles. There still is.

Just a mile from the bridge turn right to pass through the Moxa Oil Field. There is a notorious bridge over a dry wash 4.3 miles from that turn. Examine it on foot before driving across. The trail came in from the right and passed beneath the road just 4.6 miles west of the corner, then bobbed up to the north side of the blacktop again. And no wonder. The pioneers would prefer a sage-infested desert to this blacktop road, with chuckholes a foot deep. A sonovabitchin' tirebanger, as the mountain man would say. (At 2.1 and 3.1 miles past the last turn there are Oregon Trail markers, and the ruts of an alternate route are in view at both places.)

Proceed into Uinta County for 5.1 miles on that alleged highway to a little bridge. Just a half mile further is Church Butte, a gothic-inspired hunk of sandstone rising out of the plain on the left. It was a popular Mormon stopping place and the kids of today can have as much fun climbing on the parapets as they did 125 years ago.

The trail is just to the north of the collapsed buildings across the road, it having followed down the right side of the road since entering the county. Just 1.3 more miles, at another little bridge, it comes beneath the road once more, and there is a trail marker on the right.

Cross the Blacks Fork again 4.8 more miles ahead, where the emigrants did. Come over on a fine steel bridge. Note the gentleness of the river, its sandy bottom showing through the sparkling water. The third crossing is 4.4 miles from the last one, again right beneath the bridge. A mile ahead the rugged little blacktop road passes beneath I-80, then turns to parallel it. One must make somewhat of an S curve to do this; but the Oregon Trail does not. After crossing beneath the highway make a right turn, and again the trail is beneath the road, paralleling

the turnpike for a mile. Then turn to the south, but the
trail doesn't. It continues almost on a beeline to Ft.
Bridger, nine miles ahead. Proceed into the little Mormon
town of Lyman. This will involve just 2.8 more miles of
that stinking road. Emerge onto U.S. 30S and follow
it through Lyman and into Ft. Bridger.

To probe the trail in between, don't turn where highway
30 turns south in Lyman — angle to the right instead and
follow the road down into the valley of Blacks Fork. Pass
a KOA campground on the left, then its corral, and ahead
a few yards the trail crosses, now on the south bank of
Blacks Fork. The final crossing was made about two miles
northeast of Ft. Bridger.

Continue on 30S into the town of Fort Bridger. A short
distance inside the city limits is the well-marked gate into
the U.S. Army's Ft. Bridger site. Turn in.

The old fort carries the remains of the Army installation
(plus some reconstruction) that was erected in 1858, after
the Mormon occupants had burned and abandoned the
earlier fort. There is no mention of the location of the
buildings the emigrants saw. They were shabby — Old
Gabe was a lousy builder. He was able to con somebody
into writing a letter for him to Pierre Chouteau, Jr. in St.
Louis, in which the fort was described. The letter, dated
December 1843, is as follows: "I have established a small
fort with a blacksmith shop and a supply of iron in the road
of the emigrants on Blacks Fork of Green River, which
promises fairly. They, in coming out, are generally well
supplied with money, but by the time they get there are in
want of all kinds of supplies. Horses, provisions, smith
work, etc. bring ready cash from them, and should I
receive the goods hereby ordered will do a considerable
business in that way with them. The same establishment
trades with the Indians in the neighborhood, who have
mostly a good number of beaver among them."

Bridger actually built his fort in partnership with Louis
Vasquez, member of a prominent St. Louis family, and
when these two famed mountain men took to shopkeeping,
that was the absolute end of the fur trade as a big business
in the Rocky Mountains.

What kind of a fort was it? A dejecting experience for

Harold Warp Pioneer Village
Jackson's Ft. Bridger reveals a raunchy adobe emplacement surrounded by a stockade — always a disappointment to trail-weary emigrants.

most emigrants. It was built of pickets daubed over with adobe mud, which baked rock hard in the sun. Some 25 to 50 tipis might be found at certain times of the year, but always outside the walls. Inside were two or three cabins for the owners, some 40 feet long, with adobe floors. They were heated in winter by coal which Bridger found in the vicinity.

Lansford W. Hastings was there in 1842, certainly saw the first fort a mile north of town. He included data about it in the fatal 152-page guidebook published in Cincinnati in 1845; the book George Donner had in his hand when his wagons came tooling in, in 1846.

Joel Palmer, on July 25 of the prior year, described the fort as a "shabby concern built of poles and daubed with mud." Bryant didn't think much more of it: "The buildings are two or three unstable log-cabins, rudely constructed, and bearing but a faint resemblance to habitable houses."

For all the defects of construction it was sited magnificently, both from strategic and aesthetic standpoints. Against the majestic backdrop of the Uinta Mountains to the south and the Wasatch in the west, it was abundantly supplied with water, timber and mild weather. But on the other hand, anything would have looked good after what the emigrants had just been through.

Clayton said he crossed four rushing creeks getting into the fort and there would be three more on the other side before a good campsite could be found.

The most frequent complaint of the emigrants was not the appearance of the buildings, but the fact they were unoccupied. Old Gabe had to keep moving; he had trained as a smith and didn't like it anymore in 1843 than he did 20 years before in St. Louis. Old Vaskiss, as his partner was known to the mountain trade, had delusions of grandeur and frequently went for prolonged rides through the countryside in a coach and four. Rev. Parrish, in 1844, took some comfort from the fact that the mountains were covered with snow — something not often seen on the Oregon Trail in summer. The Cushing Eells party waited there a week in 1838 but, of course, that was several years before the fort was built.

So into Ft. Bridger came George Donner and his party, handbook in hand. Lansford Hastings, in his insistence that somebody take his cutoff, had sent word across South Pass to the Donners, fighting their way up the Sweetwater, that he would meet them at Ft. Bridger to personally guide them across the desert flats to California. It was now that George Donner might have learned something of the Hastings character for he was nowhere to be found. In the Donner party were 26 men, 12 women, six teenage boys and four teenage girls, 14 boys under 12 and 12 girls under 12. In the Wasatch they would link up with the Graves party of 15 more persons, including two Indians.

George Donner may have had a few doubts as he pulled into the old fort, but they soon were dispelled. He asked, first, Louis Vasquez and then Old Gabe himself, and they both confirmed Hasting's route as being bona fide. This is the only black mark against Jim Bridger, and even this is conjectural. The partners stood to realize much by a new route through their fort. Still, the Hastings reputation was considerable, and Jim, the discoverer of the Great Salt Lake, probably knew that the proposed route was passable with wagons. The Donners were tragically late — Jim knew that. What nobody knew was that the Sierra winter would be a month early.

Twenty-five years later Jim Clyman thought he recalled

a conversation with Jim Reed at Ft. Laramie, wherein he tried to dissuade Reed from the Hastings route. His recollection is questionable, however, and is not reinforced by his own diary entries.

Donner had good equipment, no doubt about that. Furthermore, he had that big wad of cash strapped inside his clothing. They all left Ft. Bridger in high spirits, following the track left only a few days before by Hastings, who was guiding a small and highly mobile party.

Within days the Donner party was in trouble. They lost the tracks left by Hastings but pushed ahead, hoping for the signs that would tell them they had reached the fabulous shortcut to California. Days dragged into weeks as they crossed mountains and blistering deserts. Dissension rose, and Reed accidentally killed one of the emigrants in a fight. One of the men raised a wagon tongue for a hanging but there was more compassion here than with the Meeker party and Reed was sentenced to go on ahead on his own — in fact, a life sentence, since most of the others soon would face death. This is the same Reed whose initials remain at the Alcove Spring, in northern Kansas.

Some of the emigrants lost their minds under the strain. Late in October, an unbelievable three months after they left Ft. Bridger, they found themselves trapped in Donner Pass in the high Sierra. They dug in and slowly starved to death, but some members of the party forged ahead on snowshoes and tried to organize a relief party from Sacramento. Heading the rescue units was Reed himself — his wife and kids were up there.

Up in the pass, in March 1847, they found little Patty Reed in a snow cave, still alive. In her bony little hand was clutched the lock of grey hair snipped from her grandmother at Alcove Spring nearly a year before. Hidden under her skirt was a tattered little doll, now a museum piece. She kept it concealed, afraid her rescuers would not let her take it out. Little Patty hadn't been outside that cave in weeks.

One of the first things to catch the eye of her father on his rescue mission was the bearded head of his old friend, Jacob Donner, severed from his body, with the brain opened and eaten by the survivors.

Only 30 of the party made it alive into the valley. And Lansford Hastings? His hopes to be governor of California smashed by the Donner tragedy, he dabbled in law, real estate and mining in California. He tried to seize California and Arizona for Jefferson Davis and died in 1870 while trying to found a Confederate colony in Brazil.

Patty Reed Lewis lived to see the monument dedicated in Donner Pass on June 6, 1918 — she was nearly 80 then. With her at the ceremony were Eliza Donner Houghton and Frances Donner Wilder. Early in this century there were still tree trunks in the pass which were cut off 10 feet above the ground by the party for cabin logs — an indication of the great depth of the snow in 1847.

There was indeed an earlier Fort Bridger about .9 mile north of town, which Jim abandoned late in 1843. The next Fort Bridger, believed to have been built in the spring of 1844, probably rose in the area which is behind the present museum building. There has been no serious excavation of the area, but Paul Henderson was able to do a bit of digging at the northern site and found considerable evidence of occupation. Aubrey Haines said the site on the bluff just south of Wall Reservoir has been turned into a borrow pit for road maintenance materials, and hence the site probably has been totally destroyed.

The state of Wyoming opened a handsome reconstruction of Bridger's old fort on July 4, 1987, near the museum, which stands on the fort's original site. The exhibits include a working blacksmith shop, where living history demonstrations are conducted during the season.

The Oregon Trail exited from old Fort Bridger headed due north. It is most unfortunate but the trail is virtually unreachable from here almost to the Idaho border. There is a road three miles to the east which goes as far north as the Fort Bridger Airport, some six miles north of town. This would provide one intercept and about a mile of driving on the trail for 16 miles of other driving, up to the little town of Carter. It simply isn't worth it, because the traveler then would have to double back the way he came.

So continue on west on U.S. 30 to an intercept with I-80, 20 miles away. Leave I-80 there and turn north on U.S. Highway 189.

It is exactly 21 miles ahead, to the northwest, that the road and the trail meet again. The trail moved due north out of Ft. Bridger and a few miles out of Carter made a gradual turn due west, to make an intercept just a few yards into Lincoln County, headed west.

Again the trail plunges into a wilderness where there are no passable roads, moving due west along the county line four miles, then north along Muddy Creek. One simply can't do this with the family car. Go on ahead into Kemmerer, and U.S. 30N. Follow 30N west for about 25 miles to Sage Junction, where Wyoming Highway 89 takes off to the left. Don't take it, as it would be a dead end probe. But 3.3 miles down that road is an intercept — the trail now is in the valley of the Bear River, with rugged deserts behind and, unfortunately, still ahead. For now the traveling would be delightful. Three miles ahead on 30N is a little bridge. Go ahead about .3 mile and turn left on a gravel road, which is marked "Pope Ranch, 2 mi." About 1.6 miles ahead, where the road curves to the right, don't. Continue across the curve to maintain a westerly heading. Exactly two miles from the highway is an Oregon Trail intercept, only a few yards away from the placid Bear River.

Return to the highway, take an odometer reading, and proceed 6.3 miles north — there the trail comes in to meet the road from the left, with the Bear River still further to the left, almost a mile from the highway. For four more miles the trail is either beneath the road or within 20 yards of the highway, right or left. Then it slants away to the right for two miles, and back to the highway again.

About 12.8 miles from the end of the last probe, Sublette Creek (or Lost Creek, or Trail Creek, or Birch Creek) passes beneath the highway — that is the junction of the Oregon Trail and the Sublette Cutoff. Unfortunately, it is now beneath the highway.

The trail proceeded to the northwest, paralleling the highway a half mile to the left, and four miles ahead the traveler will cross beautiful Smith's Fork, just a half mile east of the trail crossing of that stream. Joel Palmer, on

Aug. 1, 1845, described it as a bold, clear, beautiful stream, coming in from the east, about 15 yards wide and lined with timber and undergrowth. B.C. Clark reached the fork July 2, 1849.

This is the heart of the trapping country. Here, on the far side of the mouth of the fork, and between the Bear and the highway, some 400 lodges of Nez Perces and Flatheads camped with Andrew Drips and Osborne Russell on May 9, 1836, on the way to the rendezvous on the Green, which is a few miles to the northwest. There they would meet those two beautiful white women coming west with their missionary husbands, and it would be the first look the Indians ever had of a white woman. The year before, many of them had stood around and ogled as Dr. Whitman gave Jim Bridger a bullet to bite, rolled him over, sliced his back open and removed an iron arrowhead three inches long. It was a souvenir of his little altercation with the Blackfeet in 1832. The gallery had applauded wildly as Dr. Whitman held up the blackened object, now covered with a tough cocoon of cartilage. Old Gabe stood up and tried to make like it didn't hurt. Whitman marveled that the man hadn't died. "Shucks Doc," Bridger is reported to have said, "y'know meat don't spile in the mountains."

A mile from Smith's Fork the trail comes beneath the road and stays beneath it for another nine miles. At the little settlement of Border Junction turn to the left. Wyoming Highway 89 continues north, the trail splits the difference, then changes its mind and loops into Idaho on the right side of U.S. 30N, about 200 yards away. Proceed on into Idaho.

CHAPTER 6

The emigrants wrote with much praise of the valley of the Bear River. Ingersoll described the fine condition of the road all the way to the crossing of the Thomas Fork.

At the border the Bear will be on the left, or south, side of the highway. At this point the trail is on the right, paralleling U.S. 30, but only about a quarter of a mile away. The Thomas Fork is almost exactly one mile from the border. It comes in from the right, crossing under the highway and immediately flows into the Bear.

The emigrants had considerable trouble fording this little stream, although the reasons why are no longer in evidence. It looks no more formidable than the Big Blue in Kansas City. The character of the river obviously has changed greatly in the ensuing 140 years.

By the early 1850s there were two bridges across the Thomas Fork, the owners of which each levied a dollar for passage. In those years there were many impoverished men on the trail who resented this bitterly. Many forded, most paid the freight.

Cross the bridge over the confluence of Thomas Fork and the Bear, look ahead and slightly to the right. The ruts are plainly in evidence, snaking up the hill. At the top of that hill the emigration was 6250 feet in the air. The highway builders chose to go to the south to avoid so many turns; the emigration chose the other route because it saved them a climb of 130 more feet.

At the Thomas Fork the Bear cuts down to the south for seven miles, then winds back up toward the highway. The emigrant road crosses the fork 200 yards to the right, then it may be seen moving up and around the same mountain that the highway evades to the left. At Border Summit, where the elevation is 6,385 feet, the trail is about as high but two miles to the north.

The highway and the trail descend evenly, with the trail coming almost due west and U.S. 30 moving northwest to meet it. About 5.5 miles west of the state line, after the appearance of a broad valley at the base of the hills, the trail is off to the right only a few yards, coming around to parallel the road a few yards up the shoulder of a hill.

From this point the trail moves out through the hills in a generally northwestern direction, while the highway swings to the south to travel for several miles along the Bear River. While that course would seem to have been much preferred by the emigrants, because of the abundance of wood, water and grass, a study of the terrain will show that at many points the hills would have continued right down to the river except for the work of contemporary highway engineers. This would have been an impossible canyon for the emigrants.

The mountains to the west are the Wasatch Range. The Mormon emigrations from 1847 on penetrated those mountains southwest of Ft. Bridger on their way to the City of the Great Salt Lake. Emigrant Canyon is behind the range of high hills to the right. It is near the town of Dingle, which is 5.9 miles past the rest area, where the Bear is near the road. The trail is off to the right about 1.3 miles northeast of Dingle, headed northwest.

The site of Smith's Fort is believed to be about the same location, probably where the Union Pacific mainline is today. A mile further on is a highway sign identifying the site as "near here." It could have been to the right, left, or on, the highway.

The fort consisted of four log cabins and some Indian lodges. It was established with the idea of farming the fertile land of the Bear Valley, but there obviously was a lot more fertility in the emigration of 1849. The gold rush came to Smith's Fort too. Peg Leg Smith evidently was about as bad at fort keeping as was Jim Bridger. It was gone by 1850.

Smith was one of the legends of the Oregon Trail. A bona fide mountain man, he worked quietly and efficiently, but failed to gain the great fame of the other Smith, Jed. In the late 1820s he was forced to amputate his own leg, sealing up the arteries with a red hot bullet mold. In his younger days Smith became skillful at kidnapping Indian babies and younger children to sell as slaves to the Mexican trade. Isaac Wistar, who journeyed to California in 1849, met Smith in Independence on the way out and lived to tell about it. Smith got himself all juiced up one night during the period when the trains were forming. He ended up in one hell of a fight. Four toughs tried to keep him from entering a saloon from which he had been banned. When the smoke cleared Peg Leg had killed two of them with his wooden leg. He managed to find a gun and shoot a third as he was retreating from the saloon.

Follow the road until reaching a point about 19.6 miles west of the Wyoming border, or exactly 2.1 miles south of the heart of the town of Montpelier. Here a blacktop road proceeds due west for only a few feet, then turns northwest to parallel U.S. 30. Continue ahead on that blacktop just .8 mile, which is where the trail comes in from the hills to travel beneath this roadway. At 1.6 miles from the corner the blacktop turns right to proceed only a few feet back to the highway. The trail continued straight ahead into the beautiful little town of Montpelier, but the contemporary traveler must gain the highway again and proceed north into town.

In Montpelier the trail is exactly one block west of the highway, through town. As a matter of fact, the trail continues this way, a block or two west of the highway, almost to the Georgetown Summit. About five miles north of Montpelier the trail proceeds through the west edge of the settlement of Bennington, one block west of the highway.

In this stretch note the abundance of abandoned log cabins, a unique feature peculiar to the arid areas of Idaho. Some seem to have been deserted a century ago, yet are essentially sound today.

Exactly three miles northwest of Georgetown the trail crosses the highway from the left and continues due north as the highway heads northwest. Then, only a few yards south of the summit itself, the trail crosses again to the left side of the highway, proceeding across the 6,383-foot pass under or just to the left of the road.

About a half mile ahead the trail veers away from the highway, then again makes a due-north turn to cross the highway just 2.2 miles from the summit. The trail is quite visible during most of this stretch. It is descending at a somewhat more rapid rate than the paved road.

Note that the country is not mountainous in the true sense of the word. In fact it would seem more negotiable than many miles of the trail in Kansas.

When the highway crosses the Caribou County line the trail is off in the cultivated fields about .4 mile to the right. It closes gradually until 1.3 miles into the county, where the trail is only a few yards to the right. At 3.3 miles into the county, the highway crosses Sulphur Canyon, and at that point the trail crosses the highway to parallel it only a few yards to the left. It will continue in this manner into the town of Soda Springs.

At the east edge of Soda Springs the trail was a block to the left of the highway. As Highway 30 rises to go over the railroad tracks at the east city limits, it turns right, but the trail goes straight — one can see about a block of it going into town. Proceed around a sweeping left turn into town and, just before reaching the old Soda Springs High School on the left, turn right onto Third East Street. Continue 1.5 miles to a Y in the road and take the sweeping curve to the left for another half mile. There, shaded by a small pavilion, is Hooper Spring, one of the soda springs that so captivated the emigrations of the 19th century.

Its iron-laden, carbonated waters are perfectly clear, but as they course into the little creek just outside the pavilion, the ferric tracings of the spring branch are plainly seen far below the confluence. The edge of the main stream is colored persimmon from the mineral waters.

Return to U.S. 30 and proceed through the town, headed west. About one mile west of the city limits is a historical marker citing the springs of a bygone era.

Chester Ingersoll's 1847 letters describing the springs were printed in the *Joliet Sentinel* that fall. He placed the first spring about 1,000 feet north of the road, issuing from a mound 15 to 20 feet high, 100 yards long and 50 yards wide. (This mound no longer is in evidence; probably was bulldozed away for the development of the town.) He said that several small springs gushed from its sides. They were warm and loaded with iron, sulphur, soda and lime.

Ingersoll said that a mile further down the road, in a

grove of cedar and pine, were 20 or 30 more springs. But the best, he said, was about 1½ miles north of the road, near a mountain. That spring was 20 feet across the surface, 12 feet deep, with water about 50°. This had to be the Hooper Spring.

Ingersoll finally reported on the most famous spring of all, Steamboat. He described it as being nearly a half-mile further down the road, containing water at 88°, throwing it five or six feet in the air periodically, and foaming. Ten feet away from the mound was an opening in the crust, where steam escaped. One hundred yards further and he came to another spring, this one a chilly 50°, but containing a lot more soda. Nearby were 100 or more springs.

Most of those springs now are inundated beneath the tailwaters of the Soda Point Reservoir. This impoundment is formed by a dam across the Bear, just below Sheep Rock.

The springs were mentioned in almost every diary kept by emigrants who passed this way. Rev. Edward E. Parrish reached there Sept. 9, 1844. Joe H. Sharp in 1852 said, "By sweetening the water of those springs it made very fine drinks; one of them we considered superior to the others. Steamboat Spring emitted puffs of steam at intervals that sounded similar to the puffing of an engine on a steamboat."

Capt. Bonneville drank copiously at the Beer Spring on Nov. 10, 1833. He said it tasted like lager, and hence gave it its name. This spring evidently was just south of the roadside sign, in the reservoir waters now.

Hear Nat Wyeth: "There is also here a warm spring, which throws out water with a jet; which is like bilge-water in taste. There are also here peat beds, which sometimes take fire, and leave behind a deep, light ashe; in which animals sink deep."

On July 17, 1849, Sage wrote: ". . . theare is over a hundred of them they ar on the bank of the bear river the water when you first dip it up sparkles and fomes the same as sodo it also tasts like sodo water only a great deal stronger one mile and a half from theas springs is the steamboat spring this is the most singular one of them all this spring is on the top of a large rock and is hollowed out like a bason at regular intervals the water spouts up two or three feet high and makes a noise resembeling the scape pipe of a steam boat it then settels down slowly and in a few minutes tryes it again.''

Joel Palmer, on Aug. 4, 1845, said his first view of the Soda Springs was two or three white hillocks standing at different points to the right of the road and near a growth of cedar and pine. One was 165 feet long at the base and 50 or 60 feet wide, 25 or 30 feet above the plain. He described Steamboat, however, as having a cone only 2½ feet high and three feet in diameter. He said that the soda water swelled out at intervals of eight to 10 seconds, flowing four to five feet high, luke warm and milky in appearance, but clear as crystal when captured in a vessel. He said the steamboat-like sound could be heard a quarter of a mile away; that the sound came from a small fissure in a rock about six feet from the cone.

The most delightful quote of all is from a letter written by William J.J. Scott, on Aug. 14, 1846: ''the Sody Spring is aquite acuriosity thare is agreat many of them Just boiling rite up out of the groung take alitle sugar and desolve it in alittle water and then dip up acup full and drink it before it looses it gass it is fristrate I drank ahal of galon of it you will see several Spring Spouting up out ove the river it is quite asite to see.''

Leander V. Loomis, a member of Iowa's Birmingham Emigration Co. of 1850, gave some geographic clues in his diary entry of June 28. He said that there was a small stream leading to the Beer Spring. This would be the little creek into which the Hooper Spring branch now flows. It crosses the highway a half mile west of town, just east of the historical sign. He said that a few rods further on were more springs. A half mile further, the road turns away from the river and leads up the bluffs, but a footpath continues along the river, and after another 200 to 300 yards the Steamboat Spring is reached. That road now also is beneath the reservoir.

A short distance past the historical sign is the Soda Springs Country Club. On the far side of the grounds, .4 mile west of the entrance to the clubhouse, there is a little

The Hooper Spring, last of the big-volume springs at Soda Springs. Sparkling waters are laden with minerals and carbon dioxide.

Not even 40 feet of water could stop old Steamboat Spring, still puffing away on the bottom of Soda Point Reservoir.

gravel road at the base of a hill. Take it to the left, or southeast. There is a little surprise up ahead.

Wind exactly .3 mile in among the sage covered hills, stop the car and look to the left. There are two rust-colored, flat cones on the left side of the road. At the top of the left one, the larger of the two, is a small issuance of carbonated water inside a shallow crater. This is one of the remaining soda mounds. Note that not a sprig of vegetation grows on either mound. The other now is dry.

Another .1 mile further there is a Y in the road curving to the left. The left leg is the old Oregon Trail, leading up to the golf course to the east. On that property it is a luxuriant green swale. Here it is only two dusty ruts. Don't take it. Take the right leg of the Y, and it will wind around the Monsanto pavilion.

At the other side of the pavilion stop. Walk 10 yards to the top of the little hillock on the left, and take a bearing of 108°. Look along this sight line a quarter of

*Sheep Rock, four miles west of Soda Springs, where
the emigrants turned north toward Ft. Hall.*

the way across the reservoir. There is old Steamboat,
puffing away as always, only now 40 feet beneath the
surface of the lake. On a calm day, when the water is
still, the disturbance in the surface is pronounced. It is
difficult to see when the lake is choppy. But there she is.
The sound is gone, but all the mischief man could cook
up to obliterate a delightful national landmark couldn't
stop the Steamboat Spring.

Continue west on U.S. 30 for another three miles. The
road to Oregon is on the left, but it crosses the highway
opposite a great stone mountain on the left. Now known as
Soda Point, this is the famed Sheep Rock of the Oregon
Emigration. Around the base of it flows the Bear River,
which had been so kind to the pioneers. Now, in one majestic curve, it heads away from the trail, down south
toward the Great Salt Lake.

About .1 mile past Soda Point is the paved road west of
Alexander Station. Take it to the right and take an odometer reading. The road soon curves to the left and
this is now the Oregon Trail — the traveler will stay on it,
more or less, for the next several miles. The road looks
primitive and in spots it is. It could not be traversed by a
normal automobile within two or three days after a good

rain. It is pure dirt in many places, but hard enough in the hot dry summer.

Less than a mile from Alexander Station, just before the trail crosses a creek and heads up the mountian, is the site of the start of the famed Hudspeth Cutoff to California. The Bidwell-Bartleson party split back at Sheep Rock, with half the emigrants going on to Oregon and the balance taking an agonizing trek south through the Utah and Nevada deserts to California. The split was not tried again until 1849, and, when it was, it took place right here.

When the rushing '49ers came through, their quest for gold was so pronounced that they split again. This time the way was blazed by Benoni Hudspeth and John Myers, who reached this point July 19, 1849. Their route, however, headed straight west to intercept the Raft River road to California. It was less tortuous than the prior one and soon great hordes of gold seekers were eliminating the northern leg to Fort Hall and taking the Hudspeth Cutoff.

Chester Ingersoll described these 55 or 60 miles from Soda Springs into Fort Hall as a poor road — rocky, hilly or sandy, with water good and grass poor. This was the consensus of many emigrants and will be the consensus today also.

Continue on the Oregon Trail as it winds around the mountain and into the hills on a general bearing of 320 degrees. There is a Y in the road 1.5 miles past the Alexander Station. Take the left branch. For the first two or three miles ruts may be seen leading off the dirt road from time to time, on one side or another. These are the ruts of the Oregon Trail, as it winds to the right, left or on the contemporary road.

George B. Currey, an Oregon pioneer, reported late in the 19th century that he found a man named D. Booth there, who seemingly had been mortally wounded by Indians. Currey put him on his wagon, hauled him as far as the Salmon Falls on the Snake River, and there he died.

They buried him carelessly — other Indians exhumed the body, robbed it, and buried it again head down.

There are a number of fertile little valleys along the road after the first few miles, and the cultivation here has rendered the exact route of the trail obscure.

The Oregon Trail is bearing a steady 320 degrees. At the first opportunity turn left, around a small cluster of willow trees. Go .7 mile further to another T in the road and turn right there. Proceed one more mile straight ahead and the road quickly becomes more primitive, winding around to the left. At the point where the road turns left, the trail stays on the right for the next mile and a half.

Exactly 8.1 miles from Alexander Station there is a monument on the right side of the road, at the site of a small Mormon cemetery. This is the Ivins Pioneer Cemetery, containing 20 bodies with death dates ranging from 1883 to 1940. The trail cuts across the road .2 mile north of the cemetery, headed northwest. At 10.5 miles from the station there is a T in the road — take it to the left and make an intercept .3 mile ahead.

Exactly 4.5 miles from that corner is the highway. Turn right, or north. Four miles to the north is Eighteenmile Creek and at that point the trail crossed, then turned due north to parallel the roadway some 1,000 feet to the left. The road makes a series of turns to arrive at the little village of Chesterfield. This was a typical pioneer village — a small false-front brick general store, a brick school, and a dozen or two other buildings of logs, both dwelling and farm buildings. Almost all the structures now are abandoned.

One could go on past Chesterfield to the the point where the Oregon Trail comes to the Portneuf River. It arrived just a few yards down from the dam, and today the water covers the trail for a good many miles. One could also collect some buckshot souvenirs, as the area is posted, ''No Trespassing.'' But the primitive roadway only touches the trail once before it disintegrates to the point

Emigrants had the Three Buttes in their sights for three days approaching Ft. Hall. The view is considerably faded today due to atmospheric conditions.

of impassability.

So return on Idaho Highway 73 all the way to Bancroft and U.S. 30, and then turn right. Pass the charming town of Lava Hot Springs. Eleven miles further is I-86 — take it north, or right. In that stretch before reaching the interstate highway the Portneuf is crossed. That is all the traveler is going to see of the little river that made such a big target for the emigrants.

Proceed north through Pocatello and on to the Fort Hall exit. The trail, in the meantime, has been cutting north through and past the reservoir, then heads almost due west to hit Nat Wyeth's vindictive folly on the Snake, Fort Hall. At the overpass turn right onto the Simplot Road, to again be on the Oregon Trail, this time in reverse. (T comes in 1.3 miles to the east.) About 4.5 miles east of I-15 a small road comes in from the left a short distance west of a complex of farm buildings. At this point the trail is about 500 feet to the left and paralleling the road.

The road makes an S curve to the right and, where the road curves back to the left again, the Oregon Trail once more comes beneath it, but only for a few dozen yards. Then it turns right, and a few yards later the road does too. Exactly 8.2 miles from the highway there is a gravel road coming in from the right. This is in the center of a sweeping curve to the left on the Simplot Road. About .5 mile down this road the Oregon Trail comes in, and generally it is in the same location as the roadway all the way around the north side of North Putnam Mountain, the great bulk (8,860 feet) looming to the southeast.

One can go no further legally as the area is posted — the sign reads as follows: "No Trespassing. Stop. Notice & Warning. This is a private road for use only by enrolled Shoshone-Bannock tribe. Trespassers will be prosecuted. Department of Law and Order, Shoshone-Bannock tribe." Forget, hell. The last time the American Indian allowed trespassers on his land he lost the whole damned West.

The route around the mountain is very similar to the route north of Sheep Rock. Turn around and return to I-15.

On the way back look at the three great buttes on the northern horizon. These were noted landmarks on the Oregon Trail and signified that a rugged, dry segment of the trail was about to end. Sage, on July 19, 1849, climbed one of the hills and looked over toward the north and the famed mounds. Actually they are the Twin Buttes, 32 miles west of Idaho Falls, plus Big Southern Butte, 19 miles north-northwest of the Twin Buttes.

Proceed west across I-15 for just .5 mile and turn right onto Eagle Rd. Drive .5 mile north and turn left onto Agency Rd. Upon making that turn the trail comes beneath the roadway and follows for .3 mile west, where it veers to the northwest to cut through the center of the town of Ft. Hall. Ahead on the left are the buildings of the Indian Agency. Travelers who wish to proceed to the 1834 Ft. Hall site are asked to stop here to obtain permission to do so. Continue the balance of that mile, cross the railroad tracks and turn right. At .3 mile ahead the trail came across the highway, about through the elevator of the Russet Chemical Co. Continue another .2 mile and turn left onto the Sheepskin Road.

Just .8 mile west the trail crossed the roadway from the southeast and at the end of the first mile it is on a due west course a few yards off to the right side of the road. It continues in this manner to the end of the blacktop, which is a total of five miles west of the highway.

At the end of this stretch there is a gate and a notice to the effect that travelers must have permission to enter the tract from the Ft. Hall Indian Agency. Here the trail and the road are one and the same, and will continue to be right up to the marker. The trick is in finding the marker.

Site of old Ft. Hall, on the Snake River northwest of Pocatello. Monument is there; bronze plaque is gone.

Take another odometer reading, then go outside the car and burn every damn map in sight. If you get lost, die like a man. Don't ask any Indians for directions because all those directions will bring you right back to where you should have died in the first place. Maybe if you are lucky a Charlie Moyer will be dispatched in his earthy pickup truck from on high to guide you to the site of old Ft. Hall. That's what happened to us.

Stay on the good gravel road. Slow down and turn left exactly 1.5 miles from the fence. This also is a good gravel road.

On July 8, 1849, Bennett C. Clark of Missouri described this stretch of the trail as "a perfect bog."

Exactly three miles ahead a broad gravel road will come into the gravel road from the right. Turn right onto it. This is the Oregon Trail. Ahead another .8 miles there is a fork in the road. To the left it is rutty, so keep to the right. In recent years somebody cut a few yards further to the right to avoid deepening the old ruts; the original trail is rejoined a few hundred yards away. This is the same process that has gone on since the beginnings of the trail.

Exactly .9 miles from the Y there will be a monument on the right. There is a broad turnaround here. At one time the face of the monument bore a plaque with a legend etched on its face, but two of the smaller mosquitoes hereabouts pried it off and flew away with it.

This, then, is the site of old Fort Hall. The four corners may be located from the marker: pace 13 yards at 329 degrees; 17 yards at 027 degrees; 12 yards at 085 degrees; and four yards at 220 degrees. Nothing of Wyeth's original post was left in the late 1930s but some rotted wood from the foundations, and only slight ridges are left today.

Bitter and disillusioned, Nat Wyeth arrived at the site on July 14, 1834, and made his decision to build here the next day. Twelve men, including Osborne Russell, went to work with their axes, and soon the fort was complete. It was surrounded by a wall. Inside the stockade were houses, stores, barns, and a two-story blockhouse. Wyeth built his stockade well, along the lines of the French *poteaux en terre* style found in early Ste. Genevieve, Mo. homes, indicating that the structure still could be standing, as some are today in that old Mississippi River town, had it received minimal care. Wyeth used cottonwood logs, their butts stuck two and a half feet into the ground with 15 feet above ground.

The fort had two bastions at opposite corners, each eight feet square. It was completed Aug. 4, and the following day the Stars and Stripes was unfurled.

The first death at Fort Hall took place July 27, 1834, while the fort was still under construction. Jason Lee had just preached the first Protestant sermon in the Pacific Northwest, when a man named Casseau was bought in. A participant in a horse race, he had been thrown; the horse rolled over on him. He was cupped and bled, but he died the next morning. Wyeth reported that Lee preached over the body, the Canadians sang Catholic chants, and the relatives of his Indian wife conducted their rites at the funeral.

Narcissa Whitman arrived there late in July 1836, a year before Wyeth sold the fort to the Hudson's Bay

Harold Warp Pioneer Museum
Jackson's Ft. Hall is purely conjectural, but it is remarkably close to crude sketches left by emigrants. He was a good researcher as well as a good painter and photographer of the early West.

Company and went back to Fresh Pond and the ice business. This is part of her letter written from here: "The buildings of the fort are made of hewed logs, with roofs covered with mud brick, chimneys and fireplaces also being built of the same. No windows, except a square hole in the roof, and in the bastion a few portholes large enough for guns only. The buildings were all enclosed in a strong log wall. This affords them a place of safety when attacked by hostile Indians as they frequently are, the fort being in the Blackfeet country."

Fremont described the fort as laying in a valley 20 miles long, formed by the confluence of the Portneuf with the "Lewis Fork the Columbia [the Snake River] which enters nine miles below the fort." He listed it as 1,323 miles from Westport.

Fremont stayed only a few hours, on Sept. 22, 1843, and then forded the Portneuf. The ford was described as being 110 yards wide, only axle deep, but the passage was most uncomfortable due to a cold, high wind, and rain beating into their faces.

Marcus Whitman's wagon was the first to reach Ft. Hall. Lower on the Snake an axle snapped, and Narcissa rejoiced prematurely at the thought of finishing the journey quickly with the horses. No such luck. The dogged Whitman, determined to prove that the West could be traversed by a wagon over the Oregon Trail, turned it into a cart. The makeshift arrangement lasted only until Ft. Boise, but the point had been made by that time, whether Dr. Whitman knew it or not.

Four years later, on July 27, 1840, Rev. Cushing Eells and his diarist wife, Myra, arrived at the post, now manned by Hudsons Bay Company factors, and were introduced to "Mr. [Thomas] McKay & many Nez Perce." McKay was a principal factor of the Company. They were counseled that no wagons could be moved into the Oregon country from Ft. Hall; that the road down the Raft River to California was definitely passable with wagons, so California was the place to go. Did the Company realize the peril to British colonialism that the American emigration was causing, and was it making a concerted attempt to steer the travelers out of British-claimed territory? It might seem so, but Merle Wells of the Idaho State Historical Society is in disagreement and has plenty of documentation behind his case.

DeSmet came to Ft. Hall on Aug. 16, 1841, and was met by a huge delegation of dancing, cheering Flatheads, who had ridden several hundred miles to meet him. Contrast this to the ho-hum attitude the red man had for the Protestants.

Farnham arrived at the fort early in September, 1839, and noted that goods sold there were about 50 per cent lower than at American posts.

Marcus Whitman saw Ft. Hall many times, but the most important visit in terms of the Manifest Destiny was in 1843. W. J. Ghent, writing in 1929, states that Oregon was won for the U.S. with that visit, when the good doctor guided the caravan of 1,000 persons (including Jesse Applegate) through the fort. Whitman continued west, thus opening up the flood gates for the emigration of the next 30 years.

The British still were being accused of handing out bad advice in 1845. Joel Palmer said that they told him that many lives had been lost crossing the Snake and on the Columbia, which certainly was true. Many lives also had been lost crossing the Vermillions in Kansas, for that matter. They talked of the hostility of the debased Indian tribes, and that was true too. Palmer said they talked of the snows in the Blue Mountains, and of all those that died in that craggy wilderness. California never looked better, but still the emigration headed for Oregon.

Palmer arrived there Aug. 8, 1845, and camped about a mile southwest of the fort. The bare-breasted Snake squaws and their braves swarmed all around them. He described the river at that point as being 150 yards wide and flowing to within a half mile of the fort. They had to travel five more miles to hit the mouth of the Portneuf.

Ingersoll in 1847 said that the fort was "the worst place for emigrants that we have seen, since they [the factors] are almost destitute of honesty or human feelings." Ingersoll was there, however, in the declining years of the fort, for in its heyday the British would always subject their national well-bring to the welfare of the humanity that coursed across the plains.

By July 20, 1849, the fort was reduced to one mud building, according to Sage. It was completely abandoned in 1855 and the plain was scoured clean by a whopper of a flood in the summer of 1863.

The Oregon Trail from Ft. Hall proceeded only another half mile or so to the southwest where it plunged into the American Falls reservoir. The old ford over the mouth of the Portneuf is now several fathoms below the surface.

It was just past this ford that a band of Gros Ventres got their evens for a nasty little trick played on them at the Battle of Pierre's Hole back in 1832. A Gros Ventre chief was carrying a peace pipe to an armistice proposal before the battle, and a swarthy Iroquois named Antoine Goddin calmly rode out and shot him dead.

Goddin, now headed west from Ft. Hall, was summoned across the Portneuf to make a trade for some beaver pelts. He sat for the customary smoke with the Indians. As he reached for the pipe a Gros Ventre bullet smashed into his spine. He writhed in agony when his scalp was lifted, and just before he died the initials NJW (for his employer) were knifed into his forehead.

Joseph Ware, in his guide book, says that the Bannock River (Creek, actually) was crossed three miles from Ft. Hall, that it was 120 yards wide at the mouth with a narrow, soft bottom. Hulbert says it was six miles away. Loomis says the Portneuf was four miles distant; that the Bannock was another three miles on down the Snake. Loomis was right; the rest were wrong.

Return to I-15 and take it south, back towards Pocatello. About a mile north of town will be an interchange with I-15W. Take it. Proceed to the west through the Michaud Flats — a perfectly level area of high ground south of the Snake. The emigrants took the lower ground, and so the trail still is beneath the reservoir. Upon leaving the flats the highway will pass over Bannock Creek, which is unmarked. One more mile and there is a cluster of potato processing buildings (spud houses, they are called) on the left, identified as Shiller Siding. Exactly four miles further on the Oregon Trail starts to emerge from the reservoir, one mile to the right. The trail at that point is two miles south of the original bed of the Snake River.

American Falls to Three-Island Crossing

At the American Falls exit turn right to go into town. At the top of that exit ramp is an excellent view of the great reservoir, stretching to the northwest all the way to the horizon. There are supposed to be ruts of the trail in town, but these cannot be the main branch, which now is in the reservoir. It crossed the dam site right on the south bank of the river.

Take Business I-15 about .5 mile west to Ft. Hall Avenue, opposite the American Falls High School. Turn right on Ft. Hall Avenue and proceed to a little gravel street named "Oregon Trail." Turn left there and go a block or so to Idanha Avenue, which is on the east (near) edge of a small park. Turn right on Idanha, drive past the park, and head down the slope to the river. Turn left at a T there, and 50 yards ahead is a Meeker-like monument enclosed with a fence. It was erected in 1915. The monument probably was built right in the trail.

Ingersoll described the river above the falls as being

This dam was built just upstream from the spectacular American Falls, where, before impoundment, the Snake River plunged 50 feet in a 200-foot stretch across the entire 800-foot width of the river.

800 to 900 feet wide with a strong current. The falls themselves were a drop of 50 feet in perhaps 200 feet of length. Myra Eells camped at the falls on Aug. 2, 1838: "Mosquitoes so troublesome that we cannot go out of our tent without everything but our eyes covered. Horses are nearly black with them, and they cannot eat for them. Camped here 4½ hours." She described the falls as being 15 to 20 feet deep.

Two years earlier Narcissa Whitman wrote a letter home from the West. "We passed the American Falls on Snake river just after dinner," she said. "The roar of the water is heard at a considerable distance."

Wilson Price Hunt stopped at the American Falls on Oct. 24, 1811, and camped at the head of the falls for the night. At that time the fall was described as being about 30 feet perpendicular.

Loomis passed here on July 3, 1850, reflecting extraordinarily fast travel. He cited the water passing over a pile of rocks 75 feet high — "a grand sight. We all stopped our teams and went down to see them. At their foot was a continual rainbow while the sun was shining."

The falls were caused by a dyke of black trap rock extending across the river in horseshoe form. They were named in the days when it was unusual for Americans to be in these parts because of the total domination of the Hudson's Bay Co. over the fur business in the Pacific Northwest. Early in this period a party of American trappers were traveling down the Snake in a boat, became trapped in the current and were sucked over the falls. One survived to tell about it.

Upon returning from the river, proceed only to the I-15 Business Loop, which is also known as Fort Hall Avenue. The trail is paralleling the road and the Snake, right on the bank of the river.

Continue to the I-15W approach and start up the ramp. Turn right a few yards prior to reaching the westbound ramp, toward Neeley. The trail parallels the road about 300 yards to the right, cutting across the loops of the Snake. Proceed 4.3 miles ahead. There are good ruts a few yards off to the right of the road.

Return to the I-15 ramp and turn southwest on the highway. Just 4.7 miles ahead is the point where the trail came up from the Snake and crossed the highway.

About 6.5 miles west along I-15 the trail comes beneath or slightly south of the highway. Soon there will be a historical sign, citing the passage of the Hunt party in 1811. Stop there and walk exactly 200 yards on a bearing of 075 degrees. There is a deep swale, a cut in the earth ranging from two feet to six feet deep. This is the old emigrant road. There is 1,300 feet of it on either side of that point, wending its way down toward the highway below and Massacre Rock Pass. This is the site of the incident for which the pass is named.

John C. Hilman was on this spot, and here is the text of a letter he wrote to a friend in St. Louis on August 11, 1862:

"On the 8th of this month I wrote you and sent the letter by a Mormon to Chandler Co., Salt Lake, to be mailed.

"That was the first opportunity I got of sending a letter since the upper crossing of the Platt. I little thot when I wrote you on the 8th that an occurrence was to take place next day and the day following, and which will long impress itself upon my mind, and that we were in the very midst of a great danger and seemed to be almost entirely unconscious of it. I will relate what happened as nearly as I can: On Saturday about 5 p.m. I was riding ahead of the train a mile or so, in search of grass and a camping place at which we might remain over Sunday. On looking up the road ahead of me I saw a horseman coming toward me in a hasty manner.

"This was a rare thing to see any person coming eastward, and especially in so hasty a manner. On his approaching me I discovered that it was a man belonging to our wagon, and who had left us on the day previous to overtake a friend of his who he learned was in a train two days ahead of us. The first thing he said to me was, 'My God, John, the Indians have massacred a train and robbed them of all they had, and they are only a short distance from us.' I at once became conscious of our extreme danger and turned back to inform the train and bring up the wagons which were lagging behind and I expected an attack to be made any moment. Learning that two ox trains were ahead of us and going to camp at or near the battlefield we pushed to overtake them.

"In an hours' driving we came to the place where the horrible scene took place, but found the Indians had run off the stock, taking the provisions, clothing, etc., of the train, but left the wagons, which the ox trains ahead of us had taken and gone on, in pursuit of grass. I found quite a quantity of blood, and fragments of such things as immigrants usually carry with them, and it was evident that the Indians had done their hellish deeds in a hasty manner and left.

"The place selected by them for the attack was the best on the road and not far distant from the road which turns down to Salt Lake, which I learned is 175 miles south of us. Here we pushed on endeavoring to overtake them, but only got a short distance on account of the darkness, and were obliged to camp on the very ground where the Indians had, a few hours previous, made a ring with their pandemonium-like shouts, and [made the ground] red with the blood of innocent men and women. We at once put out

Massacre Rocks, named for an Indian attack upon a wagon train in 1862.

a strong picket guard on the surrounding hills, got a hasty supper in the dark, staked out mules in the sage brush and hoped the night would be a short one. Nothing happening, we pushed on at daybreak for the ox teams and grass, which we found in a camp five miles distant, and here we camped during the day.

"I here found three men killed and several wounded, one woman mortally wounded, and the wagons which the Indians had left. Two of the men killed were from Iowa City, A.J. Winter and an Italian whose name I did not learn. The other man was from New York City, Bulwinkle was his name, and it is said had some $6,000 which was taken from him. All were buried here but the affair did not end here.

"Some thirty men from the two ox trains and the trains attacked the previous day, started out in pursuit of the Indians and their stock. After traveling some seven miles in the direction in which the Indians went they came suddenly upon them and a fight immediately commenced. At the first fire, three-fourths of the white men ran and the red men pursued, and after a running fight of some three miles, the Indians ceased their pursuit.

"In this fight three of whites were killed and five severely wounded, one I think mortally. After we learned the fate of the last party, the greatest excitement prevailed in camp and a small party went to their assistance to recover the dead and wounded, one of which was not found and one had been scalped, the first scalped man I ever saw. Late in the evening both parties returned and two more ox trains came into camp, making now some two hundred wagons and 400 men and 300 women and children.

"This morning we all started together after burying the dead, and came 13 miles to Raft River, where we all encamped for the day, and where I am writing this. Here the road forks, one for Oregon and Washington, and the other for California.

"Truly your friend, John C. Hillman.

"P.S. The Indians I have alluded to were Snakes, and it is thought were in large force."

Abut 7.5 miles past the overpass west of American Falls is Massacre Rock State Park. Here the 20th century traveler may find some truly delightful views of some of the West's most rugged landscape. The Oregon Trail passed through the same gap the highway does.

A mile or two past Massacre Rock State Park is another Idaho park, Register Rock. Here is preserved one of innumerable "register" rocks — now safe behind a chain link fence. In it are carved countless names, most of them now illegible. They date back to 1849.

About 9 miles west of Massacre Rocks, as the trail and the highway lift out of the Snake canyon, look to the low ridge to the left of the highway. Here are some pronounced ruts left by the emigrant wagons.

Cross the line into Cassia County and at this point the trail is about a half mile south of the highway. Two and a half miles west of the county line is an exit onto a good blacktopped county road. Take it, turn left beneath the highway, and proceed 1.6 miles.

The trail makes an intercept with the road in the middle of a sweeping turn to the left. The emigrant road is bearing 240 degrees on a beeline toward the Raft River, only a mile away. The Oregon Trail crossed the Raft there, and for the excited California-bound travelers, the fabled California Trail turned south on the west bank. Ingersoll notes that, of the 750 wagons in his 1847 train, 60 to 70 turned at the Raft. Return to the highway, and just a few yards on to the west the Raft crosses beneath the road.

Another 10 miles west on the highway is a sign commemorating the California Trail. It is located there because this is the rest area nearest the Raft River. Proceed on across this desert-like expanse. The trail exactly parallels the highway, two miles to the south. At the end of I-15W, which is at its junction with I-80, take the latter route to the southeast. Just 3.4 miles from that intersection the trail crossed, still bearing almost due west. Continue to the first exit and follow the arrows to Declo. A few yards away is U.S. 30N. Take it westbound and return, almost paralleling the same I-80 stretch traveled moments before.

About 3.7 miles from this exit the highway turns due west, and it is at this point that the Oregon Trail passed beneath the highway. It stays generally with the highway until it reaches the town of Burley.

At Declo, eight miles east of Burley, the trail is a half mile north of town. Continue 2.5 miles west of Declo, and at that point the Snake comes in almost to the highway, and the trail runs beneath the road. A cluster of new homes now is located there, and the old emigrant road evidently cut through their yards.

Soon Highway 30 makes a gradual turn to the right, closely following the Snake. At this point the Oregon Trail continues straight west, to touch the south city limit of the town of Burley. Continue through Burley and 4.7 miles on past, where the highway makes a large curve to the left and away from the Snake, the emigrant road crosses, headed toward the river.

At this point there is a guard rail on the right side of the highway. The old road comes through a group of farm buildings on the left, crosses over and generally follows the course of the Union Pacific on the right.

Continue 4.5 miles southwest, then due west for three miles, and there will be a gradual left curve in the highway. At this point turn right, to go 2.1 miles to a T intersection near the Milner Dam.

This is a great reclamation project — the structure that has turned south central Idaho green and put potatoes on the plates of people all over the United States. It giveth and it taketh away. The great Snake River — one of the most picturesque in the world — is little more than a creek below this dam. The foaming cataracts, the roaring falls, the long stretches of white water — virtually gone. This is all a seasonal thing, of course. In the early spring the Snake regains a large part of its old, unharnessed meanness.

Turn west, or left, for about a half mile at that T intersection, and then turn right, just east of a grain elevator, to cross the tracks and proceed a tenth of a mile to the little bridge across the Snake below the dam. In this stretch the main irrigation canal is crossed. In July, this is brim full of fast moving water.

When the bridge leads over the Snake notice the great rocks that once served as the bed of the river and frequently tore the bottoms out of boats. Now they are high and dry. In midsummer the Snake isn't even as wide as the irrigation canal.

Idaho Historical Society
The violent Cauldron Linn on the Snake, which stopped further water passage by Wilson Price Hunt's Astorians in 1811.

Idaho Historical Society
Artifacts from the Astorians' death canoe were recovered from the Snake in 1938; now are on display in the museum of the Idaho Historical Society in Boise.

Back off the bridge, recross the tracks, and continue on west on the south lip of the chasm. At 1.5 miles the road starts to peter out — so turn left for a mile. The trail has been directly beneath the road — now it will cut diagonally across the next section of land, through the intersection and to the southwest. Turn south (left) for a mile, then west (right) for another mile, and the trail is cutting through again; this time it is just to the right of the intersection a few yards. Proceed ahead for almost a half mile and make a long jog to the left. At the right turn which completes the jog the trail touches the corner and conttinues in a west-southwest direction. Complete passage through that section and make a turn to the south, or left. Just .1 mile from that intersection the trail makes an intercept with the roadway. Continue south to the next mile road, then right, or west, another 1.3 miles, where the road turns south again. The trail is off to the right a quarter of a mile, closely following the Snake. Proceed south for one more mile to U.S. 30 and turn right.

At 1.4 miles ahead turn right, back toward the Snake. At the end of that road, which is the south lip of the chasm, turn right on a good blacktop road. Proceed .4 mile and stop. Down to the left is the once-horrible Cauldron Linn.

In 1811 Wilson Price Hunt's Astorians experienced a disaster that underscored the counsel of the Indians — don't try the Snake in a boat. On Oct. 28, one of the two canoes made it through the canyon above Cauldron

Linn without damage. The other crashed against a rock, split and overturned. Antoine Clappine died in the swirling torrent; four survived.

Retrace the route back to U.S. 30. About 1.9 miles dead ahead (to the west) the highway makes a gradual curve to the right. Ahead is a gravel road heading away from the curve, straight west. Take it. The trail crosses the highway in the middle of the curve. Continue west for 2.5 miles. The trail almost parallels the road on the left, but at the end of that first stretch, at a T in the road, it is nearly a half mile south.

Turn south, or left, to an intercept a half mile away. Proceed to the next corner and turn right on a good blacktop road. Stay on this road for the next seven miles. The trail now is near the bottom of its loop away from the Snake and soon will start back north to the river. At .6 into the first mile, the trail comes across the roadway from the right and parallels about .3 mile to the left for the next three miles. At the start of the fourth mile from the corner, it veers to the northwest and, at the end of the fifth mile, it is making an intercept in the intersection. Proceed ahead for only two more miles. At this point make a right turn.

Idaho Historical Society
Twin Falls once looked like this — a roaring cataract split by a great rock.

The north fall, left, now has only a trickle of water. The south fall, at right, is completely dry. A combination of reclamation and water power doomed the scenic attraction.

At 1.5 miles there is a bridge over an irrigation ditch — the trail crossed about here, headed northwest. Continue due north on this road now, as far as possible — that will be about 7.5 miles from the intercept.

The detour now being made is the same one that some 100,000 emigrants made 125 years ago, to see the famous Twin Falls of the Snake. There is a precipitous descent to the overlook area and one of Idaho's most handsome parks. It is not so steep that a normal recreational vehicle can't use it, with proper use of the gear train.

One would be in for a bitter disappointment if he hadn't seen the Milner Dam first. The Twin Falls, once a foaming cataract split by an enormous rock formation, are virtually dry in the irrigation season. There is a slight trickle of water over the northern fall — probably the result of a leak more than anything else. The Idaho Power Co. has harnessed the rest of the flow, diverting it away from the south fall, which now is perfectly dry.

Idaho Historical Society
*The Snake once roared over Shoshone Falls, dropping
212 feet to the deep pool below.*

Yet, all around is green. Here trees are growing where
before nothing could make it but sage. Where once there
was sterile sand, there now is a carpet of grass the color
of an emerald.

Many could argue the case against water power —
cheap electricity is often expensive when the loss of the
tourist attraction is calculated. But few could quarrel
with the reclamation project. So there is some good
news and there is some bad news.

Return out of the canyon to the first four-way
intersection and turn right, or west, onto a road marked
N4000. Proceed only two miles and turn right, or north,
onto E3300 St., and continue a mile to the famed
Shoshone Falls.

Again a steep grade is encountered. Proceed to an
overlook area and observe the falls. Note the results of a
cruel harnessment, but at least at Shoshone what is left
of the water is allowed to pass over the brink. The Snake

drops 212 feet over a horse-shoe-shaped rim about 1,000 feet wide. Visitors may walk on the rocks of the brink, where only a few isolated streams plunge to the deep pool below. At one time the water roared over the entire escarpment virtually unbroken. Thomas J. Farnham, in 1843, said that the roar could be heard three miles away.

Shoshone too is virtually dry. Both Twin Falls and Shoshone gain considerably more life in the spring, before irrigation is needed.

Return to N4000 and proceed exactly four miles south (straight ahead) from that point. Turn right, or west, for .8 mile, jog to the right, and then turn right alongside Rock Creek. The emigrants moved all this distance from the Snake just to cross this little creek, only a few feet wide and a few inches deep, with a solid rock base. The problem is that it is at the bottom of a killer canyon. The records show that the crossing was made about .8 mile west-northwest of the turn back to the north.

Proceed ahead another .8 mile and turn left, or west, for one full mile. At the end of that mile, past the Amalgamated Sugar Co., turn left, or south, and descend into the shallow Rock Creek Canyon, cross the creek and climb out with scarcely a strain on the engine. The emigrant crossing is .2 mile southeast of here. At .4 mile from the turn the trail crosses the road headed west. Proceed the rest of that mile to the south and then turn right, or west. Proceed for one mile and turn north, onto Blue Lakes Blvd. About .8 mile ahead is a probable intercept with the trail, which now is following a pipeline exactly. The location of the line is marked with steel poles painted in alternating orange and black bands.

Continue to the next corner and here make a decision.

To proceed along the Oregon Trail, turn left onto Orchard Drive. Otherwise continue on ahead on Blue Lakes Boulevard and cross the Snake chasm 476 feet above the water.

This has nothing to do with the Oregon Trail, but it is a startling illustration of the statistics of the Snake River Canyon. Return to the first four-way intersection south of the bridge, and from this point proceed exactly four miles south to Orchard Drive.

Turn right, or west, at this point, and the traveler is back on the old course again. Note a pipe line marker .3 mile to the right, marking the course of the Oregon Trail. Continue for another 1.7 miles and turn to the right, or north, on Grandview Drive South. About 1.5 miles ahead, or .1 mile past the pipe line marker, there is an intercept with the trail, which still is headed back toward the Snake. At the next corner turn left, or west, onto Addison Street, which is U.S. 30 and U.S. 93 — a four-lane expressway. Turn right, or north, on E2700, and proceed .6 mile, where the road turns half-left. The Oregon Trail comes under the roadway at this point and stays there for nearly a half mile, when the street turns half left again after an S curve.

At that point both road and trail will leave the troublesome Rock Creek Canyon. The road continues toward the west, the trail again on the logical northwest course. Go to the next corner and turn north, or right, onto E2600. A half mile ahead is another intercept with the trail. The next corner is N4100 — turn to the left, or west there and a half mile away is another intercept. Continue to the next corner and turn to the right, or north.

There is an intercept .5 mile ahead; turn left (west) again at the end of that mile. This time go almost to the next intersection, a mile away, before the trail crosses the road. It intersects just a few yards before this next intersection, headed to the northwest. Continue on another mile from that intersection and turn up toward the Snake once more. At .7 mile is another intercept, and again the high degree of cultivation of the plain, only recently covered with sage, has eradicated any trace of the trail. Turn to the left at the end of that mile and there is another intercept .4 mile west. At the stop sign at the end of that mile turn north again, or right. At .7

mile the trail crosses again. The road ends in a T up ahead, and beyond it the high edge of the black lava canyon rim told the emigrants that they had again reached the river.

Turn left at that T and proceed two miles to the west. At .3 mile of that leg the trail makes an intercept, goes up to the canyon rim and turns back south again. There was an obstruction, a steep gorge of Cedar Creek, now dry. It barred the way, as Rock Creek had done earlier. At the end of two westward miles will be another T — again the road is barred by the same canyon. Detour to the south one mile, west one mile, and north another mile. At .8 of that last mile the trail had crossed the gorge and now crosses the road headed northwest. The emigrants had crossed the gulch a half mile east of the intercept. Proceed to the corner and turn left, or west.

The trail is cutting across the cornfields now, headed toward the Snake for a second time, and it crosses the west-bound route .4 mile from the corner, through a group of farm buildings on the left side of the road.

Continue one more mile from the next mile corner and turn right, or north. The trail crosses the road at .7 mile up toward the Snake. Turn west at the next corner. Leave the blacktop here and turn onto a good, solid, gravel road. All other roads from east of Twin Falls have been blacktop. There will be another intercept at .3 mile to the west; continue on to the next mile corner and turn north, or right, at the stop sign. This is a good blacktop road. About .6 mile ahead is another intercept. Once more the black scarps above the Snake are in view to the north. At the end of this road is an arrow to the right; don't take it. Turn left instead and hang on.

There is considerable earth in the base of this road so don't try it unless the weather has been dry. As soon as the turn is completed the Oregon Trail will be beneath the road, probing and searching for a place to cross the Snake.

The grade is precipitous, requiring full use of the gear train plus plenty of brakes. As the plunge down into the canyon is completed, there will be a T in the road and a stop sign. Jog to the right here, about 100 yards, and turn left again onto another gravel road, past a huge cottonwood tree. For the better part of a mile along the Snake one may look to the right, down to a black gravel road, which is the Oregon Trail. It is coming up to meet this road, but the exact spot is no longer visible.

This is a good gravel road but it is a rough one. Even in wet weather it should be little more than uncomfortable, but no guarantees. At 1.6 miles from the cottonwood are two consecutive Y's in the road — in both cases, bear right.

At 2.9 miles there is a T in the road; turn to the right. Then turn right again to cross over Mud Creek. This still is the Oregon Trail — in fact, this is one of the longest stretches in its entire 2,000 miles where one may travel on the old road itself in an automobile.

The climb up out of Mud Creek Canyon exposes a good view of the Snake to the right — one of the few white water stretches left. The Salmon Falls must have looked something like this before the power people got to it. The falls now have water over them only occasionally. One may experience the Salmon Falls today by plugging something into a duplex receptacle. This fine piece of scenery has been reduced to a bunch of kilowatts.

At this point, about four miles from the cottonwood, the pioneers were having no trouble at all with the Snake. There was plenty of water and they were traveling in one delightful stretch, just a few feet away from it.

At 5.7 miles from the cottonwood the road surface changes to blacktop, and it will continue up into the neck of land formed by the Salmon Falls Creek and the Snake. About a half mile ahead the trail moves out to the curve to the right, but continue ahead to a 35 mph right turn, to head back to the trail.

At 6.9 miles from the tree there is a T in the road — go straight ahead there. This is the old U.S. 30 — very narrow and much in need of repair. About .2 mile straight ahead is a deep swale coming in from the right. This is the trail, now beneath the road once more.

The Salmon Falls Creek continues to separate the road from U.S. 30. Just after crossing over the creek, make a left turn to arrive at the stop sign for U.S. 30. Turn right, onto the highway, and at this point the Oregon Trail did about the same thing.

Proceed north on the highway, into the great bend of

the Snake. Observe the right bank. About 150 miles north-east of here, in the lava beds north of Pocatello, the Lost River flows into a sink and simply disappears. That river comes out here, at a place the emigrants called the Thousand Springs.

Cascades emerge from the porous rock on the north side of the canyon and plunge into the chasm below. Not a thousand, or even a hundred now, but enough to make a marvelous scenic attraction.

John Charles Fremont had his moody Preuss sketch the falls for his *Report to Congress,* then penned these lines: "Immediately opposite to us a subterranean river bursts out directly from the face of the escarpment, and falls in white foam to the river below. In the views annexed, you will find, with a sketch of this remarkable fall, a representation of the mural precipices which enclose the main river, and which form its characteristic feature along a great portion of its course. A melancholy and strange-looking country — one of fracture, and violence, and fire."

Fremont probably wrote the first part, but it must have been his talented wife Jesse who supplied the kicker.

The Oregon Trail continues across the desolate Black Mesa. The traveler could, too, if he wanted to, but only over a circuitous and wasteful route with primitive roads. One actually would be nearer to the Oregon Trail if he were across the Snake and on I-80, so that's where we're going. Cross the bridge, which is directly above Salmon Falls, and follow the signs to the little town of Glenns Ferry.

The Oregon Trail is leading a maze of five power and pipelines across the Black Mesa on the south side of the Snake, from five to eight miles south of the highway.

Proceed into Glenns Ferry and follow the signs to Three Island Crossing State Park. Follow the well-marked park entrance road down past the trailer campground to the picnic area. On the way down toward the river note the deep swale on the far side of the Snake, coming diagonally down through the hills to a barren acre of flat ground on the south bank. There the trail follows down the Snake for a mile, at the water's edge, before coming

Harold Warp Pioneer Village
Jackson's remarkable painting shows slope down to Snake at Three Island Crossing, and subsequent transversal of rapid and dangerous river.

abreast of the tail of the southernmost island. It crossed onto the island, then moved upstream to the head of the island, and here crossed the main channel, touching only the head of the second island on the way over. It pulled up the north bank on the airport property, headed northwest, but by the time it crossed U.S. 30 it was headed due north.

Samuel Hancock, whose wagon was one of a train of 245 which left Independence in 1845, was a fascinated diarist of this place: "The next day we arrived at the crossing of Snake R, when two men of the co. forded it for the purpose of hunting on the other side, and did not return that night; in the morning 4 men went in search of them, and found blood and the traces of something being dragged in the ground; they followed this and found the body of one of these men divested of its scalp, clothing, gun, etc. After looking around and making the most diligent search for the other and seeing no traces of him, they concluded that he had shared a similar fate, and burying the comrade already found as best they could, returned to camp. We now make preparations for crossing the river, which was very rapid and deep, and perhaps 200 yards wide; the crossing was effected by propping up the wagon beds above the reach of the water and having three men on horseback by the team of the first wagon, to which all the others were chained each to the preceding one, and with a man on horseback to keep the teams straight, we reached the opposite bank safely, though some of the smaller cattle were forced to swim."

Hancock, who evidently had read a lot of Poe, said that "the howling of the wolf packs made night hideous." He reported the dispatch of two young boys one day to find a better ford over the Snake — their bodies were found scalped, stripped and mutilated.

In 1852, when young Ezra Meeker's train was trying to decide whether to cross there or take the horrible passage of the south bank of the Snake, he noted that another party had caulked three wagon beds, lashed them together, and was ferrying others across at the rate of $3 to $5 a wagon. Meeker rebelled at this, caulking his own wagon, and placing the running gear in the wagon box he worked the rig into the water and across the river.

Meeker got the bright idea here, and struck off afoot and alone for the Boise River, where he bought an old wagon box, caulked it and operated his own ferry for a number of days. It took him four days to walk the distance between the rivers, and the teams took 10 days. He worked the six days at his ferry, plus several more, then caught up with his own group $110 richer.

The Three Island ford was in almost continual use, up until 1871, when Glenn's Ferry offered an easier way across the Snake. Jason Lee camped at the ford for three weeks in 1834. Fremont left a vivid description:

"About 2 o'clock, we arrived at the ford where the road crosses to the right bank of the Snake river. An Indian was hired to conduct us to the ford, which proved impracticable for us, the water sweeping away the howitzer and nearly drowning the mules, which we were obliged to extricate by cutting them out of their harness. The river here is expanded into a little bay, in which there are two islands, across which is the road of the ford; and the emigrants had passed by placing two of their heavy wagons abreast of each other, so as to oppose a considerable mass against the body of water.

The Indians informed us that one of the men, in attempting to turn some cattle which had taken a wrong direction, was carried off by the current and drowned."

Narcissa Whitman left this account for August 13, 1836: "We have come fifteen miles and have had the worst route in all the journey for the cart. We might have had a better one but for being misled by some of the company who started out before the leaders. It was two o'clock before we came into camp.

"They were preparing to cross Snake river. The packs are placed upon the tops of the highest horses and in this way we crossed without wetting. Two of the tallest horses were selected to carry Mrs. Spalding and myself over. Mr. McLeod gave me his and rode mine. The last branch we rode as much as half a mile in crossing and against the current too, which made it hard for the horses, the water being up to their sides. Husband had considerable difficulty in crossing the cart. Both cart and mules were turned upside down in the river and entangled in the harness. The mules would have been drowned but for a desparate struggle to get them ashore. Then after putting two of the strongest horses before the cart, and two men swimming behind to steady it, they succeeded in getting it across. I once thought that streams would be the most dreaded part of the journey. I can now cross the most difficult stream without the least fear. There is one manner of crossing which husband has tried but I have not, neither do I wish to. Take an elk skin and stretch it over you, spreading yourself out as much as possible, then let the Indian women carefully put you on the water and with a cord in the mouth they will swim and draw you over. Edward, how do you think you would like to travel in this way?"

Overton Johnson and William H. Winter were in the Applegate group in 1843: "After leaving the Salmon Falls, we traveled down near the river, our path frequently leading us along the sides of the almost perpendicular bluffs. Twenty-seven miles below the Salmon Falls we came to the crossing where the companies which preceded us had passed over to the North side, which is much the nearest and best way, but we, having attempted the crossing and finding it too deep, were obliged to continue down on the South. This is, perhaps, the most rugged, desert and dreary country, between the Western borders of the United States and the shores of the Pacific. It is nothing less than a wild, rocky barren wilderness, of wrecked and ruined Nature, a vast field of volcanic desolation."

On Sept. 24, 1844, Rev. Parrish had this to say: "We crossed the river safely after noon today and camped on a fine bed of grass within sight of the ford. The river is rapid and the water middling low. The bottom is gravel of the prettiest kind and the water is clear. In consequence of two islands, side by side, we had to cross three streams. Our cattle are doing well. To-morrow, it is said, we have to drive twelve miles."

P. V. Crawford found a three-day job ahead of him. July 30, 1851: "We followed the channel down to the river. Here camped, but had to swim our cattle across the river to grass. This is now called the upper crossing of Snake river. Here we decided to cross over to the north side."

July 31: "This day we spent in arranging for and crossing the river. We accomplished this by corking two wagons and lashing them together. By this means we were able to ferry over a wagon and its load at each trip. By noon we had our boat ready and began operations, but found it slow business, but succeeded in getting all over safely, but not the same day, for we had to lay by on account of wind. Leaving part of our camping on each side of the river, here we had both sides to guard."

Aug. 1: "This day we completed crossing our fifteen wagons before night. Last night we had three horses stolen, and three more shot in the shoulders with arrows. Grass is good here, but Indians are very bad."

And very late in 1851 (Aug. 21), an apprehensive Elizabeth Wood wrote this letter: "We forded the Snake River, which runs so swift that the drivers (four to a team) had to hold on to the ox yokes to keep from being swept down by the current. The water came into the wagon boxes, and after making the island we raised the boxes on blocks, engaged an Indian pilot, doubled teams, and reached the opposite bank in safety. It is best in fording this river to engage a pilot. — The 'Telegraph Company,' as we call them, who passed us in such a hurry on the Platte, have left their goods and wagons scatterd over the mountains. We find them every day. Their cattle have given out, and I have seen several head of them at a time which had been left dead at the different camping places on the road. We drove too slow on the Platte, and the 'Telegraph' hurried too fast, and while our cattle are comparatively strong and in good condition, and will enable us, if we have time before the setting in of winter, to reach our destination, theirs are so worn out from hard usage that it is doubtful if they get through at all this season. We have met some 'Packers,' and they inform us that we are too late to cross the Cascade mountains this season.''

Fremont added that the river was exactly 1,000 feet wide at the crossing, and from six to eight feet deep. He camped among the Indians on the north bank, whose lodges were ''semi-circular huts made of willow, thatched over with straw, and open to the sunny south.''

Joel Palmer arrived here Aug. 23, 1845, also very late, and advised the emigrants that they would be descending a very steep hill along the shore. He said that the two islands were covered with grass, and the traveler could go from shore to shore without great difficulty. Evidently it was not difficult to go from the south shore to the first island but on the second stretch the traveler would have to negotiate the channel itself, and Palmer advised him to turn well upstream until nearly across, then bear down to where the road pulls up out of the water.

Three-Island Crossing to Oregon Border

To view the crossing from the southwest, return to Cleveland Avenue and follow it east across the river. Continue straight ahead on the blacktop for .2 mile to a right turn signed for Rosevear Gulch. Proceed right for exactly three miles to a cattle guard, then another .6 mile will be a curve to the right. At this point the Oregon Trail comes in through one of the shallow draws on the left. Proceed another .3 mile to a second cattle guard. Another .2 mile turn right — there is a sign there: ''Three Island Xing

— 2 miles. Proceed a half mile to a point where the trail heads away from the road toward the edge of the bluffs at an angle of 320 degrees. Near the edge of the bluff is a marker indicating the trail. Proceed on the road for another .6 mile to a fork near a gravel pit excavation and start the descent to the river. The forks join again .6 mile ahead but the left one is more evenly graded. Just .2 mile past that junction there is a brief rise in the road, offering the best view of the three islands from the southwest.

Return to Glenns Ferry, turn north at the water tower and go through town to Highway 30. Turn west onto the highway, or left again. Proceed only a short distance, over the Little Canyon Creek bridge, and turn right. Proceed north under I-80, then turn left on the Bennett Road. Continue on this road for more than a dozen miles. At 1.5 miles past the highway the trail intercepts. It is headed north at that point, and soon will turn northwest to parallel the road about a mile away, for many miles.

Two miles ahead is a Y in the road — take the branch to the left. Seven miles from I-80 is a road to the right. If one were to turn right here the trail would be 1.4 miles ahead. Don't. Keep going straight ahead. At eight miles from I-80 there is another Y in the road — take the branch to the right. Make the intercept with the Oregon Trail exactly .3 miles away. It would seem that there ought to be a deep rut at this place, since the ground is unfit for cultivation. Not so. Note that the land is perfectly flat, dry, and extraordinarily dusty. The emigrants would have been crazy not to have spread out under conditions like that.

Proceed another half mile to a T in the road. Turn left there. Now the trail is following the road from 100 to 250 yards to the left, working toward the northwest and the shortcut toward the Boise River. Proceed ahead for .2 mile and turn right. Just .7 mile north turn left at a T in the road. Go one mile west and veer to the right at a Y. The trail crosses here and a fine deep rut parallels on the left. At 2.8 miles to the northwest the trail angles across the road from left to right, now parallels on the right. Four miles from the last Y is an intersection of sorts. Continue to the northwest for 1.7 miles. At this point the trail and the old Hot Springs are off to the right about 200 yards, and now the rut is continuous for the next 17 miles. Proceed ahead another 3.5 miles to the intersection with U.S. Highway 20. There is a historical marker there. Turn right.

This is the site of the Rattlesnake stage station, where the town of Mountain Home first was located.

The trail now is .3 mile southwest, ready to cut across some desolate badlands where the trail itself is the only road. It will proceed nine miles northwest before the next intercept, at the crossing of Canyon Creek.

The best road around the mesa parallels Rattlesnake Creek. Continue north on Highway 20 for 3.8 miles. At that point there will be an intersection, with an arrow directed to the left, lettered "Mayfield, 25 miles." Turn left there. This is a gravel road. The intercept of one variant of the trail is just 2.8 miles ahead, where it cuts in sharply from the left and crosses to the right.

This road is adequate for a normal passenger car but probably wouldn't work too well with a top-heavy recreational vehicle. It is very hilly and curves sharply on the downgrades. The base ranges from firm to powdery, and would be questionable in wet weather, of which there is precious little here.

Proceed west 3.6 more miles to a T in the road and bear to the right. Within the next half mile cross Canyon Creek and the main trail there veers off to the right. Continue to the northwest for two miles. A mile from the entry onto this road is a road running up from the left, identified as Martha Avenue, a rather strange name for such a desolate place. Continue ahead another mile and start a northerly direction. The trail is about a mile to the right.

At the end of this stretch, 5.9 miles from the entry, a dirt road continues on ahead. Turn left onto Foothill Road — that is the Oregon Trail. Continue on it for five miles to a T in the road and turn right.

Go .6 mile further to another Y and make another right turn. Just .6 mile north is the crossing of Souls (spelled "Soles" on the maps) Rest Creek, and another .4 mile there is a cattle guard on the descent toward the Thompson Ranch, where the trail comes beneath the road. Continue another 1.5 miles to a Y with the Bowns Creek Road; turn right at this point.

Some 2.9 miles past the turn is the nearly-abandoned town of Mayfield, now reduced to three or four buildings.

About a half mile past Mayfield is a Y in the road — bear to the right. Another 1.3 miles ahead is a road leading off to the left — don't take it; bear right instead. Fifty yards ahead is a road coming in from the right; proceed dead ahead. Twenty more yards ahead is another T in the road, from the left. Again, continue on ahead. There is a Y in the road another 4.9 miles ahead — bear to the left. There is a very small sign there pointing to the left and labeled ''Black's Creek.''

This is one of the finest stretches of the Oregon Trail It seems to have been changed only by occasional grading.

Cross Blacks Creek at the bottom of a little swale, at the same place the emigration did. At 1.1 miles from the crossing is a cattle guard, and at this point the Oregon Trail finally leaves the roadway on a beeline for Bonneville Point. The maps show no road whatsoever up to the historic knob, but there is one, if it can be called a road. Continue 2.1 miles ahead, pass under a transmission line, and go just .1 mile more. Coming to the road from the right is a dirt lane with a high center, punctuated here and there with boulders.

there with boulders. Bonneville Point bears 020 degrees. There is a radar installation bearing 035 degrees. Poke up this rutty road and it will lead to the little monument and its well-tended enclosure. It is worth the trip.

While many historical markers are insufferably dry, this is one of the best of literally hundreds along the Oregon Trail. Here is the text on the marker atop Bonneville Point:

Marker atop Bonneville Point, where Capt. Benjamin Bonneville first saw trees along the Boise River.

''From this old Indian trail, later known as the Old Oregon Trail, Capt. B.L.E.

Bonneville's party, on first sighting the river in May 1833, exclaimed, 'Les bois, les bois, voyes les bois!' meaning "The woods, the woods, see the woods!" Capt. Bonneville, therefore, named the stream Riviere Boise, also indirectly the mountains and city."

Sight down in between the mountains, and even on a hazy day the cool green of the Boise cottonwoods and willows may be seen. The trail ran to the north of the knob.

Follow the dirt road back to the gravel road and turn right. Proceed on another 2.5 miles to I-80 and take it into Boise. The Oregon Trail is following the road about three miles to the northwest, headed for the river.

Leave the highway at the Broadway exit and turn to the right, following the signs to City Center, and stay on U.S. Highways 20, 26 and 30. Follow the highway signs as they direct the traveler down Capitol Blvd. Continue down Capitol for less than a block and turn to the right onto Boise Avenue. This is the route of the Oregon Trail. Go out to meet it and bring it into town.

Proceed southeast out Boise Avenue all the way to the entrance to the Lucky Peak Recreation Area, where the road turns to the right. Stop at that turn. Look up in the hills toward Bonneville Point. The marker is too small to be seen so far away, but small binoculars bring out the nearby radar towers sharp and clear.

John Charles Fremont stood up there and looked down toward those cottonwoods on the seventh of October, 1843. He described it as a beautiful, rapid stream of clear mountain water, with a variety of timber along the banks.

Jesse Applegate wrote that the river was 100 yards wide. Two years later, on Aug. 29, 1845, Joel Palmer estimated the stream at a more realistic 40-60 yards, and abounding in salmon.

Retrace the route to Highways 20, 26 and 30, and follow them across the Boise River. Where Boise Avenue comes to the highways (and ends there), the trail continues ahead, across the beautiful Ann Morrison Park and just across the irrigation canal from the KOA campground. One cannot drive this way. Make the loop across the river, following the three highways. All three will lead back to the south bank of the river, where 20 and 26 split away to the right, toward Garden City and Caldwell. It is at that split where the trail comes in again to meet them, bows away a block to the left, and returns at about E. 46th Street. It is at the Joplin Cemetery, nearly six miles away, that the trail finally angles away from the two highways to the right, heading up toward Ft. Boise.

A mile from the cemetery and the trail will be a half mile north, but heading almost due west. It will parallel the highways all the way into Caldwell, and the crossing of the Boise River.

Continue seven miles past the Canyon County line to I-80. Take it to the northwest, or right, but follow the exit signs for Highway 20. One mile further and the trail, by this time only a quarter of a mile to the right, turns to ford the Boise River one last time just a quarter of a mile upstream from the I-80 bridge over the same river. Abandon I-80 for U.S. Highway 20 at the Parma-Nyssa exit and just past the exit the trail will come beneath the road once more.

Continue on U.S. 20 all the way through Notus and then into Parma. In the heart of Parma leave Highway 20 by taking a left onto Idaho Highway 18 to the west, then turn to the right just a few yards away onto the sportsman access road on the right side of the Union Pacific Railroad tracks. Proceed ahead for 1.6 miles. The trail stays beneath that road. At a Y in the road the trail continues dead ahead between branches of the Y. Bear right, or due north, for a half mile, then jog to the left, or west. One mile north of the point where the jog was completed, turn to the left. Proceed across the UP tracks and .8 mile ahead the blacktop ends at a wood floored bridge. Proceed another .3 mile to a triangle at the end of a T in the road. This is believed to be the site of old Ft. Boise.

Now there is a marker at the site, erected in 1972 by the Old Fort Boise Historical Society. It is about 260 yards north of the triangle. Nothing is left of the fort today, although the Idaho Historical Society has an adobe brick from the site, which probably was part of the construction.

Ft. Boise was established by the Hudsons Bay Co. in 1834 to rival Wyeth's operation at Ft. Hall. It was built by Thomas McKay, stepson of the Lion of the Columbia, Dr. John McLoughlin. Farnham, who arrived there Sept. 14,

The road to Ft. Boise. A grassy triangle at the end of this lane is the approximate site.

1839, said the fort was on the east bank of the Snake, eight miles north of the mouth of the Boise River. It was enclosed by a pole stockade 100 feet square, entered from the west side. Of log construction, the principal building contained a large dining room, bedroom and a kitchen. On the north side of the stockade was a store; on the south side, servant dwellings. An outdoor oven was back of the main building. The northeast corner of the stockade was a bastion.

The ford was said to be 400 yards below the fort. It struck the head of an island and headed to the left, toward the southern bank of the river.

Fremont reached the fort three days after he hit the Boise River, on Oct. 10, 1843. He described it as being only a simple dwelling house on the right bank of the Snake, about a mile below the mouth of the Boise.

His man, Preuss, laced his diary with the usual uncharitible remarks. On Oct. 10 he wrote: ''Half-past ten in the evening, I am sitting all alone by the fire to watch till twelve o'clock, when an immersion

Lions head on Ft. Boise marker signifies ownership by Hudsons Bay Co.

[emersion] of satellites will occur. To tell the truth, I wish the dear Lord had not attached any satellites at all to Jupiter. One can lose one's mind over it. These immersions occur so often that one forgets how to sleep."

(An emersion is when the orbiting satellite of a planet appears into view around the side of that planet. In the case of Jupiter, the major moons appear on such a regular basis that a watch could be set by them. And that is exactly why Preuss was on astronomical duty that night. If the chronometers were accurate, then the measurements of longitude would be accurate.)

The patient Narcissa Whitman, who had suffered with a balky wagon to Ft. Hall, then saw the wagon converted to a cart shortly thereafter, arrived at Ft. Boise about noon on Aug. 19, 1836. The next day she did the laundry, the third time in their long journey from Independence.

Her diary entry for Aug. 22 is as follows: "Left the Fort yesterday. Came a short distance to the crossing of the Snake river, crossed and encamped for the night. The river has three branches divided by islands, as it was when we crossed before. The first and second places were very deep, but we had no difficulty in crossing on horseback. The third was deeper still, we dared not venture on horseback. This being a fishing post of the Indians, we could easily find a canoe.

"As for the wagon, it is left at the fort, and I have nothing to say about crossing it at this time. Five of our cattle were left there also, to be exchanged for others at Walla Walla. Perhaps you will wonder why we have left the wagon, having taken it so nearly through. Our animals are failing, and the route in crossing the Blue mountains is said to be impassable for it. We have the prospect of obtaining one in exchange at Vancouver. If we do not, we shall send for it. When we have been through so much labor in getting it thus far, it is a useful article in the country."

It was at Ft. Boise that a major disaster in American history was spawned. Stephen H. L. Meek was the brother of Joe Meek. He had hired on to lead a party headed by Capt. Elijah White, in 1845. It is only conjecture but it is easy to imagine that Stephen Meek wanted to make his own name, instead of trading on his brother's. So he induced many of the party to try a new way to the Willamette, to avoid the dread Blue Mountains. The route had never been traveled by wagons before; chances are Meek had never traveled it before at all. Yet he led 150 to 200 wagons up the sinister Malheur, probing for the Columbia.

Soon the feet of the oxen were ripped and torn. There was no grass for them. The party followed a jagged ridge between the John Day and the Deschutes Rivers. They went for days on end without water. Mountain fever hit the travelers, and some of the children died. The emigrants were able to get some water by lowering buckets 200 feet into the Deschutes. They were able to build an aerial cable ferry out of an old wagon bed and cross the river that way. But they didn't know where they were nor how to get out.

Meek finally had to go on ahead for a rescue party — the thoroughly disillusioned emigrants would have blown his brains out had he stayed in camp another day. Black Harris was on the Columbia when Meek came staggering in with the bad news. He organized a rescue party. Harris, whose knowledge of the West by that time was second only to Jim Bridger's, found the desperate emigration near the mouth of Tygh Creek, and led them down the Deschutes to the Columbia River and safety. More than 75 had been lost — double that of the Donner Party. The 400 survivors came to the Methodist Mission at The Dalles, where they were fed from the winter stores.

Floods every few years, plus the decline of the fur trade, were felt at Ft. Boise. There was Indian trouble in 1854, and soon the fort was abandoned completely. A few floods later and the job was completely finished — Ft. Boise was done, for good.

Instead of turning to return to Parma, continue due east to intersect U.S. Highways 20 and 26 and follow them west to Nyssa and the crossing of the Snake into Oregon.

In Nyssa, follow the signs to Oregon Highway 201 south, leaving U.S. 20 and 26, which lead to Ontario or Vale. Pass the Nyssa High School on the right. About a mile south of town the road snakes an S curve to the right and then enters a straight southerly stretch for 1.7 miles. Then make a gentle curve to the right and approach a hard right curve. At that latter turn there will be a curve sign with a 40 mph speed limit. About where the sign stands the Oregon Trail came through from Ft. Boise and the Snake River crossing. Take a bearing of 076 degrees, .7 mile away, and that is the center of the Snake crossing.

Two miles north of Owyhee the highway curves south; don't. Leave Highway 201 by driving straight ahead down to a stop sign about .1 mile west. Turn to the right on a blacktop road and drive north for half a mile to a trail intercept. Turn left, or west, at the next corner, and proceed one mile — the trail came directly across the intersection. Proceed ahead for two more miles to the good blacktopped Lytle Avenue and follow it all the way into Vale. The eminence to the southwest is Chalk Butte, el. 3,215 ft.

One mile from the turn is an intersection. Pass through and the road makes a gentle curve to the left. Where the curve straightens out, there comes the Oregon Trail beneath the road. It will stay beneath the road or within a few yards of it all the way into Vale.

About six miles northwest of the last intersection, fully a half mile of ruts of the Oregon Trail will come into view. They will be mostly on the left of the highway, sometimes on the right. The gouge is unmistakable. Here, in Keeney Pass, is as good a place as any to get out and walk. Metal detectors ought to bring out some interesting artifacts from the 1840-1880 period. The BLM maintains an interpretive exhibit in Keeney Pass.

Note that although the country is very hilly, the trail planners used their innate engineering sense to keep the road flat, in the knowledge that it is a lot easier for an ox to make a turn in the horizontal plane than in the vertical.

Cross the Malheur (Fr.: unlucky) River just before entering the town of Vale. It was a few dozen yards east of here that the White party, with Meek as its guide, split from the trail to save 200 miles, at the eventual cost of 75 lives and several weeks. Palmer arrived here Sept. 3, 1845. Fremont came to the Malheur Oct. 11, 1843 and reported it was 50 feet wide and 18 inches deep.

Proceed into Vale and turn to follow U.S. 26. Take it 5.5 miles north of town to Fifth Street East. Bear right at the Y, then right again. One mile east is a T in the road. Turn to the left at this point. This is the Oregon Trail — it is neither to the right nor to the left. It has only been graded. Proceed ahead through the desolation for 15 miles. First come right down to a farmyard, then note that the road turns to the right around it. Then come to several stock clusters — remember that this is open range. From time to time there will be cattle asleep on the road. Hit one and you've bought yourself some fresh roast beef.

Pass through a number of gates on this road. Be sure to close them after driving through. Repeated violations of this could result in closing this road to the public.

This road definitely would not be passable by a normal automobile in rainy weather, but from the looks of the forbidding terrain the last rain couldn't have been much after 1923. The dust will pile to such thicknesses that a driver must stop from time to time to remove the powder from the windows on the lee side of the car. The dramatic swale through which the roadway is passing sometimes is two to three feet deep. The cattle, sleek and healthy looking, seem to derive adequate nourishment from desert grasses nearly a foot tall, so utterly dry they are pale gold in color. A cigarette butt here could start a range fire that could sweep across the desolation at 60 miles an hour.

Some of the emigrants said they saw the Blues from Bonneville Point, east of Boise. Perhaps they did, but this is impossible with today's atmospheric conditions. No question about it now. The Blues range up formidably all across the way. The snow can't be seen here in July, but chances are it would be most evident in mid-August, when so many of the emigrants traversed this stretch.

About a mile past the intersection with the dirt road to Moore's Hollow there is a stock corral where the road splits. The road to the left around the enclosure ought to be the better one. The one to the right sure as hell is no good.

Exactly 15 miles from the T intersection north of Vale is the Willow Springs crossing — a sharp turn to the left followed by a hairpin turn to the right. When that turn is completed, on a straight stretch, the car should be headed about 045°. About .5 mile to .7 mile from that hairpin there might be a chance to turn and leave this environment by proceeding about a mile to the northwest. The trail passes to the north of Love Reservoir. One could make an improper turn (this one did) and wander through the hills south of the reservoir for another seven miles, over increasingly menacing ruts, to strike I-80 and the Snake. At times there will be little dirt roads over deep swales that will allow about six inches of room on either side of the tires. Sometimes there are boulders concealed in the grass in the crown of the road — bad news for low slung cars. But the roads, despite the choking dust, are passable.

At the highway the traveler will be unable to turn north, because the road has a median. Turn right and follow the sign toward Weiser, and an opportunity will present itself to reverse direction and head west.

Soon there will be a rise and the Snake will pop into

First view of Farewell Bend is about like the first view gained by the emigrants. This would be their last look at the Snake River.

view ahead — the same river that was followed all across Idaho. The first view will be of the Olds Ferry site, which was a cable ferry across the Snake for the benefit of emigrants who chose to follow the right bank north out of Fort Boise. It was started in the 1850s and lasted until 1922. Just past Olds Ferry is Farewell Bend — the emigrants' last look at the river.

It was three days before Christmas 1811 when Wilson Price Hunt and his men reached Farewell Bend from the east and camped there. They killed a horse and made a bullboat of the hide. This proved too small, so they killed another to enlarge the boat. This lasted for just two trips across the Snake. The rest of the night was devoted to rebuilding the boat. The next night was the party's last on the river, which they would remember with hatred for the rest of their lives. It had taken two of their comrades. The French for years later called it *la maudite riviere enragée* — the accursed mad river.

Fremont called the Snake at this point a "fine looking stream . . . smooth current." He could see it headed into the mountains, as today, and could hear the roar of the water, which we can't because it doesn't roar anymore.

Capt. Bonneville was here Jan. 10, 1833; Nat Wyeth stopped here after leaving his new Fort Hall later in the year (Aug. 25, 1834) on the way to try to get something started with Hudsons Bay Co.

Farewell Bend marked the end of the barren Snake country, and there were nutritious grasses awaiting the trains to the west. Getting there was something else. The trail ran over some murderous dry ridges before it hit the Burnt River in Huntington, some four miles away.

The Oregon Trail passed on the western boundary of Farewell Bend State Park, and that is U.S. 30. Take the Farewell Bend exit from I-80 and go into the park to observe the river and the bend at close range.

Exit the park via U.S. 30. On the way out turn to the right and follow the signs to Huntington. Stay on U.S. 30 all the way through the town of Lime. Ignore the entrance ramps to I-80. At the park exit the Oregon Trail is just a few yards to the right. It may be seen plainly as it pulls out of the Snake River flats and up the divide to the Burnt River. Palmer said it was the most difficult road he had encountered since leaving Independence, having a number of creek crossings. This probably was one of Palmer's bad days.

The trail will stay with the highway, or within 100 yards of it, all the way through Huntington and Lime. It is, indeed, a tough pull to the ridge south of Huntington, but there surely are worse places to the east.

Just out of Huntington cross the Burnt River and start to follow it north. The bridge, as far as can be ascertained, is right where the emigrant crossing was.

For the mile or so south of Lime the trail traversed the site of present I-80. Look to the left along U.S. 30 and see the logic of this.

Just north of Lime the old trail slants off to the right. Generally, it leads the power transmission lines through the valley. It is never more than a half mile from the road and rarely is it out of sight. The ruts are as plain there as they are anywhere.

When moving north on this stretch note the tremendous bulk of the Blues hulking to the west. It scared hell out of the travelers, but the trail bore its precious cargo like a Jewish mother, weaving calmly to the right, following the topographic line and taking any curve necessary to avoid too precipitous a climb. The change in elevation of the trail is rarely discernible.

Just north of Lime one must take I-80, much of which is built over old U.S. 30; and about 7.5 miles north of Lime turn northeast onto a good gravel road. This may be followed north for about two miles as the road follows Sisley Creek. The detour was chiefly to traverse Gold Hill (a later name), which lies off to the right of I-80. The trail will be beneath the road for 2.0 to 2.3 miles. At the first opportunity make a hairpin turn left — the trail turns left immediately thereafter.

About 3.2 miles to the north start a gradual turn to the west, along with the old trail. It will come beneath the road a half mile further on and stay with it for the two miles west to I-80. It turns right onto I-80 but the traveler cannot. Turn left for about a mile, then west to cross under I-80, right to parallel the highway into Durkee, and follow the signs to regain I-80 northbound. The trail passes through Durkee about three blocks east of the highway.

About eight miles north of Durkee the trail comes into the highway at a T, but there is no travelable roadway near it today. It shoots off to the north-northwest, as the road heads west-northwest. There are no roadways into the southern part of that area known as Virtue Flat. Proceed into Baker via I-80. Exit onto State Highway 86 just north of Baker and follow it to the right, or east. Follow 86 for about 1.5 miles, where 86 and Highway 203 split; follow 86 to the right.

About 2.5 miles east of town on 86, cross the Sunnyslope Road and enter into a series of curves, climbing toward the summit of Flagstaff Hill. There is a fine stone obelisk where the road passes just below the summit, but not on the trail itself. This is within the next mile. A beautiful set of Oregon Trail ruts is visible about 100 yards down toward the valley from the obelisk. Proceed ahead to a fine gravel road knifing off to the right. This leads to a point within a few yards of the trail, but a locked gate with some forceful

No Trespassing signs impedes further progress. Those who want to press their luck, or ask the owner, might proceed down that good gravel road from Oregon 86 for 2.4 miles to a broad left turn. Leading out of that turn is a pair of ruts to the right. This is the road to the old White Swan mine, part of which is the original Oregon Trail. The gate is about a half mile ahead. If one were to go another .2 mile there would be a turn half-left, and it is at that point that the Oregon Trail comes up from the southeast. It is beneath the road for exactly one mile, where the contemporary traveler must turn half left, then full right, along a section line. A mile from the first of those turns is another half left, and again the trail is beneath the road, to stay there for another mile. There the road goes to the mine itself and ends. One can go no further. All that, of course, is the trail in reverse, headed southeast.

Back where the road knifes away from Oregon 86, turn around and return a few yards to where a pair of ruts comes up from the left side of the road, over the flat, to skirt the east side of Flagstaff Hill. These are not the ruts of the Oregon Trail. Just to the left of those ruts is a stock trail, leading toward the center of the gap through the hills. That is. Note that some very considerate people have marked the trail with a 6 x 6 post, lettered with the words "Oregon Trail." Across the

From Flagstaff Hill the optimists saw the magnificent Baker Valley; the pessimists saw the shadow of the ominous Blue Mountains.

road is a small stone marker, showing the general northwest course of the trail. The wagon road cut through the center of the pass, down toward the beautiful valley below. Undoubtedly, many did a little skylarking by going up the hill — it would have been, and still is, hard to resist.

Proceed on ahead to the marker near the summit of Flagstaff Hill. Stretching out below is one of the most memorable views along the Oregon Trail, and few are the diarists who didn't mention it.

The optimists saw the magnificent green valley; the pessimists saw the ominous Blue Mountains ahead. And all saw *l'arbre seul*, the Lone Tree. On Aug. 6, 1836, Narcissa Whitman mentioned it: "As Mr. McLeod intended to make but a days stop at Walla Walla, we came on with him, leaving Mr. and Mrs. Spalding, the hired man and most of our baggage, and the Nez Perce chief, Rottenbelly, to guide them in. We parted from them about three o'clock and came as far as the Lone Tree. The place called Lone Tree is a beautiful valley in the region of Powder River, in the center of which is a solitary tree, quite large, by the side of which travelers usually stop and refresh themselves." Then she added that they soon came in sight of the hill which leads to the Grande Ronde.

Myra Eells came into the valley on Aug. 24, 1838, after a 25 mile ride negotiated in just seven hours. They camped under the Lone Tree, "so called because it can be seen miles distant, and no other tree in sight."

Jesse A. Applegate left a splendid description during his movement west with the cow column in 1843: "The train had been moving along westward across the level country for days, it may have been, where no trees were to be seen, but looking ahead, far in the distance, we saw a bush, which as we moved along continued to grow until the shades of evening began to darken into night and we went into camp. In the morning about the first object that attracted my attention was that bush, which now appeared to have grown to be quite a sapling. By noon it had grown to be a tree, and about sunset we were under its branches, and I believe, went into camp near it. It was a very large pine tree, the round, straight trunk towering up like a great column and supporting the spreading top. This was the 'lone pine.' For several years after I could hear of the lone pine from emigrants following our trail, but later I was told that it had been cut down for firewood.''

Applegate couldn't have heard about it from very many emigrants who saw it after him. His was the last large emigration to see it at all. Shortly after Applegate left the valley Fremont arrived: ''From the heights we had looked in vain for a well-known landmark on the Powder River, which had been described to me by Mr. Payette [the factor at Ft. Boise] as *l'arbre seul* (the lone tree;) and, on arriving at the river, we found a fine tall pine stretched on the ground, which had been felled by some inconsiderate emigrant ax. It had been a beacon on the road for many years past.''

Aubrey Haines, author of *Historic Sites Along the Oregon Trail* (1983), places the tree on a bearing of 323 degrees and 3.6 miles northwest of the marker at Flagstaff Hill, but to this day no one knows (or is able to substantiate) the exact location of the old tree. However, nobody can come closer than Aubrey, either.

The mayor of Baker, Henry McKinney, planted a new pine about two miles southwest of there in April 1945 but it didn't survive.

Wilson Price Hunt gazed from these heights in late December 1811. Nat Wyeth and Jason Lee camped in the valley in 1834. Thomas Farnham dined under the tree on Sept. 19, 1839.

Return to the base of Flagstaff Hill — complete a series of curves to arrive at Sunnyslope Road. Turn right, or north. Proceed for 2.3 miles to another Oregon Trail marker. Stop and look back up toward the obelisk just below the summit of Flagstaff Hill. The ruts of the trail may be seen coming down to the left, again at the most gentle descent. It proceeds toward this marker on a beeline and will cut across the valley to the Powder River.

Continue about 1.7 more miles to the stop sign and turn left, or west, on the Medical Springs road, also Oregon Highway 203. Proceed for 1.2 miles to another intercept. Flagstaff Hill is just five miles away at this point — the traveler now is halfway through the valley.

Continue on ahead the rest of that mile. After crossing a viaduct over I-80 make a right turn onto a paved road, the so-called Slough Road, headed north. Proceed for 1.3 miles to another intercept, shortly after making a half-left turn to angle over toward the Powder River. The trail will stay beneath the road for about a half mile, then move out to the right to cross the slough, then off to the left to ignore a section line. Meanwhile, make a gentle curve back north, cross the Baldock Slough, continue another .9 mile and turn left. Proceed west for .3 mile to an intercept, then continue another .3 mile and turn right. Flagstaff Hill now is nine miles away via the trail. A half mile ahead is a set of markers. Proceed 1.5 miles further on, pass through a fence and turn left, to head west down a poor set of ruts. An irrigation pipe parallels the road on the other side of the fence. About .7 mile ahead is a pumping station for the irrigation system, and another .1 mile or less is an intercept of the trail. Dead ahead another .2 mile is a gate. Just before reaching it turn right, or north, and the ruts quickly go from bad to worse. It is imperative at this point that an accurate odometer reading be taken, and travelers without an automobile compass are urged to return 3.2 miles and turn right onto the good gravel road to Haines and U.S. 30.

The adventurous sort will proceed on north along this deteriorating set of ruts. At .8 mile a gate must be opened to pass. Precisely a quarter of a mile past this gate the ruts peter out completely and the traveler is on his own. At this point turn due west and proceed only .1 mile, looking carefully on both sides of the path. Faint ruts should reappear ahead, on the right or left of the course. Whether or not they come into view, turn back north at the end of that .1 mile and proceed a little more than a tenth of a mile further to a three-way intersection and exit from the field. (It would be a four-way intersection except the way the traveler just came doesn't count.) There is a gate just before that intersection.

The trail comes about through that intersection — maybe a little to the east. Proceed dead ahead for .2 mile and the road becomes the Oregon Trail. Turn to cross the Powder River over a bridge that has a 10-ton capacity. (The river was named for the nature of the soil found on its banks.) The emigration proceeded due north at this point, skirting the edge of the bank. The trail crossed the serpentine river nearly two miles north of this bridge, or 2.5 miles southeast of the town of North Powder. Continue about 2.5 miles northwest to U.S. 30 and turn right. When the highway is gained the trail is about 1.5 miles east, but in 2.5 miles it will come within 100 yards of the highway in the town of North Powder.

It was a short distance east (nobody knows exactly where) that Maria Dorian, on Dec. 30, 1811, excused herself from the fast-moving Astorians of Wilson Price Hunt, went off in the bushes and whelped the first native Oregonian with white blood in his veins. She washed off the little tad and rejoined the company a mile or so down the trail. Children can be such a bother. The father was Hunt's interpreter, Pierre Dorian. Lucky Pierre they called him.

Continue into North Powder and follow the signs to take I-80 northbound. The Oregon Trail will stay with the road for the first nine miles north of town. There is a pipeline following to the left of I-80 and the trail is off to the right, from 50 to 250 yards east of the highway. Nine miles from North Powder a strange thing happens. The Oregon Trail proceeds straight ahead, now following the pipeline, but I-80 takes a detour to the right, to proceed down the right side of Canyon Creek and into Ladd Canyon. About 2.5 miles further on the trail intercepts the highway, still following the pipeline, but now headed more northerly than I-80.

At this point the traveler is climbing up the southern rim of the Grande Ronde — the ''large round'' in the middle of the formidable Blue Mountains. The Ladd Canyon is the easiest way in and this is plenty tough.

Soon one of the most spectacular views in the entire West will unfold, as the traveler arrives at the southeastern rim of the great cup — a seemingly perfect circle of high mountains with a deep depression and delightfully level and green valley floor in the center, 20 miles in diameter. The emigrants saw about the same thing, only a quarter of a mile to the northeast. This is the Grande Ronde.

Capt. Bonneville described it well: "Its sheltered situation, enbosomed in mountains, renders it good pasturing ground in the winter time; when the elk come down to it in great numbers, driven out of the mountains by the snow. The Indians then resort to it to hunt. They likewise come to it in the summer to dig the camash root, of which it produces immense quantities. When this plant is in blossom, the whole valley is tinted by its blue flowers, and looks like the ocean when overcast by a cloud."

On Aug. 28, 1836, Narcissa wrote of the great basin: "We descended a very steep hill in coming into Grande Ronde, at the foot of which is a beautiful cluster of pitch and spruce pine trees, but no white pine, like that I have been accustomed to see at home. Grande Ronde is indeed a beautiful place. It is a circular plain surrounded by lofty mountains and it has a beautiful stream coursing through it, skirted by quite large timber. The scenery while passing through it is quite delightful in some places, and the soil rich. In other places we find the white sand and sedge as usual so common to this country. We nooned on the Grande Ronde river."

Farnham was unimpressed. He could write only of the frigid winds on the slopes coming down into the valley.

Many were the emigrants who would have liked to have settled in the Grande Ronde, but by this time few had any money or food, so they had to go ahead to the settlements to procure the wherewithal to last out the winter, until the crops came in the next summer.

Some sources state that the road to Dr. Whitman's mission began at the town of Cayuse, nearly 14 miles northwest of Meacham, but most place the Y about a mile north of La Grande. The road was quickly abandoned after the murder of the Whitmans late in 1847, and was never again used as an emigrant route. There probably is no way it can be precisely located today, although it is generally presumed to go through the towns of Alicel, Elgin and Tollgate. This is not, of course, the best way west, but Waiilatpu was the best location for Dr. Whitman's farm, in his opinion. If the emigrants needed help this was the best place to get it, and in the years 1836 until the burning of the mission in 1847, many of the emigrants indeed did need help.

The good doctor usually managed to get word that the vast trains were approaching through those mysterious processes of communication which existed in those pre-telegraph years. He would send Nez Perces down to the Grande Ronde to meet the emigrants and escort them to the mission. The escort was needed as protection against the Snakes — again, more theft insurance than life insurance. George B. Currey was met there on his trip to the Willamette.

It was in September, 1845, when Joel Palmer's party hit the Grande Ronde, found themselves terribly short of provisions and cash and elected to follow the escort to the mission. Palmer and a few others went ahead to the mouth of the "Umatillo," and linked up with the rest of their train there on Sept. 12. There they met Dr. and Mrs. Whitman, who had loaded a carriage with supplies for the emigrants.

It was at La Grande, on Oct. 1, 1844, that the party of Capt. Nathanial Ford, piloted by Black Harris, elected against the trip to the mission. It was getting late and the snows could hit the Blues or the Cascades at any time. The tough and knowledgeable Harris led them to the Umatilla (at present day Pendleton), down that river to the Columbia, and then on to the Willamette and safety. That cutoff was well-publicized and spelled the beginning of the end of the mission. From that time on Dr. Whitman had increasing difficulty in attracting emigrants into his Cayuse-infested lands.

On the way down the slope in the valley, the trail is off a few yards to the right. About 5.5 miles southeast of La Grande, nearly to the bottom, the trail intercepts and heads over to the hills on the left, traveling about half way over the plain from the highway.

The emigrants, generally beginning in 1845 but in

National Park Service

Jackson's view of the Blue Mountains corresponds with views today — off the highway. It was a murderous stretch, then smoothed out on the floor of the Grande Ronde.

growing numbers through 1847, turned to the west about a mile south of La Grande. Proceed through the heart of town, headed to the northwest, and all the way to Hilgard State Park, off I-80, the trail was to the left, headed over the floor of the canyon up toward the highway and the tortuous climb over and out of the Blues.

The trail passed on the southern edge of the park, then crossed I-80 about a half mile west of the interchange for the park and headed to the northwest, paralleling the highway from a few yards to a mile away on the right.

It was along this stretch that the emigrants found ripe huckleberries by the millions. Few could resist the temptation, and many pies were made. One quote from an ecstatic male still survives more than a century after his death: "Dipend alive! If I don't be jumped up if that ain't good pie!"

On into the hills the trail passed, then into the Blue Mountains again. It is difficult to understand how two pair of oxen could lug a laden wagon up those slopes, but lug them they did. The fine grass and good water along the way sustained them. It still had to be awfully tough on man and beast alike.

The trail crossed the highway just south of the Meacham exit, although there seems to have been a much-used alternate that branched into the settlement itself. The town, originally known as Lee's Encampment, was in 1848 a cantonment of soldiery dispatched by the Oregon Provisional Government to quiet the Cayuse after the Whitman massacre. Aubrey Haines says that Maj. Henry A. G. Lee, after a brief campaign against the Indians, occupied the old Methodist Mission at The Dalles.

Leaving Meacham the trail is off to the left, paralleling the road up to I-80 about a half mile away. Proceed ahead for about three miles to Emigrant Springs State Park. Take the exit there to go into the park. Come in on old U.S. 30.

Few were the travelers who could resist marveling at the massive trees in the forests of the Blue Mountains.

Just past the park entrance is a stone marker unveiled on July 4, 1923, and dedicated in person by President Warren G. Harding. Inside the park, follow the arrows to the historical marker. Then follow a bearing (from the sign) of 353 degrees for 65 yards. At that point there is a large concrete box. This is a soft bog so take one step at a time.   In this box, almost buried in the undergrowth, is a seepage spring. Scarcely more than a trickle emerges in dry weather.

The real emigrant spring is .3 mile west of the park through the wilderness, now inaccessible and virtually ruined by a pipe line coursing through its center. The spring is supposed to have been discovered by Rev. Jason Lee in 1834, on his way to the Willamette. It was in succeeding years a favorite campground for emigrants, when there were hundreds and hundreds of white tops ringed against the Snake and Cayuse for the night, with the stock pastured or staked near the delicious grasses near the spring.

Continue west on old U.S. 30. Just .2 mile north of the entrance is the familiar 6 x 6 post indicating a crossing of the Oregon Trail. Actually the trail goes beneath the highway at this point and stays there for six more miles. The trail cuts off to the right about where the power line crosses I-80. It travels due northwest while the modern highway heads south of due west. There is no way to reach the trail by automobile at this point.

Halfway between here and Pendleton the trail will be more than five air miles to the northwest. Turn to go northwest into Pendleton and the trail turns to head due west into town.

As they pulled out of the Blues, the emigrants breathed a sigh of relief. Now the worst was over. All during the spring in Kansas, as they had loitered along the trail to savor the magnificent prairies and as the pilots had cajoled, nagged and then threatened them, it was only the prospect of snow in the Blues that pulled them from the intoxicating vistas and back on the trail. And now they were past the Blues.

Some made it without having to fight the snow and some didn't. There uniformly was snow along the passes, if not actually falling. In 1844 Rev. Parrish wrote that "the rains ceased during the night and this morning it is cloudy. Glad we escaped the Blue Mts. as they are white with snow."

In the city of Pendleton follow the highway signs to the intersection of Oregon Highway 11 to Walla Walla. The traveler is unable to take the trail to get there, as no one knows exactly where that old trail was. Highway 11 will do. (It changes to Highway 125 at the state line.)

Approaching Walla Walla, the old Military Road leads to the south from the new Plaza Shopping Center. A mile down this road is the Ft. Walla Walla State Park. This is not to be confused with the original Ft. Walla Walla on the Columbia River, just up from the mouth of the Walla Walla River.

It was at this fort, however, that DeSmet in 1858 discovered the Army was holding Coeur d'Alene and Spokane families as hostage. He knew the captives, as indeed he seemed to know half the Indians in the transmontane West. He raised sufficient hell that the commandant freed the captives. The priest knew entirely too many men in high places, including the president of the United States.

Proceed into Walla Walla and follow the highway signs to U.S. Highway 12 westbound. Continue west about seven miles to the Whitman Mission National Historic Site.

Whitman Mission to Oregon City

Marcus and Narcissa Whitman were of commanding importance to the course of events in the mid-19th century, but their roles as missionaries were ridiculous to an extreme. The Cayuse no more than tolerated them; they found the melons and other produce of the farm delicious and a real ball to steal, but wanted no part of raising them. The Whitmans were important for other reasons.

In the first place the impact of their powerful personalities was felt throughout the entire United States. Dr. Whitman's personal appearances across the nation; first to get his bride and then to reinstate funding from the American Board, made deep impressions on the families who dreamed of a farm on the Willamette. Probably, of even more impact, were Narcissa's delightful letters home, given extensive publication after her death.

Take, for instance, her letter of July 5, 1836, written from a camp out west of Ft. Hall: "Husband has had a tedious time with the wagon today. It got stuck in the creek this morning when crossing and he was obliged to wade considerably in getting it out. After that, in going between the mountains, on the side of one so steep that it was difficult for horsepaths, the wagon was upset twice. Did not wonder at this at all. It was a greater wonder that it was not turning somersaults continuously. It is not very grateful to my feelings to see him wearing out with such excessive fatigue, as I am obliged to. He is not as fleshy as he was last winter. All the most difficult part of the way he has walked in laborious attempts to take the wagon "

Remember that Bill Sublette, after taking his train up the east slope of the Rockies to the rendezvous on the Popo Agie in the spring of 1830, made the comment that it would be easy for wagons to go all the way. He was wrong about the easy part, but what was important — Dr. Whitman was proving that it was not only possible but eminently feasible.

Narcissa wrote again on July 28: "One of the axletrees broke today; was a little rejoiced, for we were in hopes they would leave it and have no more trouble with it. Our rejoicing was in vain, for they are making a cart of the back wheels this afternoon, and lashing the fore wheels to it, intending to take it through in some shape or other. They are so resolute and untiring in their efforts, they probably will succeed."

Little Alice Clarissa was born at Waiilatpu on March 14, 1837, three months after Narcissa arrived. The baby was to be given life for two years, three months and nine days. Narcissa was 29 when the child was born.

On the baby's first birthday Narcissa wrote home: "Very, very dear parents: more than two years have passed since I left my father's home and not a single

National Park Service
Jackson's visualization of the Whitman Mission is fairly accurate, except for rooflines. Mill pond is at left, bend of old channel of Walla Walla River at top, main mission house at right.

word has been wafted hence, or, perhaps I should say, has greeted my ears to afford consolation in a desponding hour. This long, long silence makes me feel the truth of our situation, that we are far, very far removed from the land of our birth and Christian privileges."

Toward the end of their second summer at Waiilatpu the Whitmans had visitors of the cloth. Rev. Cushing Eells and his wife, Myra, with other missionaries, visited the struggling little farm and Myra described the emplacement as follows: "Dr. W.'s house is on the Walla Walla river which flows into the Columbia river and is about 25 miles east of Ft. Walla Walla [the first one]. It is built of adobe, mud dried in the sun in the form of brick only larger. I cannot describe its appearance as I cannot compare it with anything I ever saw. There are doors and windows but they are of the roughest kind, the boards being sawed by hand and put together by no carpenter but by one who knew nothing about such work as is evident by its appearance. There are a number of wheat, corn and potato fields about the house beside

Royal Ontario Museum, Toronto

Only authentic sketch from life is this one by Paul Kane, who visited at mission only two months before Whitmans were murdered by Cayuse. Kane drawing was found only recently.

the garden of melons and other kinds of vegetables common to a garden. There are no fences, there being no timber to make them of at this place. The furniture is very primitive, the bedstead of boards and nailed to the side of the house sink fashion. Then some blankets and husks make the bed. But it is good compared with traveling accommodations. Mr. Gray and wife have gone to Walla Walla.''

Thomas J. Farnham came in the following year, September of 1839. When he arrived he found Dr. Whitman screaming in Cayuse at the lazy Indians who were half-heartedly trying to get the cattle out of the garden. Whitman evidently had some fences up by then — Farnham refers to an enclosure of 250 acres, 200 of which was under cultivation.

As a farm the mission was in good shape by 1844, and Dr. Whitman even had a sawmill in operation 20 miles up the Mill Creek. Some of the 1,500 persons of the emigration of that year stopped at the mission, and the seven Sager children, orphaned on the trail, were left to be raised by the Whitmans. In residence then were Mary Ann Bridger, Jim's daughter, and Helen Mar Meek, daughter of old Joe himself.

Even this early, Dr. Whitman was discouraged with his missionary activities. He had utilized his practice of medicine among the Cayuse, generally with success, for all these years, and he would be hard pressed after eight of those years to name a single, honest, genuine convert to Christianity.

As a matter of fact, some of the most trusted were deserting the mission and reverting to their old nomadic ways.

It all ended in November 1847. Fort Vancouver, a part of the USA since 1846, was without either the Union Jack or Dr. McLoughlin, both of which tended to keep the Cayuse in line. A band of emigrants brought the measles with them, which ordinarly would not have been serious. Some of the kids at the mission caught the disease and were cured in a few days by Dr. Whitman. The Cayuse had no resistance to most of the diseases of the whites, including the measles, and they did not respond to treatment. Nearly half of them died. The Cayuse saw the white kids getting well and their people dying and reached the conclusion that Dr. Whitman was administering poison.

On the morning of Nov. 29, Dr. Whitman conducted Christian services for three children of a Cayuse chief who had succumbed to the measles. Shortly after noon a brave came to the mission house to ask for medicine. When Dr. Whitman turned to the cabinet to get it his skull was fractured by blows from a tomahawk. Children ran screaming from the room and Narcissa came to the door to receive her bullets. She was dead before her husband. Ten more men and two children were killed. The massacre is believed to have been engineered by a half-breed named Joe Lewis. Helen Meek, who was ill, died later when no one could care for her. Jim Bridger's girl died the next spring. There were 59 persons at the mission and 13 more at the sawmill. Six escaped; all the rest were taken captive and held for ransom by the Cayuse.

The Indians burned the mission buildings, cut down every tree in the orchard, and everything movable was consigned to the flames.

Rev. J.B.A Brouillet, a Catholic priest, evidently was immune to persecution by the Indians (he had the right medicine) because he was able to move into the mission site unmolested on the heels of the catastrophe. He helped bury the dead. Spalding was on the way to Waiilatpu and would have become the 15th victim if Brouillet hadn't made a timely interception.

The dead were hastily buried and word of the captives went down the Columbia to Ft. Vancouver. Peter Skene Ogden, the new Hudsons Bay Co. factor, established communication and arranged for the captives to be ransomed.

Ogden persuaded the chiefs to stiffen up against the young turks who had achieved domination of the Cayuse, and the ransom was paid. There were 62 blankets, 63 cotton shirts, 12 guns, 600 loads of ammunition, 37 pounds of tobacco and 12 flints.

Joe Meek saw an opportunity and took it. He saddled up and rode over the mountains in the dead of winter. He was in St. Louis by March 4 and in Washington shortly after. The ex-mountain man made a sensational report in the capital, and the need for white domination in Oregon for protection of the settlers was clearly established. Congress granted territorial status without any further delay.

Harrassment of the Cayuse continued. They knew they were in bad trouble. In the spring of 1850, five of them surrendered to Joe Meek in Oregon City. It was on the

National Park Service has found foundations for all the Whitman buildings and marked their lines with concrete blocks in the rich turf.

Bodies were buried immediately after raid, soon were disinterred by wolves. They were re-buried early in 1848 beneath the inverted box of an old wagon. In 1897, bodies were moved here, to this great grave on mission site. Narcissa was easy to identify — she was the only woman killed. Dr. Whitman's skull showed the fracture from the tomahawk. Curiously, it also had been cut open neatly with one of his own surgical saws. Obelisk in background, behind slab, is for William H. Gray.

third day of June that Joe Meek personally hung each of the five, one by one, until they were dead and the Christian church was avenged.

The National Park Service has done a splendid job of re-capturing the feeling of the old mission and the American tragedy that occured there. Three separate teams of archaeologists have combed the site to unearth artifacts from the mission site, even including a bottle containing an iodine mixture used by Dr. Whitman. Although a farmhouse dating to about 1880 had been built over a portion of the main mission building, foundations of the balance of the original structure were discovered and now are plainly marked with concrete blocks in the carefully tended lawns. The millpond has been restored, and the old channel of the little Walla Walla River is clearly visible. It was near the bend that little Alice Clarissa drowned. Dr. Whitman's irrigation ditch has been re-dug in the same place and again is filled with water.

The adobe foundation of the first house built, where the missionary carried his pregnant wife across the threshold on her 29th birthday, has been discovered, and one three-foot section has been unearthed, visible through a sealed glass viewport. Also on exhibit are the well-marked sites of the grist mill, Gray's house (later used by the emigrants), and the blacksmith shop. On the hill back of the museum are the great graves, covered with a large stone slab, and next to it the small obelisk of Gray and his wife.

Gray was considerably more charitable toward the Whitmans after they were gone. His last years were spent in a fund-raising campaign to reinter their remains under a suitable marker. He died before the job was done.

At the top of the hill is a great spire, the Whitman Memorial Shaft, from which a commanding view of the entire mission site may be gained. It is well worth the climb. Dr. Whitman himself must have surveyed the site from that hill, to gain the overall plan and to site the buildings that would be erected.

The museum itself contains artifacts from the mission ruins as discovered by archaeological excavation, but more important it graphically tells the Whitman story in terms of its importance to national expansion. The mission site is one of the most important on the Oregon Trail. At least half a day should be allotted to let the experience soak in.

Emigrants who stopped at the Whitman Mission generally stayed a few days, then followed the little stream across the Walla Walla plain to the Columbia and Ft. Walla Walla. This installation was built of logs by the Northwest Company in 1818, and control was assumed by the Hudsons Bay Co. after the forced merger in 1821. The first fort was destroyed by floods in the early 1840s, rebuilt of adobe and finally abandoned in 1855. The fort of the 1830s, where Narcissa awaited the completion of the first mission house at Waiilatpu, was of wood.

Hunt and his Astorians saw the Columbia there for

the first time, described it as being a beautiful stream, three-quarters of a mile wide, totally free from trees; bordered in some places with steep rocks and in others with pebbled shores.

Narcissa Whitman first saw the Columbia in September, 1836. Her journalism for that Sept. 7: "The Columbia is a beautiful river. Its waters are clear as crystal and smooth as a sea of glass, exceeding in beauty the Ohio. But the scenery on each side of it is very different. There is no timber to be seen and there are high perpendicular banks of rocks in some places. While rugged bluff and plains of sand are all that greet the eye, we sailed until nearly sunset."

John Charles Fremont arrived at the mission Oct. 23, 1843, only to find Dr. Whitman absent. He hit the Columbia at Wallula two days later, described it as being 1,200 yards wide.

Fremont found Applegate and his 1843 emigration at the old fort. Applegate had nearly completed construction of a fleet of mackinaw boats, and Fremont mentioned the sudden appearance of the great fleet making far better time on the river than he did.

Preuss described Ft. Walla Walla as being built very close to the stream, on bare sand. There was no grass, no tree, nothing green in sight. Fremont camped a half mile away from the fort, near some crippled willows on the bank of the Walla Walla. Capt. Benjamin Bonneville was at the fort on March 4, 1834, found it garrisoned with six or eight men.

On Oct. 29 Fremont mentioned passing the mouth of the "Umatilah" and described its fall to the Columbia. On the 31st he wrote: "Our road was a bad one, of very loose, deep sand."

Perhaps this is one of the reasons the emigrations of later years moved west considerably south of here. The wagon road down the south bank of the Columbia to Rowena or The Dalles wasn't especially bad but it wasn't very good either. After five months of jouncing around in a wagon, both man and beast were anxious to end it all and stake their claims by the Willamette. A saving of a day or two became of vast importance. Therefore, the emigrants of the mid-1840s turned their wagons west at a point east of Pendleton.

Return to Pendleton and follow the highway signs to I-80N westbound, and turn west. Cross Highway 395, the John Day Highway, and at that point the Oregon Trail is very close, if not actually beneath the highway. A mile from there, halfway down a long hill, where the Umatilla River flows below, the trail knifes off to a due-west direction. It continues off to the left for as much as a quarter of a mile, then the highway turns southwest and an intercept is made. In the middle of a broad right curve, where the interstate turns back to the northwest, the trail makes another intercept as it heads due north, and this one is clearly visible off to the right of the highway. Nearly six miles from the John Day Highway, just after cresting a long hill, the trail makes one last crossing, headed due west. It moves across the highway from right to left. The trail parallels the road for two more miles, about a quarter of a mile to the left, and then it cuts off due west to head into the little town of Echo. The interstate is closer to the trail than the blacktop which is to the south several miles. Continue on the highway to the Echo-Lexington exit and take it, following the arrows to Echo.

In Echo turn right at the stop sign for a block or so, then left to continue out of town due west. The trail comes to meet the road at that stop sign and continues beneath it through town and for three miles west of town, first crossing the Umatilla River.

Black Harris brought his 1844 emigration up this way, but, instead of rounding the hump at Echo and turning west, they continued down the left bank of the Umatilla to the Columbia, and on downstream to The Dalles via the old wagon road.

Away from the river, the newer trail will first slant away from the road a few yards to the right, then cross under a few yards to the left, over a space of two miles. At the third mile it will knife off to the right gently and proceed in a due westerly direction, as the pavement continues to the southwest. It is nearly nine miles west of Echo that Oregon Highway 207 is reached, and at that stop sign turn right to return to the interstate. At .8 miles north the trail makes an intercept headed due west. No marker is in evidence, nor is there any evidence of the crossing.

Continue on north to I-80N and turn west toward Portland. No such luck was in store for the emigrants. They proceeded southwest, then west through what is now a U.S. bombing range. This desolation is utterly complete; there are 500 contiguous square-mile sections of land south of Boardman that do not have a single dwelling place on them. There are perhaps two dozen more miles that have only one home and only one or two that have as many as two. The arid plains are flat as a billiard table, uniformly covered with sage plants that all appear to grow to the same height and no higher.

Proceed into Boardman; the trail is some 14 miles south, on the southern boundary of the bombing range. It will continue through the desert to the west, south of Arlington. There one can meet it once again to take it on to the Columbia.

At Heppner Junction, nearly 11 miles east of Arlington, the earlier emigrants turned to the south to cross the Alkali Flats, avoiding the jagged scoria and sage-grown cliffs of the Columbia.

Take the exit from I-80N into Arlington and proceed south for about 3.5 miles on Oregon Highway 19 to a fork in the road; take the pavement to the left there, in the middle of a right curve. About 4.8 miles to the southeast turn to the right on a good gravel road that could use a visit from the grader. One and a half miles southwest of there is a farmyard, and on the near edge of it is a road leading to the right, or west. Take it; that is the Oregon Trail. There are wonderful ruts in Four-Mile Canyon. Stop at the BLM marker and take a hike.

Proceed one mile; the trail stays beneath the road. Then it angles slightly to the left — seldom more than 30 or 40 yards. Turn left and proceed .3 miles south.

There is one of the most beautiful trail markers in the

West. It commemorates the journey of W. W. Weatherford, who returned to develop a ranch near here and became a prosperous stockman.

Return to the north, pass the shaft of the T and less than a half mile further north turn left on Cedar Springs Road, the first good gravel road. Exactly 1.2 miles ahead the Oregon Trail knifes in from the left to meet the roadway and stays beneath it until the Blalock Road is reached at a T.

The official maps are in error — they show a bridge across the John Day River where there is none; only increasingly menacing "No Trespassing" signs and increasingly poor, rutted dirt roads.

The name John Day never stood for anything lucky anyway. Day, a backwoodsman from Virginia, was a member of the Astorians. He and Robert Crooks fell behind the main party on the Snake River in Idaho and wintered there. In the spring of 1812 the Indians robbed them of everything they had in the world, and they were left naked on the banks of the Columbia. After reaching Astoria, Day decided to return to St. Louis with Robert Stuart, that same trip which would discover the Oregon Trail (in reverse.) Day got only as far as the Willamette when he went completely bananas. The Stuart party had to entrust his care to the two Indians who promised to return him to Astoria.

The John Day River possibly could be forded,

Sam Barlow, angry at gouging rivermen of the Lower Columbia, hacked the Barlow Road out around the south shoulder of Mt. Hood in 1845.

but certainly it shouldn't be tried unless one has an amphibious all-terrain vehicle. It would be worthwhile, for just across the river is the start of the Barlow toll road, the hell-raiser of a trail created by Samuel K. Barlow and William Rector. His 1845 route actually started at The Dalles — this is the beginning of his later road, which opened the following year.

Turn right and proceed north through Blalock Canyon to I-80N and turn west. Cross the mouth of the John Day River and the Sherman County line. Exit into the town of Rufus, pass southward beneath the highway to a T, then turn right, or west, to the Scott Canyon Road. Turn left, taking a horseshoe curve to the southwest, then up into the hills on a good blacktop road headed southeast. Here pick up the trail again, headed west. About 2.5 miles from Rufus is a broad right curve, and at the end of that curve will be a good gravel road leading off to the left. A sign is there giving the distance to Klondike. Take it for 3.6 miles to a four-point intersection and proceed on ahead for a half mile more. There the road turns due south for a half mile, then to the left, or east, again for one mile. Now it turns right, or south, again for a half mile, and then turns right, or west, for another half mile. Again it turns south for a full mile, and at that point turns west, at which time the traveler is back on the trail again. The markers on both sides of the road are 100 yards west of that corner, showing that the trail headed northwest from there. A mile away and it is .8 mile north, but starting a curve that will bring it across the road again soon. Turn left, or south, for a half mile there, and the road will curve due west at that point. Two miles west of there the trail has come down to within 100 yards of the road and will parallel it out there for the next mile. At the end of that third mile it crosses the road headed southwest — there is a marker there.

It is along this stretch that the emigrants, who had first seen the tip of the cone of Mt. Hood east of the John Day River, became aware of the awesome bulk of the mountain looming so many miles ahead.

Turn south at the T in the road and proceed on into Wasco. A half mile ahead is another intercept, but there is no marker. A few yards before reaching Wasco there is a stop sign and U.S. Highway 97. Turn right, or north. About 2.5 miles ahead is another intercept with the trail, but there is neither trace nor marker here. Continue on to Biggs and I-80N. The trail generally follows the road, ranging up to a mile away to the left. It closes in toward Biggs, and at the highway only a small hill separates it from the road. Turn to the west on the interstate, cross the Deschutes River into Wasco Co. and proceed to the Celilo fishing grounds. Cross under the highway but instead of turning to the Celilo community, take the road to the left, following the signs to the Deschutes recreation area. Go almost to the bridge over the mouth of the river and turn right onto a gravel road. Follow it only a tenth of a mile or so and it will turn back to the west. This is the Oregon Trail again, and this is the original — it is neither to the right nor left. The emigration crossed the Deschutes immediately to the east, but at that time the mouth was fairly narrow, and neither that river nor the Columbia was backed up by the series of dams that exist today.

Proceed 2.3 miles up this terrible grade, where the oxen must have had their rumps high and their noses low to haul the wagons over the ruts. The view from the top is stupendous. Several hundred feet below is the broad sweep of the Columbia, now despoiled by the dams but still a magnificent sight. A short distance further is another of those friendly little "No Trespassing" signs,

Just after crossing mouth of Deschutes River (right), emigrants were forced up steep hill, but were rewarded with find view of broad Columbia River (left).

so stop right there.

Retrace the trail down to the Deschutes, get back on I-80N and proceed to The Dalles. Take the City Center exit, cross over the interstate and turn left onto Second Street. Follow the signs to U.S. 197, toward Bend, but turn off onto N.E. Fremont Drive a mile or so from the freeway entrance road.

Continue on to the Fulton Farms, which once was the little town of Petersburg. This is the Oregon Trail again — it cut to the southwest here to head into The Dalles. This leg will follow the trail again but in the opposite direction. At the farm do not take the road to the left. Go to the right instead for 1.9 miles; this is the trail itself. There is a Y in the road at that point — bear left, and 3.3 more miles is a T. Turn to the left there. At the next intersection, Company Hollow Road, turn right and proceed nearly a mile into Fairbanks. Then cross a T in the road. The Oregon Trail continues straight ahead, to go through a farm house. The gravel road deteriorates rapidly from here on, and the traveler would have to head into the anti-trespasser farmer. Turn around at that T in the road; do not proceed ahead to the farmhouse. Return to The Dalles. Shortly after arriving at U.S. 197 the trail comes beneath the highway from the southeast, rapidly headed toward the river.

Turn left on U.S. 30W (Second Street) just before reaching I-80N. Proceed 3.5 miles west to Webber. Turn right at the ''Port Property'' sign — the National Guard Armory is across the street on the left. Cross the UP tracks and proceed 1.6 miles north to the Wasco County Animal Shelter. (Webber changes to Old River Road.) Turn right on a gravel road along the south bank of Chenowith Creek for .3 mile to the Columbia River and the end of the wagon road to Oregon.

Re-enter I-80N at Webber Street and proceed to the exit at Mayer State Park, at Rowena. Travel trailers aren't allowed in the section of the park north of the highway, due to an ancient bridge over I-80 which must be crossed. Go as far as possible to the north and the road ends in a group of park maintenance buildings on the riverbank. The wagons could go no further west than here. Near here many emigrants took to their rafts but no one knows exactly where. Probably all along these shores. The majority took to the water up at Chenowith Creek.

And many, of course, came down the Columbia from as far up as Ft. Walla Walla. Rev. Parrish was with the 1844 emigration. He related driving hard to reach "the doctor's" at night, staying a week, and taking two more days to reach the Columbia, where he arrived on Nov. 3. He opted for the land route, leaving the Columbia. On Nov. 20 the minister celebrated his 53rd birthday on the banks of the Columbia, four days east of The Dalles. That is where he lost his options — he had to board at The Dalles.

Narcissa Whitman, who went first to Ft. Vancouver by water before returning to Ft. Walla Walla to await completion of the house at the mission, wrote that 20 Indians were utilized to carry their canoe at one portage. "Below the main fall of water are rocks, deep narrow channels, and many frightful precipices. We walked deliberately among the rocks, viewing the scene with astonishment, for this once-beautiful river seemed to be cut up and destroyed by these huge masses of rock. Indeed, it is difficult to find where the main body of water passes. In high water we are told that these rocks are covered with water, the river rising to such an astonishing height."

On Sept. 9, 1836, she described The Dalles: "We came to The Dalles just before noon. Here our boat was stopped by two rocks of immense size and height, all the water in the river passing between them in a narrow channel and in great rapidity. Here we were obliged to land and make a portage of 2½ miles, carrying the boat also."

Fremont left the river on Nov. 2, 1843, heading inland to avoid the bluffs above The Dalles. He crossed the John Day River on the Oregon Trail on that day, and two days later he was at The Dalles. He described the area as having walls 25 feet above the water, which at that point was only 58 yards wide, with the whole force of the Columbia gushing through. Shortly before Fremont arrived Jesse Applegate had lost his boat there; two of his children and one man drowned in the accident.

On Sept. 26, 1845, Joel Palmer complained about crossing the John Day River. He described it as being a

*Emigrants had to make the choice at The Dalles —
whether to move over the south shoulder of Mt. Hood
(seen here from The Dalles) via the Barlow Road, or
whether to pay confiscatory tolls for water passage to
Oregon City.*

violent stream, but only 10 yards wide. Two days later
he was at the Deschutes, also described as rapid, but at
that time 100 yards wide, with its walls of basaltic rock.
He described a cascade on that stream only 400 yards
from the mouth of the river, and because of its
treacherous condition they had to ferry there.

Palmer arrived at The Dalles Sept. 29, 1845, where he
found 60 families awaiting water passage, with only two
boats plying between there and the Cascades. That
meant a 10-day wait at least. Palmer was tired and angry.
He learned that Sam Barlow was already six days into
the mountains, so he hightailed it after him, and his 30
wagons were among the first to force a passage around
Mt. Hood. They arrived in Oregon City Nov. 1 after a
strenuous passage.

Some of the difficulties faced by the emigrants are
described by George A. Waggoner: "We left our wagon
on the Umatilla. We packed our bedding on Old Nig, the
last ox left us, and started on afoot. My father sold him
[Old Nig] at The Dalles for $20 to buy food. We
stopped two weeks at The Dalles. Father found an old
stove and rigged up a table counter for the soldiers and
civilians who were building the military post there."

Elizabeth and Cornelius W. Smith were at The Dalles
Oct. 29, 1850. They saw men making rafts, women
cooking and washing, children crying. Indians were
giving a half peck of potatoes for a good shirt. The rafts

the emigrants were making were of pine logs 40 feet long.

Fremont described the portage ground at The Dalles as being thick with emigrant families, their "thin and insufficient clothing, bare-headed and bare-footed children attesting to the length of journey, showing not much preparation." This was in 1843.

At any rate, here it ended. The oxen would pull no more. Some of the travelers let their worn-out beasts go to the boatmen to help pay their passage to the Willamette. If it was late in the year and the boatmen were gone, or if it was the year 1844, Dr. McLoughlin would take care of all that by sending rescue craft to The Dalles. British or American, they still were people. Money or no money, they had to live.

All who wanted passage somehow managed to get it. Ezra Meeker says that after the terrible trials of the Snake, and then the canyons and dusty deserts of Oregon, that a heavy drowsy lassitude settled on the emigrants as they sat on the rafts in a stupor. The exhaustion was complete and so was the silence.

Oregon Historical Society

Commercial boatmen frequently made a nice living ferrying emigrants and their wagons down the Columbia. Bluffs closed off further land passage west of The Dalles. Raft is shown at Beacon Rock, near Skamania, Wash.

Suddenly someone on Meeker's raft started singing "Home, Sweet Home." Soon all 500 voices in the water-borne caravan joined in without restraint, and strong men found themselves sobbing like babies.

With good connections at the six or seven portages, the float to Ft. Vancouver could be made in a day, but more often it took three days. Rev. Parrish portaged at the Cascades, some 40 miles downstream from The Dalles, on Nov. 24, 1844, a day after taking to the river. He didn't land at Ft. Vancouver until Nov. 29.

The portage at the Cascades was quite necessary in any kind of water. The river at that point was full of great rocks deposited by a gigantic landslide about 1300 A.D. (and not by the collapse of a natural bridge, as chambers of commerce will say.) The river was so treacherous there as to be impassable to navigation until a series of locks were built a century ago. Now the great rocks are far below the surface, as the Bonneville dam has raised the water level so that the Columbia navigation system can function effectively.

The drive down the Columbia River from Rowena can be a thrilling trip or it can be humdrum, depending upon whether the choice is I-80N, a high-speed, limited-access expressway, or old U.S. 30. The freeway is built right at waters' edge much of the way, and sometimes it is even out over the river. Old U.S. 30 winds up the walls of one of the world's most stunning gorges, alternately offering views of little wooded glades, frightful vistas of the broad Columbia far below, spectacular glimpses of ribbon-like falls, and up close examination of the ornamental concrete work that characterized major paved roadways during the first years of this century.

Pass the Horsetail Falls, the Oneonta Gorge, the Multnomah Falls, and a dozen other scenic attractions that are a little maddening if one is in a hurry. Few can resist stopping. It could take the better part of a day to drive the 75 miles of the gorge into Portland.

Arrive in Portland on I-80N and leave it on I-5 north-bound, heading toward Seattle. Travel down the east bank

National Park Service

This is the reconstruction by the National Park Service of old Ft. Vancouver at its peak. It was key North American outpost for Hudsons Bay Co.

of the Willamette, then across the Columbia River. A short distance into Washington is the Mill Plain Blvd. exit. Take it east, and at the first electric signal turn right on Ft. Vancouver Way. At the first stop sign, East Evergreen Blvd., turn left and proceed a mile to the entrance of the Ft. Vancouver National Historic Site.

What is left of old Ft. Vancouver is largely still beneath the earth. Archaeological teams now are carefully excavating the foundations and are not expected to complete their work until the mid-1970s. Today there is only a stockade fence, a reconstruction of the original north wall of the emplacement. The National Park Service is a thorough-going bunch, and, if any reconstruction is done, it will not be started until the project has been researched exhaustively.

Ft. Vancouver never was more than a trading post as far as its owners, the Hudsons Bay Co., were concerned. But it was the economic, social, cultural and political hub of the British Empire west of the Rocky Mountains. This structure was built on this site in 1829. It was under the personal command of Dr. John McLoughlin. A British subject, McLoughlin probably had more to do with beefing up the American claim to the Oregon country than any Yankee. Yet, his name is virtually unknown to any but the students of the history of the Pacific Northwest. Probably he was more important than James K. Polk, Tom Benton or Dr. Linn put together. This man won Oregon for the United States, more than any other man.

With a visage like this it is no wonder Dr. John McLoughlin held absolute power over the Pacific Northwest for nearly four decades.

McLoughlin, possessed of a commanding appearance with his flowing white hair and six-foot four-inch height, had a hypnotic effect on the Indians. Known as "White Eagle," he led the Company to a virtual monopoly of the fur trade west of the Rockies. McLoughlin's men, red and white alike, ranged from what is now northern Alaska to the California border, from the Great Salt Lake to Hawaii. His forts peppered the west coast, and all were effective in providing the investors in London with handsome profits. That was the business end.

Dr. McLoughlin wanted a little more out of life than a good balance sheet. He started a civilization program on the land. Acres and acres were planted in apple trees. In came sheep, cattle and horses to graze the pasturelands. He built a sawmill up the Columbia, harvested and pickled the salmon, built ironworks, put in cash crops. He started a school, a circulating library, a theater, churches. His steamboat, *Beaver*, became the first on western waters on May 17, 1836.

The fort itself, a stockade enclosing a rectangle 732 feet by 325 feet, had a bastion in the northwest corner with several three-pounders, any one of which could scare hell out of a whole tribe of Indians. There were 22 major buildings in there and several small structures. The doctor's house was there, plus four large storehouses, a trade house for the Indians, a granary, some houses, and even a small jail.

Since the Indians held the chief factor in the utmost respect, the fort was never attacked. The control of the

The National Park Service has erected only this stockade, showing the front wall of the old fort.

White Eagle was so complete that most of the fort's employees lived in their own little town just outside the walls of the fort. There, on the plain to the south and southwest of the fort, were 30 to 50 log buildings.

This was a thrilling thing for the emigrants to see. Even the most bitter Yankee would thrill to the sight of civilization after 2,020 miles of almost complete wilderness. It looked good. It would have looked better with the Stars and Stripes on the mast, but even with the Union Jack, it looked good.

To John Charles Fremont it sounded good too. He heard the whine of the sawmill while he still was miles upstream and listened with pleasure to the sounds of civilization. He camped just before midnight on a November evening in 1843, one mile above the fort. In the morning he saw the barque *Columbia*, ready to sail to England with a cargo of furry wealth. Dr. McLoughlin took time out to throw out the red carpet for him, knowing full well that he was a) a military opportunist, b) the son-in-law of the leading Britain-baiter in the U.S. Senate, and c) an Army officer interested in any publicity he could get to further his own chances for the Presidency some day. But to McLoughlin he was just another human being — the welcome was sincere and impressive, as usual. Fremont found the fort full of emigrants, ready to sail across the Columbia and into the mouth of the Willamette.

By the mid-1840s there were enough settlers in the valley to enable them to perform their own rescue duty if they wanted to. Dr. McLoughlin's forces were often supplemented by newly-settled emigrants who felt obligated to proceed up the Columbia to provide stores and transportation to those stranded at The Dalles without much of either.

Narcissa Whitman first saw the fort Sept. 14, 1836: "Have ridden 15 miles this afternoon. We visited the barn, stock, etc. They estimated their wheat crops at 4,000 bushels this year, peas the same, oats and barley between 1,500 and 1,700 bushels each. The potato and turnip fields are large and fine. Their cattle are numerous, estimated at 1,000 head at all the settlements. They have swine in abundance, also sheep and goats, but the sheep are of an inferior kind. They also have hens, turkeys and pigeons, but no geese. You ask what kind of beds they had. I can tell you what kind of bed they made for us, and I have since found it a form of fashionable bed in this country. The bedstead is in the form of a bunk with a rough board bottom upon which I laid about a dozen Indian blankets. These with a pair of pillows covered with calico cases, constitute our beds, sheets and covering. There are several feather beds in the place made of the feathers of wild ducks, geese, cranes and the like. There is nothing here suitable for ticking. The best and only material is brown linen sheeting. The Indians make theirs of deer skin.''

One emigrant reported that the farm was nine miles square, supporting 3,000 milk cows, 2,500 head of sheep and 300 brood mares.

DeSmet, on his way down the river from Fort Colville, made one of his several visits there in 1842. He and Peter Skene Ogden arrived together on June 9. He said the palisade was 750 feet by 500 feet and contained 40 buildings, including a Catholic chapel, and he reported that there were 60 more buildings out on the plain, a farm of nine square miles with 1,500 acres under cultivation. DeSmet stayed until August 14.

He was back two years later, went down to the Methodist mission founded a decade earlier by Jason and Daniel Lee, about 12 miles north of Salem. He could see no future for a mission at that site, turned down an offer for the land. He was back in Fort Vancouver again in 1846 when his powderhorn exploded, giving him some severe burns on the face and head. He was back on the trail in a few weeks.

Nat Wyeth, here to do a little business with John Bull after getting a doublecross from the Americans on the Green River, and founding his Ft. Hall on the Snake, got the news that his ship, the *May Dacre*, had been crippled in the southern hemisphere and would miss the salmon season by 90 days. So for him, everything now was lost. His fort on the Snake was virtually worthless and he knew it. He would found another shortly, down from the mouth of the Willamette, then head back to Cambridge and Fresh Pond. Somehow he didn't have so much grief in the ice business.

There are few who would discount Nat Wyeth's ideas. They were all sound, if daring to an extreme. He took a fairly good risk and hedged himself as best he could in all directions. It was perhaps a 5 to 1 shot that all would fall through, but all did, and that's what made the old ice biz look so good again.

Joe Meek, veteran mountain man and free trapper, saw the fur trade slipping away and wanted a piece of the permanent action west of the Snake. He knew a lot

Oregon City in 1848 shows the impact of settlement. This was just five years after the first large emigration.

of people and a lot of people liked and respected him. The tough American frontiersman saw an opportunity and took it. He rallied the settlers at the now-vanished village of Champoeg, up the Willamette from Oregon City, and formed a provisional government in 1843, and at last Oregon had some laws.

By 1845, the little town of Oregon City had a Methodist church, a Catholic chapel, two grist mills (including one owned by Dr. McLoughlin) with a sawmill at each, four stores, two taverns, a hatter, a tanner, a physician, three lawyers, a printing office and newspaper, a lath machine and a good brickyard. There were plenty of carpenters and masons constantly employed at good money. The population was about 600 whites plus a few Indians. On the west side of the river were two villages — Multinoma City and Linn City, named for Dr. Linn.

By 1846, there were nearly 7,000 emigrants in Oregon, more of them from Missouri than anywhere else, and almost all of them in the valley of the Willamette. The population of Oregon City had grown to 1,000, and already 100 had located in the little town of Portland.

Head back to I-5 and take it south to where U.S. 99E peels off to the left, only a mile or so south of the Columbia. Follow 99E south, right into Oregon City, and follow the signs up to the house Dr. McLoughlin built for himself when he retired from the Hudsons Bay Co. in 1846, after Oregon was won by the United States. The house is at 711 Center St.

McLoughlin in 1829 filed a claim for the land on which much of Oregon City stands. In 1846, he applied for American citizenship and built this house on the bottom lands near the falls of the Willamette.

The house stands now on ground he donated to the city in 1850 as a park. It was moved from the original location in 1909, after much damage from flooding. His claim to citizenship was recognized in 1851, six years before his death. The house is open to the public daily except Mondays.

Return to 99E and follow it south, through the tunnel beneath the yards of the Southern Pacific, and to

The house of Dr. John McLoughlin, the Lion of the Columbia, still stands in Oregon City, now is open to the public.

the scenic overlook. There, high on the bluff, is the commanding view of the broad Willamette River. Less than a decade ago the stream was an open sewer — now there is no major river in the United States that is more clean. Flowing 95 per cent pure, it probably is as clean as it was when the emigrants first settled the area.

This, then, is the end of the Oregon Trail, as far as it can be traced. There was a little mileage left for each

Haze still clouds Oregon's air, but the broad Willamette River in Oregon City now flows 95 per cent pure, due to intensive pollution abatement program.

family, but they no longer traveled in mutual assistance caravans. Once at Oregon City the emigration societies were no more, and it wasn't until 25 years later that worshipping sons and daughters got them together again in Pioneer Societies, and the Oregon Historical Society was born, with the publication of volume after volume of their reminiscences.

From Oregon City the emigrant families fanned to the south, starting as early as February. Somewhere near the banks of the storied river they found their section of land, the blades bit in and exposed the black dirt that would succor the West.

The visitor of today can leave Oregon City via I-205, crossing the Willamette and on west to I-5, and shoot straight south past Salem and Albany to Eugene. All along the way are the lands of the pioneers; here they lived their last years and here they are buried, far from the land of their birth, but in the bosom of the land they called home.

The Speed Trip

It takes three to four weeks to make the trip described above, and many people cannot spare the time to enjoy a vacation like that. Those who cannot are urged to make half the trip one year; the other half at a later date. But for those who do not choose to do this, a speed trip is offered. This trip may be made in about 10 days. The experience will not have the impact of the four-week trip, but it will be a lot more worthwhile and thrilling than two weeks at the beach.

Take I-70 to the Tucker Prairie, on the south side of the highway 15 miles east of Columbia, Mo. Examine the prairie. Refer to pages 74-75.

Continue west on I-70 to Missouri Highway 291, east of Independence. Turn north (right) and follow the directions on page 79 to the Independence Landing.

Continue following those directions as they lead the traveler down to the square in Independence, and see as much of the square as possible. Then pick up the narrative on page 95 and follow the Independence-Westport Road to old Westport. See as much of Westport as time will allow, then pick up on page 108, proceeding down Wornall Road to Santa Fe Road and New Santa Fe. Continue into Kansas, as described on page 130.

Proceed west into Kansas only as far as U.S. Highway 69, as described on page 130. There, turn north for about 15 miles. (The highway number changes to I-635 enroute.) Cross the Kansas River to the interchange with I-70, the Kansas Turnpike. Turn west and proceed to the East Topeka exit of the turnpike and exit onto I-70. Follow that highway into the central city and turn right, or north, onto U.S. Highway 75. This coincides with the data on page 144. Continue north across the bridge, but keep on going to intersect U.S. Highway 24 north of the river. Turn left, or west, on U.S. 24.

Continue west on Highway 24 to Kansas Highway 99, and then turn right, or north, for 36 miles to Kansas Highway 9, at Frankfort. Turn left there and proceed 13 miles west to U.S. Highway 77. Turn north, or right, for 5.5 miles and then turn left on a gravel road that leads to the Alcove Spring, as described beginning on page 159. Spend as much time as possible there.

Return to Highway 77 and proceed north, across the Nebraska state line to Nebraska Highway 8. Turn left on Highway 8 and proceed west into Fairbury, in Jefferson County. In Fairbury turn north on Nebraska Highway 15 and proceed to I-80. Turn left on I-80 and drive to the Platte River, crossing it south of Grand Island. Exit on U.S. 35 north, to visit the Stuhr Museum of the Prairie Pioneer, in Grand Island. Return to I-80 and continue on up the north bank to Kearney. Turn south on Nebraska Highway 44 in Kearney, cross the Platte, and follow the signs to the east to Ft. Kearny State Park. Upon entering the grounds pick up the narrative on page 184.

Return to I-80 and continue west, crossing the Platte again just before reaching the forks east of North Platte. Continue west on I-80, right next to the old trail, to the town of Ogallala. Turn north on Nebraska Highway 61 and U.S. Highway 26; cross the South Platte and turn left on U.S. Highway 26. Proceed northwest and stop about 38 miles west of Ogallala, at the Ash Hollow sign, and pick up the narrative on page 200.

Follow the text to the town of Oshkosh, and from there continue northwest on U.S. Highway 26 instead of crossing the North Platte. Nearing Bridgeport, note the great Courthouse and Jail rocks on the left. North of Bridgeport turn left on U.S. Highway 385 and proceed south across the North Platte River and into town. Continue south on Nebraska Highway 88, and pick up the narrative on page 206.

Follow the text to Chimney Rock, and then into the town of Gering, on Nebraska Highway 92. Do not turn south to the Robidoux Pass in Gering; continue west on Highway 92, per the narrative on page 218, to Mitchell Pass and Scotts Bluff National Monument.

When leaving Scotts Bluff National Monument return to Gering instead of moving west through the pass. Turn north on Nebraska Highway 71 and cross the North Platte to Scottsbluff, then turn left, or west, on U.S. 26 and cross into Wyoming.

Stay on U.S. 26 to the town of Fort Laramie. Follow the signs in town to Ft. Laramie National Historic Site. Where U.S. 26 turns to the right, continue ahead, cross the North Platte and follow that road to the old fort. Pick up the narrative on page 229. Spend as much time at the fort as possible, and if another half hour can be spared to visit Mary Homsley's grave, so much the better. Then return to U.S. 26 and proceed west into Guernsey. In Guernsey leave the highway by turning south, following the signs to Register Cliff. Pick up the narrative on page 239, to explore Register Cliff, the deep ruts, and the grave of Lucindy Rollins, but do not visit the warm spring. Return to U.S. 26 and follow it west, or to the left.

Continue west to I-25 and turn right, proceeding north and west to the town of Glenrock. Then refer to the text on page 247 to find the graves of A. H. Unthank and Ada Magill. Now follow the narrative right on in to old Ft. Caspar, and down past the Red Buttes to the Bessemer Bend turnoff described on page 252. Don't turn there — continue south on Wyoming Highway 220 to Independence Rock. Turn into the parking lot on the north side of the rock and start reading on page 257.

Follow the text to Devils Gate, Split Rock, and on past the bridge over the Ice Slough. Delete the probe described on page 270; continue on U.S. Highway 287 to the intersection with Wyoming Highway 28, and turn

left, or south. Do not turn in toward Atlantic City. Follow
the highway signs to visit the beautifully restored South
Pass City, just south of Highway 28.

Several miles farther is the bridge over the Sweetwater
River, and exactly .7 mile ahead is a little gravel road to
the left. Take it, and follow the narrative beginning in the
last paragraph on page 272, over the South Pass.

Return to the highway and proceed to the left, or southwest, for 4.2 miles to the South Pass overlook. Park and
examine the pass from this vantage point. The narrative
begins on page 274.

Continue southwest on Wyoming Highway 28, ignore
the misplaced "Parting of the Ways" marker in Sublette
County, and turn left at Farson onto U.S. 191. Proceed
south to I-80, north of Rock Springs, and turn right, or
west. Continue west to the intersection of Wyoming highways 410 and 412. Turn south on 410 toward Mountain
View. Three miles south of the interstate turn right, or
west, on U.S. Highway 30, the Lincoln Highway, and proceed into the town of Fort Bridger. Visit the old fort, which
is right on U.S. 30. Pick up the narrative on page 284.
Continue on west until U.S. 30 joins I-80, then go west on I-80
to the intersection with U.S. Highway 189. Turn right, or
north, on U.S. 189 and pick up the narrative beginning on
page 289. Follow the text out of Wyoming to Sheep Rock,
four miles west of Soda Springs. Instead of turning north
at Sheep Rock continue west on U.S. Highway 30N to I-15,
then turn north, or right, through Pocatello to the Fort
Hall exit. At the overpass over I-15 turn left and pick up
the narrative on page 302.

Return to I-15 and turn right, or south. North of Pocatello turn west, or right, on I-15W. Follow the narrative
beginning on page 308, but do not turn in to American
Falls or the Stuart marker east of Massacre Rocks. Turn
in at Massacre Rocks State Park, still following the narrative. Continue west on I-15W over the Raft River and onto
I-80N. Drive west on I-80N to U.S. 93 north of Twin Falls.
Turn left, or south, and cross the bridge leading to the city
of Twin Falls for a magnificent view of the Snake Canyon.

The road makes a half-left turn immediately after crossing the bridge, and less than a half mile away it heads back due south again. There is a four-way intersection there. Proceed on south exactly one mile and turn left, or east. Exactly five miles from that corner turn left on a road which leads directly to the Twin Falls. Pick up the narrative on page 318. Continue the text through the Shoshone Falls.

From Shoshone Falls return to the south, only to the first road, which is the same road to Twin Falls (to the east) and to the City of Twin Falls (to the west.) Turn right and proceed west into Twin Falls, cross the Snake River bridge again and return to I-80N. Proceed northwest on I-80N to the town of Glenns Ferry. Exit there and follow the narrative beginning on page 324.

Return to I-80N and resume the course to the northwest. The interstate here follows closely the route of the trail, as it leaves the Snake River and cuts up to the Boise River. Continue on I-80 through Boise and across the Snake River into Oregon, to Farewell Bend. Take the Farewell Bend State Park exit and pick up the text starting on page 340.

Return to I-80N and follow it to the northwest. At Baker, take the second exit (Oregon Highway 86) to the right, or east. This leads around the crown of Flagstaff Hill, with its beautiful view of the Baker Valley. Pick up the narrative on page 344. Return to I-80N and follow it to the northwest, through La Grande. North of La Grande take the Hilgard Junction exit into Hilgard Junction State Park. The trail cut right through the small picnic area on the bank of the Grande Ronde River. Return to I-80N, picking up the text on page 351, through Emigrant Springs State Park, and Pendleton. Follow the text to the Whitman Mission in Walla Walla, returning through Pendleton. Leave the narrative before the last sentence of paragraph one, page 363, and continue northwest on I-80N all the way through The Dalles and Rowena, to the exit just past Bonneville Dam. This will be identified as the "Scenic Route," or old U.S. 30. Take the old highway to Troutdale and rejoin I-80N.

Continue west on I-80N to the interchange with I-5 in Portland. Turn right, or north, on I-5 to Vancouver, and pick up the narrative on page 372. Continue the narrative to the end of the book.

Bibliography

"Along Nebraska Pioneer Trails." Mimeographed, Lincoln, Nebr.: Nebraska State Historical Society, undated.

Anderson, Richard L. "Jackson County in Early Mormon Descriptions." *Missouri Historical Review,* Vol. 65, No. 3 (April 1971) Columbia, Mo.

Andrews, Thomas F. "Lansford W. Hastings and the Promotion of the Salt Desert Cutoff: A Reappraisal." *Western Historical Quarterly,* Vol. 4, No. 2 (April 1973) Logan, Utah.

Applegate, Jesse. *A Day With the Cow Column in 1843.* Chicago: The Caxton Club, 1934.

Berry, Myrtle D. *Ft. Kearny.* Lincoln, Nebr.: Nebraska State Historical Society, undated.

Bidwell, John; Bancroft, Hubert H.; & Longmire, James. *First Three Wagon Trains.* Portland, Ore.: Binfords & Mort, 1956.

Brown, A. Theodore. *Frontier Community; Kansas City to 1870.* Columbia, Mo.: University of Missouri Press, 1963.

Brown, Jennie Broughton. *Ft. Hall on the Oregon Trail.* Caldwell, Idaho: The Caxton Printers, Ltd., 1932.

Campbell, William C. "Heritage Has New Look." *The Kansas City Star,* Sept. 27, 1970.

Canaday, Golda. Personal Communications. Feb. 28, 1971.

Carpenter, Miss Estaline. Personal Communications. Feb. 28, 1971.

Case, Robert Ormond. *The Empire Builders.* Garden City, N. Y.: Doubleday & Co., Inc., 1947.

Chick, Washington Henry. "The Vicissitudes of Pioneer Life." *The Westport Historical Quarterly* Vol. 6, No. 2 (Sept., 1970) Kansas City, Mo.: Westport Historical Society.

Chimney Rock. National Park Service, 1969.

Chittenden, Hiram Martin. *The American Fur Trade of the Far West.* 3 vols. New York: Francis P. Harper, 1902.

Chouteau, Frederick. "Reminiscences." *The Westport Historical Quarterly* Vol. 6, No. 4 (March, 1971) Kansas City, Mo.: Westport Historical Society.

Christopher, Adrienne T. "James Bridger as Westport Knew Him." *Westport Historical Society Quarterly* Vol. 4, No. 2 (Sept., 1968) Kansas City, Mo.: Westport Historical Society.

——. "The Old Vogel Saloon." *Westport Historical Society Quarterly* Vol. 5, No. 4 (March, 1970) Kansas City: Westport Historical Society.

——. "What I Remember of Virginia Bridger Wachsmann-Hann." *Westport Historical Society Quarterly* Vol. 4, No. 2 (Sept., 1968) Kansas City, Mo.: Westport Historical Society.

Clark, B. C. "Diary of a Journey From Missouri to California in 1849." *Missouri Historical Review* Vol. 23 (Oct., 1928) Columbia: State Historical Society of Missouri.

Clayton, William. *Journal.* Salt Lake City: Legal Printing Co., 1928.

——. *The Latter-Day Saints' Emigrants' Guide.* St. Louis: Chambers & Knapp, 1848.

Clinkenbeard, Anna Dell. *Across the Plains in '64.* New York: Exposition Press, 1953.

Clough, Wilson O. "Mini-Aku, Daughter of Spotted Tail." *Annals of Wyoming* Vol. 39, No. 2 (Oct., 1967) Cheyenne: Wyoming Historical Society.

Currey, George B. *Transactions.* Portland: Oregon Pioneer Association, 1887.

DeVoto, Bernard. *Across the Wide Missouri.* Cambridge, Mass.: Houghton Mifflin Co., 1947.

——. *The Year of Decision: 1846.* Boston: Houghton Mifflin Co., 1942.

Dielman, Cindy. "Baker County's Past is Colorful and Exciting." *Democrat-Herald* Baker, Ore., July 30, 1970.

Dowling, Colista. *Oregon's Historic Trails and "Story Spots."* James Kearns & Abbott Co.

Driggs, Howard R. *Westward America.* New York: J. B. Lippencott, 1942.

Eells, Mrs. Myra. "Diary." *Transactions.* Portland: Oregon Pioneer Association, 1889.

Evening and The Morning Star. Vol. 1, No. 1. Independence, Mo. June, 1832.

——. Vol. 1, No. 5. Independence, Mo. Oct., 1832.

Farnham, Thomas J. *Travels in the Great Western Prairies.* London: Richard Bentley, 1843. (Thwaites, R. G. *Early Western Travels.*)

Federal Writers' Project. *The Oregon Trail.* New York: Hastings House, 1939.

Field, Matthew C. *Prairie and Mountain Sketches.* Norman: University of Oklahoma Press, 1957.

Ft. Bridger Historic Site. Cheyenne: Wyoming State Archives & Historical Dept., 1967.

Ft. Laramie. National Park Service, 1968.

Ft. Laramie Historical Association. *Ft. Laramie's Historic Buildings,* undated.

Ft. Vancouver. National Park Service, 1971.

Fowler, Mrs. Frank E. Personal Communications. In 1971: April 8, 20 & 29; May 3, 6, 10, 15, 17 & 22; June 5 & 26; Aug. 17 & 26; & Sept. 12. In 1972: Jan. 31, Feb. 9 & 14.

Franzwa, Gregory M. *Florissant Old Town.* St. Louis: Leo A. Daly Comprehensive Services, 1967.

——. *The Old Cathedral.* St. Louis: Archiodecese of St. Louis, 1965.

———. *The Story of Old Ste. Genevieve.* St. Louis: Patrice Press, Inc., 1967.

Friedman, Barbara. Personal Communications. June 9, 1971.

Fuller, George W. *A History of the Pacific Northwest.* New York: Alfred A. Knopf, 1931.

Fremont, John Charles (with Jessie Benton Fremont). *Memoirs of My Life.* Chicago & New York: Belford, Clarke & Co., 1886.

Fremont, John Charles. *Report of the Exploring Expedition to the Rocky Mountains.* Ann Arbor, Mich.: University Microfilms, Inc., 1966.

Ghent, W. J. *The Road to Oregon.* New York: Longmans, Green & Co., 1929.

Goff, William A. "Pierre D. Papin." *The Mountain Men and the Fur Trade of the Far West* Vol. 9. Glendale, Cal.: Arthur H. Clark Co., 1972.

———, Personal Communications. In 1971: Feb. 9, Feb. 10, May 20 & July 4. In 1972: Jan. 2, Feb. 5 & Feb. 12.

Gregg, Josiah. *Commerce of the Prairies.* New York: J. and H. G. Langley, 1845. (Thwaites, R. G. *Early Western Travels.*)

Gregg, J. R. *A History of the Oregon Trail, Santa Fe Trail, and Other Trails.* Portland, Ore.: Binfords & Mort, 1955.

Hansen, William A. "Thomas Hart Benton and the Oregon Question." *Missouri Historical Review* Vol. 63, No. 4 (July, 1969). Columbia: State Historical Society of Missouri.

Harned, Michael E. Personal Communications. July 14, 1971.

Harper, J. Russell (ed.) *Paul Kane's Frontier.* Austin: University of Texas Press, 1971.

"Harris Hotel . . . Comes Down." *Kansas City Star* Nov. 19, 1922.

Henderson, Paul C. "The Grave of Joel J. Hembree, 1843." *Annals of Wyoming* Vol. 35, No. 2 (Oct., 1963.) Cheyenne: Wyoming State Historical Society.

——. *Landmarks on the Oregon Trail*. New York: The Westerners, 1953.

——. Personal Communications. Aug. 31, 1971; Feb. 8, 14 & 20, 1972.

Henry, Bill. Personal Communications. July 30, 1971.

Hicks, John Edward. "Story of a Famous Westport Corner Traced." *Kansas City Times* June 8, 1966.

——. "Chouteau's Trail Was First to Bisect The City." *Kansas City Times* May 3, 1967.

——. Personal Communications. Feb. 10, 1971.

Hieb, David L. *Ft. Laramie*. Washington, D. C.: National Park Service, 1954.

Historic Missouri. Columbia, Mo.: State Historical Society of Mo., 1959.

Historical Markers in Kansas. Topeka: Kansas State Printing Plant, 1966.

Hollenberg Pony Express Station. Topeka: Kansas State Historical Society, 1970.

Honig, Louis O. *Westport; Gateway to the Early West*. Kansas City, Mo.: The Lowell Press, 1950.

Hulbert, Archer Butler, ed., *Crown Collection of American Maps*. 3 vol. Colorado Springs, Colo.: Stewart Commission on Western History, 1925.

——. *Forty-Niners*. Boston: Little, Brown, & Co., 1931.

Ingersoll, Chester. *Overland to California in 1847*. Chicago: Black Cat Press, 1937.

Irving, Washington. *Astoria, or Anecdotes of an Enterprise Beyond the Rocky Mountains*. Norman: University of Oklahoma Press, 1964 (1836.)

——. *The Adventures of Captain Bonneville*. New York & London: The Cooperative Publishing Society, Inc., 1843.

Jefferson National Expansion Memorial. National Park Service, 1971.

Judge, Bill. Personal Communications. July 31, 1971.

"Kansas City's First Baptismal and Marriage Records." *Westport Historical Society Quarterly* Vol. 2, No. 3 (Nov., 1966.) Kansas City, Mo.: Westport Historical

Society.

Kucera, Clair L. Personal Communications. May 5, 1971.

Larkin, Lewis. *Missouri Heritage.* Columbia, Mo.: American Press, Inc., 1968.

Larson, Art & Kay. "Early Snake 'Christmas Bridge' Thing of Willows, Ice." *Oregon Journal,* Portland, Dec. 24, 1970.

Laut, Agnes C. *The Overland Trail.* New York: Frederick A. Stokes Company, 1929.

Lavender, David. *Westward Vision; The Story of the Oregon Trail.* New York: McGraw-Hill Book Company, Inc., 1963.

Lecompte, Janet. "Don Benito Vasquez in Early St. Louis." *The Bulletin* Vol. 26, No. 4, Part 1 (July, 1970.) St. Louis: Missouri Historical Society.

Lewis, Wayne. Personal Communications. July 31, 1971.

Long, Luman H., ed. *The World Almanac.* New York: Newspaper Enterprise Association, Inc. 1971.

Long, Margaret. *The Oregon Trail.* Denver: W. H. Kistler Stationery Co., 1954.

Loomis, Leander V. *A Journal of the Birmingham Emigrating Company.* Salt Lake City: Legal Printing Company, 1928.

Lowell, Arthur E. Personal Communications. Nov. 21, 1971.

Main, Mrs. Mildred Miles. "Ezra Meeker — Apostle of the Oregon Trail." *The Westport Historical Society Quarterly* Vol. 5, No. 4 (March, 1970) Kansas City, Mo.: The Westport Historical Society.

Mansfield, Philip. *Preliminary Map of the Oregon Trail and the Principal Pioneer Routes to California.* Washington, D. C.: Public Roads Administration, Federal Works Agency, Feb., 1940.

Marcy, Capt. Randolph B., U.S.A. *The Prairie Traveler.* New York: Harper & Brothers, 1859.

"Marker Placed By D.A.R." *Kansas City Star,* June 13, 1926.

Mattes, Merrill J. *Scotts Bluff.* Washington, D. C.: National Park Service, 1958.

Maximilian, Prince of Weid. *Travels in the Interior of North America.* London: Ackermann & Company, 1843. (Thwaites, R. G. *Early Western Travels.*)

Meeker, Ezra. *The Ox Team; or the Old Oregon Trail, 1852-1906.* New York: published by the author, 1907.

Miele, John R. Personal Communications. July 22 & 27, 1971.

Moody, Ralph. *The Old Trails West.* New York: Thomas Y. Crowell Co., 1963.

Morgan, Dale, ed., *Overland in 1846.* 2 vol., Georgetown, Cal.: The Talisman Press, 1963.

Morgan, Dale L. & Harris, Eleanor Towles, eds. *The Rocky Mountain Journals of William Marshall Anderson.* San Marino, Cal.: The Huntington Library, 1967.

Morley, Gregory H. Personal Communications, July 13, 1971.

Moyer, Charles. Personal Communications. July 13, 1971.

Old Ft. Caspar. Casper, Wyo.: Ft. Caspar Commission.

Olson, Joan and Gene *Oregon, Times and Trails.* Grants Pass, Ore.: Windyridge Press, 1965.

Orchard, Vance. "Emigrant Spring Was Prime Stop on Trail." *Walla Walla (Wash.) Union-Bulletin* Aug. 15, 1971.

Paden, Irene D. *The Wake of the Prairie Schooner.* Carbondale & Edwardsville, Ill.: Southern Illinois University Press, 1970.

Page, Elizabeth. *Wagons West, A Story of the Oregon Trail.* New York: Farrar & Rinehart, Inc., 1930.

Palmer, Joel. *Journal of Travels Over the Rocky Mountains (1845-46).* Cincinnati: J. A. and U. P. James, 1847. (Thwaites, R. G. *Early Western Travels.*)

Parkman, Francis. *The Oregon Trail.* New York: New American Library of World Literature, Inc., 1964.

Parrish, Rev. Edward Evans. "Diary." *Transactions.* Portland: Oregon Pioneer Association, 1888.

Parrish, Philip H. *Wagons West.* Portland: Old Oregon Trail Centennial Commission, 1943.

Phelps, W. W. *The History of the Reorganized Church of Jesus Christ of Latter Day Saints 1805-35.* Independence, Mo.: Herald Publishing House.

Porter, R. L. Personal Communications. April 23, 1971.

Preuss, Charles. *Exploring with Fremont.* (translated & edited by Erwin G. & Elisabeth K. Gudde) Norman: University of Oklahoma Press, 1958.

Reed, Duane J. Personal Communications. July 30, 1968.

Reed, Preston & Marguerite. Personal Communications. July 20 − 21, 1971.

Rice, Manley M. Personal Communications. April 11, 1971.

Richmond, Robert W. Personal Communications. April 22, 1971.

Rush, Karen. *Southeast Democrat-Herald.* Baker, Ore. July 30, 1970.

Russell, Osborne. *Journal of a Trapper.* Lincoln. University of Nebraska Press, 1969.

Ruxton, George F. A. *Mountain Men.* New York: Holiday House, Inc., 1966.

Sage, Rufus B. *Rocky Mountain Life.* Boston: Wentworth & Company, 1857.

Sharp, Joe H. ''Crossing the Plains in 1852.'' *Transactions.* Portland: Oregon Pioneer Association, 1895.

Smith, Peggy. *Historic Points in Greater Kansas City.* Kansas City, Mo.: Missouri Valley Room, Kansas City Public Library, 1970.

——. Personal Communications. Nov. 20 & 23, 1971.

Snoddy, Donald D. Personal Communications. Jan. 20, 1971.

Starbird, Ethel A. ''A River Restored: Oregon's Willamette.'' *National Geographic Magazine.* June, 1972.

Stephens, Miles. Personal Communications. July 13, 1971.

Stewart, George R. *Donner Pass.* Menlo Park, Cal.: Lane Books, 1964.

Stewart, Gordon & Patricia. *Baker County Sketch Book.* Published privately, 1966.

Stiff, Cary. "Register Cliff: History's Guest Book." *Empire Magazine, The Denver Post.* Aug. 18, 1968.

Stuart, Robert. *On The Oregon Trail.* Edited by Kenneth A. Spaulding. Norman: University of Oklahoma Press, 1953.

Survey of Historic Sites & Structures in Kansas. Topeka: Kansas State Historical Society, 1957.

Sutherland, Ronald R. Personal Communications. Dec. 2, 1970.

Terrell, John Upton. *Black Robe.* Garden City, N. Y.: Echo Books, 1966.

Thruston, Ethylene Ballard. "Aunt Sophie's Cabin Weathers Span of Years." *Journal.* Independence, Mo.: Jackson County Historical Society, Spring, 1967.

Walton, Elisabeth, Personal Communications. Sept. 10, 1971.

Ware, Joseph E. *The Emigrants' Guide to California.* Princeton: Princeton University Press, 1932 (1849).

Weaver, Kenneth F. "Voyage to the Planets." *National Geographic Magazine* Aug., 1970. Washington, D. C.: National Geographic Society.

Webb, W. L. *The Centennial History of Independence, Mo.* Published by the Author. Independence, 1927.

Wells, Merle W. Personal Communications. Feb. 18, 1972.

Westing, Wilbur B. Personal Communications. Feb. 24, 1971.

White, Berenice. "Part of Jason White Home Built in 1845." *Journal.* Independence, Mo.: Jackson County Historical Society, Spring, 1967.

Whitman Mission. Washington, D. C.: National Park Service, 1970.

Whitman, Mrs. Narcissa. "Diary." *Transactions.* Portland: Oregon Pioneer Association, 1891.

Williams, Mrs. Frances R. Personal Communications. May 30, 1971.

Wimmer, Edward. "Preservation Potential in Kansas City." *Skylines.* Kansas City: Kansas City Chapter, American Institute of Architects, Spring, 1970.

Winther, Oscar Osburn. *The Old Oregon Country.* Lincoln: University of Nebraska Press, 1969.

Wood, Dean Earl. *The Old Santa Fe Trail From the Missouri River.* Kansas City: E. L. Mendenhall, Printers, 1951.

Woodbridge, Ross. *A Prentiss/Whitman Folio.* Published by the Author. Pittsford, N. Y., 1970.

Wornall, Frank C. "The Harris House Story." *Westport Historical Quarterly.* June, 1970, Kansas City, Mo.: Westport Historical Society.

Index

A

B

C

D

E

F

G

H

I

J

K

L

M

N

O

P

R

S

T

U

V

W

Y

Z

Matches east edge of map in front of book

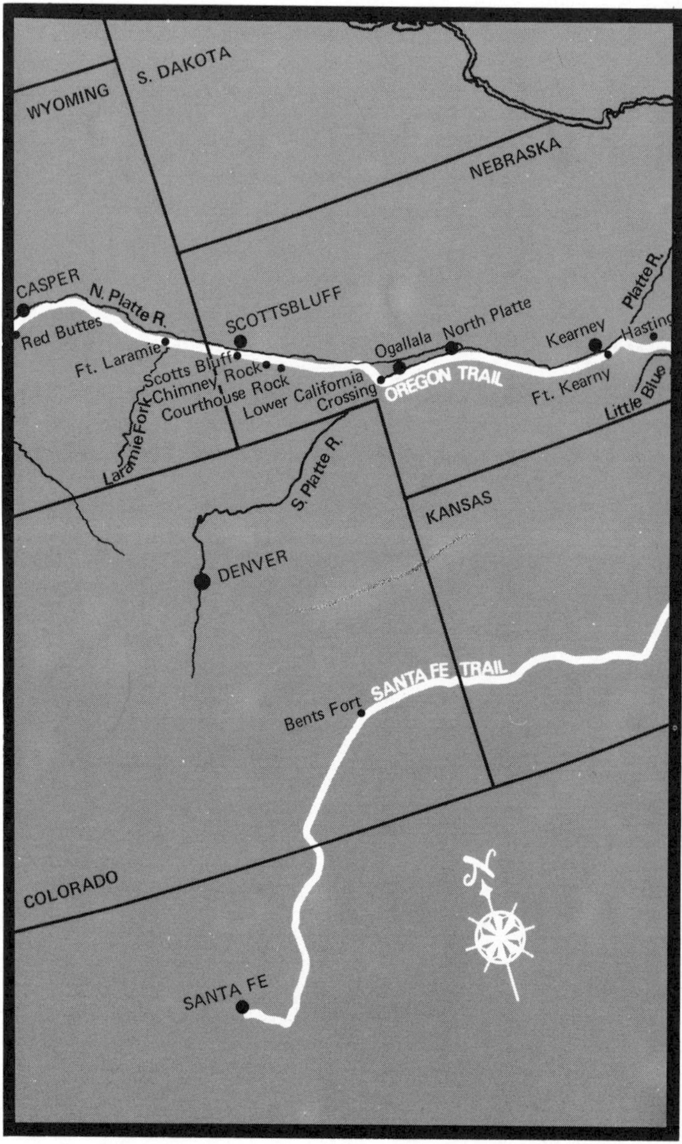

WYOMING
S. DAKOTA
NEBRASKA

CASPER
N. Platte R.
Red Buttes
SCOTTSBLUFF
Ft. Laramie
Laramie Fort
Scotts Bluff
Chimney Rock
Courthouse Rock
Lower California Crossing
Ogallala
North Platte
OREGON TRAIL
Ft. Kearny
Kearney
Hasting
Platte R.
Little Blue

S. Platte R.
DENVER
KANSAS

Bents Fort
SANTA FE TRAIL

COLORADO

SANTA FE

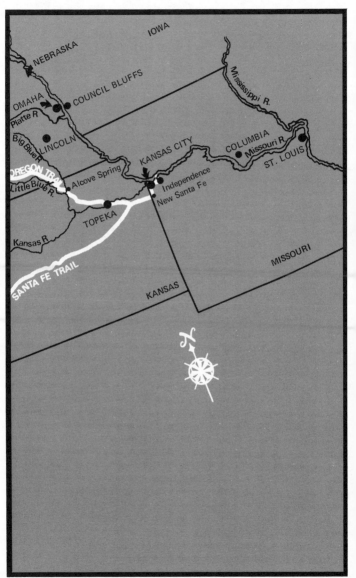

Cartography by the author.

The Patrice Press
Offers the Following Portfolio
of Western Trails Materials

Check with your favorite bookseller. If they do not stock the books you want, order directly from us: The Patrice Press, 1701 South Eighth, St. Louis MO 63104. Add $2.00 shipping for the first book and 75 cents for each additional book. Missouri customers: please add 6.1% sales tax.

Call toll-free for current prices:
1-800-367-9242

**TRAIL OF THE FIRST WAGONS
OVER THE SIERRA NEVADA**
Charles K. Graydon
80 pages; Paper, $14.95
ISBN 0-935284-47-8

In *Trail of the First Wagons* Charles K. Graydon pinpoints the location of trails used by California-bound emigrants to surmount their final and most awesome barrier — the Sierra Nevada.

Key sections of USGS topographic maps are reproduced in this book, upon which the pioneers' routes are superimposed. The text gives a brief history of the crossing and describes present-day accessibility to the trails — by car, on foot, or on skis.

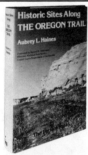

**HISTORIC SITES ALONG
THE OREGON TRAIL**
Aubrey L. Haines
439 pages
Cloth, $24.95; Paper, $12.95
ISBN 0-935284-21-4

In this single volume the reader may obtain complete information on virtually all sites of historic importance along the Oregon Trail, from Independence, Mo., to Oregon City, Oreg. Each site description includes its name, location (to a tolerance of 200 yards), distance from Independence, a general summation, and materials extracted from the journals of the 19th century emigrants and 20th century visitors. Haines usually has remarks of his own to add and closes with the name of the map on which that particular site may be found.

On The Move West

Taken together, these four books provide a vivid picture of nineteenth century American westward expansion.

In lively narrative styles, three renowned western historians take the experience through successively finer filters, describing in turn the interchangable role of the military fort as a center for trade, diplomacy, and warfare; the trailblazing of the first explorers across the vast trans-Mississippian subcontinent; the settlement of the land that cemented the claims to the region; and the imprint of Manifest Destiny on individuals' lives from the perspective of an Indian, a soldier, and a settler.

Full color and black & white illustrations, as well as maps, lavishly illustrate each work. Available in paperback only, each book may be purchased individually; subtract $5 from the total if purchasing the set.

Fort Larmie, David Lavender, 159 pages, $8.95; *Exploring the American West,* William H. Goetzmann, 128 pages, $7.95; *The Overland Migrations,* David Lavender, 111 pages, $7.95; *Indian, Soldier, and Settler,* Robert M. Utley, 84 pages, $8.95.

Old Oregon Trail Map

This decorative map, suitable as a wall hanging at 16″ x 24″, makes a handy reference for the classroom, study, or office.

Sixteen western trails are shown — not only larger ones, such as the Oregon Trail, the Santa Fe Trail, and Lewis and Clark's routes, but also smaller trails, such as the Applegate, the Bozeman, and the Naches Pass. $2.95.

**The Latter-day Saints'
EMIGRANTS' GUIDE**
Wm. Clayton
Stanley B. Kimball, Ph.D., Editor
107pp; Paper only, $9.95
ISBN 0-935284-27-3

William Clayton was a member of the original Mormon pioneer company which traveled overland in 1847 to found Salt Lake City. He published a guidebook of the Mormon Trail in 1848. This 117-page volume reproduces the original exactly, with exhaustive annotation by Stanley Kimball, Ph.D., the award-winning Mormon journalist and historian.

An American Vision

Cathedral Rock, near San Diego, Calif., *from the chromolithograph collection of the Detroit Publishing Co.*

As chief photographer and production manager of the Detroit Publishing Co., William Henry Jackson, a pioneer photographer of the West, oversaw the production of full color lithographs from his own and his assistants' glass-plate negatives.

These chromoliths were extremely popular at the turn of the century, thrilling the public with bright, colorful views of their world. Today, they offer us a vision from an earlier era shared by many of its inhabitants.

After sitting in a warehouse for sixty years, these prints were uncovered in 1984 by The Patrice Press. Hundreds of outstanding views from the American West are in the collection — Colorado mountain landscapes, Yellowstone geysers and springs, missions of the Southwest, California coastline and settlements, and many others.

Contact the Press, stating your areas of interest, for information on acquiring prints from this remarkable historic collection.

TO THE LAND OF GOLD AND WICKEDNESS
The 1848-1859 Diary of Lorena Hays
Jeanne Watson, Editor
1988 Price: Cloth, $27.95
ISBN 0-935284-53-2

Lorena Hays, who came of age in the Victorian era, left behind a diary recounting her role in the migration across the American subcontinent. She traveled west with her family, settling eventually in the California goldfields. Before her life was prematurely cut short, she had begun a family and settled somewhat reluctantly into a domestic routine.

Editor Jeanne Watson has done exhaustive research and cites scores of journals, magazine and newspaper articles from the period, as well as innumerable other sources, in order to place Lorena's experience in the larger context of her time. Watson's introductory essay will be of special interest to social historians.

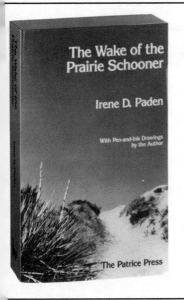

THE WAKE OF THE PRAIRIE SCHOONER
Irene D. Paden
514 pages
Cloth, $24.95;
ISBN 0-935284-40-0
Paper, $12.95;
ISBN 0-935284-38-9

Irene Paden traveled along the route of the Oregon Trail several times between 1935 and 1942, recording her adventures in a diary as well as a sketchbook. This facsimile edition, published in 1985, includes a bibliography and index.

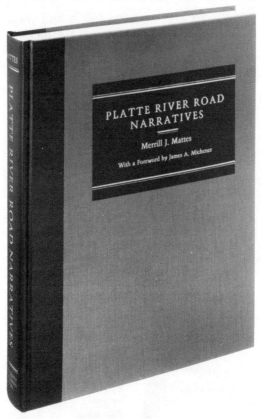

PLATTE RIVER ROAD NARRATIVES
Merrill J. Mattes
672 pages; Cloth, $95.

In an unusual endeavor Merrill Mattes spent nearly ten years poring over emigrants' journals found in private and public collections thoroughly the United States.

This effort resulted in the the publication of *Platte River Road Narratives,* a 672-page, 8 1/2″ x 11″ volume containing a concise description, synopsis, and analysis of all known significant Western trail accounts — over 2000 entries in all.

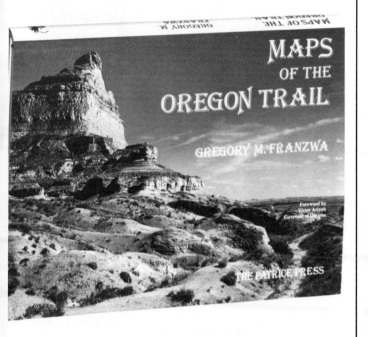

MAPS OF THE OREGON TRAIL
Gregory M. Franzwa
292 pages
Cloth, $24.95; ISBN 0-935284-30-3
Paper, $14.95; ISBN 0-935284-32-X
Looseleaf, $27.95; ISBN 0-935284-31-1

This volume reproduces the route of the Oregon Trail as a thin red line over a base of county maps, on a scale of ½″ : 1 mile. The route is from Independence, Mo., to Oregon City, Oreg., with the Barlow Cutoff and the South Snake River routes included as alternates. Also shown is the Sublette Cutoff and several of its branches.

In its 292 pages are found 133 full page trail maps, 9 detail maps, and 8 photographs.

THE GREAT PLATTE RIVER ROAD
Merrill J. Mattes
583 pages
Cloth, $36.95; Paper, $16.95

How did the pioneers cope with crime or accidents on the trail? Or with the need for food and clothing? How were wagon trains organized and equipped for the journey?

Drawing from the journals of over 700 travelers, Merrill Mattes addresses the obvious difficulties emigrants had with the topography, with the Indians, with the sheer effort of traveling a thousand miles or more across the plains and mountains of America. But he also discusses the myriad of other concerns confronted by those on the trek West.

FOLLOWING THE SANTA FE TRAIL
Marc Simmons, Ph.D.
1988 Price: Paper, $12.95

The Santa Fe Trail is unique among western routes, for its impetus was commerce rather than settlement, and that commerce was international. Marc Simmons, Ph.D., has extensively researched the trail, and he shares its colorful history in this drivers' guide.

Maps and local site descriptions direct the modern traveler to the better- and lesser-known existing sites along the trail with a minumum of guesswork.